# Conference of the North American Chapter of the Association for Computational Linguistics: Human Language Technologies (NAACL HLT 2021)



## Demonstrations

Online
6 – 11 June 2021

ISBN: 978-1-7138-3011-5

**Printed from e-media with permission by:**

Curran Associates, Inc.
57 Morehouse Lane
Red Hook, NY 12571

CURRAN ASSOCIATES INC.
proceedings
.com

**Some format issues inherent in the e-media version may also appear in this print version.**



Association for Computational Linguistics
209 N. Eighth Street
Stroudsburg, Pennsylvania 18360

Phone: 1-570-476-8006
Fax: 1-570-476-0860

acl@aclweb.org

**Additional copies of this publication are available from:**

Curran Associates, Inc.
57 Morehouse Lane
Red Hook, NY 12571 USA
Phone: 845-758-0400
Fax: 845-758-2633
Email: curran@proceedings.com
Web: www.proceedings.com

NAACL-HLT 2021

# The 2021 Conference of the North American Chapter of the Association for Computational Linguistics: Human Language Technologies

## Demonstrations

June 6 - 11, 2021

# Introduction

Welcome to the proceedings of the system demonstration track of NAACL-HLT 2021 on Jun 6th - Jun 11th, 2021. NAACL-HLT 2021 will be a virtual conference.

The system demonstration track invites submissions ranging from early prototypes to mature production-ready systems. This year we received 42 submissions, of which 17 were selected for inclusion in the program (acceptance rate 40.5%) after reviewed by three members of the program committee.

This is the first year NAACL-HLT incorporates ethical considerations in the review process. In the standard review stage, members of the program committee are given the option to flag a paper as needing separate ethics reviews. Papers flagged as needing separate ethics reviews by at least one members from the program committee are subsequently reviewed by two members from the NAACL-HLT 2021 ethics committee. In total, 4 papers went through the subsequent ethics review stage, of which 1 was offered conditional acceptance, 2 were accepted as it is and 1 was deemed as a false positive flag. The conditionally accepted paper was re-reviewed by the ethics committee post camera-ready submission and accepted to the program based on addressed ethical concerns.

We would like to thank the members of the program committee and ethics committee for their timely help in reviewing the submissions. We also thank the many authors who submitted their work to the demonstration track. The demonstration paper will be presented through pre-recorded talks (12 minutes) and one live online Q&A session (80 minutes).

Best,
Avi Sil and Xi Victoria Lin
NAACL-HLT 2021 Demonstration Track Chairs

**Organizing Committee:**

Avi Sil, IBM Research AI
Xi Victoria Lin, Facebook AI Research

**Program Committee:**

Ahmed Abdelali, Qatar Computing Research Institute
Alan Akbik, Humboldt-Universität zu Berlin
Zeynep Akkalyoncu, University of Waterloo
Bo An, Institute of Software, Chinese Academy of Sciences
Eleftherios Avramidis, German Research Center for Artificial Intelligence (DFKI)
Gianni Barlacchi, Amazon Alexa
Bernd Bohnet, Google
Georgeta Bordea, Université de Bordeaux
Aljoscha Burchardt, DFKI
José G. C. de Souza, Unbabel
Christos Christodoulopoulos, Amazon Research
Montse Cuadros, Vicomtech
Giovanni Da San Martino, University of Padova
Marina Danilevsky, IBM Research
Joseph P. Dexter, Harvard University
Chenchen Ding, NICT
James Fan, Google
Nicolas Rodolfo Fauceglia, IBM Research AI
Ming Gong, STCA NLP Group, Microsoft (China)
Ben Hachey, Harrison.ai
Masato Hagiwara, Octanove Labs LLC
Xianpei Han, Institute of Software, Chinese Academy of Sciences
Xu Han, Tsinghua University
Barbora Hladka, Charles University
Ales Horak, Masaryk University
Shajith Ikbal, IBM Research AI, India.
Philipp Koehn, Johns Hopkins University
Mamoru Komachi, Tokyo Metropolitan University
Valia Kordoni, Humboldt-Universität zu Berlin
Vishwajeet Kumar, IBM Research AI
Mark Last, Ben-Gurion University of the Negev
John Lee, City University of Hong Kong
Hao Li, ByteDance
Marina Litvak, Shamoon College of Engineering
Changsong Liu, University of California, Los Angeles
Wei Lu, Singapore University of Technology and Design
Suraj Maharjan, University of Houston
Wolfgang Maier, Mercedes-Benz AG
Benjamin Marie, NICT
David McClosky, Google
Marie-Jean Meurs, Université du Québec à Montréal
Ivan Vladimir Meza Ruiz, Insituto de Investigaciones en Matemáticas Aplicadas y en Sistemas (IIMAS-UNAM)
Margot Mieskes, University of Applied Sciences, Darmstadt
Hamdy Mubarak, Qatar Computing Research Institute

Aldrian Obaja Muis, None
Philippe Muller, IRIT, University of Toulouse
Diane Napolitano, The Associated Press
Denis Newman-Griffis, University of Pittsburgh
Pierre Nugues, Lund University
Yusuke Oda, LegalForce
Siddharth Patwardhan, Apple
Oren Pereg, AI Lab, Intel Labs
Prokopis Prokopidis, ILSP/Athena RC
Saurav Sahay, Intel Labs
Sebastin Santy, Microsoft Research
Liang-Hsin Shen, National Taiwan University
Michal Shmueli-Scheuer, IBM Research
Sunayana Sitaram, Microsoft Research India
Konstantinos Skianis, BLUAI
Dezhao Song, Thomson Reuters
Yuanfeng Song, Hong Kong University of Science and Technology, WeBank Co., Ltd
Michael Stewart, The University of Western Australia
Natalia Vanetik, Shamoon College of Engineering
Andrea Varga, CUBE
Changhan Wang, Facebook AI Research
Rui Wang, VIP.com
Deyi Xiong, Tianjin University
Qiongkai Xu, The Australian National University and Data61
Tae Yano, Expedia Group
Wenlin Yao, Tencent AI Lab
Seid Muhie Yimam, Universität Hamburg
Dian Yu, University of California, Davis
Mo Yu, IBM Research
Liang-Chih Yu, Yuan Ze University
Jun Zhao, Chinese Academy of Sciences
Guangyou Zhou, School of Computer Science, Central China Normal University
Imed Zitouni, Google

## Table of Contents

# Conference Program

**Jun 8th, 2021**

**620pm PST–740pm PST**

*PhoNLP: A joint multi-task learning model for Vietnamese part-of-speech tagging, named entity recognition and dependency parsing*
Linh The Nguyen and Dat Quoc Nguyen

*Machine-Assisted Script Curation*
Manuel Ciosici, Joseph Cummings, Mitchell DeHaven, Alex Hedges, Yash Kankanampati, Dong-Ho Lee, Ralph Weischedel and Marjorie Freedman

*NAMER: A Node-Based Multitasking Framework for Multi-Hop Knowledge Base Question Answering*
Minhao Zhang, Ruoyu Zhang, Lei Zou, Yinnian Lin and Sen Hu

*DiSCoL: Toward Engaging Dialogue Systems through Conversational Line Guided Response Generation*
Sarik Ghazarian, Zixi Liu, Tuhin Chakrabarty, Xuezhe Ma, Aram Galstyan and Nanyun Peng

*FITAnnotator: A Flexible and Intelligent Text Annotation System*
Yanzeng Li, Bowen Yu, Li Quangang and Tingwen Liu

*Robustness Gym: Unifying the NLP Evaluation Landscape*
Karan Goel, Nazneen Fatema Rajani, Jesse Vig, Zachary Taschdjian, Mohit Bansal and Christopher Ré

*EventPlus: A Temporal Event Understanding Pipeline*
Mingyu Derek Ma, Jiao Sun, Mu Yang, Kung-Hsiang Huang, Nuan Wen, Shikhar Singh, Rujun Han and Nanyun Peng

**Jun 9th, 2021**

**9am PST–1020am PST**

*COVID-19 Literature Knowledge Graph Construction and Drug Repurposing Report Generation*
Qingyun Wang, Manling Li, Xuan Wang, Nikolaus Parulian, Guangxing Han, Jiawei Ma, Jingxuan Tu, Ying Lin, Ranran Haoran Zhang, Weili Liu, Aabhas Chauhan, Yingjun Guan, Bangzheng Li, Ruisong Li, Xiangchen Song, Yi Fung, Heng Ji, Jiawei Han, Shih-Fu Chang, James Pustejovsky, Jasmine Rah, David Liem, Ahmed ELsayed, Martha Palmer, Clare Voss, Cynthia Schneider and Boyan Onyshkevych

*Multifaceted Domain-Specific Document Embeddings*
Julian Risch, Philipp Hager and Ralf Krestel

*Improving Evidence Retrieval for Automated Explainable Fact-Checking*
Chris Samarinas, Wynne Hsu and Mong Li Lee

*Interactive Plot Manipulation using Natural Language*
Yihan Wang, Yutong Shao and Ndapa Nakashole

*ActiveAnno: General-Purpose Document-Level Annotation Tool with Active Learning Integration*
Max Wiechmann, Seid Muhie Yimam and Chris Biemann

*TextEssence: A Tool for Interactive Analysis of Semantic Shifts Between Corpora*
Denis Newman-Griffis, Venkatesh Sivaraman, Adam Perer, Eric Fosler-Lussier and Harry Hochheiser

*Supporting Spanish Writers using Automated Feedback*
Aoife Cahill, James Bruno, James Ramey, Gilmar Ayala Meneses, Ian Blood, Florencia Tolentino, Tamar Lavee and Slava Andreyev

*Alexa Conversations: An Extensible Data-driven Approach for Building Task-oriented Dialogue Systems*
Anish Acharya, Suranjit Adhikari, Sanchit Agarwal, Vincent Auvray, Nehal Belgamwar, Arijit Biswas, Shubhra Chandra, Tagyoung Chung, Maryam Fazel-Zarandi, Raefer Gabriel, Shuyang Gao, Rahul Goel, Dilek Hakkani-Tur, Jan Jezabek, Abhay Jha, Jiun-Yu Kao, Prakash Krishnan, Peter Ku, Anuj Goyal, Chien-Wei Lin, Qing Liu, Arindam Mandal, Angeliki Metallinou, Vishal Naik, Yi Pan, Shachi Paul, Vittorio Perera, Abhishek Sethi, Minmin Shen, Nikko Strom and Eddie Wang

*RESIN: A Dockerized Schema-Guided Cross-document Cross-lingual Cross-media Information Extraction and Event Tracking System*
Haoyang Wen, Ying Lin, Tuan Lai, Xiaoman Pan, Sha Li, Xudong Lin, Ben Zhou, Manling Li, Haoyu Wang, Hongming Zhang, Xiaodong Yu, Alexander Dong, Zhenhailong Wang, Yi Fung, Piyush Mishra, Qing Lyu, Dídac Surís, Brian Chen, Susan Windisch Brown, Martha Palmer, Chris Callison-Burch, Carl Vondrick, Jiawei Han, Dan Roth, Shih-Fu Chang and Heng Ji

*MUDES: Multilingual Detection of Offensive Spans*
Tharindu Ranasinghe and Marcos Zampieri

**Jun 9th, 2021 (continued)**

# PhoNLP: A joint multi-task learning model for Vietnamese part-of-speech tagging, named entity recognition and dependency parsing

**Linh The Nguyen** and **Dat Quoc Nguyen**
VinAI Research, Hanoi, Vietnam
{v.linhnt140, v.datnq9}@vinai.io

## Abstract

We present the first multi-task learning model—named PhoNLP—for joint Vietnamese part-of-speech (POS) tagging, named entity recognition (NER) and dependency parsing. Experiments on Vietnamese benchmark datasets show that PhoNLP produces state-of-the-art results, outperforming a single-task learning approach that fine-tunes the pre-trained Vietnamese language model PhoBERT (Nguyen and Nguyen, 2020) for each task independently. We publicly release PhoNLP as an open-source toolkit under the Apache License 2.0. Although we specify PhoNLP for Vietnamese, our PhoNLP training and evaluation command scripts in fact can directly work for other languages that have a pre-trained BERT-based language model and gold annotated corpora available for the three tasks of POS tagging, NER and dependency parsing. We hope that PhoNLP can serve as a strong baseline and useful toolkit for future NLP research and applications to not only Vietnamese but also the other languages. Our PhoNLP is available at https://github.com/VinAIResearch/PhoNLP.

## 1 Introduction

Vietnamese NLP research has been significantly explored recently. It has been boosted by the success of the national project on Vietnamese language and speech processing (VLSP) KC01.01/2006-2010 and VLSP workshops that have run shared tasks since 2013.[1] Fundamental tasks of POS tagging, NER and dependency parsing thus play important roles, providing useful features for many downstream application tasks such as machine translation (Tran et al., 2016), sentiment analysis (Bang and Sornlertlamvanich, 2018), relation extraction (To and Do, 2020), semantic parsing (Nguyen et al., 2020), open information extraction (Truong et al., 2017) and question answering (Nguyen et al., 2017; Le-Hong and Bui, 2018). Thus, there is a need to develop NLP toolkits for linguistic annotations w.r.t. Vietnamese POS tagging, NER and dependency parsing.

VnCoreNLP (Vu et al., 2018) is the previous public toolkit employing traditional feature-based machine learning models to handle those Vietnamese NLP tasks. However, VnCoreNLP is now no longer considered state-of-the-art because its performance results are significantly outperformed by ones obtained when fine-tuning PhoBERT—the current state-of-the-art monolingual pre-trained language model for Vietnamese (Nguyen and Nguyen, 2020). Note that there are no publicly available fine-tuned BERT-based models for the three Vietnamese tasks. Assuming that there would be, a potential drawback might be that an NLP package wrapping such fine-tuned BERT-based models would take a large storage space, i.e. three times larger than the storage space used by a BERT model (Devlin et al., 2019), thus it would not be suitable for practical applications that require a smaller storage space. Jointly multi-task learning is a promising solution as it might help reduce the storage space. In addition, POS tagging, NER and dependency parsing are related tasks: POS tags are essential input features used for dependency parsing and POS tags are also used as additional features for NER. Jointly multi-task learning thus might also help improve the performance results against the single-task learning (Ruder, 2019).

In this paper, we present a new multi-task learning model—named PhoNLP—for joint POS tagging, NER and dependency parsing. In particular, given an input sentence of words to PhoNLP, an encoding layer generates contextualized word embeddings that represent the input words. These contextualized word embeddings are fed into a POS tagging layer that is in fact a linear prediction layer (Devlin et al., 2019) to predict POS tags for the corresponding input words. Each predicted POS

[1] https://vlsp.org.vn/



*Proceedings of NAACL-HLT 2021: Demonstrations*, pages 1–7
June 6–11, 2021. 

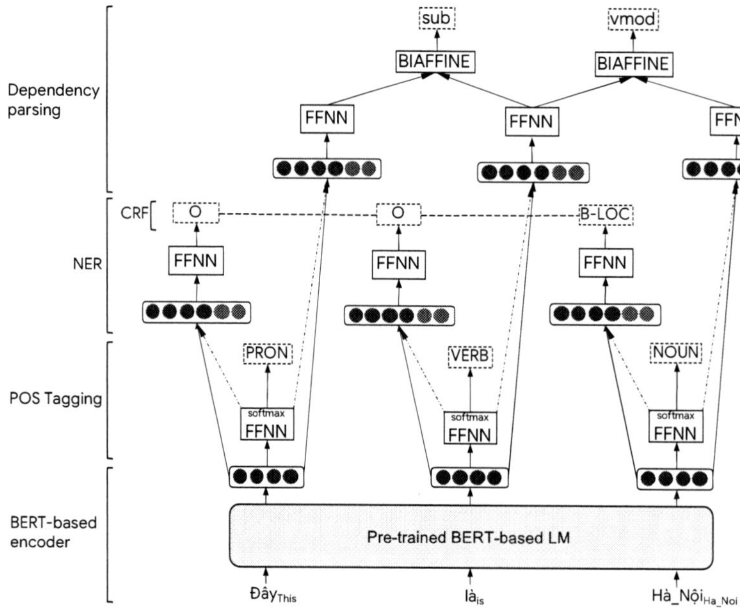


| ID | Form | POS | NER | Head | DepRel |
|---|---|---|---|---|---|
| 1 | Đây$_{\text{This}}$ | PRON | O | 2 | sub |
| 2 | là$_{\text{is}}$ | VERB | O | 0 | root |
| 3 | Hà_Nội$_{\text{Ha_Noi}}$ | NOUN | B-LOC | 2 | vmod |

Figure 1: Illustration of our PhoNLP model.

tag is then represented by two "soft" embeddings that are later fed into NER and dependency parsing layers separately. More specifically, based on both the contextualized word embeddings and the "soft" POS tag embeddings, the NER layer uses a linear-chain CRF predictor (Lafferty et al., 2001) to predict NER labels for the input words, while the dependency parsing layer uses a Biaffine classifier (Dozat and Manning, 2017) to predict dependency arcs between the words and another Biaffine classifier to label the predicted arcs. Our contributions are summarized as follows:

- To the best of our knowledge, PhoNLP is the first proposed model to jointly learn POS tagging, NER and dependency parsing for Vietnamese.
- We discuss a data leakage issue in the Vietnamese benchmark datasets, that has not yet been pointed out before. Experiments show that PhoNLP obtains state-of-the-art performance results, outperforming the PhoBERT-based single task learning.
- We publicly release PhoNLP as an open-source toolkit that is simple to setup and efficiently run from both the command-line and Python API. We hope that PhoNLP can serve as a strong baseline and useful toolkit for future NLP research and downstream applications.

## 2 Model description

Figure 1 illustrates our PhoNLP architecture that can be viewed as a mixture of a BERT-based encoding layer and three decoding layers of POS tagging, NER and dependency parsing.

### 2.1 Encoder & Contextualized embeddings

Given an input sentence consisting of $n$ word tokens $w_1, w_2, ..., w_n$, the encoding layer employs PhoBERT to generate contextualized latent feature embeddings $\mathbf{e}_i$ each representing the $i^{th}$ word $w_i$:

$$\mathbf{e}_i = \text{PhoBERT}_{\text{base}}\big(w_{1:n}, i\big) \quad (1)$$

In particular, the encoding layer employs the **PhoBERT$_{\text{base}}$** version. Because PhoBERT uses BPE (Sennrich et al., 2016) to segment the input sentence with subword units, the encoding layer in fact represents the $i^{th}$ word $w_i$ by using the contextualized embedding of its first subword.

### 2.2 POS tagging

Following a common manner when fine-tuning a pre-trained language model for a sequence labeling task (Devlin et al., 2019), the POS tagging layer is a linear prediction layer that is appended on top of the encoder. In particular, the POS tagging layer feeds the contextualized word embeddings $\mathbf{e}_i$ into a feed-forward network (FFNN$_{\text{POS}}$) followed by a softmax predictor for POS tag prediction:

$$\mathbf{p}_i = \mathsf{softmax}\big(\text{FFNN}_{\text{POS}}(\mathbf{e}_i)\big) \tag{2}$$

where the output layer size of FFNN$_{\text{POS}}$ is the number of POS tags. Based on probability vectors $\mathbf{p}_i$, a cross-entropy objective loss $\mathcal{L}_{\textbf{POS}}$ is calculated for POS tagging during training.

### 2.3 NER

The NER layer creates a sequence of vectors $\mathbf{v}_{1:n}$ in which each $\mathbf{v}_i$ is resulted in by concatenating the contextualized word embedding $\mathbf{e}_i$ and a "soft" POS tag embedding $\mathbf{t}_i^{(1)}$:

$$\mathbf{v}_i = \mathbf{e}_i \circ \mathbf{t}_i^{(1)} \tag{3}$$

where following Hashimoto et al. (2017), the "soft" POS tag embedding $\mathbf{t}_i^{(1)}$ is computed by multiplying a label weight matrix $\mathbf{W}^{(1)}$ with the corresponding probability vector $\mathbf{p}_i$:

$$\mathbf{t}_i^{(1)} = \mathbf{W}^{(1)}\mathbf{p}_i$$

The NER layer then passes each vector $\mathbf{v}_i$ into a FFNN (FFNN$_{\text{NER}}$):

$$\mathbf{h}_i = \text{FFNN}_{\text{NER}}(\mathbf{v}_i) \tag{4}$$

where the output layer size of FFNN$_{\text{NER}}$ is the number of BIO-based NER labels.

The NER layer feeds the output vectors $\mathbf{h}_i$ into a linear-chain CRF predictor for NER label prediction (Lafferty et al., 2001). A cross-entropy loss $\mathcal{L}_{\textbf{NER}}$ is calculated for NER during training while the Viterbi algorithm is used for inference.

### 2.4 Dependency parsing

The dependency parsing layer creates vectors $\mathbf{z}_{1:n}$ in which each $\mathbf{z}_i$ is resulted in by concatenating $\mathbf{e}_i$ and another "soft" POS tag embedding $\mathbf{t}_i^{(2)}$:

$$\mathbf{z}_i = \mathbf{e}_i \circ \mathbf{t}_i^{(2)} \tag{5}$$
$$\mathbf{t}_i^{(2)} = \mathbf{W}^{(2)}\mathbf{p}_i$$

Following Dozat and Manning (2017), the dependency parsing layer uses FFNNs to split $\mathbf{z}_i$ into *head* and *dependent* representations:

$$\mathbf{h}_i^{(\text{A-H})} = \text{FFNN}_{\text{Arc-Head}}(\mathbf{z}_i) \tag{6}$$
$$\mathbf{h}_i^{(\text{A-D})} = \text{FFNN}_{\text{Arc-Dep}}(\mathbf{z}_i) \tag{7}$$
$$\mathbf{h}_i^{(\text{L-H})} = \text{FFNN}_{\text{Label-Head}}(\mathbf{z}_i) \tag{8}$$
$$\mathbf{h}_i^{(\text{L-D})} = \text{FFNN}_{\text{Label-Dep}}(\mathbf{z}_i) \tag{9}$$

To predict potential dependency arcs, based on input vectors $\mathbf{h}_i^{(\text{A-H})}$ and $\mathbf{h}_j^{(\text{A-D})}$, the parsing layer uses a Biaffine classifier's variant (Qi et al., 2018) that additionally takes into account the distance and relative ordering between two words to produce a probability distribution of arc heads for each word. For inference, the Chu–Liu/Edmonds' algorithm is used to find a maximum spanning tree (Chu and Liu, 1965; Edmonds, 1967). The parsing layer also uses another Biaffine classifier to label the predicted arcs, based on input vectors $\mathbf{h}_i^{(\text{L-H})}$ and $\mathbf{h}_j^{(\text{L-D})}$. An objective loss $\mathcal{L}_{\textbf{DEP}}$ is computed by summing a cross entropy loss for unlabeled dependency parsing and another cross entropy loss for dependency label prediction during training based on gold arcs and arc labels.

### 2.5 Joint multi-task learning

The final training objective loss $\mathcal{L}$ of our model PhoNLP is the weighted sum of the POS tagging loss $\mathcal{L}_{\text{POS}}$, the NER loss $\mathcal{L}_{\text{NER}}$ and the dependency parsing loss $\mathcal{L}_{\text{DEP}}$:

$$\mathcal{L} = \lambda_1\mathcal{L}_{\text{POS}} + \lambda_2\mathcal{L}_{\text{NER}} + (1-\lambda_1-\lambda_2)\mathcal{L}_{\text{DEP}} \tag{10}$$

**Discussion:** Our PhoNLP can be viewed as an extension of previous joint POS tagging and dependency parsing models (Hashimoto et al., 2017; Li et al., 2018; Nguyen and Verspoor, 2018; Nguyen, 2019; Kondratyuk and Straka, 2019), where we additionally incorporate a CRF-based prediction layer for NER. Unlike Hashimoto et al. (2017), Nguyen and Verspoor (2018), Li et al. (2018) and Nguyen (2019) that use BiLSTM-based encoders to extract contextualized feature embeddings, we use a BERT-based encoder. Kondratyuk and Straka (2019) also employ a BERT-based encoder. However, different from PhoNLP where we construct a hierarchical architecture over the POS tagging and dependency parsing layers, Kondratyuk and Straka (2019) do not make use of POS tag embeddings for dependency parsing.[2]

[2]In our preliminary experiments, not feeding the POS tag embeddings into the dependency parsing layer decreases the performance.

| Task | #train | #valid | #test |
|---|---|---|---|
| POS tagging (leakage) | 27000 | 870 | 2120 |
| POS tagging (re-split) | 23906 | 2009 | 3481 |
| NER | 14861 | 2000 | 2831 |
| Dependency parsing | 8977 | 200 | 1020 |

Table 1: Dataset statistics. **#train**, **#valid** and **#test** denote the numbers of training, validation and test sentences, respectively. Here, "POS tagging (leakage)" and "POS tagging (re-split)" refer to the statistics for POS tagging before and after re-splitting & sentence duplication removal, respectively.

## 3 Experiments

### 3.1 Setup

#### 3.1.1 Datasets

To conduct experiments, we use the benchmark datasets of the VLSP 2013 POS tagging dataset,[3] the VLSP 2016 NER dataset (Nguyen et al., 2019) and the VnDT dependency treebank v1.1 Nguyen et al. (2014), following the setup used by the VnCoreNLP toolkit (Vu et al., 2018). Here, VnDT is converted from the Vietnamese constituent treebank (Nguyen et al., 2009).

**Data leakage issue:** We further discover an issue of data leakage, that has not yet been pointed out before. That is, all sentences from the VLSP 2016 NER dataset and the VnDT treebank are included in the VLSP 2013 POS tagging dataset. In particular, 90+% of sentences from both validation and test sets for NER and dependency parsing are included in the POS tagging training set, resulting in an unrealistic evaluation scenario where the POS tags are used as input features for NER and dependency parsing.

To handle the data leakage issue, we have to re-split the VLSP 2013 POS tagging dataset to avoid the data leakage issue: The POS tagging validation/test set now only contains sentences that appear in the union of the NER and dependency parsing validation/test sets (i.e. the validation/test sentences for NER and dependency parsing only appear in the POS tagging validation/test set). In addition, there are 594 duplicated sentences in the VLSP 2013 POS tagging dataset (here, sentence duplication is not found in the union of the NER and dependency parsing sentences). Thus we have to perform duplication removal on the POS tagging dataset. Table 1 details the statistics of the experimental datasets.

[3] https://vlsp.org.vn/vlsp2013/eval

#### 3.1.2 Implementation

PhoNLP is implemented based on PyTorch (Paszke et al., 2019), employing the PhoBERT encoder implementation available from the transformers library (Wolf et al., 2020) and the Biaffine classifier implementation from Qi et al. (2020). We set both the label weight matrices $\mathbf{W}^{(1)}$ and $\mathbf{W}^{(2)}$ to have 100 rows, resulting in 100-dimensional soft POS tag embeddings. In addition, following Qi et al. (2018, 2020), FFNNs in equations 6–9 use 400-dimensional output layers.

We use the AdamW optimizer (Loshchilov and Hutter, 2019) and a fixed batch size at 32, and train for 40 epochs. The sizes of training sets are different, in which the POS tagging training set is the largest, consisting of 23906 sentences. Thus for each training epoch, we repeatedly sample from the NER and dependency parsing training sets to fill the gaps between the training set sizes. We perform a grid search to select the initial AdamW learning rate, $\lambda_1$ and $\lambda_2$. We find the optimal initial AdamW learning rate, $\lambda_1$ and $\lambda_2$ at 1e-5, 0.4 and 0.2, respectively. Here, we compute the average of the POS tagging accuracy, NER $F_1$-score and dependency parsing score LAS after each training epoch on the validation sets. We select the model checkpoint that produces the highest average score over the validation sets to apply to the test sets. Each of our reported scores is an average over 5 runs with different random seeds.

### 3.2 Results

Table 2 presents results obtained for our PhoNLP and compares them with those of a baseline approach of single-task training. For the single-task training approach: (i) We follow a common approach to fine-tune a pre-trained language model for POS tagging, appending a linear prediction layer on top of PhoBERT, as briefly described in Section 2.2. (ii) For NER, instead of a linear prediction layer, we append a CRF prediction layer on top of PhoBERT. (iii) For dependency parsing, predicted POS tags are produced by the learned single-task POS tagging model; then POS tags are represented by embeddings that are concatenated with the corresponding PhoBERT-based contextualized word embeddings, resulting in a sequence of input vectors for the Biaffine-based classifiers for dependency parsing (Qi et al., 2018). Here, the single-task training approach is based on the $\text{PhoBERT}_{\text{base}}$ version, employing the same hyper-

| | Model | POS | NER | LAS | UAS |
|---|---|---|---|---|---|
| Leak. | Single-task | 96.7† | 93.69 | 78.77† | 85.22† |
| | PhoNLP | **96.76** | **94.41** | **79.11** | **85.47** |
| Re-spl | Single-task | 93.68 | 93.69 | 77.89 | 84.78 |
| | PhoNLP | **93.88** | **94.51** | **78.17** | **84.95** |

Table 2: Performance results (in %) on the test sets for POS tagging (i.e. accuracy), NER (i.e. $F_1$-score) and dependency parsing (i.e. LAS and UAS scores). "Leak." abbreviates "leakage", denoting the results obtained w.r.t. the data leakage issue. "Re-spl" denotes the results obtained w.r.t. the data re-split and duplication removal for POS tagging to avoid the data leakage issue. "Single-task" refers to as the single-task training approach. † denotes scores taken from the PhoBERT paper (Nguyen and Nguyen, 2020). Note that "Single-task" NER is not affected by the data leakage issue.

parameter tuning and model selection strategy that we use for PhoNLP.

Note that PhoBERT helps produce state-of-the-art results for multiple Vietnamese NLP tasks (including but not limited to POS tagging, NER and dependency parsing in a single-task training strategy), and obtains higher performance results than VnCoreNLP. However, in both the PhoBERT and VnCoreNLP papers (Nguyen and Nguyen, 2020; Vu et al., 2018), results for POS tagging and dependency parsing are reported w.r.t. the data leakage issue. Our "Single-task" results in Table 2 regarding "Re-spl" (i.e. the data re-split and duplication removal for POS tagging to avoid the data leakage issue) can be viewed as new PhoBERT results for a proper experimental setup. Table 2 shows that in both setups "Leak." and "Re-spl", our joint multi-task training approach PhoNLP performs better than the PhoBERT-based single-task training approach, thus resulting in state-of-the-art performances for the three tasks of Vietnamese POS tagging, NER and dependency parsing.

## 4 PhoNLP toolkit

We present in this section a basic usage of our PhoNLP toolkit. We make PhoNLP simple to setup, i.e. users can install PhoNLP from either source or pip (e.g. `pip3 install phonlp`). We also aim to make PhoNLP simple to run from both the command-line and the Python API. For example, annotating a corpus with POS tagging, NER and dependency parsing can be performed by using a simple command as in Figure 2.

Assume that the input file "`input.txt`" in Figure 2 contains a sentence "Tôi đang làm_việc tại VinAI ." (I$_{\text{Tôi}}$ am$_{\text{đang}}$ working$_{\text{làm_việc}}$ at$_{\text{tại}}$ VinAI). Table 3 shows the annotated output in plain text form for this sentence. Similarly, we also get the same output by using the Python API as simple as in Figure 3. Furthermore, commands to (re-)train and evaluate PhoNLP using gold annotated corpora are detailed in the PhoNLP GitHub repository. Note that it is absolutely possible to directly employ our PhoNLP (re-)training and evaluation command scripts for other languages that have gold annotated corpora available for the three tasks and a pre-trained BERT-based language model available from the transformers library.

```
python3 run_phonlp.py --save_dir
./pretrained_phonlp --mode
annotate --input_file input.txt
--output_file output.txt
```

Figure 2: Minimal command to run PhoNLP. Here "save_dir" denote the path to the local machine folder that stores the pre-trained PhoNLP model.

| | | | | | |
|---|---|---|---|---|---|
| 1 | Tôi | P | O | 3 | sub |
| 2 | đang | R | O | 3 | adv |
| 3 | làm_việc | V | O | 0 | root |
| 4 | tại | E | O | 3 | loc |
| 5 | VinAI | Np | B-ORG | 4 | pob |
| 6 | . | CH | O | 3 | punct |

Table 3: The output in the output file "`output.txt`" for the sentence "Tôi đang làm_việc tại VinAI ." from the input file "`input.txt`" in Figure 2. The output is formatted with 6 columns representing word index, word form, POS tag, NER label, head index of the current word and its dependency relation type.

**Speed test:** We perform a sole CPU-based speed test using a personal computer with Intel Core i5 8265U 1.6GHz & 8GB of memory. For a GPU-based speed test, we employ a machine with a single NVIDIA RTX 2080Ti GPU. For performing the three NLP tasks jointly, PhoNLP obtains a speed at 15 sentences per second for the CPU-based test and 129 sentences per second for the GPU-based test, respectively, with an average of 23 word tokens per sentence and a batch size of 8.

## 5 Conclusion and future work

We have presented the first multi-task learning model PhoNLP for joint POS tagging, NER and dependency parsing in Vietnamese. Experiments on Vietnamese benchmark datasets show that PhoNLP outperforms its strong fine-tuned PhoBERT-based

```
import phonlp
# Automatically download the pre-trained PhoNLP model
# and save it in a local machine folder
phonlp.download(save_dir='./pretrained_phonlp')
# Load the pre-trained PhoNLP model
model = phonlp.load(save_dir='./pretrained_phonlp')
# Annotate a corpus
model.annotate(input_file='input.txt', output_file='output.txt')
# Annotate a sentence
model.print_out(model.annotate(text="Tôi đang làm_việc tại VinAI ."))
```

Figure 3: A simple and complete example code for using PhoNLP in Python.

single-task training baseline, producing state-of-the-art performance results. We publicly release PhoNLP as an easy-to-use open-source toolkit and hope that PhoNLP can facilitate future NLP research and applications. In future work, we will also apply PhoNLP to other languages.

## References


Tran Sy Bang and Virach Sornlertlamvanich. 2018. Sentiment classification for hotel booking review based on sentence dependency structure and sub-opinion analysis. *IEICE Transactions on Information and Systems*, E101.D(4):909–916.

Yoeng-Jin Chu and Tseng-Hong Liu. 1965. On the Shortest Arborescence of a Directed Graph. *Science Sinica*, 14:1396–1400.

Jacob Devlin, Ming-Wei Chang, Kenton Lee, and Kristina Toutanova. 2019. BERT: Pre-training of deep bidirectional transformers for language understanding. In *Proceedings of NAACL*, pages 4171–4186.

Timothy Dozat and Christopher D. Manning. 2017. Deep Biaffine Attention for Neural Dependency Parsing. In *Proceedings of ICLR*.

Jack Edmonds. 1967. Optimum Branchings. *Journal of Research of the National Bureau of Standards*, 71:233–240.

Kazuma Hashimoto, Caiming Xiong, Yoshimasa Tsuruoka, and Richard Socher. 2017. A Joint Many-Task Model: Growing a Neural Network for Multiple NLP Tasks. In *Proceedings of EMNLP*, pages 1923–1933.

Dan Kondratyuk and Milan Straka. 2019. 75 Languages, 1 Model: Parsing Universal Dependencies Universally. In *Proceedings of EMNLP-IJCNLP*, pages 2779–2795.

John D. Lafferty, Andrew McCallum, and Fernando C. N. Pereira. 2001. Conditional Random Fields: Probabilistic Models for Segmenting and Labeling Sequence Data. In *Proceedings of ICML*, pages 282–289.

Phuong Le-Hong and Duc-Thien Bui. 2018. A Factoid Question Answering System for Vietnamese. In *Companion Proceedings of the The Web Conference 2018*, page 1049–1055.

Zuchao Li, Shexia He, Zhuosheng Zhang, and Hai Zhao. 2018. Joint Learning of POS and Dependencies for Multilingual Universal Dependency Parsing. In *Proceedings of the CoNLL 2018 Shared Task*, pages 65–73.

Ilya Loshchilov and Frank Hutter. 2019. Decoupled Weight Decay Regularization. In *Proceedings of ICLR*.

Anh Tuan Nguyen, Mai Hoang Dao, and Dat Quoc Nguyen. 2020. A Pilot Study of Text-to-SQL Semantic Parsing for Vietnamese. In *Findings of EMNLP 2020*, pages 4079–4085.

Dat Quoc Nguyen. 2019. A neural joint model for Vietnamese word segmentation, POS tagging and dependency parsing. In *Proceedings of ALTA*, pages 28–34.

Dat Quoc Nguyen and Anh Tuan Nguyen. 2020. PhoBERT: Pre-trained language models for Vietnamese. In *Findings of EMNLP 2020*, pages 1037–1042.

Dat Quoc Nguyen, Dai Quoc Nguyen, and Son Bao Pham. 2017. Ripple Down Rules for Question Answering. *Semantic Web*, 8(4):511–532.

Dat Quoc Nguyen, Dai Quoc Nguyen, Son Bao Pham, Phuong-Thai Nguyen, and Minh Le Nguyen. 2014. From Treebank Conversion to Automatic Dependency Parsing for Vietnamese. In *Proceedings of NLDB*, pages 196–207.

Dat Quoc Nguyen and Karin Verspoor. 2018. An improved neural network model for joint POS tagging and dependency parsing. In *Proceedings of the CoNLL 2018 Shared Task*, pages 81–91.

Huyen Nguyen, Quyen Ngo, Luong Vu, Vu Tran, and Hien Nguyen. 2019. VLSP Shared Task: Named Entity Recognition. *Journal of Computer Science and Cybernetics*, 34(4):283–294.

Phuong-Thai Nguyen, Xuan-Luong Vu, Thi-Minh-Huyen Nguyen, Van-Hiep Nguyen, and Hong-Phuong Le. 2009. Building a Large Syntactically-Annotated Corpus of Vietnamese. In *Proceedings of LAW*, pages 182–185.

Adam Paszke, Sam Gross, et al. 2019. PyTorch: An Imperative Style, High-Performance Deep Learning Library. In *Proceedings of NeurIPS 2019*, pages 8024–8035.

Peng Qi, Timothy Dozat, Yuhao Zhang, and Christopher D. Manning. 2018. Universal Dependency parsing from scratch. In *Proceedings of the CoNLL 2018 Shared Task*, pages 160–170.

Peng Qi, Yuhao Zhang, Yuhui Zhang, Jason Bolton, and Christopher D. Manning. 2020. Stanza: A python natural language processing toolkit for many human languages. In *Proceedings of ACL: System Demonstrations*, pages 101–108.

Sebastian Ruder. 2019. *Neural Transfer Learning for Natural Language Processing*. Ph.D. thesis, National University of Ireland, Galway.

Rico Sennrich, Barry Haddow, and Alexandra Birch. 2016. Neural Machine Translation of Rare Words with Subword Units. In *Proceedings of ACL*, pages 1715–1725.

Huong Duong To and Phuc Do. 2020. Extracting triples from vietnamese text to create knowledge graph. In *Proceedings of KSE*, pages 219–223.

Viet Hong Tran, Huyen Thuong Vu, Thu Hoai Pham, Vinh Van Nguyen, and Minh Le Nguyen. 2016. A reordering model for Vietnamese-English statistical machine translation using dependency information. In *Proceedings of RIVF*, pages 125–130.

Diem Truong, Duc-Thuan Vo, and Uyen Trang Nguyen. 2017. Vietnamese open information extraction. In *Proceedings of SoICT*, page 135–142.

Thanh Vu, Dat Quoc Nguyen, Dai Quoc Nguyen, Mark Dras, and Mark Johnson. 2018. VnCoreNLP: A Vietnamese Natural Language Processing Toolkit. In *Proceedings of NAACL: Demonstrations*, pages 56–60.

Thomas Wolf, Lysandre Debut, et al. 2020. Transformers: State-of-the-Art Natural Language Processing. In *Proceedings of EMNLP 2020: System Demonstrations*, pages 38–45.

# Machine-Assisted Script Curation

**Manuel R. Ciosici Joseph Cummings, Mitchell DeHaven, Alex Hedges, Yash Kankanampati, Dong-Ho Lee, Ralph Weischedel, Marjorie Freedman**
manuelc@isi.edu, weisched@isi.edu, mrf@isi.edu
Information Sciences Institute, University of Southern California

## Abstract

We describe Machine-Aided Script Curator (MASC), a system for human-machine collaborative script authoring. Scripts produced with MASC include (1) English descriptions of sub-events that comprise a larger, complex event; (2) event types for each of those events; (3) a record of entities expected to participate in multiple sub-events; and (4) temporal sequencing between the sub-events. MASC automates portions of the script creation process with suggestions for event types, links to Wikidata, and sub-events that may have been forgotten. We illustrate how these automations are useful to the script writer with a few case-study scripts.

## 1 Introduction

Scripts have been of interest for encoding procedural knowledge and understanding stories for over 40 years (Schank and Abelson, 1977). In the form of checklists, recording procedural knowledge has revolutionized fields like medicine and aviation by encoding expert knowledge and best practices (Degani and Wiener, 1993; Gawande, 2010). In the last few years, researchers have turned their attention to automatic script discovery from text (Chambers, 2013; Weber et al., 2020, 2018). However, exclusively data-driven sub-event discovery methods face the challenge that narrative descriptions often omit common knowledge.[1]

We aim for a process for building a library of scripts through human-machine collaboration leveraging NLP techniques to augment human background knowledge. The resulting demonstration system serves two related purposes. First, it is a knowledge acquisition tool that supports the development of a repository of scripts for use by downstream applications. Second, it is an annotation tool that supports the creation of a library to aid our understanding of how people create scripts. Such a library can inform and/or benchmark future script discovery approaches. Each script includes a natural language description of the steps in the complex event with links to an ontology. Events within a script are connected by (a) temporal order (e.g., negotiating the price of a car happens *before* buying the car) and (b) by shared argument (e.g., the person buying a car is also the person who negotiated its price). We designed *Machine-Aided Script Curator (MASC)*, our script-creation tool, to be used by non-NLP experts.

While approaches to script discovery suffer from the incompleteness of text, human attempts to write machine-interpretable scripts suffer from the writer's own tendency to omit steps and, where required, the challenge of mapping to a formal ontology. To assist the script creators, MASC makes three types of suggestions: (1) the ontological type for each event; (2) a fine-grained ontological type for suggested arguments; and (3) steps that the curator might have forgotten.

In the following sections, we describe the process of creating a script in MASC and the NLP components that support suggestions.[2] While a large-scale script repository is beyond this paper's scope, we have created five sample scripts, which we use as case studies for understanding the script creation process and the suggestion capabilities. In Section 4, we use these scripts to measure the utility of MASC's suggestion capabilities. In Section 5, we describe the scripts' characteristics.

## 2 Related Work

Schank and Abelson (1977) proposed organizing knowledge about human behavior using scripts. Recent approaches attempt to "induce" scripts from

[1] Common knowledge might be missing from narrative descriptions due to the *quantity* and *relevance* maxims (Grice, 1975).

[2] A video of MASC is available at https://youtu.be/slvZWAYkRmA, and the source code and the sample scripts are at https://github.com/isi-vista/MASC.



*Proceedings of NAACL-HLT 2021: Demonstrations*, pages 8–17
June 6–11, 2021. ©2021 Association for Computational Linguistics

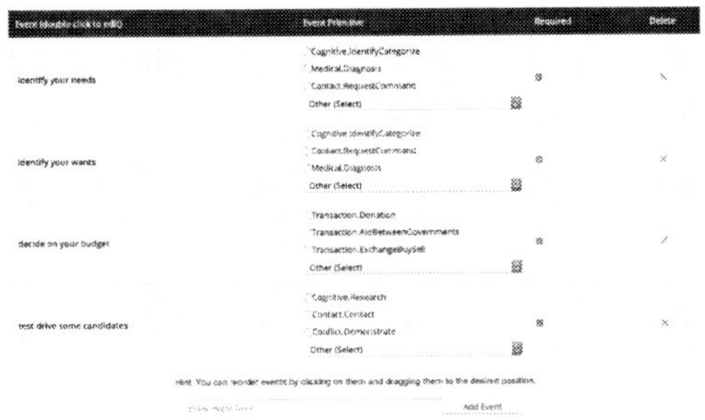

Figure 1: Adding events to the *buying a car* script.

large amounts of data rather than write scripts manually (Rudinger et al., 2015; Weber et al., 2018). Although improving year over year, these models still perform poorly (Recall@100 of ~7%, Weber et al., 2020) at predicting next events, given a set of preceding events - a necessary building block of scripts. These models' training data was obtained by asking human annotators to decide if event B happened because of event A. In contrast, the scripts produced by our curation tool incorporate the complexities of many different events in various causal orderings.

Both symbolic and neural approaches suffer from the lack of generic knowledge to "fill-in-the-blanks" or reject impossible events. Training systems to incorporate common-sense knowledge (Lin et al., 2019; Shwartz et al., 2020) has not yet addressed script creation. Another source of information for script discovery could be extraction from multiple languages and modalities. While some extraction systems have incorporated these other sources (Li et al., 2020), such extractions have not yet fed into script discovery. Resolving the co-occurrence of events or entities between languages and modalities often relies on a common mapping, e.g., a structured ontology, such as ACE (Walker et al., 2006) or ERE (Song et al., 2015). While our Machine-Aided Script Curator (MASC) does employ a structured ontology, it does not currently incorporate multi-modal or non-English sources. However, the limited ontology allows the event-sequencing background knowledge we encode to be used as a supplement to state-of-the-art information extraction systems, like OneIE (Lin et al., 2020) and DYGIE++ (Wadden et al., 2019), providing connections between otherwise disconnected extractions.

## 3 Overview of Script Creation

The curator initiates script creation by providing a name and description for the script and then enters, as text, the events in the script (Figure 1). Step entry is free-form, but we have noticed a tendency for curators to enter short, imperative sentences around a central agent's actions (e.g., *go to a car dealership, take a test drive*). Currently, script creation, unlike traditional annotation, is decoupled from any particular document. In cases where the curator is not familiar with a topic, we have used external resources to provide context (e.g., a Wikihow page open in a different window). In this setting, curation is akin to annotation that encourages the annotator to use both the material they read and prior knowledge.

The curators assign an ontology type to the main event in each step (e.g., *Movement* for both *go to a car dealership* and *take a test drive*). The ontology is configurable and can be replaced. We include a project-specific ontology with MASC's source code. When saved, scripts include both the curators' description and the selected ontology type (described in Section 4.1). This choice allows type decisions to be revisited if the ontology changes and limits the degree to which the small number of event types constrains the script's expressiveness. Downstream applications can choose whether to use the linguistic representation of the events or the normalized ontology types.

After the curators finish entering events, they encode connections between the events (Figure 2). There are two ways to connect events: the first, traditionally the focus of scripts, is temporal order; and the second is shared arguments (e.g., the same person is the agent of both *Movement* events *go to a car dealership* and *take a test drive*). To add sequential order, the curators enter pairwise *before* relations. Alternatively, they select multiple events and anchor them as coming before or after a single event. The latter method is convenient when the complete order is under-defined.[3] The curators add shared arguments to the script by selecting multiple events with the same argument, naming the argument (e.g., *buyer, seller* in Figure 2), and assigning an entity type (e.g., *PER* in Figure 2) and ontological role to each argument

[3]For example, after arriving at the car dealership, the potential buyer is likely to both walk around looking at cars and talk to a salesperson, but there is no defined order between the walking and talking.

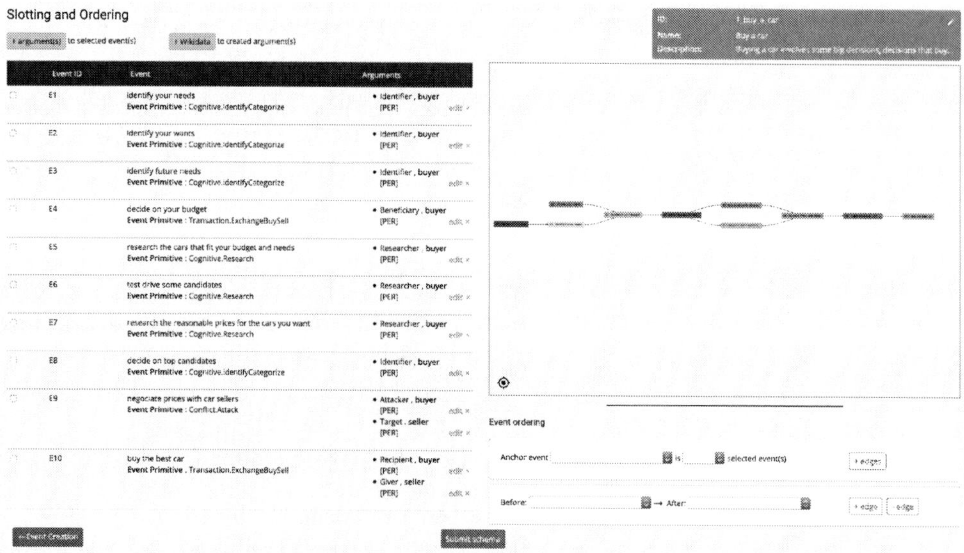


Figure 2: Adding details to events. For each event on the left, curators can add arguments. On the right side, curators can establish temporal order and visualize the script as an interactive graph.

(e.g., *Identifier, Researcher* in Figure 2). While this process is mostly manual, MASC uses the ontology's constraints to limit the available label options. In addition to project-specific entity types, MASC suggests links to the much larger set of types available using Wikidata entities (e.g., suggesting Q786803 for *car dealership*). These links provide a connection to an extensive knowledge graph and can provide additional information when the scripts are applied.

Finally, the curators review events that are automatically generated based on the manually entered description and initial script (described in Section 4.3). The suggestions can add intermediate steps that the curators may have missed, complete a script that was intentionally unfinished by the curator, or suggest alternative related paths (e.g., leasing instead of purchasing a car).

## 4 Suggestion Capabilities

To aid script creation, MASC incorporates three suggestion capabilities: suggestions for the ontological event type, suggestions for links to Wikidata, and suggestions for additional events to incorporate in the script. Below, we describe the models behind these capabilities and, for each model, report the accuracy using the five sample scripts created for this paper. Given the small sample size, the five sample scripts are best thought of as case studies, not a benchmark. Table 1 provides per-script analysis.

### 4.1 Event Type Classification

Each sub-event is ontologized with one of 41 event types through a semi-automated process. The ontology labels support connecting information to extraction engines and thus allow a script to provide potential event-event relations given information extraction output. Furthermore, the ontology labels provide language- and media-independent knowledge for identifying potential instances of the scripts.

There has been much work on automatic detection of event types (and triggers) in text (e.g., Bronstein et al. (2015); Lin et al. (2020); Peng et al. (2016)). Here, our input data (and goals) are slightly different. The ontology we use, while overlapping with ACE (Walker et al., 2006), introduces several new event types for which we do not have annotated training examples. Instead, the ontology provides a short definition and template for each event type. The curator's input events tend to be short imperative sentences with different linguistic characteristics than the text annotated in, e.g., ACE. Unlike standard information extraction, we need not identify a specific trigger phase.[4] Thus, we use a different approach to event labeling.

[4]Triggers are often used as a means to identify arguments of interest. But here, partly because of the telegraphic nature of the text entries, the arguments are often missing and, therefore, explicitly added.

To map from the curators' description of an event to the ontology, we use a version of Sentence-RoBERTa (Reimers and Gurevych, 2019)[5] to estimate the similarity of the curators' text input to the prose description of each action in the ontology. For example, for the user input *go to a car dealership*, the action description *Explicit mention of granting or allowing entry or exit from a location* receives the highest similarity score, and the corresponding action type *Movement.Transportation* becomes one of the recommendations. MASC suggests the three ontology actions most similar to the user's description. The user can accept one of the suggestions or pick a different type from the ontology (Figure 1, second column).

As mentioned earlier, the event type similarity depends on the ontology event type definitions and the event type templates. In preliminary experiments, we found using both together outperformed using either only the definitions or only the templates. While MASC's event type classification does not require training data, it depends on both the presence of templates and definitions in the ontology and their quality.

**Performance on Case-Study Scripts** The five scripts contain 58 events. We measure how often the model correctly predicts the event type that the curator selects. Accuracy of the top-1, -3, and -5 are 24, 48, and 55, respectively.[6] MASC presents the top-three suggestions to the curator; thus, accuracy at top-3 most closely relates to the curator's experience.

### 4.2 KGTK

In Section 2, we describe identifying the key repeating arguments of script events and labeling those arguments with their entity type and their role in each event using an ontology. That ontology provides only coarse distinctions between entities (e.g., a single category for facilities that does not distinguish *a car dealership* from *a school* or *a bank*). To support finer-grained distinctions and, in the future, leverage external knowledge sources, we incorporate connections to Wikidata[7] using KGTK (Ilievski et al., 2020). MASC's links aim to ground descriptive noun phrases (e.g., *car dealership*) in the large Wikidata ontology and do not require grounding specific, named entities (e.g., *Toyota*).

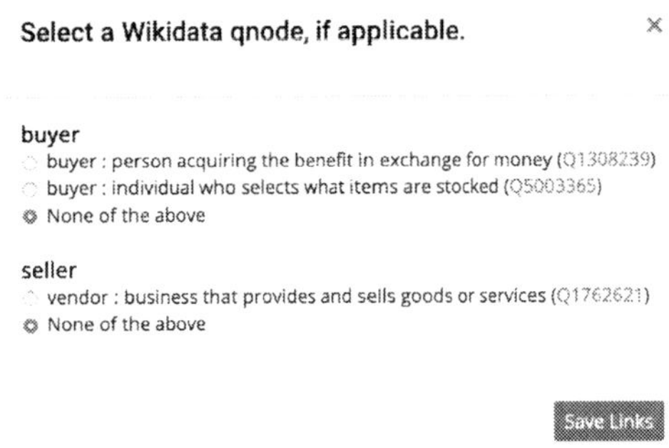


Figure 3: Reviewing the Wikidata link suggestions.

KGTK is an open-source toolkit that simplifies searching and interacting with various knowledge graphs, including Wikidata. KGTK provides a simple API for searching Wikidata entries, via Elasticsearch,[8] based on their titles and aliases (e.g., the Wikidata entry *motor car* also has the aliases *auto*, *automobile*, and *car*). KGTK also provides filtering functionality for candidate Wikidata entries. Since we are not interested in grounding specific named entities, we only return Wikidata entries representing Wikidata classes. Within MASC, KGTK allows users to link terms used in events to Wikidata. During argument creation, the curator provides a text label for each key argument. A background process then queries KGTK using the text label assigned to each argument. Candidates from KGTK are reranked using the Sentence-RoBERTa model to generate similarity scores between the label strings and the candidate Wikidata text descriptions. Before finishing a script, for each term in the script, the curator can select one of the candidates from KGTK or *None of the above* (Figure 3).

**Performance on Case-Study Scripts**. To evaluate entity linking, we treat the scripts created by the curators (and the mapping from the reference variables to Wikidata) as the labels. This is necessary since we do not have a ground-truth mapping from strings to Wikidata entities, and curators can use the same string to reference different entities. For example, *car* can refer to an automobile, a railway carriage, or a streetcar. The metric we use measures the ratio of reference variables linked to a specific Wikidata entity to the total number of

[5]Our Sentence-RoBERTa model is trained on more data. We use the two data sets in the original paper, SNLI (Bowman et al., 2015) and MNLI (Williams et al., 2018), and add the newer ANLI (Nie et al., 2020).

[6]The mean reciprocal rank (MRR, Radev et al., 2002) was 0.35 on the top three model predictions.

[7]`https://www.wikidata.org`

[8]`https://www.elastic.co/elasticsearch/`

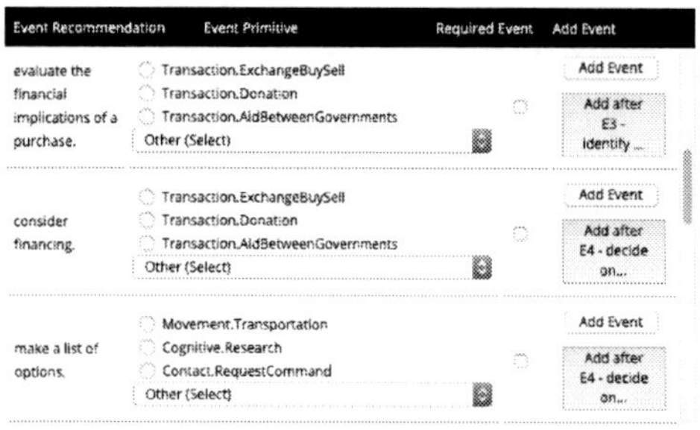


Figure 4: GPT-2 recommendations for *buying a car.*

reference variables used. We find that curators link 67% of the unique reference variables to Wikidata (e.g., *buyer* in Figure 3). We have not measured the ceiling on using Wikidata as an argument ontology. However, we suspect that refining the linking approach could yield more connections to Wikidata. Even at this low level of recall, at least a few concept-specific elements match for most scripts. In the future, these connection points could support script augmentation using common-sense and domain knowledge from Wikidata.

### 4.3 Event Recommendations

Since even the most experienced curators may overlook an action in an event script, we explored hypothesizing omitted events using GPT-2 (Radford et al., 2019) *without any fine-tuning*.

The first challenge is formulating input to GPT-2. We provide the title/name of the schema (e.g., *buying a car*), a description of the complex event (e.g., *Purchasing a car is a large investment that requires careful documentation and consideration of transportation requirements.*), and a request (e.g., *Describe steps of buying a car.*), followed by the first few events of the script. In the initial version, we used a form of the events as *First, Identify your needs. Then, Decide on your budget. Next, Identify car models you can afford.* However, a numerical formulation proved much more effective (e.g., *1. Identify your needs 2. Decide on your budget 3. Identify car models you can afford 4.*) and resulted in more coherent events.

To filter undesirable or redundant output, we pass GPT-2 outputs through a sequence of filters. We remove undesired strings characteristic of neural text generation, like empty strings (Stahlberg and Byrne, 2019), and outputs that are invalid in the context of schema creation: strings of less than two words and those with sequences of non-alphabetic characters. We address duplicated output, a considerable concern for GPT-2, especially given the short and similar inputs.[9] The filters eliminate strings with duplicates in the alternatives or the human-curated schema. To account for semantic duplicates, such as *go to dealership* and *go to the car dealership*, we use a variant of Gestalt Pattern Matching (Ratcliff and Metzener, 1988) through Python's *difflib*. For usability, we suggest at most 12 sub-events per script. Figure 4 shows the interface for reviewing event recommendations.

**Performance on Case Studies.** We measure the performance of GPT-2 recommendations in two ways. First, we generate recommendations for five scripts created by curators and ask the curators to accept relevant GPT-2 recommendations. We instruct curators to accept recommendations even if the recommended events represent alternative paths (or are semantically redundant). With these instructions, the curators accept 98% of GPT-2's recommendations. The high acceptance rate indicates that even with our simple setup for event recommendation using a language model, the system suggests domain-relevant events.

For the second evaluation, we instruct the curators to accept only those GPT-2 recommendations that add to their existing script. In other words, they only accept events that add details to the scripts or supply some missing information. We instruct curators to reject recommendations for alternative script scenarios. With these instructions, curators accept 23% of GPT-2's recommendations. This result illustrates the feasibility of supplementing human knowledge with generations from language models. Since MASC uses GPT-2 *after* the human felt the script was complete, the machine identifies events previously overlooked by the human.

**Mixed-Initiative script curation.** Given the success of GPT-2 recommendations after script curation, a natural next step is for curators to work with GPT-2 interactively. In the *mixed-initiative mode*, a curator specifies a script's name, definition, and first step. GPT-2 then suggests multiple options for the next step. The curator can use one of the suggestions, edit it, or ignore all the suggestions and manually input the next step. Every time the curator adds a step to the script, GPT-2 follows with suggestions for the next step. We found that

[9]GPT-2 often generates strings with a similar meaning, but lexically different, e.g., for a script on buying a car, it might generate *buy*, *buy the car*, and *purchase the car*. It is superfluous to show users all three suggestions.

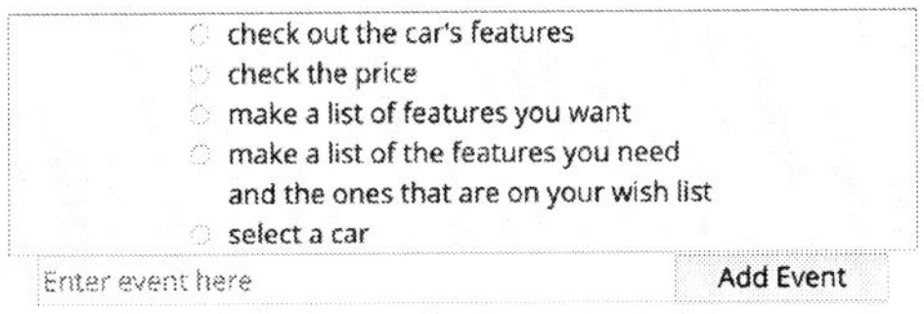


Figure 5: Mixed-Initiative: GPT-2's suggestions for the script *buying a car*, given the first step *Identify your needs*.

automated step generation took less than 3 seconds in the slowest case on modern hardware (NVIDIA GeForce RTX2080Ti).

To evaluate the effectiveness of mixed-initiative mode, we asked four curators to create a total of twelve scripts using the mode. We instructed the curators to accept event suggestions only when they are a natural continuation of the script. Out of GPT-2's 105 suggestion sets, the curators accepted an event from 50 sets (48% acceptance rate). In six more cases, the curators used a GPT-2 suggestion as a starting point and edited the suggestions to suit the script better. We found the mixed-initiative scripts to be just as comprehensive as the scripts detailed in Table 1, where GPT-2 suggested missing events only after the curators created an initial script.

## 5 Discussion and Future Work

With this demonstration system, we provide an approach to human-machine collaboration for building a repository of scripts. Having such a repository, for a diverse set of events, will allow us to investigate how procedural knowledge introduced to the AI community 40 years ago (Schank and Abelson, 1977) can be broadly applied. By facilitating the human creation of scripts, we can better understand what is required to develop automatic script discovery approaches.

While we have not yet created a large repository of scripts, we have created five scripts with which we start this analysis. The scripts cover topics with varying degree of "common knowledge": *Planning and Managing an Evacuation* (EVAC), *Ordering Food at a Restaurant* (FOOD), *Finding and Starting a New Job* (JOB), *Obtaining Medical Treatment* (MED), and *Corporate Merger or Acquisition* (MERGER). A single curator created these scripts, which we use to illustrate future directions for MASC and interesting properties of the scripts themselves. Having multiple curators for even a small number of scripts would provide insights into the diversity, prior knowledge, and level of detail a script author uses. In our analysis, we have seen that the scripts created with MASC encode knowledge that is uncommon in news-like data sets. For example, our curator included *sign confidentiality agreement* as an event in the script for a MERGER. While news frequently reports the final step of a merger, the full process is rarely described.

Table 1 summarizes the key characteristics of each of these scripts. They vary in (a) the number of steps initially created (row 1), with only 5 steps for MED and 16 for both EVAC and JOB; and (b) the time required for initial script creation (row 6). The script that took the longest was not the one with the most steps (or the most arguments). Instead, it was the domain that the curator knew the least about (and thus chose to research). For all five scripts, there were cases where the event type suggestions were correct, but for three of the five, MASC suggested the correct type less than half the time, suggesting that better automatic event typing could increase the curators' speed.

All scripts contain entities that play a role in multiple events (row 3, first and second numbers). For example, in EVAC, the evacuation manager plays some role in all events, while the evacuee plays a role in most but not all. While some arguments cannot be linked to Wikidata, all five scripts contain at least one argument that can be linked (row 3, last number). Future work could both improve linking accuracy and use Wikidata as a source of knowledge to provide additional context (and suggestions) to the curator.

While the prototypical script is a timeline with complete order between all pairs of events, we see sub-graphs with unordered steps in our data. Three of the five sample scripts display this behavior; for example, in JOB, *searching for open positions* and *notifying network that they are looking for a job* are unordered. The visualization of the schema in Figure 2 illustrates this pattern with no order between *E2* and *E3*.

MASC incorporates machine suggestions of unrecorded events. In four of the five scripts, the curator accepted at least one suggestion. Interestingly, the curator incorporated more suggestions for two events that one thinks of as everyday experiences (FOOD and MED) than they did for the script they were unfamiliar with (MERGER). This suggests that the recommendation functionality can be useful even in a familiar domain; by capturing

| | | EVAC | FOOD | JOB | MED | MERGER |
|---|---|---|---|---|---|---|
| 1 | # Events in initial script | 16 | 9 | 16 | 5 | 12 |
| 2 | Accuracy at top-1, 3, 5 for event types | 25/44/50 | 11/33/67 | 13/44/44 | 20/60/60 | 50/67/67 |
| 3 | # Entity instances, occurrences of those entities, and unique links to Wikidata | 2/26/1 | 5/18/3 | 2/24/2 | 3/11/3 | 3/24/2 |
| 4 | # Event suggestions selected for single script and all relevant (max. 12 per script) | 4/8 | 3/12 | 0/11 | 5/12 | 2/12 |
| 5 | Non-linear path | Y | Y | Y | N | N |
| 6 | Self-reported time | 1.5 hrs | 0.5 hr | 1 hr | 0.5 hr | 2.5 hrs |

Table 1: Characteristics of five sample scripts.

what the curator omits through forgetfulness or because they assume common knowledge. Further exploration of how a machine can aid a person whose knowledge may be incomplete or may forget to be explicit seems promising. Examples of possible research directions include incorporating suggestions from approaches that discover scripts (e.g., Rudinger et al. (2015); Weber et al. (2018, 2020)) and leveraging background knowledge (e.g., Wikidata).

## 6 Ethical Considerations

Many technological innovations require ethical considerations, even more so for those involving machine learning while also being a demonstration paper that provides working technology. Below we address the review questions raised in the NAACL Ethics Review Questions.[10]

*Bias.* The bias in generative language models has been well documented. In general, using a human-in-the-loop process means that rather than treating an automatically generated label or event as correct, we treat it as a suggestion that the curator can ignore. Still, the suggestions can influence the curator. Thus it is vital that the metrics reported in this paper be interpreted with an understanding of the potential for bias and any use of MASC account for bias.

MASC incorporates both a predefined ontology and the ability to link to an extensive external resource (Wikidata). Given the size of the predefined ontology is small, to apply MASC to a new domain, users would likely need to update the ontology. MASC's approach to aligning English descriptions to the ontology makes adding new event classes easy. Wikidata, while much larger and growing, is also subject to the bias of Wikidata's editors, their knowledge, and their choices about what to include. Wikidata over-represents some issues, while some socially important ones are under-represented or missing. Wikidata linking is optional; thus in a domain that is not well covered, a curator can skip the linking step or replace Wikidata with a domain-relevant resource.

The suggestion capabilities described in Section 4 use pretrained language models (GPT-2 and RoBERTa). The bias of these algorithms, measuring that bias, and mitigating it is an active area of work. Recent work has provided data sets for measuring bias (Nadeem et al., 2020) and meta-studies of the approaches taken to study and address bias (Blodgett et al., 2020). Much work has focused on bias as it impacts demographic groups. MASC focuses on events, not individuals. The publicly available GPT-2 models have learned from data that might not cover current events (e.g., GPT-2 was trained before the COVID-19 epidemic), represents only English dialects from the inner-circle (Dunn and Adams, 2020), and contains toxic language (Gehman et al., 2020). In our immediate context, we mitigate against the challenge presented by language model bias by requiring manual review of all automatically suggested output. If the ideas in this paper were extended to a fully automatic approach, language model and domain-specific studies of the impact of bias on LM-based suggestions would be necessary.

*Data Set.* To understand how the tool is used and future research directions, we created five sample scripts which we included in the supplementary material. These scripts provide interesting examples of what we could learn from a larger scale data set; however, they are not large enough themselves to serve as a new benchmark. The five scripts were created by full-time research staff compensated following US state and federal law. The scripts were created by a single individual and represent that individual's pre-existing knowledge (and their im-

[10] `https://2021.naacl.org/ethics/review-questions/`

plicit biases). To counter bias in a large-scale script repository, we recommend that the curator workforce is diverse and that any given activity is represented in scripts written by multiple people. Any released repository should have sufficient reporting about the data set creators to provide users with an understanding of data bias. The paper reports empirical results based on this five script sample. However, the paper acknowledges that the sample is small and treats these results as case studies for MASC, not a new benchmark.

*Intended Use.* The most immediate use of MASC is to create a repository of script information – either broadly available to researchers or within a specific research community. In some cases, e.g., the steps to plan a rescue operation, both the generation of the script and its application are generally understood as positive. In other cases, e.g., the steps in grooming an individual for human trafficking, the script's conclusion is negative, but understanding the process is necessary to prevent the activity. As AI's ability to discover and apply such knowledge increases, it will be necessary to regularly audit the use cases to ensure the focus remains a benefit to society. If the human-in-the-loop approaches used here were integrated into a fully automated system, further auditing of bias (and accuracy) would be necessary.

*Compute Time and Power.* Most of the models used for this demonstration are pretrained and publicly available. The pretraining and fine tuning described in Section 4.1 took less than 20 hours using a single GPU.

## Acknowledgment

This material is based on research supported by DARPA under agreement number FA8750-19-2-0500. The U.S. Government is authorized to reproduce and distribute reprints for Governmental purposes notwithstanding any copyright notation thereon. The views and conclusions contained herein are those of the authors and should not be interpreted as necessarily representing the official policies or endorsements, either expressed or implied, of DARPA or the U.S. Government.

## References

Su Lin Blodgett, Solon Barocas, Hal Daumé III, and Hanna Wallach. 2020. Language (technology) is power: A critical survey of "bias" in NLP. In *Proceedings of the 58th Annual Meeting of the Association for Computational Linguistics*, pages 5454–5476, Online. Association for Computational Linguistics.

Samuel R. Bowman, Gabor Angeli, Christopher Potts, and Christopher D. Manning. 2015. A large annotated corpus for learning natural language inference. In *Proceedings of the 2015 Conference on Empirical Methods in Natural Language Processing*, pages 632–642, Lisbon, Portugal. Association for Computational Linguistics.

Ofer Bronstein, Ido Dagan, Qi Li, Heng Ji, and Anette Frank. 2015. Seed-based event trigger labeling: How far can event descriptions get us? In *Proceedings of the 53rd Annual Meeting of the Association for Computational Linguistics and the 7th International Joint Conference on Natural Language Processing (Volume 2: Short Papers)*, pages 372–376, Beijing, China. Association for Computational Linguistics.

Nathanael Chambers. 2013. Event schema induction with a probabilistic entity-driven model. In *Proceedings of the 2013 Conference on Empirical Methods in Natural Language Processing*, pages 1797–1807, Seattle, Washington, USA. Association for Computational Linguistics.

Asaf Degani and Earl L. Wiener. 1993. Cockpit checklists: Concepts, design, and use. *Human Factors*, 35(2):345–359.

Jonathan Dunn and Ben Adams. 2020. Geographically-Balanced Gigaword Corpora for 50 Language Varieties. In *Proceedings of The 12th Language Resources and Evaluation Conference*, pages 2521–2529, Marseille, France. European Language Resources Association.

Atul Gawande. 2010. *The checklist manifesto: how to get things right.* Metropolitan Books, New York.

Samuel Gehman, Suchin Gururangan, Maarten Sap, Yejin Choi, and Noah A. Smith. 2020. RealToxicityPrompts: Evaluating neural toxic degeneration in language models. In *Findings of the Association for Computational Linguistics: EMNLP 2020*, pages 3356–3369, Online. Association for Computational Linguistics.

H Paul Grice. 1975. Logic and conversation, syntax and semantics. *Speech Acts*, 3:41–58.

Filip Ilievski, Daniel Garijo, Hans Chalupsky, Naren Teja Divvala, Yixiang Yao, Craig Rogers, Ronpeng Li, Jun Liu, Amandeep Singh, Daniel Schwabe, and Pedro Szekely. 2020. KGTK: A toolkit for large knowledge graph manipulation and analysis. In *The Semantic Web – ISWC 2020*, pages 278–293, Cham. Springer International Publishing.

Manling Li, Alireza Zareian, Ying Lin, Xiaoman Pan, Spencer Whitehead, Brian Chen, Bo Wu, Heng Ji, Shih-Fu Chang, Clare Voss, Daniel Napierski, and Marjorie Freedman. 2020. GAIA: A fine-grained multimedia knowledge extraction system. In *Proceedings of the 58th Annual Meeting of the Association for Computational Linguistics: System Demonstrations*, pages 77–86, Online. Association for Computational Linguistics.

Bill Yuchen Lin, Xinyue Chen, Jamin Chen, and Xiang Ren. 2019. KagNet: Knowledge-aware graph networks for commonsense reasoning. In *Proceedings of the 2019 Conference on Empirical Methods in Natural Language Processing and the 9th International Joint Conference on Natural Language Processing (EMNLP-IJCNLP)*, pages 2829–2839, Hong Kong, China. Association for Computational Linguistics.

Ying Lin, Heng Ji, Fei Huang, and Lingfei Wu. 2020. A joint neural model for information extraction with global features. In *Proceedings of the 58th Annual Meeting of the Association for Computational Linguistics*, pages 7999–8009, Online. Association for Computational Linguistics.

Moin Nadeem, Anna Bethke, and Siva Reddy. 2020. StereoSet: Measuring stereotypical bias in pretrained language models.

Yixin Nie, Adina Williams, Emily Dinan, Mohit Bansal, Jason Weston, and Douwe Kiela. 2020. Adversarial NLI: A new benchmark for natural language understanding. In *Proceedings of the 58th Annual Meeting of the Association for Computational Linguistics*, pages 4885–4901, Online. Association for Computational Linguistics.

Haoruo Peng, Yangqiu Song, and Dan Roth. 2016. Event detection and co-reference with minimal supervision. In *Proceedings of the 2016 Conference on Empirical Methods in Natural Language Processing*, pages 392–402, Austin, Texas. Association for Computational Linguistics.

Dragomir R. Radev, Hong Qi, Harris Wu, and Weiguo Fan. 2002. Evaluating web-based question answering systems. In *Proceedings of the Third International Conference on Language Resources and Evaluation (LREC'02)*, Las Palmas, Canary Islands - Spain. European Language Resources Association (ELRA).

Alec Radford, Jeffrey Wu, Rewon Child, David Luan, Dario Amodei, and Ilya Sutskever. 2019. Language models are unsupervised multitask learners. *OpenAI blog*, 1(8):9.

John W Ratcliff and David E Metzener. 1988. Pattern-matching - the gestalt approach. *Dr Dobbs Journal*, 13(7):46.

Nils Reimers and Iryna Gurevych. 2019. Sentence-BERT: Sentence embeddings using Siamese BERT-networks. In *Proceedings of the 2019 Conference on Empirical Methods in Natural Language Processing and the 9th International Joint Conference on Natural Language Processing (EMNLP-IJCNLP)*, pages 3982–3992, Hong Kong, China. Association for Computational Linguistics.

Rachel Rudinger, Pushpendre Rastogi, Francis Ferraro, and Benjamin Van Durme. 2015. Script induction as language modeling. In *Proceedings of the 2015 Conference on Empirical Methods in Natural Language Processing*, pages 1681–1686, Lisbon, Portugal. Association for Computational Linguistics.

Roger C Schank and Robert P Abelson. 1977. *Scripts, plans, goals, and understanding: An inquiry into human knowledge structures*. Lawrence Erlbaum Associates.

Vered Shwartz, Peter West, Ronan Le Bras, Chandra Bhagavatula, and Yejin Choi. 2020. Unsupervised commonsense question answering with self-talk. In *Proceedings of the 2020 Conference on Empirical Methods in Natural Language Processing (EMNLP)*, pages 4615–4629, Online. Association for Computational Linguistics.

Zhiyi Song, Ann Bies, Stephanie Strassel, Tom Riese, Justin Mott, Joe Ellis, Jonathan Wright, Seth Kulick, Neville Ryant, and Xiaoyi Ma. 2015. From light to rich ERE: Annotation of entities, relations, and events. In *Proceedings of the The 3rd Workshop on EVENTS: Definition, Detection, Coreference, and Representation*, pages 89–98, Denver, Colorado. Association for Computational Linguistics.

Felix Stahlberg and Bill Byrne. 2019. On NMT search errors and model errors: Cat got your tongue? In *Proceedings of the 2019 Conference on Empirical Methods in Natural Language Processing and the 9th International Joint Conference on Natural Language Processing (EMNLP-IJCNLP)*, pages 3356–3362, Hong Kong, China. Association for Computational Linguistics.

David Wadden, Ulme Wennberg, Yi Luan, and Hannaneh Hajishirzi. 2019. Entity, relation, and event extraction with contextualized span representations. In *Proceedings of the 2019 Conference on Empirical Methods in Natural Language Processing and the 9th International Joint Conference on Natural Language Processing (EMNLP-IJCNLP)*, pages 5784–5789, Hong Kong, China. Association for Computational Linguistics.

Christopher Walker, Stephanie Strassel, Julie Medero, and Kazuaki Maeda. 2006. ACE 2005 Multilingual Training Corpus LDC2006T06. Web Download. Philadelphia: Linguistic Data Consortium.

Noah Weber, Rachel Rudinger, and Benjamin Van Durme. 2020. Causal inference of script knowledge. In *Proceedings of the 2020 Conference on Empirical Methods in Natural Language Processing (EMNLP)*, pages 7583–7596, Online. Association for Computational Linguistics.

Noah Weber, Leena Shekhar, Niranjan Balasubramanian, and Nathanael Chambers. 2018. Hierarchical quantized representations for script generation. In *Proceedings of the 2018 Conference on Empirical Methods in Natural Language Processing*, pages

3783–3792, Brussels, Belgium. Association for Computational Linguistics.

Adina Williams, Nikita Nangia, and Samuel Bowman. 2018. A broad-coverage challenge corpus for sentence understanding through inference. In *Proceedings of the 2018 Conference of the North American Chapter of the Association for Computational Linguistics: Human Language Technologies, Volume 1 (Long Papers)*, pages 1112–1122, New Orleans, Louisiana. Association for Computational Linguistics.

# NAMER: A Node-Based Multitasking Framework for Multi-Hop Knowledge Base Question Answering

**Minhao Zhang**[1] **Ruoyu Zhang**[1] **Lei Zou**[1,2] **Yinnian Lin**[1] **Sen Hu**[1]
[1]Peking University, China;
[2]National Engineering Laboratory for Big Data Analysis Technology and Application (PKU), China;
{zhangminhao,ry_zhang,zoulei,linyinnian,husen}@pku.edu.cn

## Abstract

We present NAMER, an open-domain Chinese knowledge base question answering system based on a novel node-based framework that better grasps the structural mapping between questions and KB queries by aligning the nodes in a query with their corresponding mentions in question. Equipped with techniques including data augmentation and multitasking, we show that the proposed framework outperforms the previous SoTA on CCKS CKBQA dataset. Moreover, we develop a novel data annotation strategy that facilitates the node-to-mention alignment, a dataset[1] with such strategy is also published to promote further research. An online demo of NAMER[2] is provided to visualize our framework and supply extra information for users, a video illustration[3] of NAMER is also available.

## 1 Introduction

With the rapid popularization of knowledge bases (KB), knowledge base question answering (KBQA) (Unger et al., 2014) has witnessed much research effort to fulfill a robust system to simplify users' access to KBs. For any given factoid question in natural language, KBQA system utilizes its background KB for answers. Recently, many SoTA KBQA systems adopt a semantic parsing (Kwiatkowski et al., 2013; Yih et al., 2014) framework, in which they convert the question to a KB query (e.g. SPARQL, Prud'hommeaux, 2008) to get answers.

Since queries are highly structured, a robust KBQA system needs to grasp the structural mapping (Figure 1) between a question and its query. However, most previous works either adopted an end-to-end model that failed to directly use such mappings (Ge et al., 2019; Ji et al.) or devised a template or rule-based pipeline (Hu et al., 2018; Cui et al., 2017) that may lose generality in real-world applications. To preserve generality, Shen et al. (2019) incorporated a pointer generator (See et al., 2017) into the pipeline to learn the mapping between an entity and its mention. Nevertheless, the system failed to utilize the mappings of variables, literals, and types in a query.

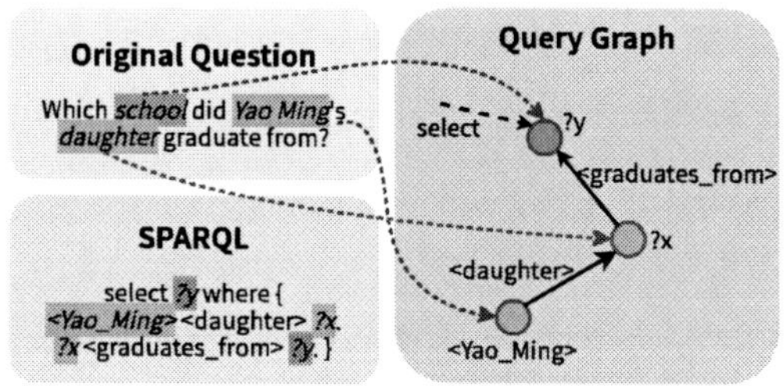


Figure 1: Structural mapping between a question and its corresponding SPARQL query.

In this paper, we argue that learning the complete question-query mapping (i.e. the alignments of all nodes to their mention, as in Figure 1) aids the system to achieve better performance. Hence, we supplement an open-domain complex Chinese KBQA dataset with annotations of all node mentions. Based on the additional data, we propose a novel node-based multi-hop KBQA framework that fully grasps the mappings of entities, variables, literals, and types. Unlike prior works, we generate the pointer of all query nodes to their mention to represent the mapping and exploit such mappings in downstream relation extraction task. Also, we explore techniques including multitasking to further improve model performance. Based on the framework, we implement a publicly available Chinese KBQA system, NAMER, for users to query KBs by natural language, which offers convenience for non-expert users to use KB and is thus fairly useful in practice. In short, the contributions of this work are: 1) we propose a novel KBQA framework with a strong ability to grasp structural mapping,

[1]https://github.com/ridiculouz/CKBQA
[2]http://kbqademo.gstore.cn
[3]https://youtu.be/yetnVye_hg4



*Proceedings of NAACL-HLT 2021: Demonstrations*, pages 18–25
June 6–11, 2021. 

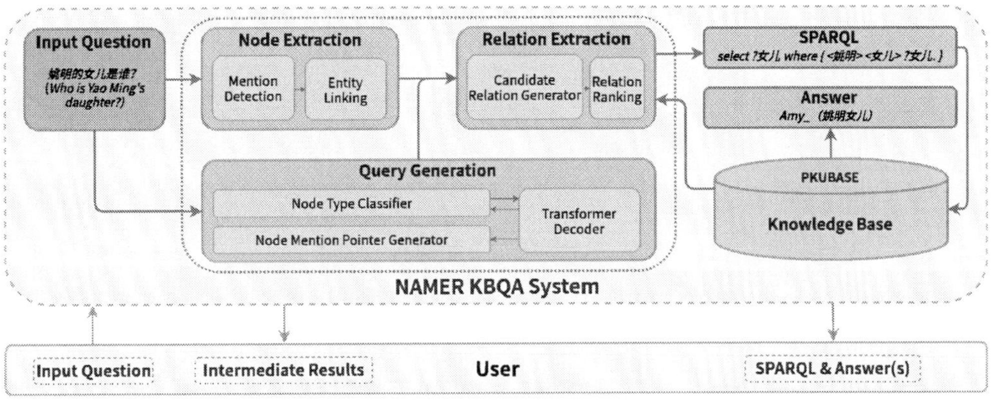


Figure 2: Architecture of the proposed system

the approach reaches SoTA results on a Chinese KBQA dataset, 2) we present a new data annotation format to better train KBQA models and publish a supplementary dataset of this format to prompt future research and 3) we implement an online demonstration of NAMER that can visualize our framework and aid users to explore KBs.

## 2 System Overview

This section explains the overall architecture of the proposed framework and the UI of the system.

### 2.1 Framework Architecture

Figure 2 illustrates the architecture of our framework. Basically, the framework can be divided into three modules, namely node extraction (NE), query generation (QG) and relation extraction (RE). Given a natural language question, NE extracts mentions of entities, variables, literals, types and performs entity linking. Meanwhile, QG generates a node sequence (i.e. vertices in the KB query, see Section 3.1 and 3.2 for more details) corresponding to the given question. Each node generated in QG consists of its type and the pointer to its mention in the input question, such pointer is replaced by the node extracted in NE when fusing NE and QG results. Up to now, we can generate the vertices of a SPARQL query, i.e. the head and tail of all its triples; to form a complete SPARQL output, RE (Section 3.3) is introduced to decide the edges (i.e. the relation of all triples). For each pair of nodes given by NE+QG, RE takes the raw question and mentions of the head and tail node as inputs to decide the relation between them. Combining all three modules, a SPARQL query is finally composed and sent to a knowledge base to get answers.

### 2.2 User Interface

An example of the interaction between users and our system is illustrated in Figure 3. With this UI, users can not only consult NAMER to answer their questions but also acquire more information around their interested entities and understand how NAMER works to compose the generated query.

## 3 Model

Consider the question "*Where was Yao Ming's daughter born?*", the following section elaborates how each module process the question to compose the correct SPARQL "*select ?y where { <Yao_Ming> <daughter> ?x. ?x <place_of_birth> ?y. }*".

### 3.1 Node Extraction (NE)

We define nodes as entities, variables, literals and types in a SPARQL query, namely the entity *<Yao_Ming>* and the variable *?x* and *?y* in the case above. The NE module aims to detect mentions of all nodes in a question, i.e. "Yao Ming", "daughter", and "where" respectively. To achieve this, we utilize a transformer (Vaswani et al., 2017) encoder with a sequence-tagging head of tag space {O, Eb, Ei, Vb, Vi, VTb, VTi, Tb, Ti, VLb, VLi, Lb, Li} (VL/VT denotes variable-literal/variable-type since mentions of multiple nodes may overlap) to tag the question. Afterward, NE performs entity linking on extracted entities via a mention-to-entity dictionary corresponding to the KB. For each entity

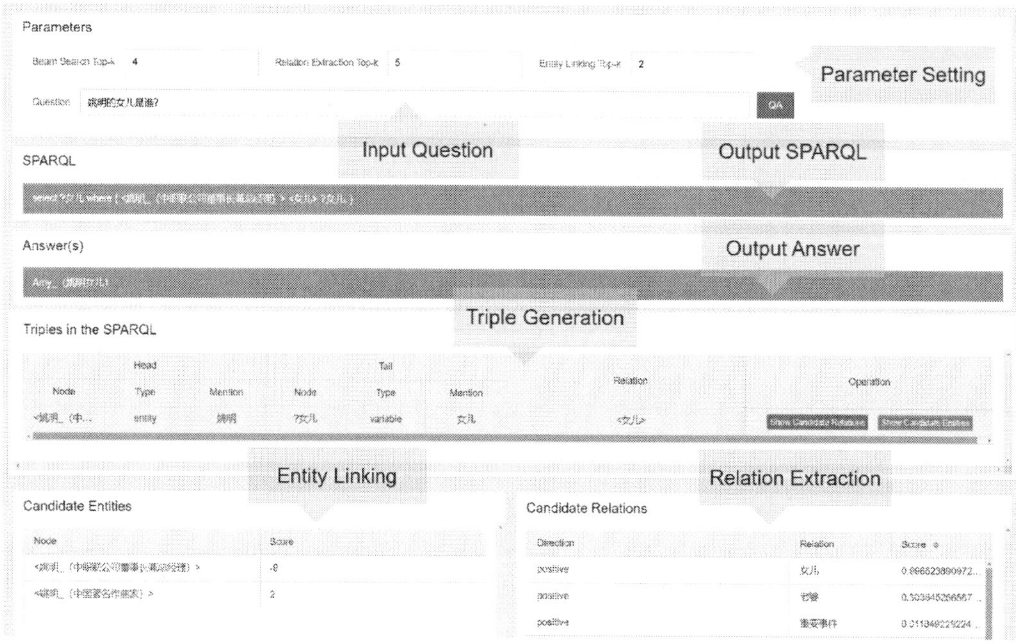


Figure 3: The user interface of NAMER. By entering a question and setting up a few parameters, a user can receive the output SPARQL and answer with intermediate results to visualize our framework. For instance, a user can check "Triples in the SPARQL" for the structure of the generated triples. Besides, after clicking the "Show Candidate Relations" button of each triple, its top score candidate relations would be displayed below; after clicking the "Show Candidate Entities", the scores of candidate entities in entity linking are also provided.

mention, we select its longest substring that appears in the dictionary and view the entities linked to such substring as candidate entities.

### 3.2 Query Generation (QG)

In QG, we want to generate the node sequence of the expected SPARQL, i.e. [*?y*, *<Yao_Ming>*, *?x*, *?x*, *?y*] for the instance above (the first node is the selected variable). One direct method to do so is to adopt a decoder that directly generates such sequence. However, as mentioned before, such an approach poses difficulties for models to grasp the query-question mapping. Hence, we adopt a pointer network (See et al., 2017) to generate a sequence of <type (entity, variable, etc.), pointer> to represent node sequence.

More specifically, QG model is based on a transformer encoder and decoder. Let $H_E \in R^{n \times d_h}$ be the encoder output given the question as input, let $T \in N^q$ be the previously generated node types ($n$ is the question length, $d_h$ denotes hidden dimension, $q$ is the length of the node sequence) by the decoder. At each decoding step, hidden vector $h_q$ of the current node is generated, which is then fed to an FFN to represent the type of next node $T_{next} \in \{E, V, L, T, Start, End\}$. We concatenate $T_{next}$ to $T$ for the next decoding step.

$$h_q = Decoder(T, H_E) \in R^{d_h}$$
$$P_{next} = softmax(FFN(h_q)) \in R^6$$
$$T_{next} = \arg\max_i P_{next}$$

An attention matrix $W^{att} \in R^{d_h \times d_h}$ is trained to calculate attention score of each input token and the pointer $Ptr_{cur}$ being the input with max score.

$$S_{cur} = h_q * W^{att} * H_E^T \in R^n$$
$$Ptr_{cur} = \arg\max_i S_{cur}$$

When combining NE and QG results, we can replace each pointer with the node it points to given by NE, e.g. replacing <var, 5> with a variable node "?daughter" with mention "daughter". Consequently, the expected node sequence [*?where*, *<Yao_Ming>*, *?daughter*, *?daughter*, *?where*] can now be formed.

### 3.3 Relation Extraction (RE)

RE module aims to determine the relation of each node pair generated in QG, i.e. determining the

| System | Dev Set | | | Test Set | | |
|---|---|---|---|---|---|---|
| | P | R | F1 | P | R | F1 |
| Team JCHL | / | / | .707 | .742 | .752 | .736 |
| gAnswer | .593 | .598 | .589 | .554 | .560 | .549 |
| NAMER | **.774** | **.770** | **.761** | **.772** | **.771** | **.757** |

Table 1: Performance on CCKS CKBQA dataset. The official metrics are average answer-level F1 while we also report Precision and Recall. "Team JCHL" refers to the contest winner whose dev P&R wasn't published.

relation *<daughter>* between *<Yao_Ming>* and *?x* and *<place_of_birth>* between *?x* and *?y* for the aforementioned case. We complete this in a ranking manner, which is, we first generate candidate relations for each node pair $n_1$ and $n_2$ (next paragraph), then, we concatenate each candidate with the raw question and the mentions of head and tail nodes to form model input. Such input is encoded by a transformer encoder and converted to a number $S \in [0, 1]$ to represent the score of such candidate relation. RE module selects top-scored candidates of each node pair to form output SPARQL. More specifically, since relations are directional in KB, we obtain candidates of both positive (from $n_1$ to $n_2$) and reversed (from $n_2$ to $n_1$) directions, marked as $R_{pos}$ and $R_{rev}$ respectively. Suppose a positive relation $r^*$ is the correct choice and $q$ is the question, for each $r_1/r_2$ in $R_{pos}/R_{rev}$ excluding $r^*$, we construct $(q, n_1, n_2, r_1)/(q, n_2, n_1, r_2)$ as negative samples and $(q, n_1, n_2, r^*)$ as a positive sample to train our model.

For each node pair, we query KB to obtain candidate relations. For pairs with an entity, literal or type (deterministic) node in it, we view those relations around that node in KB as candidates; for pairs merely consist of variables, we trace back the route from these variables to any deterministic node and view the relations k-hop away from the deterministic node as candidates. For instance, if three pairs (*<Yao_Ming>*, *?x*), (*?x*, *?y*) and (*?y*, *?z*) are generated, their candidates are 1, 2 and 3-hop away from entity *<Yao_Ming>* in KB respectively.

Additionally, we propose an augmentation method when training RE model. Back to the case above, we also add $(q, n_2, n_1, r_1)/(q, n_1, n_2, r_2)$ and $(q, n_2, n_1, r^*)$ to negative samples when training. Consequently, the model learns the effects of mention order to the prediction, through which it may learn a better scoring policy. See further analysis in Section 4.4.

### 3.4 Multitasking

Clearly, since all modules above have an encoder, we can share it across different models in the hope of better comprehension and less error propagation. Let $loss_{NE}, loss_{type}, loss_{ptr}, loss_{RE}$ be the losses of NE, QG-type, QG-pointer, and RE respectively, we can co-train the models by minimizing the weighted sum over all losses.

$$loss = \gamma * loss_{NE} + \alpha * loss_{type} + \beta * loss_{ptr} + \theta * loss_{RE}$$

We can also multitask on a subset of modules by setting some hyperparameters $(\gamma, \alpha, \beta, \theta)$ to zero.

## 4 Experiments

### 4.1 Experimental Setup

**Dataset** We utilize the dataset published in CCKS Chinese KBQA Contest[4] for evaluation. The dataset consists of various Chinese open-domain complex (multi-hop) questions that require deep comprehension of questions and strong generalization ability, its background KB is PKUBASE[5], a Chinese KB based on Baidu Baike. We follow the raw separation of 2.2k/0.76k/0.76k train/dev/test data, note that no information in dev or test set are used when training.

**Annotations** We manually label the mention of all SPARQL nodes in the question required by our framework in the train and dev set. When multiple mentions co-refer a node, all mentions are accepted but we recommend annotators to choose a more informative one, e.g. for the question "*Who is Yao Ming's daughter?*" and SPARQL "*select ?x where {<Yao_Ming> <daughter> ?x.}*", both "*daughter*" and "*who*" refer to *?x*, but the former is preferred. When no mention refers to a node, annotators leave the mention as "*None*". We perform a brief double-check on 420 randomly selected questions and >93% of which are annotated correctly. See more details of the annotation process in Ethical Considerations.

**Baselines** We compare our results with the top ranking team *"jchl"*[6](Luo et al., 2019) in the contest and a competitive KBQA system gAnswer[7] (Hu

[4] `https://www.biendata.xyz/competition/ccks_2019_6/data/`

[5] A KB endpoint: `http://pkubase.gstore.cn/`

[6] Team *"luoxiao1"* was disqualified in final ranking so we compare with the team that won the contest

[7] `https://github.com/pkumod/gAnswer`

| Methods | NE | | | QG | | RE | | Overall F1 | |
|---|---|---|---|---|---|---|---|---|---|
| | P | R | F1 | EM Acc. | Actual Acc. | Hit@5 | MRR | Dev Set | Test Set |
| Separate | .840 | .855 | .843 | .654 | .773 | .971 | .895 | .730 | .715 |
| NE+QG+RE | .839 | **.862** | .846 | .668 | **.795** | .957 | .866 | .726 | .705 |
| NE+QG | **.843** | .861 | **.847** | **.678** | .792 | **.971** | **.895** | **.761** | **.757** |

Table 2: Performance details of different multitasking strategies. "Methods" refer to co-trained modules, "Separate" means no multitasking. Metrics in NE refers to the P/R/F1 of the extracted node list. In QG, EM (exact-match) and Actual Acc. means the accuracy of generated node sequence (yield of NE&QG); the former counts when the generated sequence is identical to gold sequence while the latter counts when two sequences are equivalent semantically, e.g. when gold and generated sequence are [*?daughter*, *<Yao_Ming>*, *?daughter*] and [*?who*, *<Yao_Ming>*, *?who*], EM Acc. does not count due to false pointer of the variable but they are semantically equal since the name of a variable does not effect query results. For RE, Hit@5 denotes the ratio of node pairs whose score of gold relation is among top-5 in all candidates; MRR was defined in Craswell, 2009. Overall F1 is explained in Table 1. We evaluate all NE, QG, and RE-related metrics on dev set.

et al., 2018) that reached first place in QALD-9 (Ngomo, 2018). Since the NE and RE module in gAnswer does not officially support Chinese, we replace them with those in our system. Hence, the gAnswer evaluated can be partly viewed as our system with a rule-based QG module and its comparison with us indicates the effectiveness of our generative QG module.

**Setup** We adopt Chinese RoBERTa-large (Cui et al., 2020) in transformers library (Wolf et al., 2020) released by HFL[8] as encoder and a 6-layer 8-head transformer as decoder. For our best results, we co-train the NE and QG models, remaining RE as a separate model. For NEQG, we train the encoder and decoder with learning rate 1e-6 and 4e-6 respectively with an Adam (Kingma and Ba, 2015) optimizer, setting hyperparameters to $\gamma = 1, \alpha = \beta = 2.5, \theta = 0$ and batch size to 40. For RE model, we set the learning rate and batch size to 1e-5 and 96 respectively with $\gamma = \alpha = \beta = 0, \theta = 1$. Both models are trained until no progress on validation accuracy for at most 10k steps.

### 4.2 Overall Performance Evaluation

Table 1 compares the performance of our system and the baselines on official F1 metrics as well as precision and recall. As shown, our system consistently outperforms the contest winner *"jchl"* on dev and test set while significantly surpass the modified version of gAnswer, setting up a new state-of-the-art performance on the evaluated dataset.

We attribute the improvement to the effectiveness of the proposed framework. With the cooperation of NE and QG, NAMER learns the direct mapping between question and query, making it possible for models to deeply grasp their supervision signals even in case of complex questions and insufficient training data, which is exactly the case for the current dataset. Since the evaluated gAnswer can be viewed as replacing QG with a rule-based subgraph matching module, our advantage over it also implies the superiority of a trainable generative module in KBQA which, we speculate, has better generalization ability facing the highly diversified questions. Finally, based on NEQG, our RE module can naturally deal with complex multi-hop questions by processing a triple (instead of a question) at a time, resulting in an accurate relation scoring for every node pair.

### 4.3 Analysis of Multitasking

In his section, we try to discuss the impact of different multitasking strategies (Section 3.4) on the framework performance. The results of each module and the overall metrics are given in Table 2. Evidently, multitasking NE and QG consistently improves performance over no multitasking; this is probably due to the shared supervise signals across NE and QG offer extra information for models to better comprehend their tasks. E.g., the supervision in NE tells QG model the semantics of a pointer (since it provides the node mention of a pointer) which assists QG to predict pointers. However, when multitasking all three modules, the performance fails to improve. In detail, although NE and QG metrics resemble our best results, RE encounters a considerable drop on both metrics. We

[8]Pretrained weights: `https://github.com/ymcui/Chinese-BERT-wwm`

| Methods | RE | | Overall F1 | |
|---|---|---|---|---|
| | Hit@5 | MRR | Dev-set | Test-set |
| Ours | **.971** | **.895** | **.761** | **.757** |
| w/o Aug. | .943 | .863 | .736 | .740 |

Table 3: Effects of RE data augmentation. "w/o Aug." denotes the RE model trained without augmentation.

| Methods | $n_1$ to $n_2$ | | $n_2$ to $n_1$ | |
|---|---|---|---|---|
| | Relation | Score | Relation | Score |
| Ours | *Elder_Brother* | .998 | *Younger_Brother* | .801 |
| w/o Aug. | *Elder_Brother* | .999 | ***Elder_Brother*** | .999 |

Table 4: A case study for the top-scored relation in both directions between a node pair. False answer is in bold.

speculate that the different input format of NEQG and RE results in a different semantic space on the tasks, which harms the performance when we forcibly co-train them. Anyway, multitasking notably reduces the storage cost of our system by sharing one encoder across various tasks, which is significant for a system in practice.

### 4.4 Analysis of Data Augmentation

A data augmentation technique is introduced in Section 3.3, we inspect its effect in Table 3 and provide further discussion in this section. As illustrated, removing augmentation from RE results in a drop on both RE metrics and overall performance, indicating the positive effect of augmentation. To explain, we perform a case study on the question *What's the nickname of Tom's elder brother?*[9]. Consider the node pair $n_1 = Tom, n_2 = elder\ brother$, we compare the top-scored relation from $n_1$ to $n_2$ and from $n_2$ to $n_1$ given by the model with and without augmentation. As shown in Table 4, the augmented model outputs two antonymous relations in two directions while its counterpart makes two same predictions. Hence, we argue that the augmented training data help the model to concurrently learn 1) the topic-level relationship between a relation and a node pair in question and 2) the effect of node direction to relation (i.e. $r^*$ is only the correct choice from $n_1$ to $n_2$, not conversely). The extra supervise signal enables a deeper comprehension of RE which, in turn, improves model performance.

Interestingly, we find a similar discussion in Lan et al. (2019) on the advantage of SOP over NSP, since sentence order provides additional supervision on discourse-level coherence (which largely resembles the coherence between node direction and relation in our case). Thus, we speculate that similar augmentation methods may work in more scenarios in future research.

[9] We translate raw Chinese input to English in this case.

## 5 Related Work

**Semantic parsing-based KBQA** A semantic parser in KBQA converts a question to a KB query. Previously, some works (Petrochuk and Zettlemoyer, 2018; Mohammed et al., 2018) only focus on answering one-hop questions. To process multi-hop questions, Cui et al. (2017) proposed a template-based pipeline in which a question is converted to a template to further decide its predicate. Hu et al. (2018) and Jin et al. (2019) adopted a subgraph-matching-based model in the pipeline to form a query graph. Ge et al. (2019) used a seq2seq transformer to directly generate queries. To help models directly comprehend the structural mapping, Wang et al. adopted a query template generator as well as an entity and relation extractor to represent the mentions of entities and relations; however, they failed to utilize the mention of variables and literals. Similar to our approach, Shen et al. (2019) used a pointer-generator and entity extractor to grasp the mapping between an entity and its mention, but the mappings of other types of nodes are omitted in their work, also, unlike us, the mappings failed to directly assist downstream RE task. Different from the above, we propose a framework that grasps the mappings of all node types and use them to aid downstream tasks.

**Public KBQA systems** Prior to us, several online KBQA systems are available for the public. However, most systems focused on domain-specific KBs, e.g. E-commerce (Li et al., 2019) and food (Haussmann et al., 2019). On open-domain KBs, Cui et al. (2016) published a system that can answer complex questions and visualize their answers. However, few systems on open-domain Chinese KBQA provide a publicly available web page with detailed visualization of the framework pipeline as in NAMER.

## 6 Conclusion

We present a robust Chinese KBQA system, NAMER, based on a novel node-based multitasking framework. With three cooperative modules, our system grasps the structural mapping between a question and its corresponding query. Hence, NAMER reaches superior performance compared to previous SoTA on an open-domain Chinese complex KBQA dataset. Further experiments also demonstrate the effectiveness of the architecture and the techniques adopted in NAMER. As a system intended for easier access to KB for all users, the UI of NAMER provides not only the answers to a given question but also the query structure accompanied by a series of intermediate results (e.g. candidates & scores), assisting users to visualize our system pipeline and explore more KB information to their interest.

For the future, we will incorporate more visualization functions into NAMER to further reduce the barrier to KB for nonspecialist users. Since extra data annotations are required to support NAMER, we also plan to study the effects of the scale of annotated data on system performance. Moreover, we expect to implement and optimize NAMER in multilingual scenarios.

## Ethical Considerations

### Data Collection

**Annotation Guideline** SPARQL queries usually include several triples, restricting the range of target answers. Nodes are defined as the entities, variables, literals, and types in a SPARQL (including the select variable). For instance, the SPARQL *select ?x where {<Yao_Ming> <daughter> ?x.}* corresponds to the node sequence [*?x*, *<Yao_Ming>*, *?x*]. Given a natural language question "*Who is Yao Ming's daughter?*" and its corresponding SPARQL, annotators are asked to annotate the mention span of every node in the question, i.e. "*Yao Ming*" for *<Yao_Ming>* and "*daughter*" for *?x*.

**Annotation Details** The questions were distributed evenly to seven annotators with substantial knowledge of NLP. To ensure that the annotators were comfortable with the task, annotation guidance was given before the task began. After the primary annotation, two annotators double-checked the annotation to ensure consistency. All annotators worked part-time on the task.

### System Output

We provide an online Chinese KBQA system as shown in Figure 3. The system uses PKUBASE as its supportive KB and accepts Chinese questions as possible input. Despite our efforts to eliminate biased and offensive output, NAMER retains the potential to generate answers that may be wrong or trigger offense. This failure may be induced by the deficiency of PKUBASE, implicit bias of the pretrained model and the limitation of training data. These are known issues in current state-of-the-art neural network-based language models and automatically constructed knowledge base. In no case should inappropriate answers generated by NAMER be construed to reflect the views or values of the authors.

## Acknowledgements

We would like to thank Yanzeng Li and Wenjie Li for the valuable assistance on system design and implementation. We also appreciate anonymous reviewers for their insightful and constructive comments. This work was supported by NSFC under grants 61932001, 61961130390, U20A20174. This work was also partially supported by Beijing Academy of Artificial Intelligence (BAAI). The corresponding author of this work is Lei Zou (zoulei@pku.edu.cn).

## References

Nick Craswell. 2009. Mean reciprocal rank. *Encyclopedia of database systems*, 1703.

Wanyun Cui, Yanghua Xiao, Haixun Wang, Yangqiu Song, Seung-won Hwang, and Wei Wang. 2017. Kbqa: Learning question answering over qa corpora and knowledge bases. *Proceedings of the VLDB Endowment*, 10(5).

Wanyun Cui, Yanghua Xiao, and Wei Wang. 2016. Kbqa: An online template based question answering system over freebase. In *IJCAI*, volume 16, pages 09–15.

Yiming Cui, Wanxiang Che, Ting Liu, Bing Qin, Shijin Wang, and Guoping Hu. 2020. Revisiting pre-trained models for Chinese natural language processing. In *Proceedings of the 2020 Conference on Empirical Methods in Natural Language Processing: Findings*, pages 657–668, Online. Association for Computational Linguistics.

Donglai Ge, Junhui Li, and Muhua Zhu. 2019. A transformer-based semantic parser for nlpcc-2019 shared task 2. In *CCF International Conference on Natural Language Processing and Chinese Computing*, pages 772–781. Springer.

Steven Haussmann, Yu Chen, Oshani Seneviratne, Nidhi Rastogi, James Codella, Ching-Hua Chen, Deborah L McGuinness, and Mohammed J Zaki. 2019. Foodkg enabled q&a application. In *ISWC Satellites*, pages 273–276.

S. Hu, L. Zou, J. X. Yu, H. Wang, and D. Zhao. 2018. Answering natural language questions by subgraph matching over knowledge graphs. *IEEE Transactions on Knowledge and Data Engineering*, 30(5):824–837.

Guangxi Ji, Shujun Wang, Ding Zhang, Xiaowang Zhang, and Zhiyong Feng. A fine-grained complex question translation for kbqa.

Hai Jin, Yi Luo, Chenjing Gao, Xunzhu Tang, and Pingpeng Yuan. 2019. Comqa: Question answering over knowledge base via semantic matching. *IEEE Access*, 7:75235–75246.

Diederik P. Kingma and Jimmy Ba. 2015. Adam: A method for stochastic optimization. In *3rd International Conference on Learning Representations, ICLR 2015, San Diego, CA, USA, May 7-9, 2015, Conference Track Proceedings*.

Tom Kwiatkowski, Eunsol Choi, Yoav Artzi, and Luke Zettlemoyer. 2013. Scaling semantic parsers with on-the-fly ontology matching. In *Proceedings of the 2013 conference on empirical methods in natural language processing*, pages 1545–1556.

Zhenzhong Lan, Mingda Chen, Sebastian Goodman, Kevin Gimpel, Piyush Sharma, and Radu Soricut. 2019. Albert: A lite bert for self-supervised learning of language representations. In *International Conference on Learning Representations*.

Feng-Lin Li, Weijia Chen, Qi Huang, and Yikun Guo. 2019. Alime kbqa: Question answering over structured knowledge for e-commerce customer service. In *China Conference on Knowledge Graph and Semantic Computing*, pages 136–148. Springer.

Jinchang Luo, Cunxiang Yin, Xiaohui Wu, Lifang Zhou, and Huiqiang Zhong. 2019. Hunhe yuyi xiangsidu de zhongwen zhishitupu wenda xitong [a chinese knowledge base question answering system based on mixed semantic similarity]. *Proceedings of the 2019 China Conference on Knowledge Graph and Semantic Computing: Evaluation Papers*.

Salman Mohammed, Peng Shi, and Jimmy Lin. 2018. Strong baselines for simple question answering over knowledge graphs with and without neural networks. In *Proceedings of the 2018 Conference of the North American Chapter of the Association for Computational Linguistics: Human Language Technologies, Volume 2 (Short Papers)*, pages 291–296.

Ngonga Ngomo. 2018. 9th challenge on question answering over linked data (qald-9). *language*, 7(1).

Michael Petrochuk and Luke Zettlemoyer. 2018. Simplequestions nearly solved: A new upperbound and baseline approach. In *Proceedings of the 2018 Conference on Empirical Methods in Natural Language Processing*, pages 554–558.

Eric Prud'hommeaux. 2008. Sparql query language for rdf, w3c recommendation. *http://www. w3. org/TR/rdf-sparql-query/*.

Abigail See, Peter J Liu, and Christopher D Manning. 2017. Get to the point: Summarization with pointer-generator networks. In *Proceedings of the 55th Annual Meeting of the Association for Computational Linguistics (Volume 1: Long Papers)*, pages 1073–1083.

Tao Shen, Xiubo Geng, QIN Tao, Daya Guo, Duyu Tang, Nan Duan, Guodong Long, and Daxin Jiang. 2019. Multi-task learning for conversational question answering over a large-scale knowledge base. In *Proceedings of the 2019 Conference on Empirical Methods in Natural Language Processing and the 9th International Joint Conference on Natural Language Processing (EMNLP-IJCNLP)*, pages 2442–2451.

Christina Unger, André Freitas, and Philipp Cimiano. 2014. An introduction to question answering over linked data. In *Reasoning Web International Summer School*, pages 100–140. Springer.

Ashish Vaswani, Noam Shazeer, Niki Parmar, Jakob Uszkoreit, Llion Jones, Aidan N Gomez, Łukasz Kaiser, and Illia Polosukhin. 2017. Attention is all you need. In *Advances in neural information processing systems*, pages 5998–6008.

Shujun Wang, Jie Jiao, Yuhan Li, Xiaowang Zhang, and Zhiyong Feng. Answering questions over rdf by neural machine translating.

Thomas Wolf, Lysandre Debut, Victor Sanh, Julien Chaumond, Clement Delangue, Anthony Moi, Pierric Cistac, Tim Rault, Rémi Louf, Morgan Funtowicz, Joe Davison, Sam Shleifer, Patrick von Platen, Clara Ma, Yacine Jernite, Julien Plu, Canwen Xu, Teven Le Scao, Sylvain Gugger, Mariama Drame, Quentin Lhoest, and Alexander M. Rush. 2020. Transformers: State-of-the-art natural language processing. In *Proceedings of the 2020 Conference on Empirical Methods in Natural Language Processing: System Demonstrations*, pages 38–45, Online. Association for Computational Linguistics.

Wen-tau Yih, Xiaodong He, and Christopher Meek. 2014. Semantic parsing for single-relation question answering. In *Proceedings of the 52nd Annual Meeting of the Association for Computational Linguistics (Volume 2: Short Papers)*, pages 643–648.

# DiSCoL: Toward Engaging *Di*alogue *S*ystems through *Co*nversational *L*ine Guided Response Generation

**Sarik Ghazarian,[1] Zixi Liu,[1] Tuhin Chakrabarty,[2]**
**Xuezhe Ma,[1] Aram Galstyan,[1] Nanyun Peng[1, 3]**
[1] University of Southern California / Information Sciences Institute
[2] Computer Science Department of Columbia University
[3] Computer Science Department of University of California, Los Angeles
{sarik, zixiliu, xuezhema, galstyan}@isi.edu
tuhin.chakr@cs.columbia.edu violetpeng@cs.ucla.edu

## Abstract

Having engaging and informative conversations with users is the utmost goal for open-domain conversational systems. Recent advances in transformer-based language models and their applications to dialogue systems have succeeded in generating fluent and human-like responses. However, those systems still lack control over the generation process toward producing contentful responses and achieving engaging conversations. To address this, we present **DiSCoL** (**Di**alogue **S**ystems through **Co**versational **L**ine guided response generation). DiSCoL is an open-domain dialogue system that leverages conversational lines (briefly **convlines**) as controllable and informative content-planning elements to guide the generation model in producing engaging and informative responses. Two primary modules in DiSCoL's pipeline are conditional generators trained for 1) predicting relevant and informative convlines for dialogue contexts and 2) generating high-quality responses conditioned on the predicted convlines. Users can also change the returned convlines to *control* the direction of the conversations toward topics that are more interesting for them. Through automatic and human evaluations, we demonstrate the efficiency of the convlines in producing engaging conversations.

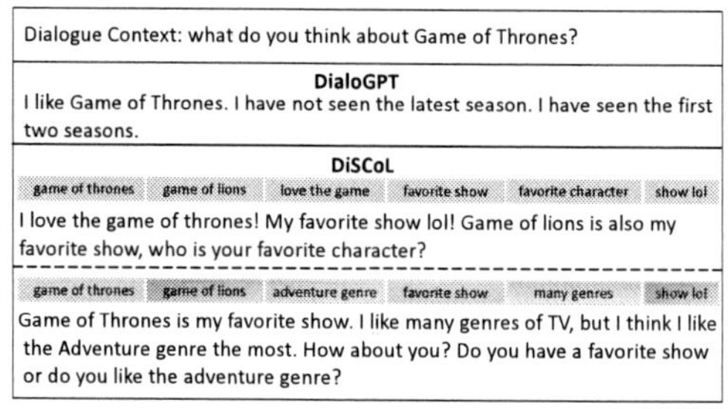


Figure 1: A dialogue context and its three responses generated based on DialoGPT and our proposed DiSCoL system using originally inferred and manipulated convlines, respectively. DiSCoL leverages convlines (depicted in colored boxes) to guide the generation model to encapsulate those informative contents. Our demo enables the user to edit or remove the inferred convlines (shown in blue for edits and red for removal) to guide the conversation towards its desired directions.

## 1 Introduction

Over the past decade, users have actively engaged with dialogue systems to fulfill a wide range of requirements. *Task-oriented dialogue systems* have assisted users in accomplishing specific tasks such as finding apartments (Gustafson et al., 2000) and restaurants (Gruenstein and Seneff, 2007) or even booking movie tickets (Li et al., 2017). While, *Open-domain dialogue systems* have been extensively leveraged for psychotherapy counseling, entertainment, and even teaching foreign languages to users (Zhou et al., 2020; Oh et al., 2017; Sarosa et al., 2020). In this work, we focus on the second group.

In the context of open-domain dialogue systems, neural-network-based generative models have outperformed retrieval-based systems by generating diverse and novel responses. More recently, large-scale language models with transformer-based architectures, such as GPT-2 (Radford et al., 2019) and BART (Lewis et al., 2019), have advanced the state of the art in Natural Language Generation and Dialogue Systems. Such models can be further enhanced by fine-tuning them on task-specific data, as it is the case of DialoGPT (dialogue generative pre-trained transformer) (Zhang et al., 2019), a neural conversational response generation model, trained on 147M conversation-like exchanges extracted from Reddit. Although responses generated by such models are fluent and locally coherent, they usually suffer from content poverty (e.g., generating non-informative content), which can negatively impact user engagement. Furthermore, these models do not allow the users to exert control on the generation process and guide the conversation to-



*Proceedings of NAACL-HLT 2021: Demonstrations*, pages 26–34
June 6–11, 2021. 

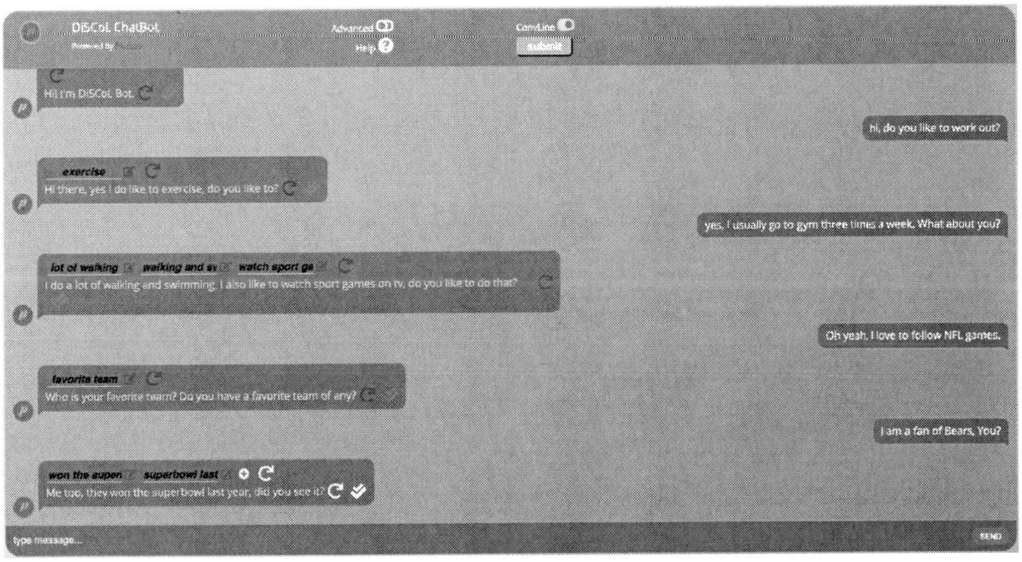


Figure 2: A snapshot of the proposed DiSCoL system

ward users' desired direction. The first block in Figure 1 depicts an example of a generated response by DialoGPT.

To alleviate this issue, here we propose DiSCoL, an open-domain dialogue system, which leverages **convlines** as primary elements to add *control* for generating informative and content-rich responses. Convlines are abstract representations of utterances in the dialogues that can be used as content planning elements to form high-level content of an utterance and guide the generator to incorporate these informative units in the generation (See colored boxes in Figure 1). Content planning has been shown to be beneficial in the story generation task. These abstract representations known as storylines or story plots have been successful to guide the language models produce more coherent and fluent stories (Yao et al., 2019; Goldfarb-Tarrant et al., 2019; Fan et al., 2019; Goldfarb-Tarrant et al., 2020; Rashkin et al., 2020; Brahman et al., 2020).

DiSCoL is composed of four main neural-network-based modules (See Figure 3). The first two modules are designed to extract entities and topics of the dialogue context. The third module is a fine-tuned conditional generator that learns to take the dialogue context and previously extracted information and predict convlines that would be leveraged in the response generator module. Similar to convline generator, response generator is a conditional auto-regressive language model that generates response conditioned on the dialogue context and its convlines, entities, and topics extracted from previous modules. The middle block of Figure 1 exhibits the generated response for the inferred convlines shown in green boxes. In the interactive setting of our devised demo from which a snapshot is shown in Figure 2, we provide the users with the facility to manipulate the predicted convlines to direct the conversation toward its topics of interest. The last block in Figure 1 depicts the removed and edited convlines (red and blue boxes) that led the generator to generate a slightly different response by taking into account the applied adjustments.

We validate DiSCoL on the Topical chat dataset (Gopalakrishnan et al., 2019) using both human and automatic evaluations. Our results demonstrate the superiority of DiSCoL over DialoGPT in terms of generating higher quality responses, thus indicating the usefulness of convlines as dialogue control mechanisms for generating more engaging responses. We release the source code and trained models to facilitate the future dialogue research. [1]

## 2 system Architecture

The architecture of our proposed DiSCoL demo system and its modules are depicted in Figure 3. A user converses with the system by writing an utterance as an input. This utterance passes through all the modules and in each module some new information such as its extracted entities, topics, and convlines are augmented. The last module, response

[1]Github Link: `https://github.com/PlusLabNLP/Dialogue_System_Hackathon`

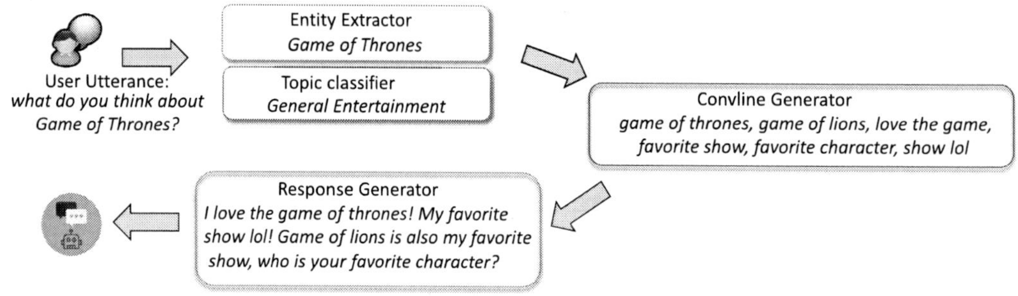


Figure 3: Architecture of DiSCoL system

generator, incorporates all this information to generate a response as the output of the system. In this section, we explain each module in detail.

### 2.1 Entity Extractor

One of the principal components in the conversational systems is the set of entities that both interlocutors are interested to converse about. It is crucial that the system can identify the main entities from the dialogue context and try to continue the conversation by providing more relevant information or even expressing its opinions and impressions regarding them. Therefore, in DiSCoL we take the user's utterance as the dialogue context and extract its entities. This task is known as a named entity recognition (NER) task, where each token in the text is classified into one of the predefined classes such as a person, organization, location or other.

Toward this goal, we leverage the BERT model (Devlin et al., 2019) fine-tuned on CoNLL-2003 dataset (Sang and De Meulder, 2003), which is a well-known corpus for NER task.[2] We detokenize the output of the fine-tuned BERT model to get the original version of entities' tokens and disregard the predefined classes of entities since in our case they do not augment additional benefits. As shown in Figure 3, all entities with labels other than *O* are returned from the entity extractor module.

### 2.2 Topic Classifier

Knowing the topic that the user is enthusiastic to discuss is essential for the dialogue system to generate utterances about that specific topic. The blue box in Figure 3 represents the topic classifier that takes the user's utterance and predicts the most relevant topics from a predefined set. These topics are later used for predicting convlines and consequently generating responses.

Due to the proven effectiveness of the BERT model (Devlin et al., 2019) and its wide applicability in many classification tasks, we incorporate it into the topic classifier module of DiSCoL. We fine-tune BERT model on pairs of utterances and their aligned topics with the main goal of minimizing the cross-entropy loss.

### 2.3 Convline Generator

DiSCoL's main contribution is in the convline generator module that is depicted as the purple box in Figure 3. Convlines are abstract representations or content plans of utterances throughout the conversation. These representations, which are also known as storylines or story plots in the context of story generation, have recently posited their efficiency in generating higher quality stories (Yao et al., 2019; Fan et al., 2019; Goldfarb-Tarrant et al., 2020; Rashkin et al., 2020). Story generation models leverage plan-and-write framework that is successful in generating fluent and informative stories by the intervention of storylines as an intermediate step. In this work, we follow the same idea but in the context of conversational systems. In particular, we aim to show that the controlled generation of high-quality utterances by planning in advance and leveraging useful abstract-level convlines can be beneficial for dialogue systems as well.

To compose the convlines as the main component in the convline generator module, we extract sequences of important words in each utterance from existing human-human conversational data. We use the YAKE (Campos et al., 2018) method that relies on the text's statistical features to extract the most important keywords of an utterance, as it has shown its superiority over other state-of-the-art unsupervised approaches such as TF-IDF and RAKE (Rose et al., 2010).

[2]We leverage fine-tuned BERT model provided by Huggingface (`https://github.com/huggingface/transformers`).

To train the convline generator, we extract pairs of $(u_i, r_i)$ as a set of consecutive pairs of dialogue context utterances and their corresponding ground-truth responses in the human-human conversational data. For each dialogue context utterance $(u_i)$, we extract its entities $(e_i)$ and topics $(t_i)$ using the entity extractor and topic classifier modules. Each response $(r_i)$ is replaced by its convlines $(c_i)$ obtained by the YAKE algorithm. The constructed input data are in $(u_i, e_i, t_i, c_i)$ format.

The convline generator is a conditional model that generates the most probable convlines given the provided dialogue context utterance together with its entities and topics. To this end, we apply BART (Lewis et al., 2019), which is a state-of-the-art pre-trained sequence-to-sequence generative model. It combines a bidirectional encoder as that of BERT (Devlin et al., 2019) to encode the input and a GPT like (Radford et al., 2018) auto-regressive decoder model to generate convlines as the output. The top block in Figure 4 encapsulates the training process of the convlines module. We fine-tune BART on the constructed training data with the objective of minimizing the negative log likelihood shown in Equation (1).

$$L_{line\_gen} = -log \sum_{i=1}^{n} P(c_i|u_i, t_i, e_i) \quad (1)$$

During inference, the fine-tuned BART model takes the user's utterance augmented with its inferred entities and topics to predict the most probable convlines, as depicted in the bottom block of Figure 4. We use top-k sampling (Fan et al., 2019) with $k = 5$ and a temperature of 0.7 for the generation.

### 2.4 Response Generator

The last module in DiSCoL system's pipeline is the response generator that is identical to convline generator except for the type of inputs and outputs. The response generator takes the dialogue context utterance, its convlines and topics as inputs and generates response conditioned on those data.

$$L_{resp\_gen} = -log \sum_{i=1}^{n} P(r_i|u_i, t_i, c_i) \quad (2)$$

During training, we provide utterances, their topics and convlines extracted from YAKE to the BART model and fine-tune this pre-trained conditional generator. As it is shown in Equation (2), the training objective is to maximize the probability of generating ground-truth responses given their context utterances, topics, and the convlines.

During inference, the generator attempts to produce the most probable responses that include convlines returned by the convline generator module.

## 3 System Implementation

We test our system on Topical-Chat dataset (Gopalakrishnan et al., 2019) that includes knowledge-grounded human-human conversations covering a set of 8 different topics. This dataset has been collected by employing Amazon Mechanical Turk (AMT) workers who have been provided with specific entities and some external knowledge (Wikipedia lead sections, Washington Post articles, or some Reddit fun facts) to chat about. Therefore, each utterance in the conversation is either based on provided knowledge sources or the user's personal knowledge. Overall, 261 popular entities spanning 8 various topics (Fashion, Sports, Books, Politics, General Entertainment, Music, Science & Technology and Movies) have been selected for the dataset collection. We add *General* topic for utterances (e.g. greetings) that do not include any specific contents such as *"hi, how are you today?"*.

### 3.1 Topic Classification Data

Although each utterance in the Topical-Chat dataset comes from either provided external knowledge or interlocutor's personal knowledge about some specified entities, it lacks determined topic labels, which are necessary for DiSCoL modules. To infer topics, we first manually match all 261 entities in the external knowledge to one of the topics in the predefined set (Fashion, Sports, Books, Politics, and etc.). Next, we label all utterances talking about those entities to their corresponding topics. This simple labeling scheme produces topics for about 78% of the 188,378 (*easy_set*) total utterances. As an example, the utterance *"Do you know Tom Brady"* is about *"Tom Brady"* entity that is an indication of the *"Sports"* topic. Therefore, we label this utterance with the *"Sports"* topic.

The remaining challenging utterances are mainly the continuation of the dialogue history without directly containing any entities. Take *"I guess they live up to their name then!"* as an example of such utterances with no mentioned entities. We pursue the following context-based heuristics to label such *challenging_set* utterances with their relevant topics. If the utterance's neighbors (utterances right before or after the current utterance) are from *easy_set* and both share the same entity, we assign

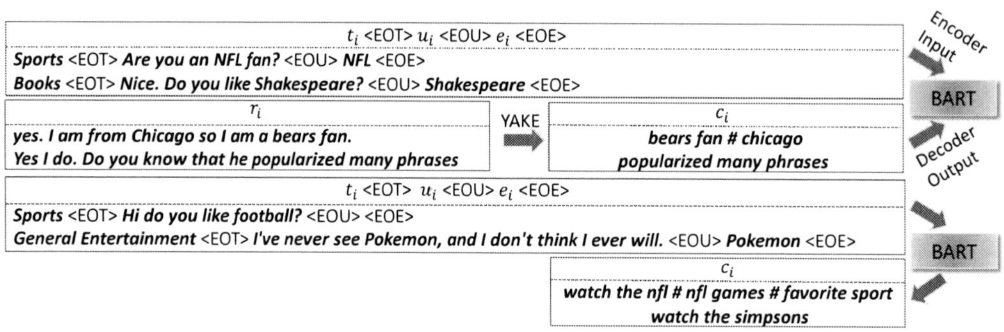


Figure 4: Architecture of the convline generator during training and inference time

| Uttr. | Easy_set | Challenging_set | General_uttr. |
|---|---|---|---|
| 188,378 | 146,370 | 5,323 | 5,966 |

Table 1: Statistics of different groups of utterances (uttr.) in the Topical chat dataset

that entity's topic to the current utterance, while in the case of neighbors containing different entities, we label the given utterance with both utterances' topics. If the previous rules do not apply to an utterance in the *challenging_set*, we use the most frequent topic in the dialog as its topic.

In parallel to the above heuristics and in order to improve the quality of assigned topics, we also apply a keyword-based classifier that classifies *challenging_set* utterances with appropriate topics. The keyword-based classifier retrieves the most similar entity from the overall 261 entities to each utterance's keywords using their BERT embeddings. Then, the manually matched topics for the retrieved entity are assigned to the utterance. We only consider 5323 *challenging_set* utterances that their adapted labels based on both approaches: 1) context-based heuristics and 2) keyword-based classifier are the same (See statistics in Table 1).

The remaining utterances shown in the last column of Table 1 are mainly general utterances for starting or ending conversations without any specific content such as *"Good Morning! How are you today?"* or *"It was nice chatting with you!"*. We fine-tune the BERT model as the topic classifier for 10 epochs and get an accuracy of 85.55 on the validation set.

### 3.2 Convline Generator Data

Convlines are the central components in the training of the DiSCoL system. We leverage YAKE (Campos et al., 2018) for retrieving discourse keywords representing convlines. YAKE assigns an importance score to tokens in a text by following an unsupervised approach that builds upon features extracted from the text (Campos et al., 2018). In this model, a set of features are computed for each term in the text. Subsequently, a list of candidates (n-grams of tokens) is created. Next, the Levenshtein distance is used to remove duplicate keywords. Finally, the aggregation of token scores in each keyword is used to represent the keyword's score. Keywords with lower scores are returned as the text's salient convlines. We use YAKE to generate a contiguous sequence of 1, 2, and 3-grams candidate convlines. We extract 3-grams convlines, followed by extracting 2-grams and 1-gram that are not included in the previously returned keywords. We fine-tune BART-large for both convlines and response generator models for 3 epochs and checkpoint the best epoch based on validation perplexity.[3]

| Dialogue Context | Annotators | Kappa | Pearson |
|---|---|---|---|
| 100 | 33 | 0.44 | 0.5 |

Table 2: Statistics and inter-annotator agreements of AMT evaluations on DiSCoL and DialoGPT performances.

## 4 Experimental Results

We evaluate the performance of DiSCoL system against DialoGPT, which is one of the strongest recent baselines that has shown its efficiency in generating consistent and relevant responses.

### 4.1 Metrics

To explore the efficiency of our proposed controlled response generation, we apply both automatic and human evaluations.

[3]We fine-tune BART model using https://github.com/pytorch/fairseq

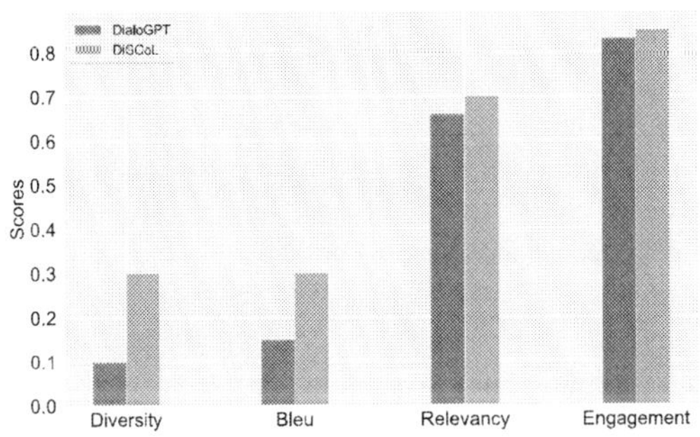


Figure 5: Automatic evaluations on responses generated by DiSCoL and DialoGPT systems

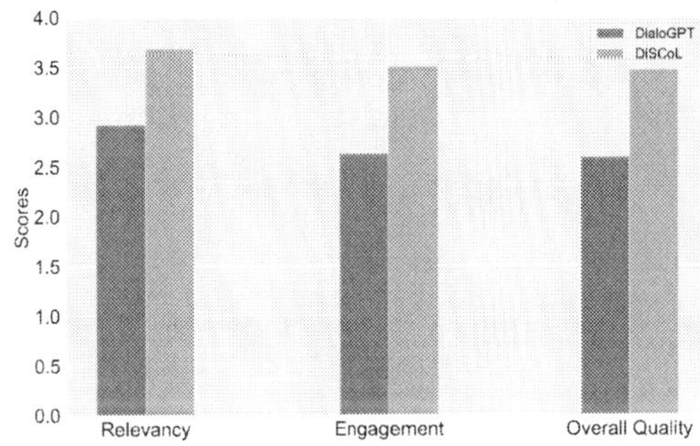


Figure 6: Human evaluations on responses generated by DiSCoL and DialoGPT systems

### 4.2 Automatic Evaluations

Due to the multi-faceted nature of dialogue quality, it is necessary to do the evaluation from different aspects (See et al., 2019; Mehri and Eskenazi, 2020). To this end, we compare the quality of DiSCoL and DialoGPT generated responses through computing different metrics. We conduct automatic evaluations and compute evaluation metrics on 23,530 consecutive utterance pairs (dialogue context utterances and their ground-truth responses) of the Topical chat test set. The measured metrics are averaged over all utterance pairs within the test set. We compute BLEU-3 (Papineni et al., 2002) to evaluate the similarity of generated responses to ground-truth responses based on the 3-grams overlaps. Due to the one-to-many essence of open-domain dialogue systems and the imperfection of such word-overlap metrics (Liu et al., 2016; Ghazarian et al., 2019; Mehri and Eskenazi, 2020), we also focus on three main aspects: diversity, relevancy, and engagingness as better indications of systems performances.

Diversity measures the percentage of distinct generated tokens by each model. Li et al. (2015) proposed distinct-2 that computes distinct bi-grams divided by the total number of generated words. Relevancy utilizes both dialogue context utterance and the generated response to deliberate how much it is relevant to the given utterance (Tao et al., 2018; Ghazarian et al., 2019). We use the contextualized Ruber metric for this purpose (Ghazarian et al., 2019). At the end, since in open-domain dialogue systems, it is necessary to have both relevant and interesting responses to make the user feel satisfied (Ghazarian et al., 2020), we further validate systems based on the engagingness of responses. We compute engagingness as the probability score of the engaging class predicted by Ghazarian et al. (2020)'s proposed engagement classifier.

### 4.3 Human Evaluations

We extend our evaluations by running AMT experiments to report human judgments on the quality of system-generated responses. We randomly select 100 dialogue context utterances from the Topical chat test set. For each given dialogue context utterance, we ask three AMT workers to rate DiSCoL and DialoGPT's generated responses by keeping these systems anonymous. Participants rate the relevancy, engagingness, and overall quality of each response on a 5-point Likert scale (1 indicating irrelevant/not engaging and low-quality response). The statistics of the AMT experiment are shown in Table 2.

### 4.4 Results

**Automatic Evaluation.** Figure 5 depicts the average scores of diversity, BLEU, relevancy, and engagingness resulted from automatic evaluation metrics for all the generated responses of DiSCoL and DialoGPT systems. The strength of DiSCoL is noticeable from its higher BLEU score and more diverse, relevant, and engaging responses. Overall, the diversity is low due to the limited distinct topics considered in the Topical chat dataset. The BLEU metric is low for both systems which shows its inadequacy in the open-domain evaluations; where a response can be super appropriate and at the same time not similar to the ground-truth response.

**Human Evaluation.** The bars in Figure 6 demonstrate the average of human annotations for different qualities of generated utterances. Each response's score is the mean aggregation of three annotators' ratings. According to Figure 6, annotators appraise responses generated by DiSCoL with higher scores in terms of relevancy, engagingness, and overall quality. This could be an evidence for the positive impact of incorporating convlines to guide the dialogue system towards generating controllable, relevant, and contentful responses that infuse the user to converse for a longer time.

## 5 Conclusion

We have introduced DiSCoL, an open domain dialogue system that leverages convline as an intermediate step toward generating more informative and controllable responses in dialogues. The convlines are predicted and subsequently leveraged in the response generation process. Additionally, DiSCoL allows users to manipulate convlines towards their favorite conversational direction. Our findings show that in contrast to other transformer-based dialogue systems that do not incorporate content planning, DiSCoL takes the advantage of such a principled structure to generate better and more engaging conversations with users.

In the future, we imagine an open path of possible research in the controllable conversations which would guide the dialogue toward having pleasant features such as empathy and bias-free or even personalized convlines to generate dialogues with such aspects. It is also expecting to train dialogue models to converse by following specific styles such as generating formal conversations by predicting more formal convlines.

## 6 Ethics

Through the entire phases of the conducted research and developed DiSCoL system, all co-authors were agreed and adhered to *ACM Code of Ethics*. Our effort was to ensure we stuck to the conscience of the profession and considered the Code principles. We certify that this system and all the presented evaluations are compatible with the provided code. In the following, we discuss two main spots in the development and evaluation of our system that could be targeted for encompassing abusive and improper conversations and having biased evaluations.

**DiSCoL System's Development** The main contribution of our proposed DiSCoL system is to augment controllable response generation with the intervention of convlines that leads the generation towards producing more relevant and interesting responses. Indeed, DiSCoL provides an opportunity for users to manipulate the convlines and guide the system to continue the conversation in the user's favorite direction. All DiSCoL's modules leverage pre-trained large language models such as BART (Lewis et al., 2019) and fine-tune them on recently proposed Topical chat dataset (Gopalakrishnan et al., 2019). One potential harm that DiSCoL could cause is its feasibility to generate improper responses conditioned on the inferred convlines with abusive contents. Since the convline and response generators are BART models finetuned on human-human conversations that do not encompass profanity and inappropriate content ((Gopalakrishnan et al., 2019)), hence the convlines that indeed are important informative units of the utterances would be free of bias and obscene content. However, there still is a possibility of dual-usage attacks by augmenting conversations with offensive languages to fine-tune the generators and teach them to generate such inappropriate content. The identification of such attacks that could occur in almost all learnable models and the way to overcome them by itself is a distinct and huge research area that is out of this paper's scope.

**DiSCoL System's Evaluation** Alongside the automatic evaluation for demonstrating the efficiency of controllable generations using convlines, we further collected human annotations by conducting Amazon Mechanical Turk (AMT) experiments. We provided different systems responses for given utterances while keeping systems anonymous and asked users to rate responses by considering different aspects that had been explained in the AMT surveys. We estimated the average time users would spend on each survey and fairly compensated them according to the hourly wage.

We kept the privacy of all AMT turkers who participated in the experiments. Our experiments did not have the requisite to know the user's personal information, therefore their personal information including their genre, ethnicity, and etc. are not revealed. This fades the necessity for IRB approvals.

At the end, we want to note that our system's target is NLP open-domain conversational AI community with the main goal of achieve engaging conversations with the incorporation of convlines and increasing the user's ability to control the generation process. Likewise other proposed dialogue systems, we anticipate specific failure modes specifically for novel conversations on new topics. Lifelong learning in dialogue systems which is not the focus of this work is a research area that attempts to enhance conversation systems' ability to deal with such novel scenarios.

## Acknowledgment

This work is supported by the CwC program under the Contract W911NF-15-1-0543 with the US Defense Advanced Research Projects Agency (DARPA) and is the result of a hackathon in PLUSlab from USC/UCLA. We would like to thank all members of PLUSlab from USC/UCLA, specifically Johnny Wei, and Zhubo Deng for their constructive help. We also want to appreciate the anonymous reviewers for their helpful comments.

## References

Faeze Brahman, Alexandru Petrusca, and Snigdha Chaturvedi. 2020. Cue me in: Content-inducing approaches to interactive story generation. In *Asia-Pacific Chapter of the Association for Computational Linguistics (AACL)*.

Ricardo Campos, Vítor Mangaravite, Arian Pasquali, Alípio Mário Jorge, Célia Nunes, and Adam Jatowt. 2018. Yake! collection-independent automatic keyword extractor. In *European Conference on Information Retrieval*, pages 806–810. Springer.

Jacob Devlin, Ming-Wei Chang, Kenton Lee, and Kristina Toutanova. 2019. Bert: Pre-training of deep bidirectional transformers for language understanding. In *North American Chapter of the Association for Computational Linguistics (NAACL-HLT)*.

Angela Fan, Mike Lewis, and Yann Dauphin. 2019. Strategies for structuring story generation. In *Association for Computational Linguistics (ACL)*.

Sarik Ghazarian, Johnny Tian-Zheng Wei, Aram Galstyan, and Nanyun Peng. 2019. Better automatic evaluation of open-domain dialogue systems with contextualized embeddings. In *Proceedings of the Methods for Optimizing and Evaluating Neural Language Generation (NeuralGen workshop of NAACL-HLT)*.

Sarik Ghazarian, Ralph M Weischedel, Aram Galstyan, and Nanyun Peng. 2020. Predictive engagement: An efficient metric for automatic evaluation of open-domain dialogue systems. In *AAAI*, pages 7789–7796.

Seraphina Goldfarb-Tarrant, Tuhin Chakrabarty, Ralph Weischedel, and Nanyun Peng. 2020. Content planning for neural story generation with aristotelian rescoring. In *Empirical Methods in Natural Language Processing (EMNLP)*.

Seraphina Goldfarb-Tarrant, Haining Feng, and Nanyun Peng. 2019. Plan, write, and revise: an interactive system for open-domain story generation. In *2019 Annual Conference of the North American Chapter of the Association for Computational Linguistics (NAACL-HLT 2019), Demonstrations Track*, volume 4, pages 89–97.

Karthik Gopalakrishnan, Behnam Hedayatnia, Qinglang Chen, Anna Gottardi, Sanjeev Kwatra, Anu Venkatesh, Raefer Gabriel, Dilek Hakkani-Tür, and Amazon Alexa AI. 2019. Topical-chat: Towards knowledge-grounded open-domain conversations. In *INTERSPEECH*.

Alexander Gruenstein and Stephanie Seneff. 2007. Releasing a multimodal dialogue system into the wild: User support mechanisms. In *Proceedings of the 8th SIGdial Workshop on Discourse and Dialogue*, pages 111–119.

Joakim Gustafson, Linda Bell, Jonas Beskow, Johan Boye, Rolf Carlson, Jens Edlund, Björn Granström, David House, and Mats Wirén. 2000. Adapt—a multimodal conversational dialogue system in an apartment domain. In *The Sixth International Conference on Spoken Language Processing (ICSLP), Beijing, China*, pages 134–137.

Mike Lewis, Yinhan Liu, Naman Goyal, Marjan Ghazvininejad, Abdelrahman Mohamed, Omer Levy, Ves Stoyanov, and Luke Zettlemoyer. 2019. Bart: Denoising sequence-to-sequence pre-training for natural language generation, translation, and comprehension. In *Association for Computational Linguistics (ACL)*.

Jiwei Li, Michel Galley, Chris Brockett, Jianfeng Gao, and Bill Dolan. 2015. A diversity-promoting objective function for neural conversation models. In *North American Chapter of the Association for Computational Linguistics (NAACL-HLT)*.

Xiujun Li, Yun-Nung Chen, Lihong Li, Jianfeng Gao, and Asli Celikyilmaz. 2017. End-to-end task-completion neural dialogue systems. In *International Joint Conference on Natural Language Processing (IJCNLP)*.

Chia-Wei Liu, Ryan Lowe, Iulian V Serban, Michael Noseworthy, Laurent Charlin, and Joelle Pineau. 2016. How not to evaluate your dialogue system: An empirical study of unsupervised evaluation metrics for dialogue response generation. In *Empirical Methods in Natural Language Processing (EMNLP)*.

Shikib Mehri and Maxine Eskenazi. 2020. Unsupervised evaluation of interactive dialog with dialogpt. In *Proceedings of the 21th Annual Meeting of the Special Interest Group on Discourse and Dialogue*.

Kyo-Joong Oh, Dongkun Lee, Byungsoo Ko, and Ho-Jin Choi. 2017. A chatbot for psychiatric counseling in mental healthcare service based on emotional dialogue analysis and sentence generation. In *2017 18th IEEE International Conference on Mobile Data Management (MDM)*, pages 371–375. IEEE.

Kishore Papineni, Salim Roukos, Todd Ward, and Wei-Jing Zhu. 2002. Bleu: a method for automatic evaluation of machine translation. In *Proceedings of the 40th annual meeting of the Association for Computational Linguistics*, pages 311–318.

Alec Radford, Karthik Narasimhan, Tim Salimans, and Ilya Sutskever. 2018. Improving language understanding by generative pre-training.

Alec Radford, Jeffrey Wu, Rewon Child, David Luan, Dario Amodei, and Ilya Sutskever. 2019. Language models are unsupervised multitask learners. *OpenAI blog*, 1(8):9.

Hannah Rashkin, Asli Celikyilmaz, Yejin Choi, and Jianfeng Gao. 2020. PlotMachines: Outline-conditioned generation with dynamic plot state tracking. In *Proceedings of the 2020 Conference on Empirical Methods in Natural Language Processing (EMNLP)*.

Stuart Rose, Dave Engel, Nick Cramer, and Wendy Cowley. 2010. Automatic keyword extraction from individual documents. *Text mining: applications and theory*, 1:1–20.

Erik F Sang and Fien De Meulder. 2003. Introduction to the conll-2003 shared task: Language-independent named entity recognition. *arXiv preprint cs/0306050*.

M Sarosa, M Kusumawardani, A Suyono, and MH Wijaya. 2020. Developing a social media-based chatbot for english learning. In *IOP Conference Series: Materials Science and Engineering*, page 012074. IOP Publishing.

Abigail See, Stephen Roller, Douwe Kiela, and Jason Weston. 2019. What makes a good conversation? how controllable attributes affect human judgments. In *North American Chapter of the Association for Computational Linguistics (NAACL-HLT)*.

Chongyang Tao, Lili Mou, Dongyan Zhao, and Rui Yan. 2018. Ruber: An unsupervised method for automatic evaluation of open-domain dialog systems. In *Proceedings of the AAAI Conference on Artificial Intelligence*.

Lili Yao, Nanyun Peng, Weischedel Ralph, Kevin Knight, Dongyan Zhao, and Rui Yan. 2019. Plan-and-write: Towards better automatic storytelling. In *The Thirty-Third AAAI Conference on Artificial Intelligence (AAAI-19)*.

Yizhe Zhang, Siqi Sun, Michel Galley, Yen-Chun Chen, Chris Brockett, Xiang Gao, Jianfeng Gao, Jingjing Liu, and Bill Dolan. 2019. Dialogpt: Large-scale generative pre-training for conversational response generation. In *Proceedings of the 58th Annual Meeting of the Association for Computational Linguistics*.

Li Zhou, Jianfeng Gao, Di Li, and Heung-Yeung Shum. 2020. The design and implementation of xiaoice, an empathetic social chatbot. *Computational Linguistics*, 46(1):53–93.

# FITAnnotator: A Flexible and Intelligent Text Annotation System

**Yanzeng Li, Bowen Yu, Quangang Li, Tingwen Liu***
Institute of Information Engineering, Chinese Academy of Sciences
School of Cyber Security, University of Chinese Academy of Sciences
{liyanzeng, yubowen, liquangang, liutingwen}@iie.ac.cn

## Abstract

In this paper, we introduce FITAnnotator, a generic web-based tool for efficient text annotation. Benefiting from the fully modular architecture design, FITAnnotator provides a systematic solution for the annotation of a variety of natural language processing tasks, including classification, sequence tagging and semantic role annotation, regardless of the language. Three kinds of interfaces are developed to annotate instances, evaluate annotation quality and manage the annotation task for annotators, reviewers and managers, respectively. FITAnnotator also gives intelligent annotations by introducing task-specific assistant to support and guide the annotators based on active learning and incremental learning strategies. This assistant is able to effectively update from the annotator feedbacks and easily handle the incremental labeling scenarios. [1]

## 1 Introduction

Manually-labeled gold standard annotations are the first prerequisite for the training and evaluation of modern Natural Language Processing (NLP) methods. With the development of deep learning, neural networks have achieved state-of-the-art performance in a variety of NLP fields. These impressive achievements rely on large-scale training data for supervised training. However, building annotation requires a significant amount of human effort and incurs high costs, and can place heavy demands on human annotators for maintaining annotation quality and consistency.

To improve annotation productivity and reduce the financial cost of annotation, many text annotation softwares are developed by constraining user actions and providing an effective interface. In the early days, platforms for linguistic annotations such as O'Donnell (2008), BART (Stenetorp et al., 2012), WebAnno-13 (Yimam et al., 2013) mainly focused on providing a visual interface for user labeling process, making annotation accessible to non-expert users. Recently, integrating active learning into annotation systems for providing suggestions to user has became mainstream (TextPro (Pianta et al., 2008), WebAnno-14 (Yimam et al., 2014), Active DOP (van Cranenburgh, 2018), INCEpTION (Klie et al., 2018), etc), but most of these works focus on English text and rarely consider the multi-lingual setting, which is necessary due to the growing demand for annotation in other languages. In addition to the interface and efficiency, incremental annotation is also necessary in real-world scenarios since the pre-defined annotation standards and rules cannot handle rapidly emerging novel classes in the real world, while being less addressed in existing annotation tools.

To address the challenges above, we propose FITAnnotator, a generic web-based tool for text annotation, which fulfills the following requirements:

- Extremely flexible and configurable: our system architecture is fully modular, even the user interface is a replaceable module. Which means it is model-agnostic and supports annotation on a variety of linguistic tasks, including tagging, classification, parsing, etc.

- Active learning: learning from small amounts of data, and selecting by itself what data it would like the user to label from an unlabeled dataset. Annotators label these selected instances and add them to the training set. A new model is automatically trained on the updated training set. This process repeats and results in dramatic reductions in the amount of labeling required to train the NLP model.

- Expansible data provider: the previous annotation tools are compatible with the static corpus for annotation, which is not convenient

*Corresponding author

[1] A video demonstration of FITAnnotator is available at https://vimeo.com/499446008



*Proceedings of NAACL-HLT 2021: Demonstrations*, pages 35–41
June 6–11, 2021. 

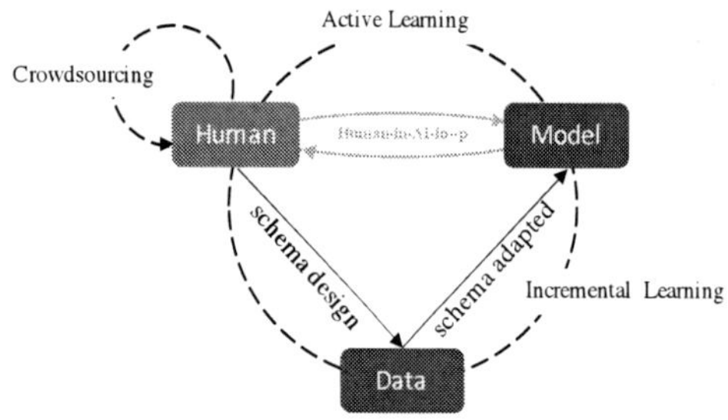


Figure 1: The interaction of the three major elements of the intelligent annotation system

for annotating from sketch and expansion. FITAnnotator sets up an independent data loader and data provider, which can continuously import data to the corpus in bulk. The flexible data provider also brings new problems, such as dynamic labeling schema, which should be solved by incremental learning.

- Incremental learning: creating a prototype for each category and enabling the prototypes of the novel categories far from the prototypes of the original categories while maintaining features to cluster near the corresponding category prototypes, which makes the tool suitable for annotating with new classes added incrementally.

- Collaboration & crowdsourcing: the system is designed for the multi-user scenario, where multiple annotators can work collaboratively at the same time. When multiple users cooperate in annotation, the dismountable crowdsourcing algorithm interface can be used to allocate overlapping data in apiece task packages, for evaluating the annotation quality of each user. Also, the system provides a manual review interface, which can perform sampling inspection and evaluation on various users' annotation.

Figure 1 reflects our design philosophy and comprehension of the interaction between the three major elements in our annotation system.

## 2 Related Works

In recent years, the NLP community has developed several annotation tools (Neves and Ševa, 2019). Yedda (Yang et al., 2018b) provides an easy-to-use and lightweight GUI software for collaborative text annotation, and provides certain administrator analysis for evaluating multi-annotators. FLAT[2] introduces generalised paradigm and well-defined annotation format defined in folia (van Gompel, 2012), and provides web-based annotation interface. Doccano (Nakayama et al., 2018) is an open-source, web-based text annotation tool that provides collaboration, intelligent recommendation functions, and includes a user-friendly annotation interface. INCEpTION (Klie et al., 2018) is a comprehensive text annotation system, which is also web-based and open-source, integrates active learning algorithms and provides various interfaces for different annotation tasks, and it is developing for more tasks (de Castilho et al., 2018), more convenient (Boullosa et al., 2018) and low-resource scenarios (Klie et al., 2020).

In addition, commercial annotation tools such as prodigy[3], tagtog[4] , LightTag[5] also provide powerful active learning support, team-collaboration functions, efficient user interfaces, and provide more related commercial solutions, which have gained appreciable business achievement.

All of these intelligent text annotation tools have several common features: supporting active learning and a rich variety of tasks. And commercial annotation tools pay more attention to user experience and collaboration.

## 3 Architecture

The architecture of FITAnnotator is influenced by the ideas of functional programming and, in particular, by the desire to combine functional with object-oriented programming. The adherence to the programming principles such as immutability and modularity, FITAnnotator is developed by hybrid programming language Python. An overview of our system is shown in Figure 2, which has four main modules:

1. `core` module controls all data flow and provides the gateway for other modules. Tasks and projects are stored in the database of this module, and there are some fields to specify the URI of each related module. The system is based on these URIs to transfer and process data between modules. This module also

[2] `http://github.com/proycon/flat`
[3] `https://prodi.gy/`
[4] `http://www.tagtog.net`
[5] `https://www.lighttag.io/`

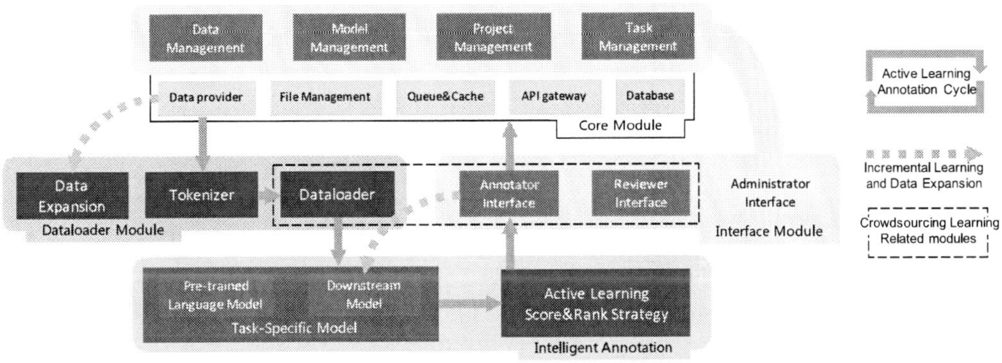


Figure 2: The overall architecture of the system

provides an administrator control panel for managing the system and database.

2. `data-loader` module contains fundamental tokenizer and data-loader of specific machine learning model. By deploy multifarious data-loader module with different tokenizers, we can adapt this system to different languages and tasks. In addition, we also provide data expansion function in this module. Expanded data would be cleaned in this module and passed to `core` module.

3. `intelligent annotation` module acts as the assistant which provides a pre-built machine learning model according to the type of tasks. This model could be simple as FastText (Joulin et al., 2017) or complex as BERT (Devlin et al., 2019). With such a model, we can obtain automatic labeling results for unlabeled data, and calculate their ranking scores according to the active learning strategy. By reordering the unlabeled data before pushing them to annotators, the annotation speed could be accelerated. Besides, incremental learning is also implemented in this module. We describe the details of this module in Section 4.

4. `interface` module contains three separate web interfaces: annotator, reviewer and administrator. The annotator interface presents the ranked unlabeled instances based on the recommendation score provided by the active learning module. Upon annotating a new sentence, the annotator is presented with the most probable labels recommended by the active learning model (see Figure 4). When the annotators make a decision for confirming model recommendation or altering the labels, the operations will be fed back to the backend system and update the parameters of the active learning model. In the reviewer interface, the users monitor the progress of the annotation and see statistics such as the number of annotated instances, and the remaining unlabeled data. The reviewers can also review these already annotated instances and introduce corrections if necessary. In the administrator interface (shown in Figure 3), the project manager defines the annotation standards and sets all parameters for the annotation process, including the configures of active learning models, the management of annotators and reviewers, the assignment of tasks and so on.

The system is written with a modular design intended to be easily modifiable. Modules and interfaces (except `core` module and `administrator interface`) can be replaced easily for specific requirements. The flexibility it easy to adapt to multiple tasks and languages. FITAnnotator has three built-in annotation templates now: text classification, sequence tagging and semantic structure annotation, which cover most common NLP tasks, including sentence classification, sentence pair matching, named entity recognition and semantic role annotation. Users can also migrate to other tasks through simple modification of the framework.

## 4 Intelligent Annotation

Creating high-quality annotated corpora is a laborious process and requires experts who are highly familiar with the annotation schemes and stan-

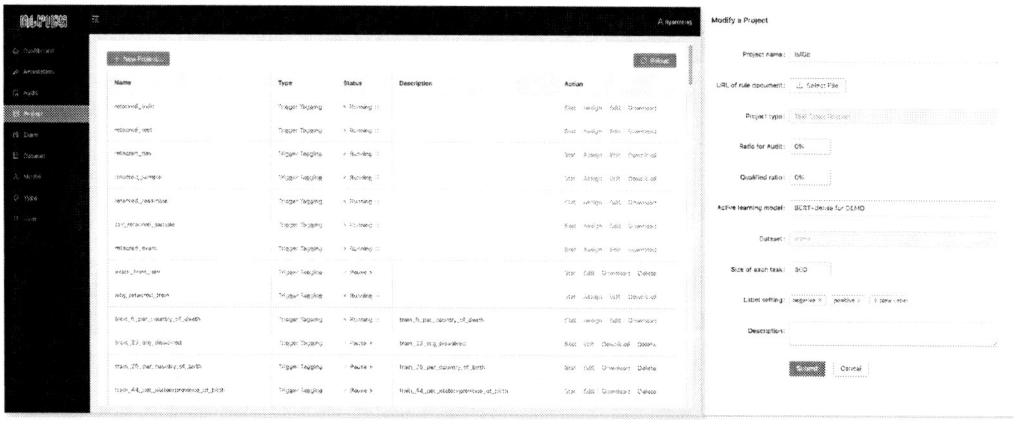

Figure 3: Screenshot of administrator interface

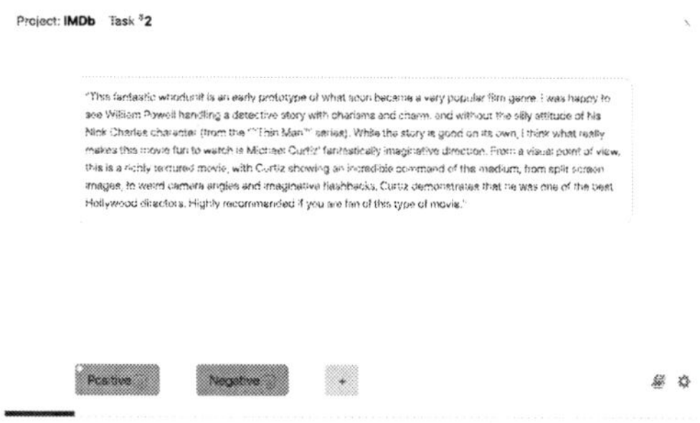


(a) Text classification.

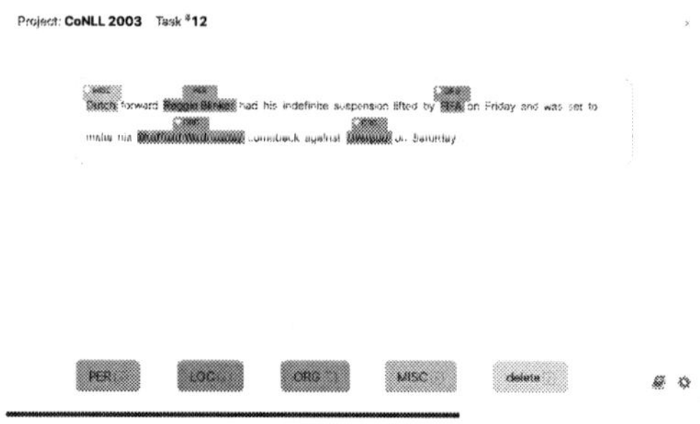


(b) Named entity recognition.

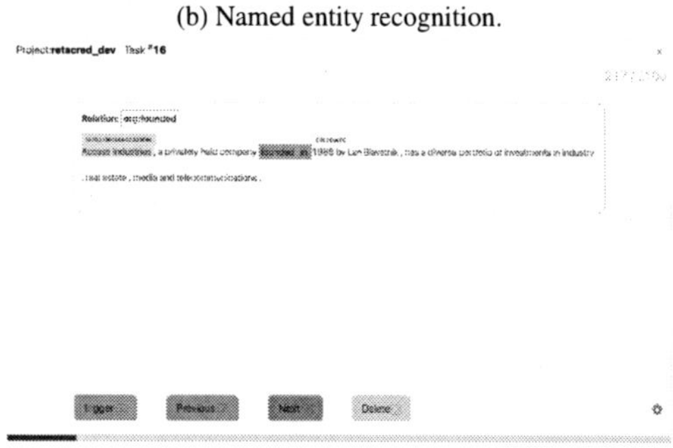


(c) Sequence tagging.

Figure 4: Screenshots of annotator interface for different tasks.

dards. To accelerate the annotation process, we introduce the intelligent assistant that incorporates task-specific neural networks which actively assist and guide annotators. The cores of intelligent annotation are two adaptive learning mechanisms: active learning and incremental learning.

### 4.1 Active Learning

A framework where a model learns from small amounts of data, and optimizes the selection of the most informative or diverse sample to annotate in order to maximize training utility value, is referred to as active learning (Gal et al., 2017; Schröder and Niekler, 2020). In particular, we employ a fused active learning method as a default strategy for evaluating, re-ranking and re-sampling data, which considers uncertainty and diversity at the same time (Zhou et al., 2017; Lutnick et al., 2019). Using such a strategy, the most difficult and diverse instances will be annotated first, which are more valuable for model learning with respect to the rest of the corpus. After the instances have been selected by active learning, the system displays them in the annotator interface with the highlighted suggestion labels. The annotator can then accept or modify the suggestion. The choices are stored and passed to the active learning module as new training data to update the parameters.

For analyzing the effectiveness of active learning strategies in FITAnnotator, we conduct a simple but representative comparative experiment based on the IMDb movie reviews sentiment classification task (Maas et al., 2011). In this experiment, we respectively explore the effectiveness of the uncertainty sampling and the diversity sampling in active

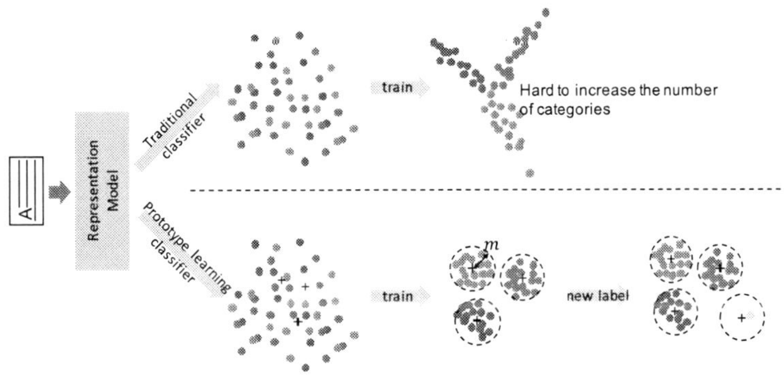


Figure 5: 2-dim sketch of prototype-based incremental learning

learning (Fu et al., 2013), and employ a random sampling strategy as the baseline method. Two kinds of popular text classification models (FastText (Joulin et al., 2017) and BERT (Devlin et al., 2019)) are respectively implemented as the backbone of active learning. We use $accuracy+$ as the indicator to measure the performance (Lu et al., 2019):

$$accuracy+ = \frac{TP^H + TN^H + TP^M + TN^M}{N}$$

where $N$ is the size of dataset, $H$ and $M$ represent the human-annotated labels and the model-predicted labels respectively. The evaluation is continuously carried out with the annotation process of the IMDb training set. Every 100 new annotation samples are generated, the performance of the backbone is evaluated on the standard test set. The results are shown in Figure 6. Apparently, the BERT-based active learning method outperforms the FastText-based method. In terms of training convergence speed, the sampling strategy based on the uncertainty criterion is similar to the diversity criterion, but both of them are obviously faster than the random sampling baseline. After plenty of samples are labeled, the accuracy of those sampling methods tends to be approximate. This observation demonstrates that our system is able to accelerate the training process of the models by introducing active learning algorithms, so as to provide users with label recommendations more quickly and accurately.

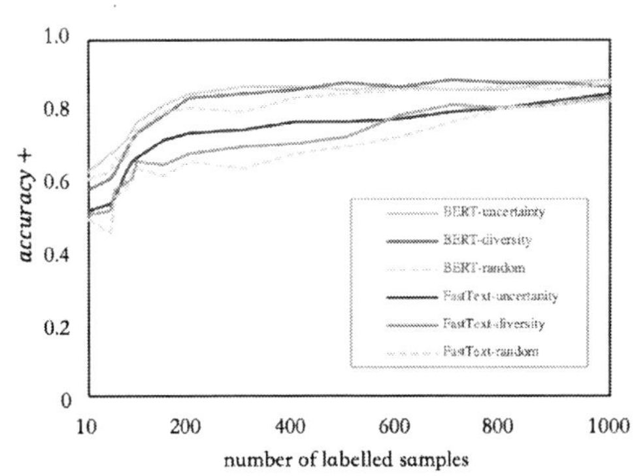


Figure 6: Results of different active learning strategies and models over imdb dataset. Curves start from 10 at along x-axis.

## 4.2 Incremental Learning

Existing annotation tools focus on labeling instances based on a fixed annotation scheme. However, the pre-defined standards may not cover all the cases met in the annotation process, especially for the classification task with constantly updated source data. Take the case of aspect category classification (ACC). In E-commerce platforms, online reviews are valuable resources for providers to get feedback for their services. ACC aims to identify all the aspects discussed in a given review. Yet in the real world, new reviews and products are rapidly emerging, and it is impossible to annotate reviews with a pre-defined set of aspect categories once to cover all aspects (Toh and Su, 2015; Wu et al., 2018).

Considering the enormous cost of re-labeling the entire corpus, in an ideal annotation system, the new classes should be integrated into the existing labeled instances, sharing the previously learned parameters of active learning. To this end, we introduce an incremental learning mechanism into our annotation system. As Figure 5 shown, by creating a prototype for each category, the classification problem is converted into a problem of matching the samples to the prototypes (Yang et al.,

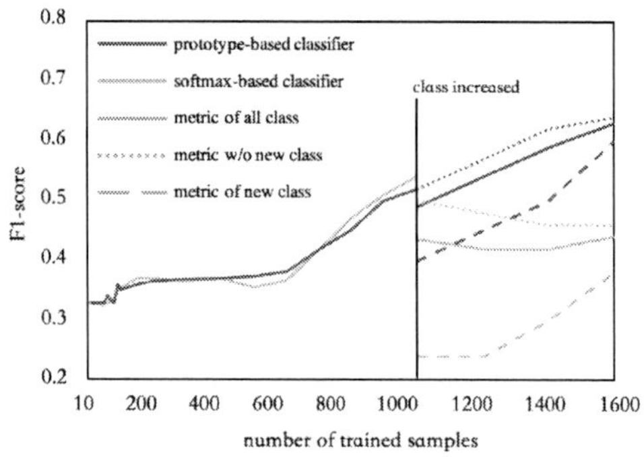


Figure 7: Results of different classifier (softmax-based and prototype-based) in class-incremental scenario.

2018a). During the training process, the loss function is designed to minimize the distance between the sample and the prototype ($m$ in Figure 5 is the minimal margin between prototypes) and maximize the distance between prototypes. Thus the space of representation is sparse and clear outside of prototype clusters, a new prototype of the category can be added easily (Rebuffi et al., 2017).

To verify the effectiveness of FITAnnotator combined with incremental learning, we conduct experiments on the AG News dataset[6], which is collected from the news corpus with four classes. In order to simulate the real-world scenario, we first use samples belonging to three of the four categories for annotation. After labeling 1000 samples, we import the data of the fourth category, and use the class-incremental function provided by FITAnnotator to change the annotation schema. For evaluation, we construct a word-level LSTM + CNN representation model with glove word embedding (Pennington et al., 2014) as the encoder, and compare our prototype-based method with the classic softmax-based classifier. The micro-F1 score is chosen as the evaluation metric.

Figure 7 illustrates the experimental results. In the ordinary text classification task, the performance of the softmax-based classifier and the prototype-based classifier is relatively approximate. After introducing the fourth class (new class), the performance of the softmax-based classifier occurs a catastrophic recession. On the contrary, the prototype-based method shows impressive results in the class-incremental scenario, and the negative effect of the newly introduced class is negligible.

[6] http://groups.di.unipi.it/~gulli/AG_corpus_of_news_articles.html

## 5 Conclusion

In this paper, we present FITAnnotator, a web-based system for interactive NLP annotation. In order to reduce the workload of annotators, we integrate an active learning strategy in our system recommendation part, and introduce an incremental learning strategy to facilitate the rapid annotation of incessantly emerging novel categories. It supports a range of annotation types, and analyzing, assessing, and managing the annotations. In future work, FITAnnotator will integrate more advanced incremental learning and active learning algorithms, and be enhanced to develop more task templates.

## Acknowledgement

This work is supported by the Strategic Priority Research Program of Chinese Academy of Sciences, Grant No. XDC02040400.

## References

Beto Boullosa, Richard Eckart de Castilho, Naveen Kumar, Jan-Christoph Klie, and Iryna Gurevych. 2018. Integrating knowledge-supported search into the inception annotation platform. In *Proceedings of the 2018 Conference on Empirical Methods in Natural Language Processing*, volume Demo Papers, pages 127–132.

Richard Eckart de Castilho, Jan-Christoph Klie, Naveen Kumar, Beto Boullosa, and Iryna Gurevych. 2018. Linking text and knowledge using the inception annotation platform. In *Proceedings of the 14th eScience IEEE International Conference*, pages 327–328.

Jacob Devlin, Ming-Wei Chang, Kenton Lee, and Kristina Toutanova. 2019. Bert: Pre-training of deep bidirectional transformers for language understanding. In *NAACL-HLT 2019: Annual Conference of the North American Chapter of the Association for Computational Linguistics*, pages 4171–4186.

Yifan Fu, Xingquan Zhu, and Bin Li. 2013. A survey on instance selection for active learning. *Knowledge and information systems*, 35(2):249–283.

Yarin Gal, Riashat Islam, and Zoubin Ghahramani. 2017. Deep bayesian active learning with image data. In *International Conference on Machine Learning*, pages 1183–1192.

Armand Joulin, Edouard Grave, Piotr Bojanowski, and Tomas Mikolov. 2017. Bag of tricks for efficient text classification. In *Proceedings of the 15th Conference of the European Chapter of the Association for Computational Linguistics: Volume 2, Short Papers*, volume 2, pages 427–431.

Jan-Christoph Klie, Michael Bugert, Beto Boullosa, Richard Eckart de Castilho, and Iryna Gurevych. 2018. The inception platform: Machine-assisted and knowledge-oriented interactive annotation. In *Proceedings of the 27th International Conference on Computational Linguistics: System Demonstrations*, pages 5–9. Association for Computational Linguistics.

Jan-Christoph Klie, Richard Eckart de Castilho, and Iryna Gurevych. 2020. From Zero to Hero: Human-In-The-Loop Entity Linking in Low Resource Domains. In *Proceedings of the 58th Annual Meeting of the Association for Computational Linguistics*, pages 6982–6993, Online. Association for Computational Linguistics.

Jinghui Lu, Maeve Henchion, and Brian Mac Namee. 2019. Investigating the effectiveness of representations based on word-embeddings in active learning for labelling text datasets. *arXiv*, pages arXiv–1910.

Brendon Lutnick, Brandon Ginley, Darshana Govind, Sean D. McGarry, Peter S. LaViolette, Rabi Yacoub, Sanjay Jain, John E. Tomaszewski, Kuang-Yu Jen, and Pinaki Sarder. 2019. An integrated iterative annotation technique for easing neural network training in medical image analysis. *Nature Machine Intelligence*, 1(2):112–119.

Andrew L. Maas, Raymond E. Daly, Peter T. Pham, Dan Huang, Andrew Y. Ng, and Christopher Potts. 2011. Learning word vectors for sentiment analysis. In *Proceedings of the 49th Annual Meeting of the Association for Computational Linguistics: Human Language Technologies*, pages 142–150, Portland, Oregon, USA. Association for Computational Linguistics.

Hiroki Nakayama, Takahiro Kubo, Junya Kamura, Yasufumi Taniguchi, and Xu Liang. 2018. doccano: Text annotation tool for human. Software available from https://github.com/doccano/doccano.

Mariana Neves and Jurica Ševa. 2019. An extensive review of tools for manual annotation of documents. *Briefings in Bioinformatics*.

Mick O'Donnell. 2008. Demonstration of the uam corpustool for text and image annotation. In *Proceedings of the ACL-08: HLT Demo Session*, pages 13–16.

Jeffrey Pennington, Richard Socher, and Christopher D. Manning. 2014. Glove: Global vectors for word representation. In *Empirical Methods in Natural Language Processing (EMNLP)*, pages 1532–1543.

Emanuele Pianta, Christian Girardi, and Roberto Zanoli. 2008. The textpro tool suite. In *LREC*.

Sylvestre-Alvise Rebuffi, Alexander Kolesnikov, Georg Sperl, and Christoph H Lampert. 2017. icarl: Incremental classifier and representation learning. In *Proceedings of the IEEE conference on Computer Vision and Pattern Recognition*, pages 2001–2010.

Christopher Schröder and Andreas Niekler. 2020. A survey of active learning for text classification using deep neural networks. *arXiv preprint arXiv:2008.07267*.

Pontus Stenetorp, Sampo Pyysalo, Goran Topić, Tomoko Ohta, Sophia Ananiadou, and Jun'ichi Tsujii. 2012. brat: a web-based tool for nlp-assisted text annotation. In *Proceedings of the Demonstrations at the 13th Conference of the European Chapter of the Association for Computational Linguistics*, pages 102–107.

Zhiqiang Toh and Jian Su. 2015. Nlangp: Supervised machine learning system for aspect category classification and opinion target extraction. In *Proceedings of the 9th International Workshop on Semantic Evaluation (SemEval 2015)*, pages 496–501.

Andreas van Cranenburgh. 2018. Active dop: A constituency treebank annotation tool with online learning. In *Proceedings of the 27th International Conference on Computational Linguistics: System Demonstrations*, page 38.

Maarten van Gompel. 2012. Folia: Format for linguistic annotation. *CLIN22, Tilburg*.

Chuhan Wu, Fangzhao Wu, Sixing Wu, Zhigang Yuan, and Yongfeng Huang. 2018. A hybrid unsupervised method for aspect term and opinion target extraction. *Knowledge-Based Systems*, 148:66–73.

Hong-Ming Yang, Xu-Yao Zhang, Fei Yin, and Cheng-Lin Liu. 2018a. Robust classification with convolutional prototype learning. In *Proceedings of the IEEE Conference on Computer Vision and Pattern Recognition*, pages 3474–3482.

Jie Yang, Yue Zhang, Linwei Li, and Xingxuan Li. 2018b. Yedda: A lightweight collaborative text span annotation tool.

Seid Muhie Yimam, Chris Biemann, Richard Eckart de Castilho, and Iryna Gurevych. 2014. Automatic annotation suggestions and custom annotation layers in webanno. In *Proceedings of 52nd Annual Meeting of the Association for Computational Linguistics: System Demonstrations*, pages 91–96.

Seid Muhie Yimam, Iryna Gurevych, Richard Eckart de Castilho, and Chris Biemann. 2013. Webanno: A flexible, web-based and visually supported system for distributed annotations. In *Proceedings of the 51st Annual Meeting of the Association for Computational Linguistics: System Demonstrations*, pages 1–6.

Zongwei Zhou, Jae Shin, Lei Zhang, Suryakanth Gurudu, Michael Gotway, and Jianming Liang. 2017. Fine-tuning convolutional neural networks for biomedical image analysis: Actively and incrementally. In *2017 IEEE Conference on Computer Vision and Pattern Recognition (CVPR)*, volume 2017, pages 4761–4772.

# Robustness Gym: Unifying the NLP Evaluation Landscape

**Karan Goel**[*†]
Stanford University

**Nazneen Rajani**[†]
Salesforce Research

**Jesse Vig**
Salesforce Research

**Zachary Taschdjian**
Salesforce Research

**Mohit Bansal**
UNC Chapel-Hill

**Christopher Ré**
Stanford University

## Abstract

Despite impressive performance on standard benchmarks, natural language processing (NLP) models are often brittle when deployed in real-world systems. In this work, we identify challenges with evaluating NLP systems and propose a solution in the form of Robustness Gym (ℝ𝔾),[1] a simple and extensible evaluation toolkit that unifies 4 standard evaluation paradigms: subpopulations, transformations, evaluation sets, and adversarial attacks. By providing a common platform for evaluation, ℝ𝔾 enables practitioners to compare results from disparate evaluation paradigms with a single click, and to easily develop and share novel evaluation methods using a built-in set of abstractions. Robustness Gym is under active development and we welcome feedback & contributions from the community.

## 1 Introduction

Advances in natural language processing (NLP) have led to models that achieve high test accuracy on independent and identically distributed (i.i.d.) data. However, analyses suggest that models are not robust to data corruptions (Belinkov and Bisk, 2018), distribution shifts (Hendrycks et al., 2020; Miller et al., 2020), and harmful data manipulations (Jia and Liang, 2017), and rely on spurious patterns (McCoy et al., 2019b). In practice, these vulnerabilities hinder deployment of trustworthy systems, as seen in public-use systems that were later revealed to be systematically biased, such as chatbots (Stuart-Ulin, 2018) and recruiting tools (Hamilton, 2018).

While practitioners know of these problems, it remains common to evaluate solely on i.i.d. data. Ideally, the goal of evaluation is to perform a broad assessment of a model's capabilities on the types of examples that it is likely to see when deployed. This process is complex for practitioners, since existing tools cater to a specialized set of evaluations for a task, and provide no clear way to leverage or share findings from prior evaluations. Thus, current evaluation practices face two challenges:

1. **Idiomatic lock-in (Section 2.1).** We identify 4 distinct evaluation types or idioms supported by existing tools and research – subpopulations, transformations, adversarial attacks and evaluation sets. Existing tools use bespoke abstractions to serve a subset of these idioms (e.g., adversarial attacks on words), requiring users to glue together tools to perform a broad evaluation that mixes idioms.

2. **Workflow fragmentation (Section 2.2).** As practitioners evaluate, they need to save progress, report findings and collaborate to understand model behavior. Existing solutions to save progress are tool- and idiom-specific, lack versioning, and provide limited support for sharing. Existing reporting templates are free-form, and have not successfully incentivized users to report findings e.g. only 6% of Huggingface (Wolf et al., 2020b) models report evaluation information.

In response to these challenges, we introduce Robustness Gym (ℝ𝔾), a simple, extensible and unified toolkit for evaluating robustness and sharing findings (Figure 1). ℝ𝔾 users can:

1. **Create slices (Section 3.1)** of data in ℝ𝔾. Each slice is a collection of examples, built using one or more evaluation idioms. ℝ𝔾 scaffolds users in a two-stage workflow, separating the storage of side-information about examples (CachedOperation) from the nuts and bolts of programmatically building slices using this information (SliceBuilder). This workflow helps

* E-mail: `kgoel@cs.stanford.edu`
† Equal contribution.
[1] `https://github.com/robustness-gym/robustness-gym`



*Proceedings of NAACL-HLT 2021: Demonstrations*, pages 42–55
June 6–11, 2021. 

| | Type | Instantiation | Examples |
|---|---|---|---|
| Rule-based | Filters | HasPhrase<br>HasLength<br>Position | ▒ Subpopulation that contains negation.<br>▒ Subpopulation that is in the {X} percentile for length.<br>▒ Subpopulation that contains {TOKEN} in position {N}. |
| | Logic | IFTTT recipes<br>Symmetry<br>Consistency | ▒ If example ends in {ING} then transform with backtranslation.<br>▒ Switch the first and last sentences of a source document to create a new eval set.<br>▒ Adding "aaaabbbb" at the end of every example as a form of attack. |
| | Template | Checklist | ▒ Generate new eval set using examples of the form "I {NEGATION} {POS_VERB}." |
| Machine | Classifier | HasScore<br>HasTopic | ▒ Subpopulation with perplexity {>X} based on a LM.<br>▒ Subpopulation belonging to a certain topic. |
| | Tagger* | POS<br>NER<br>SRL<br>Coref | ▒ Subpopulation that contains {POS_NOUN} in position {N}.<br>▒ Subpopulation that contains entity names with non-English origin.<br>▒ Subpopulation where there is no {AGENT}.<br>▒ Subpopulation that contains the pronouns for a particular gender. |
| | Parser* | Constituency<br>Dependency | ▒ Transform with all complete subtrees of {POS_VP} in the input.<br>▒ Subpopulation that has at least 2 {POS_NP} dependent on {POS_VP}. |
| | Generative | Backtranslation<br>Few-shot | ▒ Using a seq2seq model for transformation using backtranslation.<br>▒ Using GPT3 like models for creating synthetic eval sets. |
| | Perturbation | Paraphrasing<br>TextAttack | ▒ Synonym substitution using EDA.<br>▒ Perturbing input using TextAttack recipes. |
| Human or Human-in-the-loop | Filtering | Figurative text | ▒ Using humans to identify subpopulation that contains sarcasm. |
| | Curation | Evaluation sets<br>Data validation | ▒ Building datasets like ANLI, Contrast sets, HANS, etc.<br>▒ Using human-in-the-loop for label verification. |
| | Adversarial | Invariant<br>Directional | ▒ Perturbing text in a way that the expected output does not change.<br>▒ Perturbing text in a way that the expected output changes. |
| | Transformation | Counterfactual | ▒ Transforming to counterfactuals for a desired target concept. |

Table 1: Sample of slice builders and corresponding data slices along with example use cases that can either be used out-of-the-box or extended from Robustness Gym. ▒ $\rightarrow$ subpopulations, ▒ $\rightarrow$ transformations, ▒ $\rightarrow$ adversarial attacks and ▒ $\rightarrow$ evaluation sets. $*$ marked are CachedOperations and the rest are SliceBuilders.

users quickly implement new ideas, minimize boilerplate code and seamlessly integrate existing tools.

2. **Consolidate evaluations (Section 3.2)** and findings for community sharing. ℝ𝔾 users add slices into a TestBench that can be versioned and shared, allowing users to collaboratively build benchmarks and track progress. For standardized reporting, ℝ𝔾 provides *Robustness Reports* that can be auto-generated from testbenches and included in paper appendices.

We close with a discussion of how Robustness Gym can benefit practitioners[2] (Section 4), describing how users with varying expertise – novice, intermediate, expert – can evaluate a natural language inference (NLI) model in ℝ𝔾.

## 2 The Landscape of Evaluation Tools

We describe two challenges facing evaluation today, and situate them in the context of existing work.

[2]See 2 minute supplementary demo video.

### 2.1 Challenge 1: Idiomatic Lock-In

When practitioners decide what they want to evaluate, they can suffer from lock-in to a particular *idiom* or type of evaluation after they adopt a tool. Our analysis suggests that most tools and research today serve a subset of four evaluation idioms:

1. **Subpopulations.** Identify subpopulations of a dataset where the model may perform poorly.

   *Example*: short reviews (< 50 words) in the IMDB sentiment dataset (Maas et al., 2011).

2. **Transformations.** Perturb data to check that the model responds correctly to changes.

   *Example*: substitute words with their synonyms in the IMDB dataset.

3. **Attacks.** Perturb data adversarially to exploit weaknesses in a model.

   *Example*: add "aabbccaa" to the end of reviews, making the model predict positive sentiment.

4. **Evaluation Sets.** Use existing datasets or author examples to test generalization and perform targeted evaluation.

| Evaluation Idiom | Tools Available | Research Literature (focusing on NLI) |
|---|---|---|
| Subpopulations | Snorkel (Ratner et al., 2017),<br>Errudite (Wu et al., 2019) | Hard/easy sets (Gururangan et al., 2018)<br>Compositional-sensitivity (Nie et al., 2019) |
| Transformations | NLPAug (Ma, 2019) | Counterfactuals (Kaushik et al., 2019), Stress test (Naik et al., 2018),<br>Bias factors (Sanchez et al., 2018), Verb veridicality (Ross and Pavlick, 2019) |
| Attacks | TextAttack (Morris et al., 2020),<br>OpenAttack (Zeng et al., 2020)<br>Dynabench (Kiela, 2020) | Universal Adversarial Triggers (Wallace et al., 2019a),<br>Adversarial perturbations (Glockner et al., 2018),<br>ANLI (Nie et al., 2020) |
| Evaluation Sets | SuperGLUE diagnostic sets<br>(Wang et al., 2019)<br>Checklist (Ribeiro et al., 2020) | FraCaS (Cooper et al., 1994), RTE (Dagan et al., 2005), SICK (Marelli et al., 2014),<br>SNLI (Bowman et al., 2015), MNLI (Williams et al., 2018),<br>HANS (McCoy et al., 2019b), Quantified NLI (Geiger et al., 2018),<br>MPE (Lai et al., 2017), EQUATE (Ravichander et al., 2019), DNC (Poliak et al., 2018),<br>ImpPres (Jeretic et al., 2020), Systematicity (Yanaka et al., 2020)<br>ConjNLI (Saha et al., 2020), SherLIiC (Schmitt and Schütze, 2019) |

Table 2: Evaluation tools and literature, focusing on NLI as a case study. Some tools support multiple types of evaluations, e.g., TextAttack supports both augmentations and attacks. For additional related work, see Section 5.

*Example*: author new movie reviews in the style of a newspaper columnist.

We note that these idioms are not exhaustive. In Table 2, we use this categorization to summarize the tools and research available today, using the well-studied natural language inference (NLI) task as a case study. As an example, TextAttack (Morris et al., 2020) users can perform attacks, while CheckList (Ribeiro et al., 2020) users author examples using templates, but cannot perform attacks.

Tools vary in whether they provide scaffolding to let users build on new evaluation ideas easily. They often provide excellent abstractions for particular idioms, e.g., TextAttack (Morris et al., 2020) scaffolds users to easily write new adversarial attacks. However, no tool that we are aware of addresses this for evaluation that cuts across multiple idioms.

All of these limitations make it difficult for practitioners, who are forced to glue together a combination of tools. Each tool meets different developer needs, and has its own abstractions and organizing principles, which takes away time from users to inject their own creativity and expertise into the evaluation process.

We address these challenges with Robustness Gym (Section 3.1), which uses an open-interface design to support all 4 evaluation idioms, and provides a simple workflow to scaffold users.

## 2.2 Challenge 2: Workflow Fragmentation

As practitioners evaluate, they need to keep track of progress and communicate findings. Evaluation tools today let users save their progress, but provide no support for semantic versioning (Preston-Werner, 2013) and sharing findings. This is made more difficult when consolidating evaluations and results across multiple tools. General-purpose data storage solutions (McKerns et al., 2012) solve this problem, but require significant user effort to customize and manage.

Reporting findings can be difficult since there is no consensus on how to report when performing evaluation across multiple idioms. To study whether existing tools incentivize reporting, we scraped *model cards* for all available Huggingface models (Wolf et al., 2020a). Model cards (Mitchell et al., 2019) are free-form templates for standardized reporting that contain an entry for "Evaluation" or "Results", but leave the decision of what to report to the user. Huggingface provides tools for users to create model cards when submitting models to their model hub.

Our findings are summarized in Table 3. Only a small fraction (6.0%) of models carry model cards with any evaluation information. Qualitatively, we found low consistency in how users report findings, even for models trained on the same task. This suggests that it remains difficult for users to report evaluation information consistently and easily.

In Section 3.2, we describe the support that Robustness Gym provides for versioning evaluations in testbenches, and easily exporting and reporting findings with reports.

| # Model Cards | | % of Models |
|---|---|---|
| Total | 2133 | 64.6% |
| Non-empty | 922 | 27.9% |
| Any evaluation info | 197 | 6.0% |
| # Models | 3301 | 100.0% |

Table 3: Prevalence of evaluations in model cards on the HuggingFace Model Hub (huggingface.co/models).

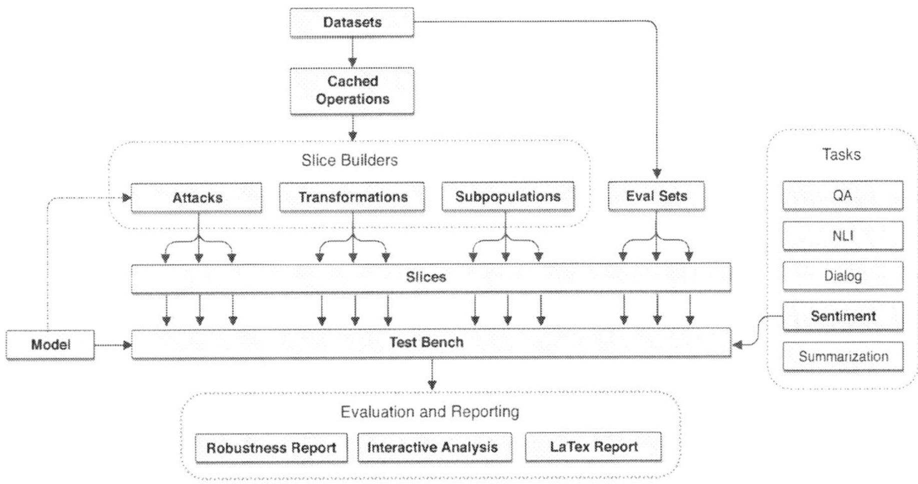


Figure 1: Robustness Gym system design and workflow.

## 3 Robustness Gym

We address the challenges highlighted in Section 2 with Robustness Gym (ℝ𝔾). We describe how users can build evaluations in Section 3.1, and version evaluations and report findings in Section 3.2. Figure 1 provides a visual depiction of the system design and workflow in ℝ𝔾, while Python examples for ℝ𝔾 are in Tables 4, 5 and 6 of the appendix.

### 3.1 Evaluation Workflow

As highlighted in Section 2.1, practitioners can get locked into a single tool that supports only a few evaluation idioms. By contrast, ℝ𝔾 enables broad evaluations across multiple idioms. At a high level, ℝ𝔾 breaks evaluation into a two-stage workflow:

1. **Caching information.** First, practitioners typically perform a set of common pre-processing operations (e.g., tokenization, lemmatization) and compute useful side information for each example (e.g., entity disambiguation, coreference resolution, semantic parsing) using external knowledge sources and models, which they cache for future analysis. An example is running the spaCy pipeline, and caching the Doc object that is generated for downstream analysis.

   A large part of practitioner effort goes into generating this side information – which can be expensive to compute – and into standardizing it to a format that is convenient for analysis.

   *RG Support.* CachedOperation is an abstraction in ℝ𝔾 to derive useful information or generate side information for each example in a dataset by (i) letting users run common operations easily and caching the outputs of these operations e.g., running spaCy (Honnibal et al., 2020); (ii) storing this information alongside the associated example so that it can be accessed conveniently; (iii) providing a simple abstraction for users to write their own operations.

2. **Building slices.** Second, practitioners use the examples' inputs and any available cached information to build *slices*, which are collections of examples used for evaluation based on any of the 4 evaluation idioms. These slices are derived from a loaded dataset by applying one of the evaluation idioms, e.g. filtering a dataset based on some criteria to construct a subpopulation.

   *RG Support.* SliceBuilder is an abstraction to retrieve information for an example and create slices of data from them by (i) providing retrieval methods to access inputs and cached information conveniently when writing custom code to build slices; (ii) providing specialized abstractions for specific evaluation idioms: transformations, attacks and subpopulations.

   Robustness Gym includes wrappers for libraries such as TextAttack and nlpaug that provide specialized support for constructing adversarial attacks and data transformations respectively. This allows users the ability to utilize external libraries in a unified toolkit and workflow.

This breakdown naturally separates the process of gathering useful information from the nuts and

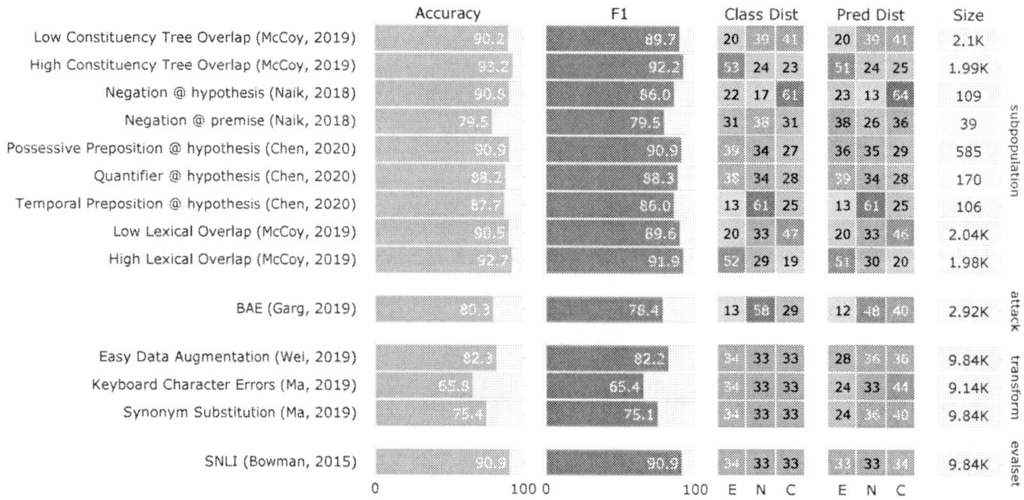


Figure 2: Robustness Report for Natural Language Inference using `bert-base` on SNLI.

bolts of using that information to build slices. Table 1 contains examples of CachedOperations and SliceBuilders that can be supported by ℝ𝔾.

ℝ𝔾 relies on a common data interface provided by the datasets library from HuggingFace (Wolf et al., 2020a), which is backed by Apache Arrow (Foundation, 2019). This ensures that all operations in ℝ𝔾 interoperate with HuggingFace models.

### 3.2 Testbenches and Reports

As highlighted in Section 2.2, users may find themselves consolidating evaluation results across several tools and evaluation idioms. ℝ𝔾 addresses this fragmentation by providing users a TestBench abstraction for storing and versioning evaluations, and a Report abstraction for sharing findings.

- **Versioning evaluations.** Users can assemble and version a collection of slices into a TestBench, which represents a suite of evaluations. A TestBench contains the slices created by the user, and users can interact with a TestBench to evaluate models and store metrics. Each TestBench has an associated semantic version that can be "bumped" as changes are made, e.g. if a user adds a new set of slices, they can change the version to indicate that the TestBench has been modified.

  ℝ𝔾 tracks the provenance or history of slices, making it easy to identify the (i) slice's original data source; (ii) sequence of SliceBuilders by which a slice was created. This makes it easy for another user to reproduce evaluations when given a TestBench, even without the original code. They can simply inspect the slices in the TestBench to look at provenance information, and use it to reproduce their evaluation process.

- **Sharing findings.** Users can create a *Robustness Report* for any model on a TestBench (Figure 2), or standalone reports for evaluations that are not performed in ℝ𝔾, using the Report abstraction. To incentivize standardized reporting, ℝ𝔾 supports *Standard Reports* for several tasks. The Standard Report is comprehensive, static and is backed by a TestBench that contains slices from all evaluation idioms. It can be generated in a PDF or LaTeX format to be added to the appendix of a paper[3]. Reports reduce user burden in communicating findings, and make it easier to standardize reporting in the community.

  ℝ𝔾 supports an interactive Streamlit tool[4] for generating standard reports, which will be expanded in the future to allow users to pick slices based on their evaluation needs.

## 4 User Personas in Robustness Gym

Next, we discuss how users with varying expertise can use ℝ𝔾. We describe how 3 user personas—beginner, intermediate, and advanced—can use ℝ𝔾

[3]See Figure 3 in the appendix.

[4]Screenshot in Figure 4 of the appendix.

to analyze the performance of an natural language inference (NLI) model. In NLI, the goal is to determine whether a premise sentence entails, is neutral to, or contradicts a hypothesis sentence.

### 4.1 Scenario I: Beginner User

**Description.** Users new to NLP and robustness, lack knowledge to choose or write specific slices.

**Example Goal.** Exploratory robustness testing.

**RG support:**

- *Visual Interface.* The user creates a report with a few clicks in the Streamlit interface[5]. They select "Standard Report", "SNLI" (dataset)[6], "Ternary Natural Language Inference" (task), "BERT-Base" (model), and click "Generate Report".
- *Standard Reports.* The Standard Report, shown in Figure 2 provides a detailed snapshot of various robustness tests for NLI. The tests may include Subpopulations (e.g., HASNEGATION, LEXICALOVERLAP), Transformations (e.g., SYNONYMAUG, KEYBOARDAUG) (Ma, 2019), Attacks (TEXTATTACK) (Morris et al., 2020; Garg and Ramakrishnan, 2020), and Evaluation Sets (Bowman et al., 2015). The user gleans several initial insights from this report. For example, their model is vulnerable to typing mistakes due to low accuracy on the KEYBOARDAUG slice; the predicted class distribution column reveals that this noise causes the model to predict `contradiction` more frequently than `entailment` or `neutral`. The user is able to easily share the generated PDF of this report.

### 4.2 Scenario II: Intermediate User

**Description.** Users familiar with NLP and robustness, willing to write minimal code.

**Example Goal.** Explore gender bias when gendered pronouns are present in the input.

**RG support:**

- *Built-in SliceBuilders.* Apply the existing HASPHRASE SliceBuilder to create subpopulations with female pronouns in the hypothesis:

```
subpopulations = HasPhrase(['her', 'she'])
slices = subpopulations(snli, ['hypothesis'])
```

- *Testbenches.* Put slices into a TestBench and make it available on GitHub for collaboration.
- *Reports.* Generate Robustness Reports for any model from the TestBench.

### 4.3 Scenario III: Advanced User

**Description.** NLP experts, need to write custom code for their task and research.

**Example Goal.** Evaluate whether NLI models rely on surface-level spurious similarities between premise and hypothesis.

**RG support:**

- *CachedOperations.* Run the spaCy pipeline for tokenization.
- *Custom SliceBuilders.* Utilize the SCORESUBPOPULATION class to construct subpopulations with arbitrary scoring functions. Write a custom scoring function `len_diff` that returns the absolute difference in length between the tokenized hypothesis and premise. Then, find examples that score in the top 10% as follows:

```
s = ScoreSubpopulation(
    intervals=[('90%','100%')], score_fn=len_diff)
```

- *Transformations.* Transform data using classes such as EASYDATAAUGMENTATION (Wei and Zou, 2019). Compose this transformation with the custom SCORESUBPOPULATION described earlier to create a larger slice.
- *Testbench.* Publish a new TestBench on GitHub for others to reuse and refine the evaluations.
- *Report.* Generate a report for immediate analysis and a LaTeX appendix to share results in a research paper (see Figure 3 in appendix).

## 5 Related Tools and Work

We highlight additional related work for evaluation and reporting, including work on interpretability.

**Evaluation and error-analysis.** Tools for evaluation and error analysis support users in understanding where their models fail. In contrast to RG, existing tools support only a subset of evaluations and analyses. Errudite (Wu et al., 2019), Snorkel (Ratner et al., 2017) support subpopulations, TextAttack (Morris et al., 2020) adversarial attacks, nlpaug (Ma, 2019) transformations, and CrossCheck (Arendt et al., 2020), Manifold (Zhang et al., 2018) focus on visualization and analysis for model comparison.

**Interpretability.** Tools for interpretability enable a better understanding of model behavior. These

[5]See supplementary demo video for example usage.

[6]The Stanford Natural Languge Inference dataset (Bowman et al., 2015).

tools serve complementary objectives to Robustness Gym, e.g., explaining why a model makes a certain prediction, rather than performing broad evaluations. Tools include the recent Language Interpretability Tool (LIT) (Tenney et al., 2020), IBM's AI Explainability 360 (Arya et al., 2019), AllenNLP Interpret (Wallace et al., 2019b), InterpretML (Nori et al., 2019), Manifold (Zhang et al., 2018), Pytorch Captum (Narine Kokhlikyan and Reblitz-Richardson), DiCE (Mothilal et al., 2020), What-if (Wexler et al., 2019), FairVis (Cabrera et al., 2019), and FairSight (Ahn and Lin, 2019). Many of these tools focus on interactive visualization, which limits their scope to interpreting small numbers of examples and makes their use susceptible to subjectivity and selection bias. By contrast, Robustness Gym can scale to large datasets, while testbenches ensure reproducibility of analyses.

## 6 Conclusion

We introduced Robustness Gym, an evaluation toolkit that supports a broad set of evaluation idioms, and can be used for collaboratively building and sharing evaluations and results. Robustness Gym is under active development and we welcome feedback and contributions from the community.

## Acknowledgements

This work was part of a collaboration between Stanford, UNC, and Salesforce Research and was supported by Salesforce AI Research grants to MB and CR. We are thankful to Samson Tan, Jason Wu, Stephan Zheng, Caiming Xiong, Han Guo, Laurel Orr, Jared Dunnmon, Chris Potts, Marco Tulio Ribeiro, Shreya Rajpal for helpful discussions and feedback. CR also gratefully acknowledges the support of NIH under No. U54EB020405 (Mobilize), NSF under Nos. CCF1763315 (Beyond Sparsity), CCF1563078 (Volume to Velocity), and 1937301 (RTML); ONR under No. N000141712266 (Unifying Weak Supervision); the Moore Foundation, NXP, Xilinx, LETI-CEA, Intel, IBM, Microsoft, NEC, Toshiba, TSMC, ARM, Hitachi, BASF, Accenture, Ericsson, Qualcomm, Analog Devices, the Okawa Foundation, American Family Insurance, Google Cloud, Swiss Re, Total, the HAI-AWS Cloud Credits for Research program, and members of the Stanford DAWN project: Facebook, Google, and VMWare. The U.S. Government is authorized to reproduce and distribute reprints for Governmental purposes notwithstanding any copyright notation thereon. Any opinions, findings, and conclusions or recommendations expressed in this material are those of the authors and do not necessarily reflect the views, policies, or endorsements, either expressed or implied, of NIH, ONR, or the U.S. Government.

## References

Yongsu Ahn and Yu-Ru Lin. 2019. Fairsight: Visual analytics for fairness in decision making. *IEEE transactions on visualization and computer graphics*, 26(1):1086–1095.

Dustin Arendt, Zhuanyi Huang, Prasha Shrestha, E. Ayton, Maria Glenski, and Svitlana Volkova. 2020. Crosscheck: Rapid, reproducible, and interpretable model evaluation. *ArXiv*, abs/2004.07993.

Vijay Arya, Rachel K. E. Bellamy, Pin-Yu Chen, Amit Dhurandhar, Michael Hind, Samuel C. Hoffman, Stephanie Houde, Q. Vera Liao, Ronny Luss, Aleksandra Mojsilović, Sami Mourad, Pablo Pedemonte, Ramya Raghavendra, John Richards, Prasanna Sattigeri, Karthikeyan Shanmugam, Moninder Singh, Kush R. Varshney, Dennis Wei, and Yunfeng Zhang. 2019. One explanation does not fit all: A toolkit and taxonomy of ai explainability techniques.

Yonatan Belinkov and Yonatan Bisk. 2018. Synthetic and natural noise both break neural machine translation. *ArXiv*, abs/1711.02173.

Samuel R Bowman, Gabor Angeli, Christopher Potts, and Christopher D Manning. 2015. A large annotated corpus for learning natural language inference. *arXiv preprint arXiv:1508.05326*.

Ángel Alexander Cabrera, Will Epperson, Fred Hohman, Minsuk Kahng, Jamie Morgenstern, and Duen Horng Chau. 2019. Fairvis: Visual analytics for discovering intersectional bias in machine learning. In *2019 IEEE Conference on Visual Analytics Science and Technology (VAST)*, pages 46–56. IEEE.

Vincent Chen, Sen Wu, Alexander J Ratner, Jen Weng, and Christopher Ré. 2019. Slice-based learning: A programming model for residual learning in critical data slices. In *Advances in neural information processing systems*, pages 9392–9402.

Robin Cooper, Dick Crouch, Jan Van Eijck, Chris Fox, Johan Van Genabith, Jan Jaspars, Hans Kamp, David Milward, Manfred Pinkal, Massimo Poesio, and et al. Pulman, Stephen. 1994. Using the framework. Technical report, Deliverable D6.

Ido Dagan, Oren Glickman, and Bernardo Magnini. 2005. The pascal recognising textual entailment challenge. In *Machine Learning Challenges Workshop*, pages 177–190. Springer.

Apache Software Foundation. 2019. Arrow: A cross-language development platform for in-memory data.

Siddhant Garg and Goutham Ramakrishnan. 2020. Bae: Bert-based adversarial examples for text classification. *ArXiv*, abs/2004.01970.

Atticus Geiger, Ignacio Cases, Lauri Karttunen, and Christopher Potts. 2018. Stress-testing neural models of natural language inference with multiply-quantified sentences. *arXiv preprint arXiv:1810.13033*.

Max Glockner, Vered Shwartz, and Yoav Goldberg. 2018. Breaking nli systems with sentences that require simple lexical inferences. In *Proceedings of the 56th Annual Meeting of the Association for Computational Linguistics (Volume 2: Short Papers)*, pages 650–655.

Suchin Gururangan, Swabha Swayamdipta, Omer Levy, Roy Schwartz, Samuel R Bowman, and Noah A Smith. 2018. Annotation artifacts in natural language inference data. *arXiv preprint arXiv:1803.02324*.

Isobel Asher Hamilton. 2018. Amazon built an AI tool to hire people but had to shut it down because it was discriminating against women.

Dan Hendrycks, Steven Basart, Norman Mu, Saurav Kadavath, Frank Wang, Evan Dorundo, Rahul Desai, Tyler Zhu, Samyak Parajuli, Mike Guo, et al. 2020. The many faces of robustness: A critical analysis of out-of-distribution generalization. *arXiv preprint arXiv:2006.16241*.

Matthew Honnibal, Ines Montani, Sofie Van Landeghem, and Adriane Boyd. 2020. spaCy: Industrial-strength Natural Language Processing in Python.

Paloma Jeretic, Alex Warstadt, Suvrat Bhooshan, and Adina Williams. 2020. Are natural language inference models imppressive? learning implicature and presupposition. *arXiv preprint arXiv:2004.03066*.

Robin Jia and Percy Liang. 2017. Adversarial examples for evaluating reading comprehension systems. In *EMNLP*.

Divyansh Kaushik, Eduard Hovy, and Zachary C Lipton. 2019. Learning the difference that makes a difference with counterfactually-augmented data. *arXiv preprint arXiv:1909.12434*.

Douwe Kiela. 2020. Rethinking AI Benchmarking.

Alice Lai, Yonatan Bisk, and Julia Hockenmaier. 2017. Natural language inference from multiple premises. In *Proceedings of the Eighth International Joint Conference on Natural Language Processing (Volume 1: Long Papers)*, pages 100–109, Taipei, Taiwan. Asian Federation of Natural Language Processing.

Edward Ma. 2019. NLP Augmentation.

Andrew L. Maas, Raymond E. Daly, Peter T. Pham, Dan Huang, Andrew Y. Ng, and Christopher Potts. 2011. Learning word vectors for sentiment analysis. In *Proceedings of the 49th Annual Meeting of the Association for Computational Linguistics: Human Language Technologies*, pages 142–150, Portland, Oregon, USA. Association for Computational Linguistics.

Marco Marelli, Luisa Bentivogli, Marco Baroni, Raffaella Bernardi, Stefano Menini, and Roberto Zamparelli. 2014. SemEval-2014 task 1: Evaluation of compositional distributional semantic models on full sentences through semantic relatedness and textual entailment. In *Proceedings of the 8th International Workshop on Semantic Evaluation (SemEval 2014)*, pages 1–8, Dublin, Ireland. Association for Computational Linguistics.

R. T. McCoy, Ellie Pavlick, and Tal Linzen. 2019a. Right for the wrong reasons: Diagnosing syntactic heuristics in natural language inference. *ArXiv*, abs/1902.01007.

R Thomas McCoy, Ellie Pavlick, and Tal Linzen. 2019b. Right for the wrong reasons: Diagnosing syntactic heuristics in natural language inference. *arXiv preprint arXiv:1902.01007*.

M. McKerns, Leif Strand, T. Sullivan, Alta Fang, and M. A. G. Aivazis. 2012. Building a framework for predictive science. *ArXiv*, abs/1202.1056.

J. Miller, Karl Krauth, B. Recht, and L. Schmidt. 2020. The effect of natural distribution shift on question answering models. *ArXiv*, abs/2004.14444.

Margaret Mitchell, Simone Wu, Andrew Zaldivar, Parker Barnes, Lucy Vasserman, Ben Hutchinson, Elena Spitzer, Inioluwa Deborah Raji, and Timnit Gebru. 2019. Model cards for model reporting. In *Proceedings of the conference on fairness, accountability, and transparency*, pages 220–229.

John X Morris, Eli Lifland, Jin Yong Yoo, and Yanjun Qi. 2020. Textattack: A framework for adversarial attacks in natural language processing. *arXiv preprint arXiv:2005.05909*.

Ramaravind K Mothilal, Amit Sharma, and Chenhao Tan. 2020. Explaining machine learning classifiers through diverse counterfactual explanations. In *Proceedings of the 2020 Conference on Fairness, Accountability, and Transparency*, pages 607–617.

Aakanksha Naik, Abhilasha Ravichander, Norman Sadeh, Carolyn Rose, and Graham Neubig. 2018. Stress test evaluation for natural language inference. *arXiv preprint arXiv:1806.00692*.

Miguel Martin Edward Wang Jonathan Reynolds Alexander Melnikov Natalia Lunova Narine Kokhlikyan, Vivek Miglani and Orion Reblitz-Richardson. Pytorch captum.

Yixin Nie, Yicheng Wang, and Mohit Bansal. 2019. Analyzing compositionality-sensitivity of nli models. In *Proceedings of the AAAI Conference on Artificial Intelligence*, volume 33, pages 6867–6874.

Yixin Nie, Adina Williams, Emily Dinan, Mohit Bansal, Jason Weston, and Douwe Kiela. 2020. Adversarial nli: A new benchmark for natural language understanding. In *ACL*.

Harsha Nori, Samuel Jenkins, Paul Koch, and Rich Caruana. 2019. Interpretml: A unified framework for machine learning interpretability. *arXiv preprint arXiv:1909.09223*.

Adam Poliak, Aparajita Haldar, Rachel Rudinger, J. Edward Hu, Ellie Pavlick, Aaron Steven White, and Benjamin Van Durme. 2018. Collecting diverse natural language inference problems for sentence representation evaluation. In *Proceedings of the 2018 Conference on Empirical Methods in Natural Language Processing*, pages 67–81, Brussels, Belgium. Association for Computational Linguistics.

Tom Preston-Werner. 2013. Semantic versioning 2.0. 0. *línea]. Available: http://semver. org*.

Alexander Ratner, Stephen H Bach, Henry Ehrenberg, Jason Fries, Sen Wu, and Christopher Ré. 2017. Snorkel: Rapid training data creation with weak supervision. In *Proceedings of the VLDB Endowment. International Conference on Very Large Data Bases*, volume 11, page 269. NIH Public Access.

Abhilasha Ravichander, Aakanksha Naik, Carolyn Rose, and Eduard Hovy. 2019. EQUATE: A benchmark evaluation framework for quantitative reasoning in natural language inference. In *Proceedings of the 23rd Conference on Computational Natural Language Learning (CoNLL)*, pages 349–361, Hong Kong, China. Association for Computational Linguistics.

Marco Tulio Ribeiro, Tongshuang Wu, Carlos Guestrin, and Sameer Singh. 2020. Beyond accuracy: Behavioral testing of nlp models with checklist. In *Association for Computational Linguistics (ACL)*.

Alexis Ross and Ellie Pavlick. 2019. How well do nli models capture verb veridicality? In *Proceedings of the 2019 Conference on Empirical Methods in Natural Language Processing and the 9th International Joint Conference on Natural Language Processing (EMNLP-IJCNLP)*, pages 2230–2240.

Swarnadeep Saha, Yixin Nie, and Mohit Bansal. 2020. Conjnli: Natural language inference over conjunctive sentences. In *Proceedings of the 2020 Conference on Empirical Methods in Natural Language Processing (EMNLP)*, pages 8240–8252.

Ivan Sanchez, Jeff Mitchell, and Sebastian Riedel. 2018. Behavior analysis of NLI models: Uncovering the influence of three factors on robustness. In *Proceedings of the 2018 Conference of the North American Chapter of the Association for Computational Linguistics: Human Language Technologies, Volume 1 (Long Papers)*, pages 1975–1985, New Orleans, Louisiana. Association for Computational Linguistics.

Martin Schmitt and Hinrich Schütze. 2019. SherLIiC: A typed event-focused lexical inference benchmark for evaluating natural language inference. In *Proceedings of the 57th Annual Meeting of the Association for Computational Linguistics*, pages 902–914, Florence, Italy. Association for Computational Linguistics.

Chloe Rose Stuart-Ulin. 2018. Microsoft's politically correct chatbot is even worse than its racist one.

Ian Tenney, James Wexler, Jasmijn Bastings, Tolga Bolukbasi, Andy Coenen, Sebastian Gehrmann, Ellen Jiang, Mahima Pushkarna, Carey Radebaugh, Emily Reif, et al. 2020. The language interpretability tool: Extensible, interactive visualizations and analysis for nlp models. *arXiv preprint arXiv:2008.05122*.

Eric Wallace, Shi Feng, Nikhil Kandpal, Matt Gardner, and Sameer Singh. 2019a. Universal adversarial triggers for nlp. *arXiv preprint arXiv:1908.07125*.

Eric Wallace, Jens Tuyls, Junlin Wang, Sanjay Subramanian, Matt Gardner, and Sameer Singh. 2019b. Allennlp interpret: A framework for explaining predictions of nlp models. *arXiv preprint arXiv:1909.09251*.

Alex Wang, Yada Pruksachatkun, Nikita Nangia, Amanpreet Singh, Julian Michael, Felix Hill, Omer Levy, and Samuel Bowman. 2019. Superglue: A stickier benchmark for general-purpose language understanding systems. In *Advances in Neural Information Processing Systems*, pages 3266–3280.

Jason W Wei and Kai Zou. 2019. Eda: Easy data augmentation techniques for boosting performance on text classification tasks. *arXiv preprint arXiv:1901.11196*.

James Wexler, Mahima Pushkarna, Tolga Bolukbasi, Martin Wattenberg, Fernanda Viégas, and Jimbo Wilson. 2019. The what-if tool: Interactive probing of machine learning models. *IEEE transactions on visualization and computer graphics*, 26(1):56–65.

Adina Williams, Nikita Nangia, and Samuel Bowman. 2018. A broad-coverage challenge corpus for sentence understanding through inference. In *Proceedings of the 2018 Conference of the North American Chapter of the Association for Computational Linguistics: Human Language Technologies, Volume 1 (Long Papers)*, pages 1112–1122. Association for Computational Linguistics.

Thomas Wolf, Lysandre Debut, Victor Sanh, Julien Chaumond, Clement Delangue, Anthony Moi, Pierric Cistac, Tim Rault, Rémi Louf, Morgan Funtowicz, Joe Davison, Sam Shleifer, Patrick von Platen, Clara Ma, Yacine Jernite, Julien Plu, Canwen Xu, Teven Le Scao, Sylvain Gugger, Mariama Drame, Quentin Lhoest, and Alexander M. Rush. 2020a. Huggingface's transformers: State-of-the-art natural language processing.

Thomas Wolf, Lysandre Debut, Victor Sanh, Julien Chaumond, Clement Delangue, Anthony Moi, Pierric Cistac, Tim Rault, Rémi Louf, Morgan Funtowicz, Joe Davison, Sam Shleifer, Patrick von Platen, Clara Ma, Yacine Jernite, Julien Plu, Canwen Xu, Teven Le Scao, Sylvain Gugger, Mariama Drame, Quentin Lhoest, and Alexander M. Rush. 2020b. Transformers: State-of-the-art natural language processing. In *Proceedings of the 2020 Conference on Empirical Methods in Natural Language Processing: System Demonstrations*, pages 38–45, Online. Association for Computational Linguistics.

Tongshuang Wu, Marco Tulio Ribeiro, J. Heer, and Daniel S. Weld. 2019. Errudite: Scalable, reproducible, and testable error analysis. In *ACL*.

Hitomi Yanaka, Koji Mineshima, Daisuke Bekki, and Kentaro Inui. 2020. Do neural models learn systematicity of monotonicity inference in natural language? *arXiv preprint arXiv:2004.14839*.

Guoyang Zeng, Fanchao Qi, Qianrui Zhou, Tingji Zhang, Bairu Hou, Yuan Zang, Zhiyuan Liu, and Maosong Sun. 2020. Openattack: An open-source textual adversarial attack toolkit. *arXiv preprint arXiv:2009.09191*.

Jiawei Zhang, Yang Wang, Piero Molino, Lezhi Li, and David S Ebert. 2018. Manifold: A model-agnostic framework for interpretation and diagnosis of machine learning models. *IEEE transactions on visualization and computer graphics*, 25(1):364–373.

## A Appendix

**Code.** We provide example code snippets for Robustness Gym in Tables 4 (CachedOperation), 5 (SliceBuilder), and 6 (TestBench, Report), below.

**LaTeX Report.** Figure 3 is an example of a report generated in a LaTeX format. The code for the figure was auto-generated and the figure was simply included in the appendix.

**Streamlit Application.** Figure 4 is a screenshot of our streamlit application for generating standard reports.

| Goal | | | Code Snippet |
|---|---|---|---|
| Caching | Create | Create Spacy cached operation | `spacy = Spacy()` |
| | | Create Stanza cached operation | `stanza = Stanza()` |
| | | Create a custom cached operation | `cachedop = CachedOperation( apply_fn=my_custom_fn, identifier=Identifier('MyCustomOp'), )` |
| | | Run a cached operation | `dataset = cachedop(dataset, columns)` |
| | Retrieve | Retrieve all Spacy info cached | `Spacy.retrieve(dataset, columns)` |
| | | Retrieve Spacy tokens | `Spacy.retrieve(batch, columns, 'tokens')` |
| | | Retrieve Stanza entities | `Stanza.retrieve( batch, columns, Stanza.entities )` |
| | | Retrieve any cached operation info after processing | `CachedOperation.retrieve( batch, columns, my_proc_fn, 'MyCustomOp' )` |

Table 4: Code for the CachedOperation abstraction in Robustness Gym.

<table>
<tr><th colspan="3">Goal</th><th>Code Snippet</th></tr>
<tr><td rowspan="10">Slice Building</td><td rowspan="3">Subpopulations</td><td>Create a subpopulation that generates three slices based on raw lengths in $[0, 10]$, $[10, 20]$ and $[20, \infty)$</td><td><pre>length_sp = Length(
    [(0, 10), (10, 20), (20, np.inf)]
)</pre></td></tr>
<tr><td>Create a subpopulation that generates two slices based on bottom 10% and top 10% length percentiles</td><td><pre>length_sp = Length(
    [('0%', '10%'), ('90%', '100%')]
)</pre></td></tr>
<tr><td>Create a custom subpopulation by binning the outputs of a scoring function</td><td><pre>custom_sp = ScoreSubpopulation(
    [('0%', '10%'), ('90%', '100%')],
    my_scoring_fn
)</pre></td></tr>
<tr><td rowspan="3">Transformations</td><td>Create EasyDataAugmentation</td><td><pre>eda = EasyDataAugmentation()</pre></td></tr>
<tr><td>Create any NlpAug transformation</td><td><pre>nlpaug_trans = NlpAugTransformation(
    pipeline=nlpaug_pipeline
)</pre></td></tr>
<tr><td>Create a custom transformation</td><td><pre>custom_trans = Transformation(
    Identifier('MyTransformation'),
    my_transformation_fn
)</pre></td></tr>
<tr><td>Attacks</td><td>Create TextAttack recipe</td><td><pre>attack = TextAttack.from_recipe(recipe, model)</pre></td></tr>
<tr><td>Evaluation Sets</td><td>Create a slice from a dataset</td><td><pre>sl = Slice(dataset)</pre></td></tr>
<tr><td>Slice Builders</td><td>Run any SliceBuilder</td><td><pre>dataset, slices, membership = slicebuilder(
    batch_or_dataset=dataset,
    columns=columns,
)</pre></td></tr>
</table>

Table 5: Code for the SliceBuilder abstraction in Robustness Gym.

| Goal | | | Code Snippet |
|---|---|---|---|
| Reporting | Testbench | Create a testbench | `testbench = TestBench( identifier=Identifier('MyTestBench'), version='0.1.0' )` |
| | | Add slices to testbench | `testbench.add_slices(slices)` |
| | | Fuzzy search testbench for slices | `top_k_matched_slices = testbench.search('len')` |
| | | Bump testbench minor version | `testbench.bump_minor()` |
| | | Save and load a testbench | `testbench.save(path)` `testbench.load(path)` |
| | Report | Evaluate model on slices and generate report | `testbench.create_report(model)` |
| | | Create a custom report | `report = Report( dataframe_with_metrics, report_columns, )` |
| | | Generate figure from report | `figure = report.figure()` |
| | | Generate LaTeXreport | `latex = report.latex()` |

Table 6: Code for the TestBench and Report abstractions in Robustness Gym.

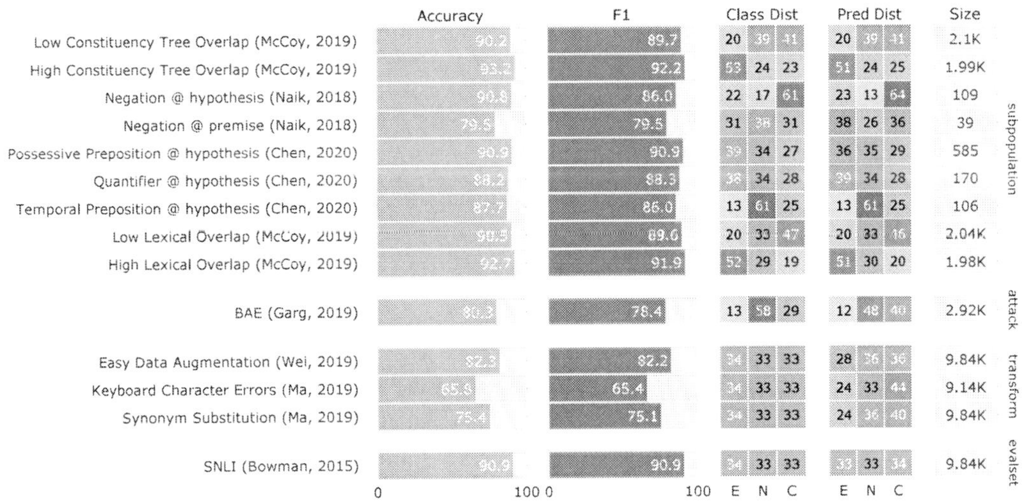


Figure 3: Robustness report for textattack/bert-base-uncased-snli model on SNLI dataset. The report lays out scores for each evaluation, broken out by category. Citations: (Chen et al., 2019; Naik et al., 2018; McCoy et al., 2019a; Wei and Zou, 2019; Ma, 2019; Bowman et al., 2015).

*Note: the LaTeX figure and caption above is auto-generated using "report.latex()".*

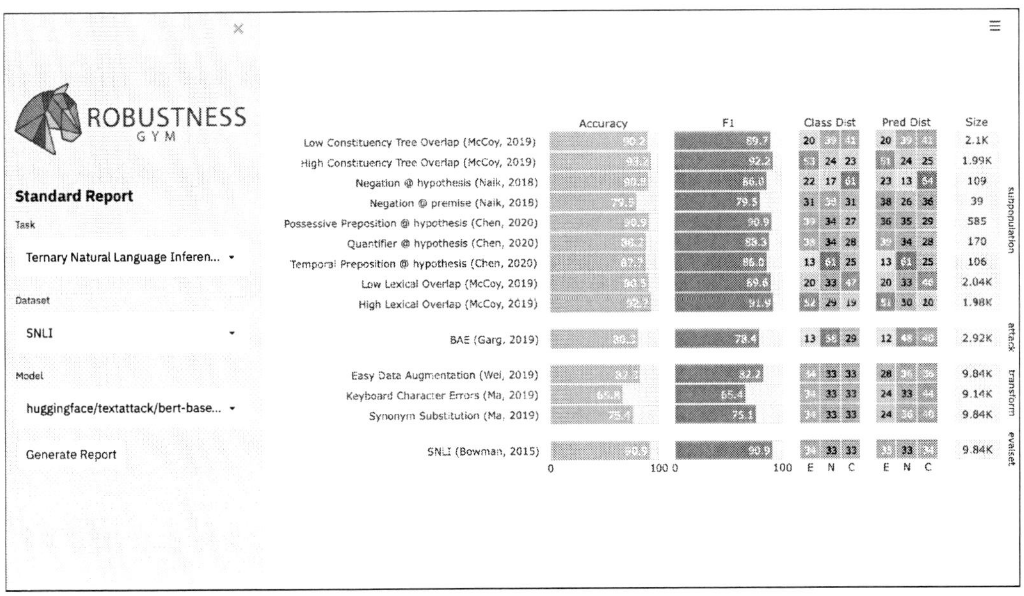


Figure 4: Screenshot of our interactive Streamlit application for creating standard reports. Users can choose a task, dataset and model on the left side, and a standard report spanning all 4 evaluation idioms – subpopulations, transformations, attacks and evaluation sets – is auto-generated on the right side.

# EventPlus: A Temporal Event Understanding Pipeline

**Mingyu Derek Ma**[1*] **Jiao Sun**[2*] **Mu Yang**[3] **Kung-Hsiang Huang**[2]
**Nuan Wen**[2] **Shikhar Singh**[2] **Rujun Han**[2] **Nanyun Peng**[1,2]
[1] Computer Science Department, University of California, Los Angeles
[2] Information Sciences Institute, University of Southern California
[3] Texas A&M University
{ma,violetpeng}@cs.ucla.edu
{jiaosun,kunghsia,nuanwen,ssingh43,rujunhan}@usc.edu
yangmu@tamu.edu

## Abstract

We present EventPlus, a temporal event understanding pipeline that integrates various state-of-the-art event understanding components including *event trigger and type detection*, *event argument detection*, *event duration* and *temporal relation extraction*. Event information, especially event temporal knowledge, is a type of common sense knowledge that helps people understand how stories evolve and provides predictive hints for future events. EventPlus as the first comprehensive temporal event understanding pipeline provides a convenient tool for users to quickly obtain annotations about events and their temporal information for any user-provided document. Furthermore, we show EventPlus can be easily adapted to other domains (e.g., biomedical domain). We make EventPlus publicly available to facilitate event-related information extraction and downstream applications.

## 1 Introduction

Event understanding is intuitive for humans and important for daily decision making. For example, given the raw text shown in Figure 1, a person can infer lots of information including *event trigger and type*, *event related arguments* (e.g., agent, patient, location), *event duration* and *temporal relations* between events based on the linguistic and common sense knowledge. These understandings help people comprehend the situation and prepare for future events. The event and temporal knowledge are helpful for many downstream applications including question answering (Meng et al., 2017; Huang et al., 2019), story generation (Peng et al., 2018; Yao et al., 2019; Goldfarb-Tarrant et al., 2019, 2020), and forecasting (Wang et al., 2017; Granroth-Wilding and Clark, 2016; Li et al., 2018).

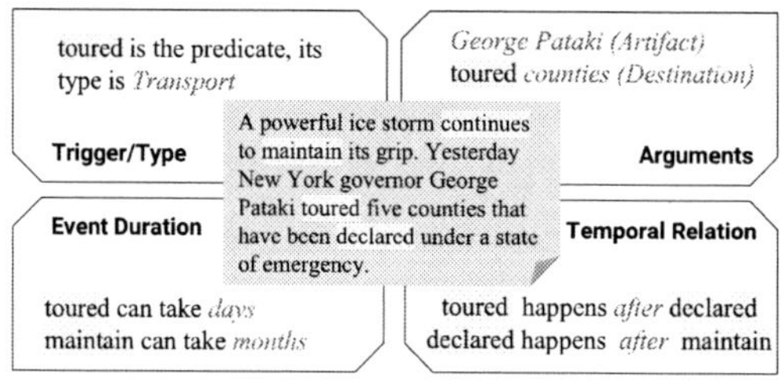


Figure 1: Event understanding components. We highlight events triggers in yellow, and mark the predicted task-related information in *Italic*.

Despite the importance, there are relatively few tools available for users to conduct text-based temporal event understanding. Researchers have been building natural language processing (NLP) analysis tools for "core NLP" tasks (Gardner et al., 2018; Manning et al., 2014; Khashabi et al., 2018). However, systems that target at semantic understanding of events and their temporal information are still under-explored. There are individual works for event extraction, temporal relation detection and event duration detection, but they are separately developed and thus cannot provide comprehensive and coherent temporal event knowledge.

We present EventPlus, the *first* pipeline system integrating several high-performance temporal event information extraction models for comprehensive temporal event understanding. Specifically, EventPlus contains event extraction (both on defined ontology and for novel event triggers), event temporal relation prediction, event duration detection and event-related arguments and named entity recognition, as shown in Figure 2.[1]

*Equal contribution.

[1]The system is publicly accessible at https://kairos-event.isi.edu. The source code is available at https://github.com/PlusLabNLP/EventPlus. We also provide an introductory video at https://pluslabnlp.github.io/eventplus.



*Proceedings of NAACL-HLT 2021: Demonstrations*, pages 56–65
June 6–11, 2021. 

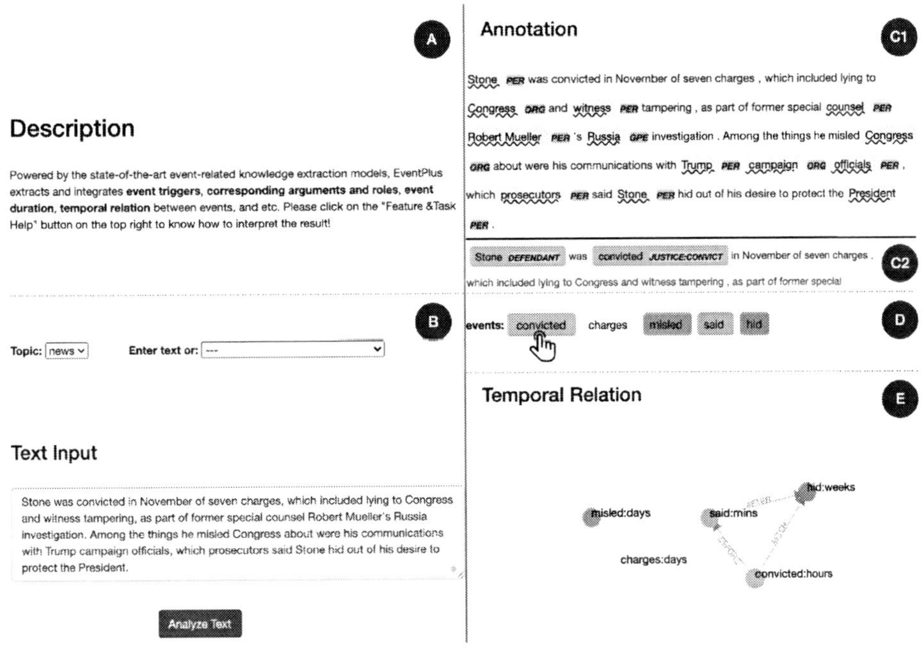

Figure 2: The interface of EventPlus. Users can either choose examples or freely input text which matches with their selected topic in $B$. $C$ shows the Name Entity Recognition (NER) results, which serve as argument candidates for events. When clicking on an event trigger in $D$, we show the selected event trigger and its corresponding *arguments* in $C2$. We show *temporal-related information* of all events in $E$, where nodes represent event triggers and edges represent their relations; we further indicate the *event duration* as labels of nodes.

EventPlus is designed with multi-domain support in mind. Particularly, we present an initial effort to adapt EventPlus to the biomedical domain. We summarize the contributions as follows:

- We present the first event pipeline system with comprehensive event understanding capabilities to extract *event triggers and argument*, *temporal relations* among events and *event duration* to provide an event-centric natural language understanding (NLU) tool to facilitate downstream applications.
- Each component in EventPlus has comparable performance to the state-of-the-art, which assures the quality and efficacy of our system for temporal event reasoning.

## 2 Component

In this section, we introduce each component in our system, as shown in Figure 3. We use a multi-task learning model for event trigger and temporal relation extraction (§ 2.1). The model introduced in § 2.2 extracts semantic-rich events following the ACE ontology, and the model introduced in § 2.3 predicts the event duration. Note that our system handles two types of event representations: one represents an event as the trigger word (Pustejovsky et al., 2003a) (as the event extraction model in § 2.1), the other represents event as a complex structure including trigger, type and arguments (Ahn, 2006) (as the event extraction model in § 2.2). The corpus following the former definition usually has a broader coverage while the latter can provide richer information. Therefore, we develop models to combine the benefits of both worlds. We also introduce a speculated and negated events handling component in § 2.4 to further identify whether an event happens or not.

### 2.1 Multi-task Learning of Event Trigger and Temporal Relation Extraction

The event trigger extraction component takes the input of raw text and outputs single-token event triggers. The input to the temporal relation extraction model is raw text and a list of detected event triggers. The model will predict temporal relationships between each pair of events. In previous literature (Han et al., 2019b), multi-task learning of these two tasks can significantly improve performance on both tasks following the intuition that

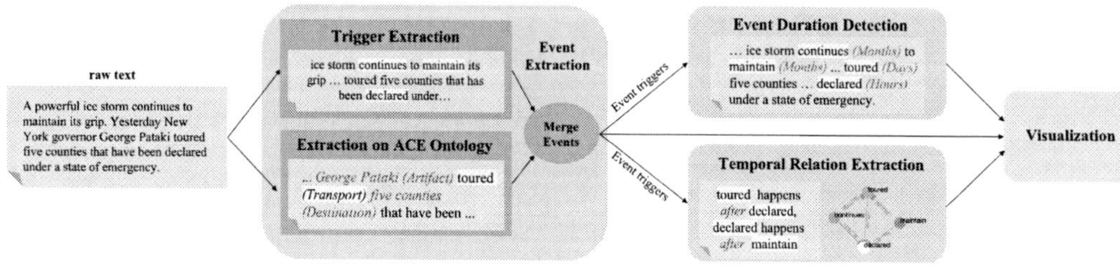


Figure 3: Overall system design of EventPlus. The raw text is first fed into two event extraction components, and then we pass the event triggers of the merged event list to event duration detection and temporal relation extraction models. Finally outputs from all models are combined for visualization.

event relation signals can be helpful to distinguish event triggers and non-event tokens.

The model feeds BERT embedding (Devlin et al., 2019) of the input text to a shared BiLSTM layer for encoding task-specific contextual information. The output of the BiLSTM is passed to an event scoring function and a relation scoring function which are MLP classifiers to calculate the probability of being an event (for event extraction) or a probability distribution over all possible relations (for temporal relation extraction). We train the multi-task model on MATRES (Ning et al., 2018a) containing temporal relations BEFORE, AFTER, SIMULTANEOUS and VAGUE. Though the model performs both tasks during training, it can be separately used for each individual task during inference.

### 2.2 Event Extraction on ACE Ontology

Although event triggers present the occurrence of events, they are not sufficient to demonstrate the semantic-rich information of events. ACE 2005[2] corpus defines an event ontology that represents an event as a structure with triggers and corresponding event arguments (participants) with specific roles (Doddington et al., 2004).[3] Our system is trained with ACE 2005 corpus, thus it is capable of extracting events with the complex structure. ACE focuses on events of a particular set of types including LIFE, MOVEMENT, TRANSACTION, BUSINESS, CONFLICT, CONTACT, PERSONNEL and JUSTICE, where each type has corresponding sub-types. Following prior works (Wadden et al., 2019; Lin et al., 2020), we keep 7 entity types (person, organization, location, geo-political entity, facility, vehicle, weapon), 33 event sub-types, and 22 argument roles that are associated with sub-types.

Similar to Han et al. (2019b), we build our event extraction component for ACE ontology upon a multi-task learning framework that consists of trigger detection, argument role detection and entity detection. These tasks share the same BERT encoder, which is fine-tuned during training. The entity detector predicts the argument candidates for all events in an input sentence. The trigger detector labels the input sequence with the event sub-types at the token level. The argument role detector finds the argument sequence[4] for each detected trigger via attention mechanism. For example, for the sentence in Figure 1, its target trigger sequence has MOVEMENT:TRANSPORT label at the position of "toured" token, and its argument sequence for this MOVEMENT:TRANSPORT event has B-ARTIFACT, I-ARTIFACT labels at the position of "George Pataki" and B-DESTINATION label at the position of "counties" respectively. The entire multi-task learning framework is jointly trained.

During inference, our system detects arguments solely based on triggers. To make our system better leverage information from argument candidates, we developed the following constraints during decoding based on the predicted entities (argument candidates) and other specific definitions in ACE:

- Entity-Argument constraint. The argument role label for a token can take one of the 22 argument roles if and only if the token at this position belongs to a predicted entity.
- Entity-Trigger constraint. The trigger label for a token can take one of the 33 event sub-types if and only if the token at this position does not belong to a predicted entity.
- Valid Trigger-Argument constraint. Based on the definitions in ACE05, each event sub-type takes

[2] `https://www.ldc.upenn.edu/collaborations/past-projects/ace`

[3] The ACE program provides annotated data for five kinds of extraction targets: entities, times, values, relations and events. We only focus on events and entities data in this paper.

[4] Argument sequences are presented using BIO encoding.

certain types of argument roles. We enforce that given the predicted trigger label, the argument roles in this sequence can only take those that are valid for this trigger.

To account for these constraints, we set the probability of all invalid configurations to be 0 during decoding.

### 2.3 Event Duration Detection

This component classifies event triggers into duration categories. While many datasets have covered time expressions which are explicit timestamps for events (Pustejovsky et al., 2003b; Cassidy et al., 2014; Reimers et al., 2018; Bethard et al., 2017), they do not target categorical event duration. To supplement this, Vashishtha et al. (2019) introduces the UDS-T dataset, where they provide 11 duration categories which we adopt for our event pipeline: INSTANT, SECONDS, MINUTES, HOURS, DAYS, WEEKS, MONTHS, YEARS, DECADES, CENTURIES and FOREVER. Pan et al. (2006) also present a news domain duration annotation dataset containing 58 articles developed from TimeBank corpus (we refer as Typical-Duration in the following), it provides 7 duration categories (a subset of the 11 categories in UDS-T from SECONDS to YEARS).

We developed two models for the event duration detection task. For a sentence, along with predicate root and span, the models perform duration classification. In the first method, we fine-tune a BERT language model (Devlin et al., 2019) on single sentences and take hidden states of event tokens from the output of the last layer, then feed into a multi-layer perceptron for classification.

The second model is adapted from the UDS-T baseline model, which is trained under the multi-task objectives of duration and temporal relation extraction. The model computes ELMo embeddings (Peters et al., 2018) followed by attention layers to compute the attended representation of the predicate given sentence. The final MLP layers extract the duration category. Even though this model can detect temporal relations, it underperforms the model we described in § 2.1, so we exclude the temporal relation during inference.

### 2.4 Negation and Speculation Cue Detection and Scope Resolution

The event extraction components described above are designed to extract all possible events, but we identify events that are indicated by speculation (e.g., *would*) or negation (e.g., *not*) keywords (Konstantinova et al., 2012). Since those events do not happen, we mark them with special labels. For example, in the sentence "The United States is *not* considering sending troops to Mozambique", we identify "send" will not happen.

We adapt the BERT-based negation and speculation cue detection model and the scope resolution model introduced by Khandelwal and Sawant (2020). To fine-tune these models, we use the SFU Review dataset with negation and speculation annotations (Taboada et al., 2006; Taboada and Grieve, 2004; Konstantinova et al., 2012), and we feed ground truth negation and speculation cues as input for the scope resolution model. We evaluate the two models on a separate testing set of the SFU Review dataset. The cue detection model yields a 0.92 F1 score, and the scope resolution model yields a 0.88 F1 score for token-level prediction, given ground truth cues as input. In EventPlus, we input cues detected by the cue detection model to the scope resolution model.

## 3 System

We design a pipeline system to enable the interaction among components with state-of-the-art performance introduced in § 2 and provide a comprehensive output for events and visualize the results. Figure 3 shows the overall system design.

### 3.1 Pipeline Design

**Event Extraction** EventPlus takes in raw text and feeds the tokenized text to two event extraction modules trained on ACE ontology-based datasets and free-formatted event triggers. The ACE ontology extraction modules will produce the output of event triggers ("toured" is a trigger), event type (it is a MOVEMENT:TRANSPORT event), argument and its role (the ARTIFACT is "George Pataki" and DESTINATION is "counties") and NER result ("New York" and "counties" are GEO-POLITICAL ENTITY and "governer" and "George Pataki" are PERSON). The trigger-only extraction model will produce all event triggers ("continues", "maintain" and "declared" are also event triggers but we do not have arguments predicted for them). Then trigger-only events will be merged to ACE-style events list and create a combined event list from the two models. For each extracted event, if it is in the negation or speculation scope predicted by the cue detection and scope resolution component, then we add a "speculation or negation" argument to that event.

**Duration Detection and Temporal Relation Extraction** The combined events list will be passed to the event duration detection model to detect duration for each of the extracted events ("tours" will take DAYS etc.) and passed to temporal relation extraction component to detect temporal relations among each pair of events ("toured" is after "declared" etc.). Note that duration and temporal relation extraction are based on the context sentence besides the event triggers themselves and they are designed to consider contextualized information contained in sentences. Therefore "take (a break)" can take MINUTES in the scenario of "Dr. Porter is now taking a break and will be able to see you soon" but take DAYS in the context of "Dr. Porter is now taking a Christmas break" (Ning, 2019).

**Visualization** To keep the resulted temporal graph clear, we remove predicted VAGUE relations since that indicates the model cannot confidently predict temporal relations for those event pairs. Finally, all model outputs are gathered and pass to the front-end for visualization.

### 3.2 Interface Design

Figure 2 shows the interface design of EventPlus.[5] We display the NER result with wavy underlines and highlight event triggers and corresponding arguments with the same color upon clicks. Besides, we represent the temporal relations among events in a directed graph using d3 [6] if there are any, where we also indicate each event's duration in the label for each event node.

## 4 Evaluation

Each capability in the pipeline has its own input and output protocol, and they require various datasets to learn implicit knowledge independently. In this section, we describe the performance for each capability on corresponding labeled datasets.

### 4.1 Event Trigger Extraction

We report the evaluation about event triggers extraction component on TB-Dense (Cassidy et al., 2014) and MATRES (Ning et al., 2018a), two event extraction datasets in the news domain (Han et al., 2019b). We show the result in Table 1. Comparing the performance on TB-Dense with CAEVO (Chambers et al., 2014), DEER (Han et al., 2020a) and MATRES performance with Ning et al. (2018b), the model we use achieves best F1 scores and yields the state-of-the-art performance.

| Corpus | Model | F1 |
|---|---|---|
| TB-Dense | Chambers et al. (2014) | 87.4 |
| | Han et al. (2020a) | 90.3 |
| | Ours | **90.8** |
| MATRES | Ning et al. (2018b) | 85.2 |
| | Ours | **87.8** |

Table 1: Evaluation for event trigger extraction

### 4.2 Event Extraction on ACE Ontology

We evaluate our event extraction component on the test set of ACE 2005 dataset using the same data split as prior works (Lin et al., 2020; Wadden et al., 2019). We follow the same evaluation criteria:

- Entity: An entity is correct if its span and type are both correct.
- Trigger: A trigger is correctly **identified** (Trig-I) if its span is correct. It is correctly **classified** (Trig-C) if its type is also correct.
- Argument: An argument is correctly **identified** (Arg-I) if its span and event type are correct. It is correctly **classified** (Arg-C) if its role is also correct.

In Table 2, we compare the performance of our system with the current state-of-the-art method OneIE (Lin et al., 2020). Our system outperforms OneIE in terms of entity detection performance. However our trigger and argument detection performance is worse than it. We leave the improvements for triggers and arguments for future work.

| Model | Entity | Trig-I | Trig-C | Arg-I | Arg-C |
|---|---|---|---|---|---|
| OneIE | 90.2 | **78.2** | **74.7** | **59.2** | **56.8** |
| Ours | **91.3** | 75.8 | 72.5 | 57.7 | 55.7 |

Table 2: Test set performance on ACE 2005 dataset. Following prior works, we use the same evaluation criteria: *-I represent Trigger or Argument Identification. *-C represent Trigger or Argument Classification.

### 4.3 Event Duration Detection

We evaluate the event duration detection models on Typical-Duration and newly annotated ACE-Duration dataset to reflect the performance on

[5] We have a walk-through instruction available to help first-time end users get familiar with EventPlus. Please see our video for more information.

[6] `https://d3js.org/`

generic news domain for which our system is optimized. Since UDS-T dataset (Vashishtha et al., 2019) is imbalanced and has limited samples for some duration categories, we do not use it as an evaluation benchmark but we sample 466 high IAA data points as training resources. We split Typical-Duration dataset and use 1790 samples for training, 224 for validation and 224 for testing.

To create ACE-Duration, we sample 50 unique triggers with related sentences from the ACE dataset, conduct manual annotation with three annotators and take the majority vote as the gold duration category. Given natural ordering among duration categories, the following metrics are employed: accuracy over 7 duration categories (Acc), coarse accuracy (Acc-c, if the prediction falls in categories whose distance to the ground truth is 1, it is counted as correct) and Spearman correlation (Corr).

| | Typical-Duration | | | ACE-Duration | | |
|---|---|---|---|---|---|---|
| Model | Acc | Acc-c | Corr | Acc | Acc-c | Corr |
| UDS-T (U) | 0.20 | 0.54 | 0.59 | 0.38 | 0.68 | 0.62 |
| UDS-T (T) | 0.52 | 0.79 | 0.71 | 0.47 | 0.67 | 0.50 |
| UDS-T (T+U) | 0.50 | 0.76 | 0.68 | **0.49** | 0.74 | 0.66 |
| BERT (T) | **0.59** | **0.81** | **0.75** | 0.31 | 0.67 | 0.64 |
| BERT (T+U) | 0.56 | **0.81** | 0.73 | 0.45 | **0.79** | **0.70** |

Table 3: Event duration detection experimental result. Typical-Duration results are from testing subset. Notations in the bracket of model names indicate resources for training, U: 466 UDS-T high IAA samples, T: Typical-Duration training set

Experimental results in Table 3 show the BERT model is better than UDS-T ELMo-based model in general and data augmentation is especially helpful to improve performance on ACE-Duration. Due to the limited size of ACE-Duration, we weight more on the Typical-Duration dataset and select BERT (T) as the best configuration. To the best of our knowledge, this is the state-of-the-art performance on the event duration detection task.

### 4.4 Temporal Relation Extraction

We report temporal relation extraction performance on TB-Dense and MATRES datasets. TB-Dense consider the duration of events so the labels are INCLUDES, INCLUDED IN, BEFORE, AFTER, SIMULTANEOUS and VAGUE, while MATRES uses start-point as event temporal anchor and hence its labels exclude INCLUDES and INCLUDED IN. In EventPlus, we augment extracted events from multiple components, so we report temporal relation extraction result given golden events as relation candidates to better reflect single task performance.

| Corpus | Model | F1 |
|---|---|---|
| TB-Dense | Vashishtha et al. (2019) | 56.6 |
| | Meng and Rumshisky (2018) | 57.0 |
| | Ours | **64.5** |
| MATRES | Ning et al. (2018b) | 65.9 |
| | Ning et al. (2018a) | 69.0 |
| | Ours | **75.5** |

Table 4: Experimental result for temporal relation extraction given golden event extraction result

Table 4 shows the experimental results.[7] Our model in § 2.1 achieves the best result on temporal relation extraction and is significantly better than (Vashishtha et al., 2019) mentioned in § 2.3.[8]

## 5 Extension to Biomedical Domain

With our flexible design, each component of EventPlus can be easily extended to other domains with little modification. We explore two approaches to extend the event extraction capability (§ 2.2) to the biomedicine domain: 1) multi-domain training (MDT) with GENIA (Kim et al., 2009), a dataset containing biomolecular interaction events from scientific literature, with shared token embeddings, which enables the model to predict on both news and biomedical text; 2) replace the current component with an in-domain event extraction component **SciBERT-FT** (Huang et al., 2020) which is a biomedical event extraction system based on fine-tuned SciBERT (Beltagy et al., 2019).

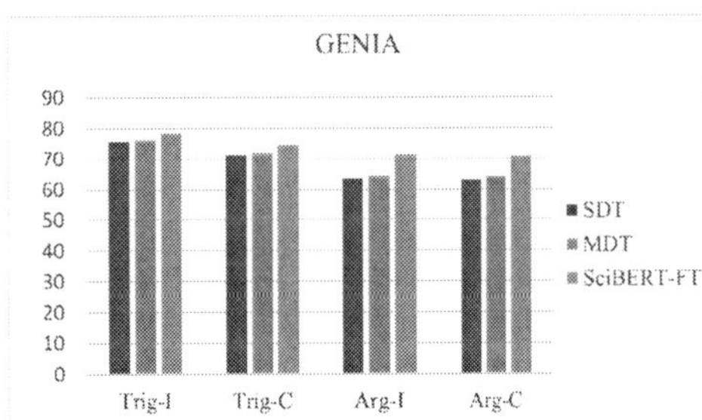


Figure 4: Performance comparison of single-domain training (SDT), multi-domain training (MDT) and SciBERT-FT on the Dev set of GENIA

[7]The MATRES experiment result in Table 4 uses 183 documents for training and 20 for testing developed from the entire TempEval-3 dataset. Han et al. (2019a) reports higher F1 score but it uses a subset of MATRES (22 documents for train, 5 for dev and 9 for test) and has different setting.

[8]The latest state-of-the-art work (Han et al., 2020a) only reports end-to-end event extraction and temporal relation extraction result, pure temporal relation extraction result given ground-truth events are not provided. We are not able to compare with it directly.

While MDT on ACE and GENIA datasets from different domains improves the performance on GENIA, it is still lower than **SciBERT-FT** (Figure 4). Therefore, we decide to pursue the second extension approach to incorporate **SciBERT-FT** and extend EventPlus to the biomedical domain.

## 6 Related Works

Existing NLP toolkits (Manning et al., 2014; Khashabi et al., 2018) provide an interface for a set of useful models. Some tools integrate several models in a pipeline fashion (Peng et al., 2015; Noji and Miyao, 2016). The majority of these systems focus on token-level tasks like tokenization, lemmatization, part-of-speech tagging, or sentence-level tasks like syntactic parsing, semantic role labeling etc. There are only a few systems that can provide capabilities of event extraction and temporal information detection (Tao et al., 2013; Ning, 2019).

For event extraction, some systems only provide results within a certain defined ontology such as AIDA (Li et al., 2019), there are also some works utilizing data from multiple modalities (Li et al., 2020a,b). Some works could handle novel events (Xiang and Wang, 2019; Ahmad et al., 2021; Han et al., 2020b; Huang and Peng, 2020), but they are either restricted to a certain domain (Yang et al., 2018) or lack of performance superiority because of their lexico-syntactic rule-based algorithm (Valenzuela-Escárcega et al., 2015). For temporal information detection, Ning et al. (2019) proposes a neural-based temporal relation extraction system with knowledge injection. Most related to our work, Ning et al. (2018b) demonstrates a temporal understanding system to extract time expression and implicit temporal relations among detected events, but this system cannot provide event-related arguments, entities and event duration information.

These previous works either are not capable of event understanding or just focus on one perspective of event-related features. There is no existing system that incorporates a comprehensive set of event-centric features, including event extraction and related arguments and entities, temporal relations, and event duration.

## 7 Conclusion and Future Work

We represent EventPlus, a pipeline system that takes raw texts as inputs and produces a set of temporal event understanding annotations, including *event trigger and type*, *event arguments*, *event duration* and *temporal relations*. To the best of our knowledge, EventPlus is the first available system that provides such a comprehensive set of temporal event knowledge extraction capabilities with state-of-the-art components integrated. We believe EventPlus will provide insights for understanding narratives and facilitating downstream tasks.

In the future, we plan to further improve EventPlus by tightly integrating event duration prediction and temporal relation extraction modules. We also plan to improve the performance for triggers and arguments detection under the ACE ontology and develop joint training models to optimize all event-related features in an end-to-end fashion.

## Acknowledgments

Many thanks to Yu Hou for the quality assessment annotations, to Fred Morstatter and Ninareh Mehrabi for feedback on the negation and speculation event handling, and to the anonymous reviewers for their feedback. This material is based on research supported by DARPA under agreement number FA8750-19-2-0500. The U.S. Government is authorized to reproduce and distribute reprints for Governmental purposes notwithstanding any copyright notation thereon. The views and conclusions contained herein are those of the authors and should not be interpreted as necessarily representing the official policies or endorsements, either expressed or implied, of DARPA or the U.S. Government.

## References

Wasi Ahmad, Nanyun Peng, and Kai-Wei Chang. 2021. Gate: Graph attention transformer encoder for cross-lingual relation and event extraction. In *The Thirty-Fifth AAAI Conference on Artificial Intelligence (AAAI-21)*.

David Ahn. 2006. The stages of event extraction. In *Proceedings of the Workshop on Annotating and Reasoning about Time and Events*, pages 1–8.

Iz Beltagy, Kyle Lo, and Arman Cohan. 2019. SciBERT: A pretrained language model for scientific text. In *Proceedings of the 2019 Conference on Empirical Methods in Natural Language Processing and the 9th International Joint Conference on Natural Language Processing (EMNLP-IJCNLP)*, pages 3615–3620, Hong Kong, China. Association for Computational Linguistics.

Steven Bethard, Guergana Savova, Martha Palmer, and James Pustejovsky. 2017. SemEval-2017 task 12: Clinical TempEval. In *Proceedings of the*

11th International Workshop on Semantic Evaluation (SemEval-2017)*, pages 565–572, Vancouver, Canada. Association for Computational Linguistics.

Taylor Cassidy, Bill McDowell, Nathanael Chambers, and Steven Bethard. 2014. An annotation framework for dense event ordering. In *Proceedings of the 52nd Annual Meeting of the Association for Computational Linguistics (Volume 2: Short Papers)*, pages 501–506.

Nathanael Chambers, Taylor Cassidy, Bill McDowell, and Steven Bethard. 2014. Dense event ordering with a multi-pass architecture. *Transactions of the Association for Computational Linguistics*, 2:273–284.

Jacob Devlin, Ming-Wei Chang, Kenton Lee, and Kristina Toutanova. 2019. Bert: Pre-training of deep bidirectional transformers for language understanding. In *Proceedings of the 2019 Conference of the North American Chapter of the Association for Computational Linguistics: Human Language Technologies, Volume 1 (Long and Short Papers)*, pages 4171–4186.

G Doddington, A Mitchell, M Przybocki, L Ramshaw, S Strassel, and R Weischedel. 2004. Automatic content extraction (ace) program: task definitions and performance measures. In *Proceedings of the Fourth International Language Resources and Evaluation Conference (LREC'04)*.

Matt Gardner, Joel Grus, Mark Neumann, Oyvind Tafjord, Pradeep Dasigi, Nelson F Liu, Matthew Peters, Michael Schmitz, and Luke Zettlemoyer. 2018. Allennlp: A deep semantic natural language processing platform. In *Proceedings of Workshop for NLP Open Source Software (NLP-OSS)*, pages 1–6.

Seraphina Goldfarb-Tarrant, Tuhin Chakrabarty, Ralph Weischedel, and Nanyun Peng. 2020. Content planning for neural story generation with aristotelian rescoring. In *the 2020 Conference on Empirical Methods in Natural Language Processing (EMNLP)*, pages 4319–4338.

Seraphina Goldfarb-Tarrant, Haining Feng, and Nanyun Peng. 2019. Plan, write, and revise: an interactive system for open-domain story generation. In *Proceedings of the 2019 Conference of the North American Chapter of the Association for Computational Linguistics (Demonstrations)*, pages 89–97.

Mark Granroth-Wilding and Stephen Clark. 2016. What happens next? event prediction using a compositional neural network model. *Proceedings of the AAAI Conference on Artificial Intelligence*, 30(1).

Rujun Han, I-Hung Hsu, Mu Yang, Aram Galstyan, Ralph Weischedel, and Nanyun Peng. 2019a. Deep structured neural network for event temporal relation extraction. In *Proceedings of the 23rd Conference on Computational Natural Language Learning (CoNLL)*, pages 666–106, Hong Kong, China. Association for Computational Linguistics.

Rujun Han, Qiang Ning, and Nanyun Peng. 2019b. Joint event and temporal relation extraction with shared representations and structured prediction. In *Proceedings of the 2019 Conference on Empirical Methods in Natural Language Processing and the 9th International Joint Conference on Natural Language Processing (EMNLP-IJCNLP)*, pages 434–444, Hong Kong, China. Association for Computational Linguistics.

Rujun Han, Xiang Ren, and Nanyun Peng. 2020a. Deer: A data efficient language model for event temporal reasoning. *arXiv preprint arXiv:2012.15283*.

Rujun Han, Yichao Zhou, and Nanyun Peng. 2020b. Domain knowledge empowered structured neural net for end-to-end event temporal relation extraction. In *the 2020 Conference on Empirical Methods in Natural Language Processing (EMNLP)*, pages 5717–5729. Association for Computational Linguistics.

Kung-Hsiang Huang and Nanyun Peng. 2020. Efficient end-to-end learning of cross-event dependencies for document-level event extraction. *ArXiv*, abs/2010.12787.

Kung-Hsiang Huang, Mu Yang, and Nanyun Peng. 2020. Biomedical event extraction with hierarchical knowledge graphs. In *Findings of the Association for Computational Linguistics: EMNLP 2020*, pages 1277–1285, Online. Association for Computational Linguistics.

Lifu Huang, Ronan Le Bras, Chandra Bhagavatula, and Yejin Choi. 2019. Cosmos qa: Machine reading comprehension with contextual commonsense reasoning. In *Proceedings of the 2019 Conference on Empirical Methods in Natural Language Processing and the 9th International Joint Conference on Natural Language Processing (EMNLP-IJCNLP)*, pages 2391–2401.

Aditya Khandelwal and Suraj Sawant. 2020. Negbert: A transfer learning approach for negation detection and scope resolution. *ArXiv*, abs/1911.04211.

Daniel Khashabi, Mark Sammons, Ben Zhou, Tom Redman, Christos Christodoulopoulos, Vivek Srikumar, Nick Rizzolo, Lev Ratinov, Guanheng Luo, Quang Do, et al. 2018. Cogcompnlp: Your swiss army knife for nlp. In *Proceedings of the Eleventh International Conference on Language Resources and Evaluation (LREC 2018)*.

Jin-Dong Kim, Tomoko Ohta, Sampo Pyysalo, Yoshinobu Kano, and Jun'ichi Tsujii. 2009. Overview of BioNLP'09 shared task on event extraction. In *Proceedings of the BioNLP 2009 Workshop Companion Volume for Shared Task*, pages 1–9, Boulder, Colorado. Association for Computational Linguistics.

Natalia Konstantinova, Sheila CM De Sousa, Noa P Cruz Díaz, Manuel J Mana López, Maite Taboada, and Ruslan Mitkov. 2012. A review corpus annotated for negation, speculation and their scope. In *Lrec*, pages 3190–3195.

Manling Li, Ying Lin, Joseph Hoover, Spencer Whitehead, Clare Voss, Morteza Dehghani, and Heng Ji. 2019. Multilingual entity, relation, event and human value extraction. In *Proceedings of the 2019 Conference of the North American Chapter of the Association for Computational Linguistics (Demonstrations)*, pages 110–115, Minneapolis, Minnesota. Association for Computational Linguistics.

Manling Li, Alireza Zareian, Ying Lin, Xiaoman Pan, Spencer Whitehead, Brian Chen, Bo Wu, Heng Ji, Shih-Fu Chang, Clare Voss, Daniel Napierski, and Marjorie Freedman. 2020a. GAIA: A fine-grained multimedia knowledge extraction system. In *Proceedings of the 58th Annual Meeting of the Association for Computational Linguistics: System Demonstrations*, pages 77–86, Online. Association for Computational Linguistics.

Manling Li, Alireza Zareian, Qi Zeng, Spencer Whitehead, Di Lu, Heng Ji, and Shih-Fu Chang. 2020b. Cross-media structured common space for multimedia event extraction. In *Proceedings of the 58th Annual Meeting of the Association for Computational Linguistics*, pages 2557–2568, Online. Association for Computational Linguistics.

Zhongyang Li, Xiao Ding, and Ting Liu. 2018. Constructing narrative event evolutionary graph for script event prediction. *arXiv preprint arXiv:1805.05081*.

Ying Lin, Heng Ji, Fei Huang, and Lingfei Wu. 2020. A joint neural model for information extraction with global features. In *Proceedings of the 58th Annual Meeting of the Association for Computational Linguistics*, pages 7999–8009, Online. Association for Computational Linguistics.

Christopher D Manning, Mihai Surdeanu, John Bauer, Jenny Rose Finkel, Steven Bethard, and David McClosky. 2014. The stanford corenlp natural language processing toolkit. In *Proceedings of 52nd annual meeting of the association for computational linguistics: system demonstrations*, pages 55–60.

Yuanliang Meng and Anna Rumshisky. 2018. Context-aware neural model for temporal information extraction. In *Proceedings of the 56th Annual Meeting of the Association for Computational Linguistics (Volume 1: Long Papers)*, pages 527–536, Melbourne, Australia. Association for Computational Linguistics.

Yuanliang Meng, Anna Rumshisky, and Alexey Romanov. 2017. Temporal information extraction for question answering using syntactic dependencies in an lstm-based architecture. In *Proceedings of the 2017 Conference on Empirical Methods in Natural Language Processing*, pages 887–896.

Qiang Ning. 2019. *Understanding time in natural language text*. Ph.D. thesis, University of Illinois at Urbana-Champaign.

Qiang Ning, Sanjay Subramanian, and Dan Roth. 2019. An improved neural baseline for temporal relation extraction. In *Proceedings of the 2019 Conference on Empirical Methods in Natural Language Processing and the 9th International Joint Conference on Natural Language Processing (EMNLP-IJCNLP)*, pages 6203–6209, Hong Kong, China. Association for Computational Linguistics.

Qiang Ning, Hao Wu, and Dan Roth. 2018a. A multi-axis annotation scheme for event temporal relations. In *ACL*.

Qiang Ning, Ben Zhou, Zhili Feng, Haoruo Peng, and Dan Roth. 2018b. CogCompTime: A tool for understanding time in natural language. In *Proceedings of the 2018 Conference on Empirical Methods in Natural Language Processing: System Demonstrations*, pages 72–77, Brussels, Belgium. Association for Computational Linguistics.

Hiroshi Noji and Yusuke Miyao. 2016. Jigg: A framework for an easy natural language processing pipeline. In *Proceedings of ACL-2016 System Demonstrations*, pages 103–108, Berlin, Germany. Association for Computational Linguistics.

F. Pan, Rutu Mulkar-Mehta, and J. Hobbs. 2006. Learning event durations from event descriptions. In *ACL*.

Nanyun Peng, Francis Ferraro, Mo Yu, Nicholas Andrews, Jay DeYoung, Max Thomas, Matthew R. Gormley, Travis Wolfe, Craig Harman, Benjamin Van Durme, and Mark Dredze. 2015. A concrete Chinese NLP pipeline. In *Proceedings of the 2015 Conference of the North American Chapter of the Association for Computational Linguistics: Demonstrations*, pages 86–90, Denver, Colorado. Association for Computational Linguistics.

Nanyun Peng, Marjan Ghazvininejad, Jonathan May, and Kevin Knight. 2018. Towards controllable story generation. In *Proceedings of the First Workshop on Storytelling*, pages 43–49.

Matthew Peters, Mark Neumann, Mohit Iyyer, Matt Gardner, Christopher Clark, Kenton Lee, and Luke Zettlemoyer. 2018. Deep contextualized word representations. In *Proceedings of the 2018 Conference of the North American Chapter of the Association for Computational Linguistics: Human Language Technologies, Volume 1 (Long Papers)*, pages 2227–2237.

James Pustejovsky, José M Castano, Robert Ingria, Roser Sauri, Robert J Gaizauskas, Andrea Setzer, Graham Katz, and Dragomir R Radev. 2003a. Timeml: Robust specification of event and temporal expressions in text. *New directions in question answering*, 3:28–34.

James Pustejovsky, Patrick Hanks, Roser Sauri, Andrew See, Robert Gaizauskas, Andrea Setzer, Dragomir Radev, Beth Sundheim, David Day, Lisa Ferro, et al. 2003b. The timebank corpus. In *Corpus linguistics*, volume 2003, page 40. Lancaster, UK.

Nils Reimers, Nazanin Dehghani, and Iryna Gurevych. 2018. Event time extraction with a decision tree of neural classifiers. *Transactions of the Association for Computational Linguistics*, 6:77–89.

Maite Taboada, Caroline Anthony, and Kimberly D Voll. 2006. Methods for creating semantic orientation dictionaries. In *LREC*, pages 427–432.

Maite Taboada and Jack Grieve. 2004. Analyzing appraisal automatically. In *Proceedings of AAAI Spring Symposium on Exploring Attitude and Affect in Text (AAAI Technical Re# port SS# 04# 07), Stanford University, CA, pp. 158q161. AAAI Press.*

Fangbo Tao, Kin Hou Lei, Jiawei Han, ChengXiang Zhai, Xiao Cheng, Marina Danilevsky, Nihit Desai, Bolin Ding, Jing Ge Ge, Heng Ji, et al. 2013. Eventcube: multi-dimensional search and mining of structured and text data. In *Proceedings of the 19th ACM SIGKDD international conference on Knowledge discovery and data mining*, pages 1494–1497.

Marco A. Valenzuela-Escárcega, Gus Hahn-Powell, Mihai Surdeanu, and Thomas Hicks. 2015. A domain-independent rule-based framework for event extraction. In *Proceedings of ACL-IJCNLP 2015 System Demonstrations*, pages 127–132, Beijing, China. Association for Computational Linguistics and The Asian Federation of Natural Language Processing.

Siddharth Vashishtha, Benjamin Van Durme, and Aaron Steven White. 2019. Fine-grained temporal relation extraction. In *Proceedings of the 57th Annual Meeting of the Association for Computational Linguistics*, pages 2906–2919, Florence, Italy. Association for Computational Linguistics.

David Wadden, Ulme Wennberg, Yi Luan, and Hannaneh Hajishirzi. 2019. Entity, relation, and event extraction with contextualized span representations. In *Proceedings of the 2019 Conference on Empirical Methods in Natural Language Processing and the 9th International Joint Conference on Natural Language Processing (EMNLP-IJCNLP)*, pages 5784–5789, Hong Kong, China. Association for Computational Linguistics.

Zhongqing Wang, Yue Zhang, and Ching Yun Chang. 2017. Integrating order information and event relation for script event prediction. In *Proceedings of the 2017 Conference on Empirical Methods in Natural Language Processing*, pages 57–67.

Wei Xiang and Bang Wang. 2019. A survey of event extraction from text. *IEEE Access*, 7:173111–173137.

Hang Yang, Yubo Chen, Kang Liu, Yang Xiao, and Jun Zhao. 2018. DCFEE: A document-level Chinese financial event extraction system based on automatically labeled training data. In *Proceedings of ACL 2018, System Demonstrations*, pages 50–55, Melbourne, Australia. Association for Computational Linguistics.

Lili Yao, Nanyun Peng, Weischedel Ralph, Kevin Knight, Dongyan Zhao, and Rui Yan. 2019. Plan-and-write: Towards better automatic storytelling. In *The Thirty-Third AAAI Conference on Artificial Intelligence (AAAI-19)*.

# COVID-19 Literature Knowledge Graph Construction and Drug Repurposing Report Generation

Qingyun Wang[1], Manling Li[1], Xuan Wang[1], Nikolaus Parulian[1], Guangxing Han[2], Jiawei Ma[2], Jingxuan Tu[3], Ying Lin[1], Haoran Zhang[1], Weili Liu[1], Aabhas Chauhan[1], Yingjun Guan[1], Bangzheng Li[1], Ruisong Li[1], Xiangchen Song[1], Yi R. Fung[1], Heng Ji[1], Jiawei Han[1], Shih-Fu Chang[2], James Pustejovsky[3], Jasmine Rah[4], David Liem[5], Ahmed Elsayed[6], Martha Palmer[6], Clare Voss[7], Cynthia Schneider[8], Boyan Onyshkevych[9]

[1]University of Illinois at Urbana-Champaign [2]Columbia University [3]Brandeis University
[4]University of Washington [5]University of California, Los Angeles [6]Colorado University
[7]Army Research Lab [8]QS2 [9]Department of Defense

hengji@illinois.edu, hanj@illinois.edu, sc250@columbia.edu

## Abstract

To combat COVID-19, both clinicians and scientists need to digest vast amounts of relevant biomedical knowledge in scientific literature to understand the disease mechanism and related biological functions. We have developed a novel and comprehensive knowledge discovery framework, **COVID-KG** to extract fine-grained multimedia knowledge elements (entities and their visual chemical structures, relations and events) from scientific literature. We then exploit the constructed multimedia knowledge graphs (KGs) for question answering and report generation, using drug repurposing as a case study. Our framework also provides detailed contextual sentences, subfigures, and knowledge subgraphs as evidence. All of the data, KGs, reports[1], resources, and shared services are publicly available[2].

## 1 Introduction

Practical progress at combating COVID-19 relies heavily on effective search, discovery, assessment, and extension of scientific research results. However, clinicians and scientists are facing two unique barriers in digesting these research papers.

The first challenge is *quantity*. Such a bottleneck in knowledge access is exacerbated during a pandemic when increased investment in relevant research leads to even faster growth of literature than usual. For example, as of April 28, 2020, at PubMed[3] there were 19,443 papers related to coronavirus; as of June 13, 2020, there were 140K+ related papers, *nearly 2.7K new papers per day* (see Figure 1). The resulting knowledge bottleneck contributes to significant delays in the development of vaccines and drugs for COVID-19. More intelligent knowledge discovery technologies need to be developed to enable researchers to more quickly and accurately access and digest relevant knowledge from the literature.

The second challenge is *quality*. Many research results about coronavirus from different research labs and sources are redundant, complementary, or even conflicting with each other, while some false information has been promoted in both formal publication venues as well as social media platforms such as Twitter. As a result, some of the public policy responses to the virus, and public perception of it, have been based on misleading, and at times erroneous claims. The relative isolation of these knowledge resources makes it hard, if not impossible, for researchers to connect the dots that exist in separate resources to gain new insights.

Let us consider drug repurposing as a case study.[4] Besides the long process of clinical trials and biomedical experiments, another major cause of the lengthy discovery phase is the complexity of the problem involved and the difficulty in drug discovery in general. The current clinical trials for drug repurposing rely mainly on reported symptoms in considering drugs that can treat diseases with similar symptoms. However, there are too many drug candidates and too much misinformation published in multiple sources. The clinicians and scientists thus urgently need assistance in obtaining a reliable ranked list of drugs with detailed evidence, and also in gaining new insights into the underlying molecular cellular mechanisms on COVID-19 and the pre-existing conditions that may affect the mortality and severity of this disease.

To tackle these two challenges we propose a new

[1]Demo video: `http://159.89.180.81/demo/covid/Covid-KG_DemoVideo.mp4`

[2]Project website: `http://blender.cs.illinois.edu/covid19/`

[3]https://www.ncbi.nlm.nih.gov/pubmed/

[4]This is a *pre-clinical phase of biomedical research* to discover new uses of existing, approved drugs that have already been tested in humans and so detailed information is available on their pharmacology, formulation, and potential toxicity.



*Proceedings of NAACL-HLT 2021: Demonstrations*, pages 66–77
June 6–11, 2021. 

framework, **COVID-KG**, to accelerate scientific discovery and build a bridge between the research scientists making use of our framework and clinicians who will ultimately conduct the tests, as illustrated in Figure 2. **COVID-KG** starts by reading existing papers to build multimedia knowledge graphs (KGs), in which nodes are entities/concepts and edges represent relations and events involving these entities, as extracted from both text and images. Given the KGs enriched with path ranking and evidence mining, **COVID-KG** answers natural language questions effectively. With drug repurposing as a case study, we focus on 11 typical questions that human experts pose and integrate our techniques to generate a comprehensive report for each candidate drug.

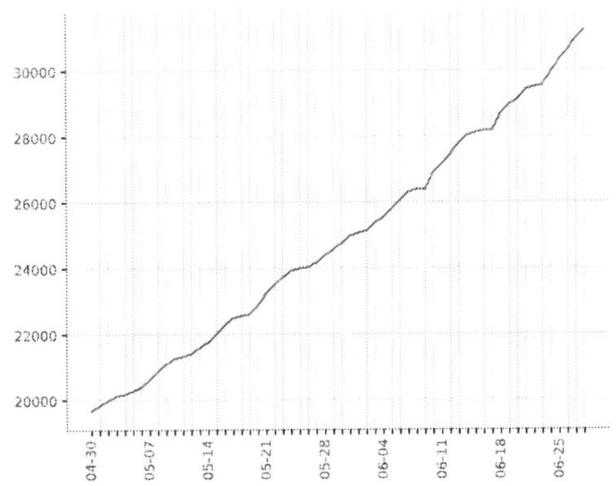


Figure 1: Increasing numbers of COVID-19 papers over time in PubMed website

## 2 Multimedia Knowledge Graph Construction

### 2.1 Coarse-grained Text Knowledge Extraction

Our coarse-grained Information Extraction (IE) system consists of three components: (1) coarse-grained entity extraction (Wang et al., 2019a) and entity linking (Zheng et al., 2015) for four entity types: *Gene nodes, Disease nodes, Chemical nodes, and Organism.* We follow the entity ontology defined in the Comparative Toxicogenomics Database (CTD) (Davis et al., 2016), and obtain a Medical Subject Headings (MeSH) Unique ID for each mention. (2) Based on the MeSH Unique IDs, we further link all entities to the CTD and extract 133 subtypes of relations such as *Gene–Chemical–Interaction Relationships, Chemical–Disease Associations, Gene–Disease Associations, Chemical–GO Enrichment Associations and Chemical–Pathway Enrichment Associations.* (3) Event extraction (Li et al., 2019): we extract 13 Event types and the roles of entities involved in these events as defined in (Nédellec et al., 2013), including *Gene expression, Transcription, Localization, Protein catabolism, Binding, Protein modification, Phosphorylation, Ubiquitination, Acetylation, Deacetylation, Regulation, Positive regulation, and Negative regulation.* Figure 3 shows an example of the constructed KG from multiple papers. Experiments on 186 documents with 12,916 sentences manually annotated by domain experts show that our method achieves 83.6% F-score on node extraction and 78.1% F-score on link extraction.

### 2.2 Fine-grained Text Entity Extraction

However, questions from experts often involve fine-grained knowledge elements, such as *"Which **amino acids** in glycoprotein are most related to Glycan (CHEMICAL)?"*. To answer these questions, we apply our fine-grained entity extraction system CORD-NER (Wang et al., 2020c) to extract 75 types of entities to enrich the KG, including many COVID-19 specific new entity types (e.g., *coronaviruses, viral proteins, evolution, materials, substrates, and immune responses*). CORD-NER relies on distantly- and weakly-supervised methods (Wang et al., 2019b; Shang et al., 2018), with no need for expensive human annotation. Its entity annotation quality surpasses SciSpacy (up to 93.95% F-score, over 10% higher on the F1 score based on a sample set of documents), a fully supervised BioNER tool. See Figure 4 for results on part of a COVID-19 paper (Zhang et al., 2020).

### 2.3 Image Processing and Cross-media Entity Grounding

Figures in biomedical papers may contain different types of visual information, for example, displaying molecular structures, microscopic images, dosage response curves, relational diagrams, and other unique visual content. We have developed a visual IE subsystem to extract the visual information from figures to enrich the KG. We start by designing a pipeline and automatic tools shown in Figure 5 to extract figures from papers in the CORD-19 dataset and segment figures into nearly half a million isolated subfigures. In the end, we perform cross-modal entity grounding, i.e., associating visual objects identified in these subfigures with entities mentioned in their captions or refer-

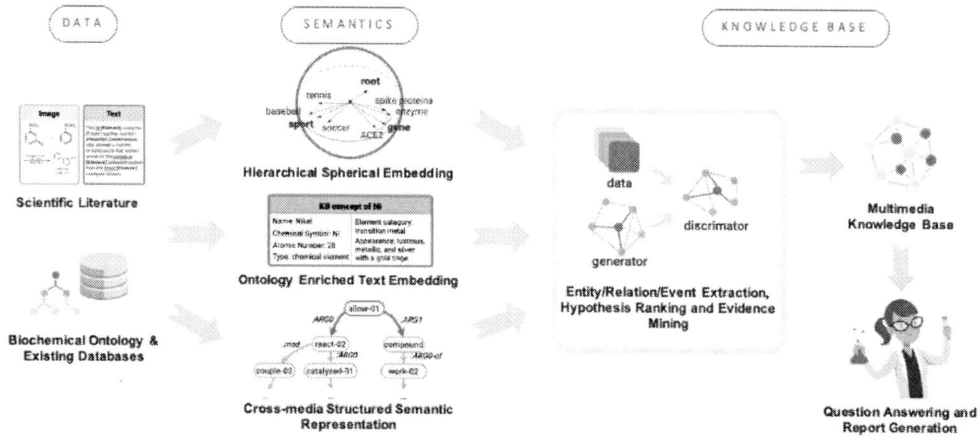


Figure 2: COVID-KG Overview: From Data to Semantics to Knowledge

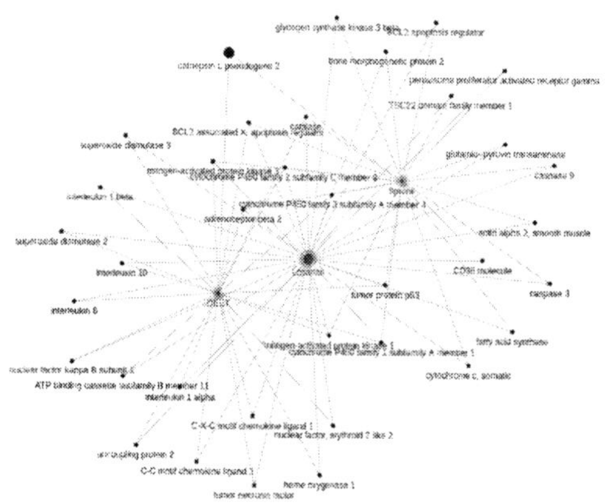

Figure 3: Constructed KG Connecting Losartan (candidate drug in COVID-19) and cathepsin L pseudogene 2 (gene related to coronavirus), where red nodes represent chemicals, grey nodes represent genes, and edges represent gene-chemical relations.

Angiotensin-converting enzyme 2 **GENE_OR_GENOME** ( ACE2 **GENE_OR_GENOME** ) as a SARS-CoV-2 **CORONAVIRUS** receptor: molecular mechanisms and potential therapeutic target. SARS-CoV-2 **CORONAVIRUS** has been sequenced [3]. A phylogenetic **EVOLUTION** analysis [3, 4] found a bat **WILDLIFE** origin for the SARS-CoV-2 **CORONAVIRUS**. There is a diversity of possible intermediate hosts for SARS-CoV-2 **CORONAVIRUS**, including pangolins **WILDLIFE**, but not mice **EUKARYOTE** and rats **EUKARYOTE** [5]. There are many similarities of SARS-CoV-2 **CORONAVIRUS** with the original SARS-CoV **CORONAVIRUS**. Using computer modeling, Xu *et al.* [6] found that the spike proteins **GENE_OR_GENOME** of SARS-CoV-2 **CORONAVIRUS** and SARS-CoV **CORONAVIRUS** have almost identical 3-D structures in the receptor binding domain that maintains Van der Waals forces **PHYSICAL_SCIENCE**. SARS-CoV spike proteins **GENE_OR_GENOME** has a strong binding affinity to human ACE2 **GENE_OR_GENOME**, based on biochemical interaction studies and crystal structure analysis [7]. SARS-CoV-2 **CORONAVIRUS** and SARS-CoV spike proteins **GENE_OR_GENOME** share identity in amino acid sequences and ......

Figure 4: Example of Fine-grained Entity Extraction

ring text. To start, since most figures are embedded as part of PDF files, we run Deepfigures (Siegel et al., 2018) to automatically detect and extract figures from each PDF document. Then each figure is associated with text in its caption or referring

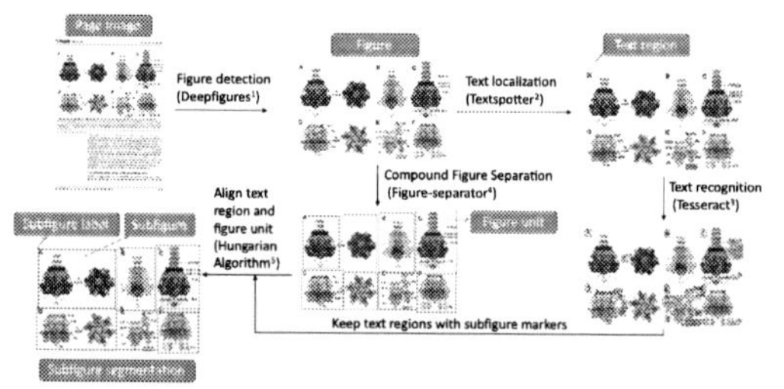


Figure 5: System Pipeline for Automatic Figure Extraction and Subfigure Segmentation. The figure image shown here is from (Kizziah et al., 2020)

context (main body text referring to the figure). In this way, a figure can be attached, at a coarse level, to a KG entity if that entity is mentioned in the associated text.

To further delineate semantic and visual information contained within each subfigure, we have developed a pipeline to segment individual subfigures and then align each subfigure with its corresponding subcaption. We run Figure-separator (Tsutsui and Crandall, 2017) to detect and separate all non-overlapping image regions. On occasion, subfigures within a figure may also be marked with alphabetical letters (e.g., A, B, C, etc). We use deep neural networks (Zhou et al., 2017) to detect text within figures and then apply OCR tools (Smith, 2007) to automatically recognize text content within each figure. To identify *subfigure marker text* and *text labels* for analyzing figure content, we rely on the distance between text labels and subfigures to locate subfigure text markers. Location information of such text markers can also be used to merge multiple image regions into a single subfigure. In

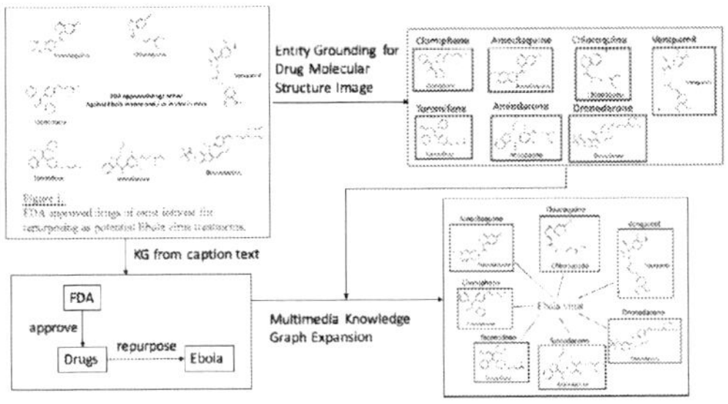


Figure 6: Expanding KG through Subfigure Segmentation and Cross-modal Entity Grounding. The figure image shown here is from (Ekins and Coffee, 2015)

the end, each subfigure is segmented, and associated with its corresponding subcaption and referring context. The segmented subfigures and associated text labels provide rich information that can expand the KG constructed from text captions. For example, as shown in Figure 6, we apply a classifier to detect subfigures containing molecular structures. Then by linking the specific drug names extracted from within-figure text to corresponding drug entities in the coarse KG constructed from the caption text, an expanded cross-modal KG can be constructed that then links images with specific molecular structures to their drug entities in the KG.

### 2.4 Knowledge Graph Semantic Visualization

In order to enhance the exploration and discovery of the information mined from the COVID-19 literature through the algorithms discussed in previous sections, we create semantic visualizations over large complex networks of biomedical relations using the techniques proposed by Tu et al. (2020). Semantic visualization allows for the visualization of user-defined subsets of these relations interactively through semantically typed tag clouds and heat maps. This allows researchers to get a global view of selected relation subtypes drawn from hundreds or thousands of papers at a single glance. This in turn allows for the ready identification of novel relations that would typically be missed by directed keyword searches or simple unigram word cloud or heatmap displays.[5]

We first build a data index from the knowledge elements in the constructed KGs, and then create a Kibana dashboard[6] out of the generated data indices. Each Kibana dashboard has a collection of visualizations that are designed to interact with each other. Dashboards are implemented as web applications. The navigation of a dashboard is mainly through clicking and searching. By clicking the protein keyword `EIF2AK2` in the tag cloud named *"Enzyme proteins participating Modification relations"*, a constraint on the type of proteins in modifications is added. Correspondingly, all the other visualizations will be changed.

One unique feature of the semantic visualization is the creation of *dense tag clouds* and *dense heatmaps*, through a process of parameter reduction over relations, allowing for the visualization of relation sets as tag clouds and multiple chained relations as heatmaps. Figure 7 illustrates such a dense heatmap that contains relations between proteins and implicated diseases (e.g., *"those proteins that are down-regulators of TNF which are implicated in obesity"*), along with their type information[7].

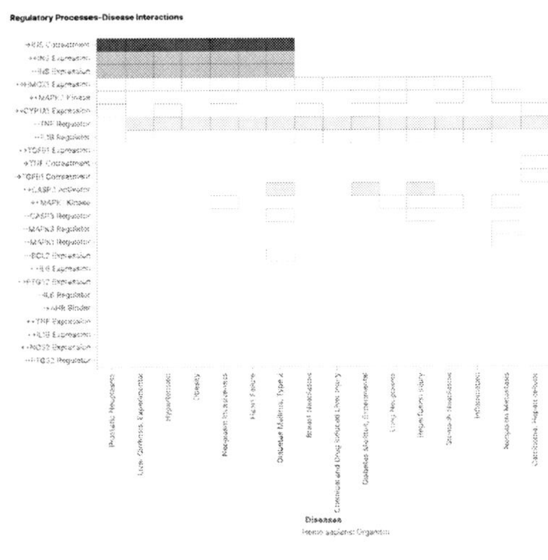


Figure 7: Regulatory Processes-Disease Interactions Heatmap

## 3 Knowledge-driven Question Answering

In contrast to most current question-answering (QA) methods which target single documents, we have developed a QA component based on a combination of KG matching and distributional semantic matching across documents. We build KG indexing and searching functions to facilitate effective and

[5] https://www.semviz.org/

[6] https://github.com/elastic/kibana

[7] We use the following symbols to indicate the "action" involved in each protein: "++" = increase, "−−" = decrease, "→" = affect.

efficient search when users pose their questions. We also support extended semantic matching from the constructed KGs and related texts by accepting multi-hop queries.

A common category of queries is the connections between two entities. Given two entities in a query, we generate a subgraph covering salient paths between them to show how they are connected through other entities. Figure 3 is an example subgraph summarizing the connections between *Losartan* and *cathepsin L pseudogene 2*. The paths are generated by traversing the constructed KG, and are ranked by the number of papers covering the knowledge elements in each path in the KG. Each edge is assigned a salience score by aggregating the scores of paths passing through it. In addition to knowledge elements, we also present related sentences and source information as evidence. We use BioBert (Lee et al., 2020), a pre-trained language model to represent each sentence along with its left and right neighboring sentences as local contexts. Using the same architecture computed on all respective sentences and the user query, we aggregate the sequence embedding layer, the last hidden layer in the BERT architecture with average pooling (Reimers and Gurevych, 2019). We use the similarity between the embedding representations of each sentence and each query to identify and extract the most relevant sentences as evidence.

Another common category of queries includes entity types, rather than entity instances, and requires extracting evidence sentences based on type or pattern matching. We have developed EVIDENCEMINER (Wang et al., 2020a,b), a web-based system that allows for the user's query as a natural language statement or an inquiry about a relationship at the meta-symbol level (e.g., CHEMICAL, PROTEIN) and then automatically retrieves textual evidence from a background corpora of COVID-19.

## 4 A case study on Drug Repurposing Report Generation

### 4.1 Task and Data

A human-written report about drug repurposing usually answers the following typical questions.

1. Current indication: what is the drug class? What is it currently approved to treat?
2. Molecular structure (symbols desired, but a pointer to a reference is also useful)
3. Mechanism of action i.e., inhibits viral entry, replication, etc. (w/ a pointer to data)
4. Was the drug identified by manual or computation screen?
5. Who is studying the drug? (Source/lab name)
6. In vitro Data available (cell line used, assays run, viral strain used, cytopathic effects, toxicity, LD50, dosage response curve, etc.)
7. Animal Data Available (what animal model, LD50, dosage response curve, etc.)
8. Clinical trials on going (what phase, facility, target population, dosing, intervention etc.)
9. Funding source
10. Has the drug shown evidence of systemic toxicity?
11. List of relevant sources to pull data from.

The answers to questions #5 and #11 are extracted based on the meta-data sections of research papers in scientific literature, including the author affiliation and acknowledgement sections. The answers for other questions are all extracted based on the knowledge graphs constructed and knowledge-driven question-answering method described above.

As in our case studies, DARPA biologists inquired about three drugs, Benazepril, Losartan, and Amodiaquine, and their links to COVID-19 related chemicals/genes as shown in Figure 8:

BM1_00870 BM1_06175 BM1_16375 BM1_17125 BM1_22385 BM1_30360 BM1_33735 BM1_56245 BM1_56735 BM1_00870 BM1_06175 BM1_16375 BM1_17125 BM1_22385 BM1_30360 BM1_33735 BM1_56245 BM1_56735 CATB-10270 CATB-1418 CATB-1674 CATB-16A CATB-16D2 CATB-1852 CATB-1874 CATB-2744 CATB-3098 CATB-348 CATB-3483 CATB-5880 CATB-84 CATB-912 CATD CATHY CATK CATL CATL-LIKE CTS12 CTS3 CTS6 CTS7 CTS7-PS CTS8 CTS8L1 CTS8-PS CTSA CTSA.L CTSB CTSBA CTSBB CTSB.L CTSB-PS CTSB.S CTSC CTSC.L CTSC.S CTSD CTSD2 CTSD.S CTSE CTSEAL CTSE.L CTSE.S CTSF CTSF.L CTSG CTSH CTSH.L CTSH-PS CTSJ CTSK CTSK1 CTSK.L CTSL CTSL.1 CTSL3 CTSL3P CTSLA CTSLB CTSLL CTSL.L CTSLL3 CTSLP1 CTSLP2 CTSLP3 CTSLP4 CTSLP6 CTSLP8 CTSM CTSM-PS CTSM-PS2 CTSO CTSO.L CTSQ CTSQL2 CTSR CTSS CTSS1 CTSS.2 CTSS2.1 CTSS2.2 CTSSL CTSS.L CTSS.S CTSV CTSV.L CTSW CTSW.L CTSZ CTSZ.L CTSZ.S LOAG_18685 SMP_013040.1 SMP_034410.1 SMP_067050 SMP_067060 SMP_085010 SMP_085180 SMP_103610 SMP_105370 SMP_158410 SMP_158420 SMP_179950 TSP_01409 TSP_02382 TSP_02383 TSP_03306 TSP_07747 TSP_10129 TSP_10493 TSP_11596 LMAN1 LMAN1L LMAN1.L LMAN1.S LMAN2 LMAN2L MBL1P MBL2 ACE2 FURIN TMPRSS2

Figure 8: COVID-19 related chemicals/genes.

Our KG results for many other drugs are visualized at our website[8]. We download new COVID-19 papers from three Application Programming Interfaces (APIs): NCBI PMC API, NCBI Pubtator API, and CORD-19 archive. We provide incremental updates including new papers, removed papers and updated papers, and their metadata information at our website[9].

[8] http://blender.cs.illinois.edu/covid19/visualization.html

[9] http://blender.cs.illinois.edu/covid19/

## 4.2 Results

As of June 14, 2020 we collected 140K papers. We selected 25,534 peer-reviewed papers and constructed the KG that includes 7,230 Diseases, 9,123 Chemicals and 50,864 Genes, with 1,725,518 Chemical-Gene links, 5,556,670 Chemical-Disease links, and 77,844,574 Gene-Disease links. The KG has received more than 1,000+ downloads. Our final generated reports[10] are shared publicly. For each question, our framework provides answers along with detailed evidence, knowledge subgraphs, image segmentation and analysis results. Table 1 shows some example answers.

Several clinicians and medical school students in our team have manually reviewed the drug repurposing reports for three drugs, and also the KGs connecting 41 drugs and COVID-19 related chemicals/genes. In checking the evidence sentences and reading the original articles, they reported that most of our output is informative and valid. For instance, after the coronavirus enters the cell in the lungs, it can cause a severe disease called Acute Respiratory Distress Syndrome. This condition causes the release of inflammatory molecules in the body named cytokines such as Interleukin-2, Interleukin-6, Tumor Necrosis Factor, and Interleukin-10. We see all of these connections in our results, such as the examples shown in Figure 3 and Figure 9. With further checks on these results, the scientists also indicated that many results were worth further investigation. For example, in Figure 3 we can see that Lusartan is connected to tumor protein p53 which is related to lung cancer.

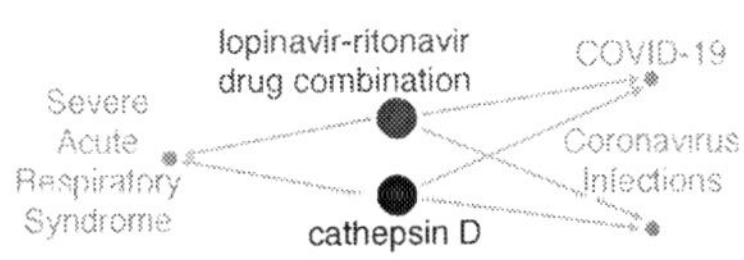


Figure 9: Connections Involving Coronavirus Related Diseases

| Question | Example Answers | |
|---|---|---|
| Q1 | Drug Class | angiotensin-converting enzyme (ACE) inhibitors |
| | Disease | hypertension |
| | Evidence Sentences | [PMID:32314699 (PMC7253125)] Past medical history was significant for hypertension, treated with amlodipine and benazepril, and chronic back pain. |
| | | [PMID:32081428 (PMC7092824)] On the other hand, many ACE inhibitors are currently used to treat hypertension and other cardiovascular diseases. Among them are captopril, perindopril, ramipril, lisinopril, benazepril, and moexipril. |
| Q4 | Disease | COVID-19 |
| | Evidence Sentences | [PMID:32081428 (PMC7092824)] By using a molecular docking approach, an earlier study identified N-(2-aminoethyl)-1 aziridine-ethanamine as a novel ACE2 inhibitor that effectively blocks the SARS-CoV RBD-mediated cell fusion. This has provided a potential candidate and lead compound for further therapeutic drug development. Meanwhile, biochemical and cell-based assays can be established to screen chemical compound libraries to identify novel inhibitors. |
| Q6 | Disease | cardiovascular disease |
| | Evidence Sentences | [PMID:22800722 (PMC7102827)] The in vitro half-maximal inhibitory concentration (IC50) values of food-derived ACE inhibitory peptides are about 1000 fold higher than that of synthetic captopril but they have higher in vivo activities than would be expected from their in vitro activities..... |
| Q8 | Disease | COVID-19 |
| | Evidence Sentences | [PMID:32336612 (PMC7167588)] Two trials of losartan as additional treatment for SARS-CoV-2 infection in hospitalized (NCT04312009) or not hospitalized (NCT04311177) patients have been announced, supported by the background of the huge adverse impact of the ACE Angiotensin II AT1 receptor axis over-activity in these patients. |
| | | [PMID:32350632 (PMC7189178)] To address the role of angiotensin in lung injury, there is an ongoing clinical trial to examine whether losartan treatment affects outcomes in COVID-19 associated ARDS (NCT04312009). |
| | | [PMID:32439915 (PMC7242178)] Losartan was also the molecule chosen in two trials recently started in the United States by the University of Minnesota to treat patients with COVID-19 (clinical trials.gov NCT04311177 and NCT 104312009). |

Table 1: Example Answers for Questions in Drug Repurposing Reports

## 5 Related Work

Extensive prior research work has focused on extracting biomedical entities (Zheng et al., 2014; Habibi et al., 2017; Crichton et al., 2017; Wang et al., 2018; Beltagy et al., 2019; Alsentzer et al., 2019; Wei et al., 2019; Wang et al., 2020c), relations (Uzuner et al., 2011; Krallinger et al., 2011; Manandhar and Yuret, 2013; Bui et al., 2014; Peng et al., 2016; Wei et al., 2015; Peng et al., 2017; Luo et al., 2017; Wei et al., 2019; Li and Ji, 2019; Peng et al., 2019, 2020), and events (Ananiadou et al., 2010; Van Landeghem et al., 2013; Nédellec et al., 2013; Deléger et al., 2016; Wei et al., 2019; Li et al., 2019; ShafieiBavani et al., 2020) from biomedical literature, with the most recent work focused on COVID-19 literature (Hope et al., 2020; Ilievski et al., 2020; Wolinski, 2020; Ahamed and Samad, 2020).

Most of the recent biomedical QA work (Yang et al., 2015, 2016; Chandu et al., 2017; Kraus et al., 2017) is driven by the BioASQ initiative (Tsatsaronis et al., 2015), and many live QA systems, including COVIDASK[11] and AUEB[12], and search en-

[10]http://blender.cs.illinois.edu/covid19/DrugRe-purposingReport_V2.0.docx

[11]https://covidask.korea.ac.kr/

[12]http://cslab241.cs.aueb.gr:5000/

gines (Kricka et al., 2020; Esteva et al., 2020; Hope et al., 2020; Taub Tabib et al., 2020) have been developed. Our work is an application and extension of our recently developed multimedia knowledge extraction system for the news domain (Li et al., 2020a,b). Similar to the news domain, the knowledge elements extracted from text and images in literature are complementary. Our framework advances state-of-the-art by extending the knowledge elements to more fine-grained types, incorporating image analysis and cross-media knowledge grounding, and KG matching into QA.

## 6 Conclusions and Future Work

We have developed a novel framework, **COVID-KG**, that automatically transforms a massive scientific literature corpus into organized, structured, and actionable KGs, and uses it to answer questions in drug repurposing reporting. With **COVID-KG**, researchers and clinicians are able to obtain informative answers from scientific literature, and thus focus on more important hypothesis testing, and prioritize the analysis efforts for candidate exploration directions. In our ongoing work, we have created a new ontology that includes 77 entity subtypes and 58 event subtypes, and we are building a neural IE system following this new ontology. In the future, we plan to extend **COVID-KG** to automate the creation of new hypotheses by predicting new links. We will also create a multimedia common semantic space (Li et al., 2020a,b) for literature and apply it to improve cross-media knowledge grounding and inference.

## Ethical Considerations

### Required Workflow for Using Our System

**Human review required.** Our knowledge discovery tool provides investigative leads for pre-clinical research, not final results for clinical use. Currently, biomedical researchers scour the literature to identify candidate drugs, then follow a standard research methodology to investigate their actual utility (involving literature reviews, computer simulations of drug mechanisms and effectiveness, in-vitro studies, cellular in-vivo studies, etc. before moving to clinical studies.). Our tool COVID-KG (and all knowledge discovery tools for biomedical applications) is not meant to be used for direct clinical applications on any human subjects. Rather, our tool aims to highlight unseen relations and patterns in large amounts of scientific textual data that would be too time-consuming for manual human effort. Accordingly, the tool would be useful for stakeholders (e.g., biomedical scientists) to identify specific drug candidates and molecular targets that are relevant in their biomedical and clinical research aims. The use of our knowledge discovery tool allows the researcher to narrow down the set of candidate drugs to investigate rapidly, but then proceed with the usual sequence of steps before kicking off expensive and time-consuming clinical tests. Failure to follow this sequence of events, and use of the system without the required human review, could lead to misguided experimental design wasting time and resources.

**Check evidence and source before using our system results.** In addition, our tool provides source, confidence values and rich evidence sentences for each node and link in the KG. To curtail potential harms caused by extraction errors, users of the knowledge graphs should double-check the source information and verify the accuracy of the discovered leads before launching expensive experimental studies. We spell out here the positive values, as well as the limitations and possible solutions to address these issues for future improvement. Moreover, any planned investigations involving human subjects should first be approved by the stakeholder's IRB (Institutional Review Board) who will oversee the safety of the proposed studies and the role of COVID-KG before any experimental studies are conducted. COVID-KG is a tool to enhance biomedical and clinical research; it is not a tool for direct clinical application with human subjects.

### Limitations of System Performance and Data Collection

**System errors.** Our system can effectively convert a large amount of scientific papers into knowledge graphs, and can scale as literature volume increases. However, none of our extraction components is perfect, they produce about 6%-22% false alarms and misses as reported in section 2. But as we described in the workflow, all of the connections and answers will be validated by domain experts by checking their corresponding sources before they are included in the drug repurposing report. COVID-KG is developed for pre-clinical research to target down drugs of interest for biomedical scientists. Therefore, no human subjects or specific populations are directly subjected to COVID-

KG unless approved by the stakeholder's IRB who oversees the safety and ethical aspects of the clinical studies in accordance with the Belmont report (https://www.hhs.gov/ohrp/regulations-and-policy/belmont-report/index.html). Accordingly, COVID-KG will not impose direct harm to vulnerable human cohorts or populations, unless misused by the stakeholders without IRB approval. With regards to potential harm in preclinical studies, users of COVID-KG are advised to verify the accuracy of the discovered leads in the source information before conducting expensive experimental studies.

**Bias in training data.** Proper use of the technology requires that input documents are legally and ethically obtained. Regulation and standards (e.g. GDPR[13]) provide a legal framework for ensuring that such data is properly used and that any individual whose data is used has the right to request its removal. In the absence of such regulation, society relies on those who apply technology to ensure that data is used in an ethical way. The input data to our system is peer-reviewed publicly available scientific articles. Additional potential harm could come from the output of the system being used in ways that magnify the system errors or bias in its training data. The various components in our system rely on weak distant supervision based on large-scale external knowledge bases and ontologies that cover a wide range of topics in the biomedical domain. Nevertheless, our system output is intended for human interpretation. We do not endorse incorporating the system's output into an automatic decision-making system without human validation; this fails to meet our recommendations and could yield harmful results. In the cited technical reports for each component in our framework, we have reported detailed error rates for each type of knowledge element from system evaluations and provide detailed qualitative analysis and explanations.

**Bias in development data.** We also note that the performance of our system components as reported is based on the specific benchmark datasets, which could be affected by such data biases. Thus questions concerning generalizability and fairness should be carefully considered. Within the research community, addressing data bias requires a combination of new data sources, research that mitigates the impact of bias, and, as done in (Mitchell et al., 2019), auditing data and models. Sections 2 and 4.1 cite data sources used for training to support future auditing. A general approach to properly use our system should incorporate ethics considerations as the first-order principles in every step of the system design, maintain a high degree of transparency and interpretability of data, algorithms, models, and functionality throughout the system, make software available as open-source for public verification and auditing, and explore countermeasures to protect vulnerable groups. In our ongoing and future work, we will keep increasing the annotated dataset size, add more rounds of user correction and validation, and iteratively incorporate feedback from domain experts who have used the tool, to create new benchmarks for retraining model and conducting more systematic evaluations. We recommend caution of using our system output until a more complete expert evaluation has occurred.

**Bias in source.** Furthermore, our system output may include some biases from the sources, by way of biases in the peer-reviewing process. In our previous work (Yu et al., 2014; Ma et al., 2015; Zhi et al., 2015; Zhang et al., 2019), we have aggregated source profile, knowledge graphs, and evidence for fact-checking across sources. We plan to extend our framework to include fact-checking to enable practitioners and researchers to access up-to-the-minute information.

**Bias in test queries.** Finally, the queries (i.e., the lists of candidate drugs and proteins/genes) are provided by the users who might have biases in their selection. Addressing the user's own biases falls outside the scope of our project, but as we have stated in the previous subsection, we direct users to carefully examine source information (author, publication date, etc.) and detailed evidence (contextual sentences and documents) associated with the extracted connections.

## Acknowledgement

This research is based upon work supported in part by U.S. DARPA KAIROS Program No. FA8750-19-2-1004, U.S. DARPA AIDA Program # FA8750-18-2-0014, .S. DTRA HDTRA I -16-1-0002/Project #1553695, eTASC - Empirical Evidence for a Theoretical Approach to Semantic Components, U.S. NSF No. 1741634, the Office of the Director of National Intelligence (ODNI), and Intelligence Advanced Research Projects Activity (IARPA) via contract FA8650-17-C-9116. The views and conclusions contained herein are

[13]The General Data Protection Regulation of the European Union https://gdpr.eu/what-is-gdpr/.

those of the authors and should not be interpreted as necessarily representing the official policies, either expressed or implied, of DARPA, or the U.S. Government. The U.S. Government is authorized to reproduce and distribute reprints for governmental purposes notwithstanding any copyright annotation therein.

## References


Sabber Ahamed and Manar Samad. 2020. Information mining for covid-19 research from a large volume of scientific literature. *Information Retrieval Repository*, arXiv:2004.02085.

Emily Alsentzer, John Murphy, William Boag, Wei-Hung Weng, Di Jindi, Tristan Naumann, and Matthew McDermott. 2019. Publicly available clinical BERT embeddings. In *Proceedings of the 2nd Clinical Natural Language Processing Workshop*, pages 72–78, Minneapolis, Minnesota, USA. Association for Computational Linguistics.

Sophia Ananiadou, Sampo Pyysalo, Jun'ichi Tsujii, and Douglas B Kell. 2010. Event extraction for systems biology by text mining the literature. *Trends in biotechnology*, 28(7):381–390.

Iz Beltagy, Kyle Lo, and Arman Cohan. 2019. SciBERT: A pretrained language model for scientific text. In *Proceedings of the 2019 Conference on Empirical Methods in Natural Language Processing and the 9th International Joint Conference on Natural Language Processing (EMNLP-IJCNLP)*, pages 3615–3620, Hong Kong, China. Association for Computational Linguistics.

Quoc-Chinh Bui, Peter MA Sloot, Erik M Van Mulligen, and Jan A Kors. 2014. A novel feature-based approach to extract drug–drug interactions from biomedical text. *Bioinformatics*, 30(23):3365–3371.

Khyathi Chandu, Aakanksha Naik, Aditya Chandrasekar, Zi Yang, Niloy Gupta, and Eric Nyberg. 2017. Tackling biomedical text summarization: OAQA at BioASQ 5B. In *BioNLP 2017*, pages 58–66, Vancouver, Canada,. Association for Computational Linguistics.

Gamal Crichton, Sampo Pyysalo, Billy Chiu, and Anna Korhonen. 2017. A neural network multi-task learning approach to biomedical named entity recognition. *Bioinformatics*, 18(1):368.

Allan Peter Davis, Cynthia J. Grondin, Robin J. Johnson, Daniela Sciaky, Benjamin L. King, Roy McMorran, Jolene Wiegers, Thomas C. Wiegers, and Carolyn J. Mattingly. 2016. The Comparative Toxicogenomics Database: update 2017. *Nucleic Acids Research*, 45(D1):D972–D978.

Louise Deléger, Robert Bossy, Estelle Chaix, Mouhamadou Ba, Arnaud Ferré, Philippe Bessières, and Claire Nédellec. 2016. Overview of the bacteria biotope task at BioNLP shared task 2016. In *Proceedings of the 4th BioNLP Shared Task Workshop*, pages 12–22, Berlin, Germany. Association for Computational Linguistics.

Sean Ekins and Megan Coffee. 2015. Fda approved drugs as potential ebola treatments. *F1000Research*, 4.

Andre Esteva, Anuprit Kale, Romain Paulus, Kazuma Hashimoto, Wenpeng Yin, Dragomir Radev, and Richard Socher. 2020. Co-search: Covid-19 information retrieval with semantic search, question answering, and abstractive summarization. *Information Retrieval Repository*, arXiv:2006.09595.

Maryam Habibi, Leon Weber, Mariana Neves, David Luis Wiegandt, and Ulf Leser. 2017. Deep learning with word embeddings improves biomedical named entity recognition. *Bioinformatics*, 33(14):37–48.

Tom Hope, Jason Portenoy, Kishore Vasan, Jonathan Borchardt, Eric Horvitz, Daniel S Weld, Marti A Hearst, and Jevin West. 2020. Scisight: Combining faceted navigation and research group detection for covid-19 exploratory scientific search. *Information Retrieval Repository*, arXiv:2005.12668.

Filip Ilievski, Daniel Garijo, Hans Chalupsky, Naren Teja Divvala, Yixiang Yao, Craig Rogers, Ronpeng Li, Jun Liu, Amandeep Singh, Daniel Schwabe, et al. 2020. Kgtk: A toolkit for large knowledge graph manipulation and analysis. *Artificial Intelligence Repository*, arXiv:2006.00088.

James L Kizziah, Keith A Manning, Altaira D Dearborn, and Terje Dokland. 2020. Structure of the host cell recognition and penetration machinery of a staphylococcus aureus bacteriophage. *PLoS pathogens*, 16(2):e1008314.

Martin Krallinger, Miguel Vazquez, Florian Leitner, David Salgado, Andrew Chatr-Aryamontri, Andrew Winter, Livia Perfetto, Leonardo Briganti, Luana Licata, Marta Iannuccelli, et al. 2011. The protein-protein interaction tasks of biocreative iii: classification/ranking of articles and linking bio-ontology concepts to full text. *BMC bioinformatics*, 12(S8):S3.

Milena Kraus, Julian Niedermeier, Marcel Jankrift, Sören Tietböhl, Toni Stachewicz, Hendrik Folkerts, Matthias Uflacker, and Mariana Neves. 2017. Olelo: a web application for intuitive exploration of biomedical literature. *Nucleic acids research*, 45(W1):478–483.

Larry J Kricka, Sergei Polevikov, Jason Y Park, Paolo Fortina, Sergio Bernardini, Daniel Satchkov, Valentin Kolesov, and Maxim Grishkov. 2020. Artificial intelligence-powered search tools and resources in the fight against covid-19. *EJIFCC*, 31(2):106.

Jinhyuk Lee, Wonjin Yoon, Sungdong Kim, Donghyeon Kim, Sunkyu Kim, Chan Ho So, and Jaewoo Kang. 2020. Biobert: a pre-trained biomedical language representation model for biomedical text mining. *Bioinformatics*, 36(4):1234–1240.

Diya Li, Lifu Huang, Heng Ji, and Jiawei Han. 2019. Biomedical event extraction based on knowledge-driven tree-LSTM. In *Proceedings of the 2019 Conference of the North American Chapter of the Association for Computational Linguistics: Human Language Technologies, Volume 1 (Long and Short Papers)*, pages 1421–1430, Minneapolis, Minnesota. Association for Computational Linguistics.

Diya Li and Heng Ji. 2019. Syntax-aware multi-task graph convolutional networks for biomedical relation extraction. In *Proc. EMNLP2019 Workshop on Health Text Mining and Information Analysis*.

Manling Li, Alireza Zareian, Ying Lin, Xiaoman Pan, Spencer Whitehead, Brian Chen, Bo Wu, Heng Ji, Shih-Fu Chang, Clare Voss, Daniel Napierski, and Marjorie Freedman. 2020a. GAIA: A fine-grained multimedia knowledge extraction system. In *Proceedings of the 58th Annual Meeting of the Association for Computational Linguistics: System Demonstrations*, pages 77–86, Online. Association for Computational Linguistics.

Manling Li, Alireza Zareian, Qi Zeng, Spencer Whitehead, Di Lu, Heng Ji, and Shih-Fu Chang. 2020b. Cross-media structured common space for multimedia event extraction. In *Proceedings of the 58th Annual Meeting of the Association for Computational Linguistics*, pages 2557–2568, Online. Association for Computational Linguistics.

Yuan Luo, Özlem Uzuner, and Peter Szolovits. 2017. Bridging semantics and syntax with graph algorithms—state-of-the-art of extracting biomedical relations. *Briefings in bioinformatics*, 18(1):160–178.

Fenglong Ma, Yaliang Li, Qi Li, Minghui Qiu, Jing Gao, Shi Zhi, Lu Su, Bo Zhao, Heng Ji, and Jiawei Han. 2015. Faitcrowd: Fine grained truth discovery for crowdsourced data aggregation. In *Proc. the 21st ACM SIGKDD Conference on Knowledge Discovery and Data Mining (KDD2015)*.

Suresh Manandhar and Deniz Yuret, editors. 2013. *Second Joint Conference on Lexical and Computational Semantics (*SEM), Volume 2: Proceedings of the Seventh International Workshop on Semantic Evaluation (SemEval 2013)*. Association for Computational Linguistics, Atlanta, Georgia, USA.

Margaret Mitchell, Simone Wu, Andrew Zaldivar, Parker Barnes, Lucy Vasserman, Ben Hutchinson, Elena Spitzer, Inioluwa Deborah Raji, and Timnit Gebru. 2019. Model cards for model reporting. In *Proceedings of the Conference on Fairness, Accountability, and Transparency*, pages 220–229.

Claire Nédellec, Robert Bossy, Jin-Dong Kim, Jung-jae Kim, Tomoko Ohta, Sampo Pyysalo, and Pierre Zweigenbaum. 2013. Overview of BioNLP shared task 2013. In *Proceedings of the BioNLP Shared Task 2013 Workshop*, pages 1–7, Sofia, Bulgaria. Association for Computational Linguistics.

Nanyun Peng, Hoifung Poon, Chris Quirk, Kristina Toutanova, and Wen-tau Yih. 2017. Cross-sentence n-ary relation extraction with graph lstms. *Transactions of the Association for Computational Linguistics*, 5:101–115.

Yifan Peng, Qingyu Chen, and Zhiyong Lu. 2020. An empirical study of multi-task learning on BERT for biomedical text mining. In *Proceedings of the 19th SIGBioMed Workshop on Biomedical Language Processing*, pages 205–214, Online. Association for Computational Linguistics.

Yifan Peng, Chih-Hsuan Wei, and Zhiyong Lu. 2016. Improving chemical disease relation extraction with rich features and weakly labeled data. *Journal of cheminformatics*, 8(1):53.

Yifan Peng, Shankai Yan, and Zhiyong Lu. 2019. Transfer learning in biomedical natural language processing: An evaluation of BERT and ELMo on ten benchmarking datasets. In *Proceedings of the 18th BioNLP Workshop and Shared Task*, pages 58–65, Florence, Italy. Association for Computational Linguistics.

Nils Reimers and Iryna Gurevych. 2019. Sentence-BERT: Sentence embeddings using Siamese BERT-networks. In *Proceedings of the 2019 Conference on Empirical Methods in Natural Language Processing and the 9th International Joint Conference on Natural Language Processing (EMNLP-IJCNLP)*, pages 3982–3992, Hong Kong, China. Association for Computational Linguistics.

Elaheh ShafieiBavani, Antonio Jimeno Yepes, Xu Zhong, and David Martinez Iraola. 2020. Global locality in biomedical relation and event extraction. In *Proceedings of the 19th SIGBioMed Workshop on Biomedical Language Processing*, pages 195–204, Online. Association for Computational Linguistics.

Jingbo Shang, Liyuan Liu, Xiaotao Gu, Xiang Ren, Teng Ren, and Jiawei Han. 2018. Learning named entity tagger using domain-specific dictionary. In *Proceedings of the 2018 Conference on Empirical Methods in Natural Language Processing*, pages 2054–2064, Brussels, Belgium. Association for Computational Linguistics.

Noah Siegel, Nicholas Lourie, Russell Power, and Waleed Ammar. 2018. Extracting scientific figures with distantly supervised neural networks. In *Proceedings of the 18th ACM/IEEE on Joint Conference on Digital Libraries*, page 223–232, New York, NY, USA. Association for Computing Machinery.

Ray Smith. 2007. An overview of the tesseract ocr engine. In *Proceedings of the 9th international conference on document analysis and recognition (ICDAR 2007)*, volume 2, pages 629–633.

Hillel Taub Tabib, Micah Shlain, Shoval Sadde, Dan Lahav, Matan Eyal, Yaara Cohen, and Yoav Goldberg. 2020. Interactive extractive search over biomedical corpora. In *Proceedings of the 19th SIGBioMed Workshop on Biomedical Language Processing*, pages 28–37, Online. Association for Computational Linguistics.

George Tsatsaronis, Georgios Balikas, Prodromos Malakasiotis, Ioannis Partalas, Matthias Zschunke, Michael R Alvers, Dirk Weissenborn, Anastasia Krithara, Sergios Petridis, Dimitris Polychronopoulos, et al. 2015. An overview of the bioasq large-scale biomedical semantic indexing and question answering competition. *BMC bioinformatics*, 16(1):138.

Satoshi Tsutsui and David J Crandall. 2017. A data driven approach for compound figure separation using convolutional neural networks. In *Proceedings of the 2017 14th IAPR International Conference on Document Analysis and Recognition (ICDAR)*, volume 1, pages 533–540.

Jingxuan Tu, M. Verhagen, B. Cochran, and J. Pustejovsky. 2020. Exploration and discovery of the covid-19 literature through semantic visualization. *ArXiv*, abs/2007.01800.

Özlem Uzuner, Brett R South, Shuying Shen, and Scott L DuVall. 2011. 2010 i2b2/va challenge on concepts, assertions, and relations in clinical text. *Journal of the American Medical Informatics Association*, 18(5):552–556.

Sofie Van Landeghem, Jari Björne, Chih-Hsuan Wei, Kai Hakala, Sampo Pyysalo, Sophia Ananiadou, Hung-Yu Kao, Zhiyong Lu, Tapio Salakoski, Yves Van de Peer, et al. 2013. Large-scale event extraction from literature with multi-level gene normalization. *PloS one*, 8(4):e55814.

Qingyun Wang, Lifu Huang, Zhiying Jiang, Kevin Knight, Heng Ji, Mohit Bansal, and Yi Luan. 2019a. PaperRobot: Incremental draft generation of scientific ideas. In *Proceedings of the 57th Annual Meeting of the Association for Computational Linguistics*, pages 1980–1991, Florence, Italy. Association for Computational Linguistics.

Xuan Wang, Yingjun Guan, Weili Liu, Aabhas Chauhan, Enyi Jiang, Qi Li, David Liem, Dibakar Sigdel, John Caufield, Peipei Ping, et al. 2020a. Evidenceminer: Textual evidence discovery for life sciences. In *Proceedings of the 58th Annual Meeting of the Association for Computational Linguistics: System Demonstrations*, pages 56–62.

Xuan Wang, Weili Liu, Aabhas Chauhan, Yingjun Guan, and Jiawei Han. 2020b. Automatic textual evidence mining in covid-19 literature. *Computation and Language Repository*, arXiv:2004.12563.

Xuan Wang, Xiangchen Song, Yingjun Guan, Bangzheng Li, and Jiawei Han. 2020c. Comprehensive named entity recognition on cord-19 with distant or weak supervision. *Computation and Language Repository*, arXiv:2003.12218.

Xuan Wang, Yu Zhang, Qi Li, Xiang Ren, Jingbo Shang, and Jiawei Han. 2019b. Distantly supervised biomedical named entity recognition with dictionary expansion. In *Proceedings of the 2019 IEEE International Conference on Bioinformatics and Biomedicine (BIBM)*, pages 496–503.

Xuan Wang, Yu Zhang, Xiang Ren, Yuhao Zhang, Marinka Zitnik, Jingbo Shang, Curtis Langlotz, and Jiawei Han. 2018. Cross-type biomedical named entity recognition with deep multi-task learning. *Bioinformatics*, 35(10):1745–1752.

Chih-Hsuan Wei, Alexis Allot, Robert Leaman, and Zhiyong Lu. 2019. PubTator central: automated concept annotation for biomedical full text articles. *Nucleic Acids Research*, 47(W1):587–593.

Chih-Hsuan Wei, Yifan Peng, Robert Leaman, Allan Peter Davis, Carolyn J Mattingly, Jiao Li, Thomas C Wiegers, and Zhiyong Lu. 2015. Overview of the biocreative v chemical disease relation (cdr) task. In *Proceedings of the 5th BioCreative challenge evaluation workshop*, volume 14.

Francis Wolinski. 2020. Visualization of diseases at risk in the covid-19 literature. *Information Retrieval Repository*, arXiv:2005.00848.

Zi Yang, Niloy Gupta, Xiangyu Sun, Di Xu, Chi Zhang, and Eric Nyberg. 2015. Learning to answer biomedical factoid & list questions: Oaqa at bioasq 3b. *CLEF (Working Notes)*, 1391.

Zi Yang, Yue Zhou, and Eric Nyberg. 2016. Learning to answer biomedical questions: OAQA at BioASQ 4B. In *Proceedings of the Fourth BioASQ workshop*, pages 23–37, Berlin, Germany. Association for Computational Linguistics.

Dian Yu, Hongzhao Huang, Taylor Cassidy, Heng Ji, Chi Wang, Shi Zhi, Jiawei Han, Clare Voss, and Malik Magdon-Ismail. 2014. The wisdom of minority: Unsupervised slot filling validation based on multi-dimensional truth-finding. In *Proc. The 25th International Conference on Computational Linguistics (COLING2014)*.

Haibo Zhang, Josef M Penninger, Yimin Li, Nanshan Zhong, and Arthur S Slutsky. 2020. Angiotensin-converting enzyme 2 (ace2) as a sars-cov-2 receptor: molecular mechanisms and potential therapeutic target. *Intensive care medicine*, 46(4):586–590.

Xiaomei Zhang, Yibo Wu, Lifu Huang, Heng Ji, and Guohong Cao. 2019. Expertise-aware truth analysis and task allocation in mobile crowdsourcing. *IEEE Transactions on Mobile Computing*.

Jin Guang Zheng, Daniel Howsmon, Boliang Zhang, Juergen Hahn, Deborah McGuinness, James Hendler, and Heng Ji. 2014. Entity linking for biomedical literature. In *BMC Medical Informatics and Decision Making*.

Jin Guang Zheng, Daniel Howsmon, Boliang Zhang, Juergen Hahn, Deborah McGuinness, James Hendler, and Heng Ji. 2015. Entity linking for biomedical literature. In *Proceedings of the BMC Medical Informatics and Decision Making*, volume 15.

Shi Zhi, Bo Zhao, Wenzhu Tong, Jing Gao, Dian Yu, Heng Ji, and Jiawei Han. 2015. Modeling truth existence in truth discovery. In *Proc. the 21st ACM SIGKDD Conference on Knowledge Discovery and Data Mining (KDD2015)*.

Xinyu Zhou, Cong Yao, He Wen, Yuzhi Wang, Shuchang Zhou, Weiran He, and Jiajun Liang. 2017. East: an efficient and accurate scene text detector. In *Proceedings of the IEEE conference on Computer Vision and Pattern Recognition*, pages 5551–5560.

# Multifaceted Domain-Specific Document Embeddings

**Julian Risch** and **Philipp Hager** and **Ralf Krestel**
Hasso Plattner Institute, University of Potsdam
Potsdam, Germany
firstname.lastname@hpi.de

## Abstract

Current document embeddings require large training corpora but fail to learn high-quality representations when confronted with a small number of domain-specific documents and rare terms. Further, they transform each document into a single embedding vector, making it hard to capture different notions of document similarity or explain why two documents are considered similar. In this work, we propose our Faceted Domain Encoder, a novel approach to learn multifaceted embeddings for domain-specific documents. It is based on a Siamese neural network architecture and leverages knowledge graphs to further enhance the embeddings even if only a few training samples are available. The model identifies different types of domain knowledge and encodes them into separate dimensions of the embedding, thereby enabling multiple ways of finding and comparing related documents in the vector space. We evaluate our approach on two benchmark datasets and find that it achieves the same embedding quality as state-of-the-art models while requiring only a tiny fraction of their training data.

## 1 Introduction

Many documents have an inherently multifaceted nature, a characteristic that domain experts could exploit when searching through large document collections. For example, doctors could search through medical archives for documents containing similar disease descriptions or related uses of a specific drug. However, one of the major challenges of information retrieval in such document collections is domain-specific language use:

1. Training datasets to learn document representations are limited in size,
2. documents might express the same information by using completely different terms (vocabulary mismatch) or different levels of granularity (granularity mismatch),
3. and the lack of context knowledge prevents drawing even simple logical conclusions.

Domain-specific embeddings are available for a variety of domains, including scientific literature (Beltagy et al., 2019), patents (Risch and Krestel, 2019), and the biomedical domain (Kalyan and Sangeetha, 2020). However, these approaches require large amounts of training data and computing resources. In this paper, we introduce and demonstrate our Faceted Domain Encoder, a document embedding approach that produces comparative results on considerably smaller document collections and requires fewer computing resources. Further, it provides a multifaceted view of texts while also addressing the challenges of domain-specific language use. To this end, we introduce external domain knowledge to the embedding process, tackling the problem of vocabulary and granularity mismatches. A screenshot of the demo is shown in Figure 1. The interactive demo, our source code, and the evaluation datasets are available online: https://hpi.de/naumann/s/multifaceted-embeddings and a screencast is available on YouTube: https://youtu.be/HHcsX2clEwg.

## 2 Related Work

A popular approach for introducing external domain knowledge to the embedding process uses retrofitting of word vectors based on a graph of semantic relationships as a post-processing step (Faruqui et al., 2015). Similarly, Zhang et al. (2019) train fastText embeddings on biomedical journal articles and additionally on sequences of medical terms sampled from a knowledge graph. Dis2Vec uses a lexicon of medical terms to bring Word2Vec vectors of domain terms closer together and to push out-of-domain vectors further away (Ghosh et al., 2016). Unlike Dis2Vec, which concerns only whether a word is in the domain vocabulary or not, our approach handles diverse types



*Proceedings of NAACL-HLT 2021: Demonstrations*, pages 78–83

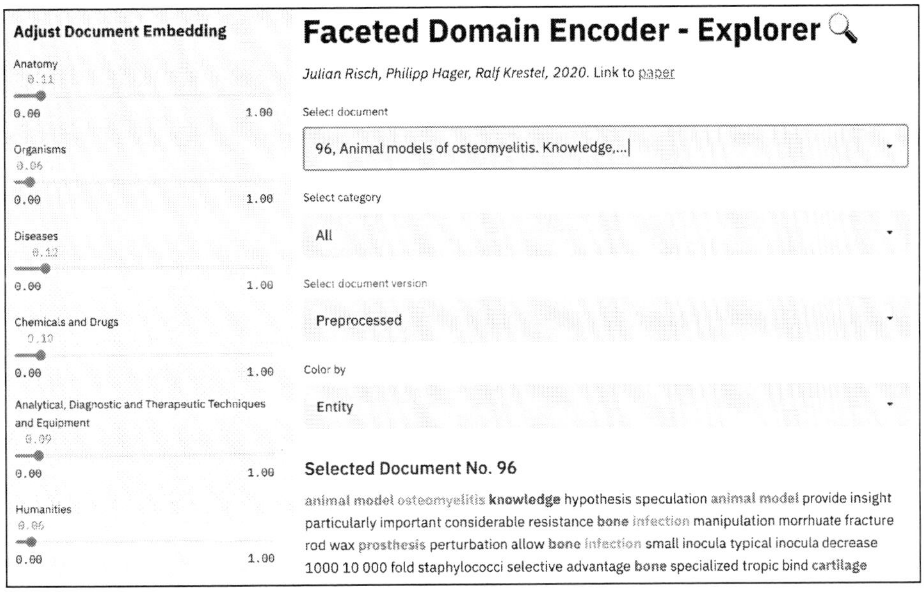


Figure 1: The demo shows nearest neighbor documents and highlights entities within the same categories ("facets"). Stop word removal and lemmatization can be turned off for increased readability. The user interface allows to adjust the weights of the facets of the document embeddings.

of relationships between domain terms. Nguyen et al. (2017) propose an extension of Doc2Vec, adding vectors for domain concepts as input for learning medical document embeddings. Roy et al. (2017) annotate words in the input text with a list of matching entities and relationships from a knowledge graph and extend Word2Vec to jointly learn embeddings for words and annotations. Their abstraction of the graph structure as text annotations enables the inclusion of different node types and edge connections into word embeddings. Another work (Liu et al., 2020) proposed K-BERT, which extends BERT (Devlin et al., 2019) by expanding input sentences with entities from a knowledge graph.

Multifaceted embeddings capture more than one view of a document. Yang et al. (2018) propose a multifaceted network embedding and apply community detection algorithms to learn separate embeddings for each community. Liu et al. (2019) suggest an extension to the deepwalk graph embedding, which learns separate node embeddings for different facets of nodes in a knowledge graph. Similar to our approach, they propose to concatenate the obtained facet embeddings into a single representation. We learn separate embeddings for types of domain knowledge and concatenate them into an overall document representation.

## 3 Faceted Domain Encoder

Our Faceted Domain Encoder is a supervised learning approach using a Siamese neural network to encode documents and a knowledge graph as a source for additional domain information. The architecture is visualized in Figure 2.

### 3.1 Overview

The network encodes two documents at-a-time with a bidirectional GRU layer and predicts a similarity score for each pair. By computing the pair's target similarity score based on our knowledge graph, we train the network to adjust its document representations to the relationships between domain terms in the graph. We introduce multiple facets in this process by grouping nodes in the graph into multiple categories. Our model represents different aspects of domain knowledge in different category embeddings by learning not a single embedding vector but an embedding per graph category. We train one embedding for each graph category per document and concatenate them into a single embedding vector to represent the entire document. This representation enables the fast discovery of related documents by performing a conventional nearest neighbor search either based on the whole document or specific category embeddings. To control which category contributes the most to the doc-

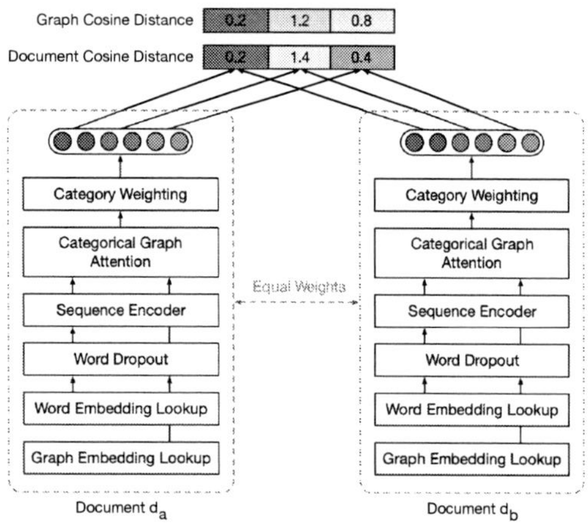


Figure 2: Our model is based on a Siamese network architecture, which encodes two documents in parallel and compares them in the last (top) layer. It is trained to minimize the difference between the documents' cosine distance in the embedding space and their graph-based ground-truth distance. Colors symbolize different facets of the embeddings, which are learned based on node categories in the knowledge graph.

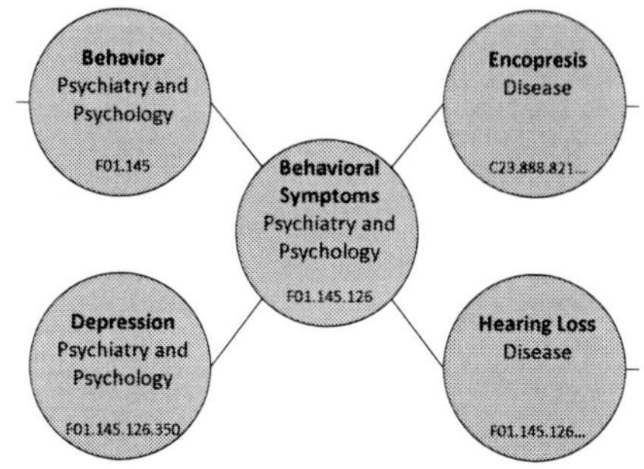


Figure 3: This excerpt of our graph representation of the Medical Subject Headings (MeSH) hierarchy visualizes entities as nodes with their color corresponding to categories ("facets"). The edges and the node numbers reveal the hierarchical relationships, e.g., the broader concept of "Behavior" and the specific mental illness "Depression".

ument vector's overall direction, we apply corpus normalization inspired by Liu et al. (2019).

To cope with limited amounts of training data, our approach leverages external domain knowledge during the training process. We represent this external domain knowledge in the form of a knowledge graph. Each node in the graph represents an entity, e.g., the name of a disease. Each entity belongs to a category, modeled as a node attribute. For example, entities in a medical graph are grouped into diseases, chemicals, or body parts. Categories define the different types of domain knowledge that the model learns to embed into different subparts of the document embedding. Edges between nodes represent relationships, e.g., chemicals in the same group in the periodic table. The entity linking requires a dictionary mapping from words to entities and handles synonyms mapping to the same entity. For the demo, we created a knowledge graph from the taxonomy underlying Medical Subject Headings (MeSH). Figure 3 shows a small excerpt of the graph.

After parsing and deduplicating the official dataset, MeSH comprises 29,641 concepts (entities) and 271,846 synonyms, which are organized in a hierarchy ranging from broad concepts to specific sub-concepts. Following previous work (Guo et al., 2020), we transform the hierarchy into a network graph prevailing the relationships between concepts.

### 3.2 Equally Weighted Categories

Our approach learns separate embeddings for different categories of domain terms. However, not all categories might be useful when it comes to representing the overall document. We illustrate this problem with a fictional example from the medical domain. Our approach might learn that an article covers a seldom form of cancer (disease category) in the lung and stomach (anatomy category), and the study originates in the United States (location category). Concatenating these three embeddings gives equal weight to each category. The closest document in embedding space needs to be similar in all of the three categories. This might lead to counterintuitive results with the most relating article covering a stomach disease in a small town in Ohio, instead of a document just covering lung cancer. When reading the text again, we might weigh the given information differently based on its specificity and expect the form of cancer to be more important than the geographic location of the study. Note that this problem is magnified when combining up to sixteen categories in the case of our medical dataset. We illustrate the problem with an actual example from our demo in Figure 4.

A second problem can arise when a single, seemingly unimportant category dominates the document embedding. Some documents mention a single term very often, e.g., the word "patient". A high frequency of less-informative words can lead to individual categories collecting vastly more word embeddings than others and taking over the entire document embedding.

The root cause of both issues is an unintended difference in magnitude between the category embeddings. When concatenating multiple embeddings into a new vector, the category embeddings with the highest magnitude will decide the overall direction of the embedding vector. We address this issue with a simple normalization and weighting process to control which category embeddings contribute the most to the overall direction of the document vector. This approach is similar to what Liu et al. proposed in their work on multifaceted graph embeddings but differs in that we also apply normalization and propose new weighting strategies.

### 3.3 Category Normalization Strategies

We propose two strategies to compute category weights: corpus-idf and document-tfidf. The first strategy, corpus-idf, sums the inverse-document-frequency of all terms in the category across the entire vocabulary. We normalize the resulting values for all categories to sum to one. This strategy applies the same category weights to all documents in the entire corpus. The motivation is to identify categories that contain the most important words in a collection of documents. This strategy is closely related to the number of unique mentioned tokens in each category.

The second strategy, document-tfidf, computes category weights for individual documents by summing the inverse-document-frequency value of all category terms in the document. Since terms can occur multiple times, the result is similar to the tf-idf value when computed for each category. Additionally, we sum the idf of all words without a category and split the weight equally among all categories. Thereby, we avoid zero weights for categories in the overall embedding. The idea behind this weighting scheme is to have a document-level proxy metric to indicate which categories are important for the document.

## 4 Experiments

For our experiments, we use two Semantic Textual Similarity (STS) benchmarks from the biomedical domain, BIOSSES (Soğancıoğlu et al., 2017) and Med-STS (Wang et al., 2020). The benchmarks comprise sentence pairs with relatedness scores assigned by domain experts. They measure embedding quality by comparing the annotator score with the embedding similarity of both sentences based on Pearson correlation.

To this end, BIOSSES contains 100 sentence pairs collected from medical articles and judged by five domain experts at a scale of 0 to 4. We perform stratified 10-fold cross-validation as proposed by the benchmark authors. We divide the dataset into ten equally-sized subsets using the annotator scores for stratification. Stratification ensures that each split has a similar distribution of related and unrelated sentence pairs. We train ten separate models on the subsets, always using one subset for testing and the remaining nine for training. Note that we still use 30 percent of the training dataset for validation and early stopping: we stop the training process after the first epoch in which the loss on the validation set stops decreasing. Med-STS contains 1,068 sentence pairs from medical records collected internally in the U.S. Mayo Clinics. Two domain experts judged each sentence pair on a scale from 0 to 5. The dataset authors proposed a train-test split of 750 to 350 sentence pairs. Additionally, we use 30 percent, or 225 pairs, of our training set for validation and early stopping.

The experiment results listed in Table 1 show that our Faceted Domain Encoder outperforms the domain-agnostic embeddings from fastText (Bojanowski et al., 2017) and Universal Sentence Encoder (Cer et al., 2018) on both benchmarks. The corpus-idf normalization is better than the document-tfidf normalization strategy on the BIOSSES dataset but not on the Med-STS dataset. In comparison with the domain-specific embeddings from BioWordVec (Zhang et al., 2019) and BioSentVec (Chen et al., 2019), our approach achieves almost the same performance on Med-STS, which is remarkable given that our Faceted Domain Encoder requires no pre-training on large corpora in contrast to the other presented models. For BIOSSES, only BioSentVec outperforms our approach by a large margin.

## 5 Interactive User Interface

The user interface comprises three main parts: top center, bottom center, and sidebar. In the top center, the user can select a source document and one or all of the categories ("facets"). Further, either a preprocessed (stop word removal, lemmatization) or a raw document version can be selected for the viewed documents and word highlighting can be

Table 1: Pearson correlation on STS benchmarks (* marks results reported by Chen et al. (2019)).

| Embedding | Pre-Trained | BIOSSES | Med-STS |
|---|---|---|---|
| Avg. fastText English (Bojanowski et al., 2017) | ✓ | 0.51 | 0.68 |
| Universal Sentence Encoder (Cer et al., 2018) | ✓ | 0.35* | 0.71* |
| Avg. BioWordVec (Zhang et al., 2019) | ✓ | 0.69* | 0.75* |
| BioSentVec (Chen et al., 2019) | ✓ | 0.82* | 0.77* |
| Faceted Domain Encoder, Document Normalization | | 0.53 | 0.75 |
| Faceted Domain Encoder, Corpus Normalization | | 0.62 | 0.72 |

switched between coloring by entities and coloring by attention scores. The bottom center shows the selected document and the top ten documents that are closest to the selected document in the embedding space. Depending on the selected facet, the documents' distance is calculated based on one specific facet or on the entire document embedding. The sidebar at the left-hand side provides an option to adjust the document embedding in detail. It allows the user to specify what impact the individual facets have on the document's overall embedding.

## 6 Conclusion

Current document embeddings require large amounts of training data and provide only a single view of document similarity, which prevents searches with different notions of similarity. In this paper, we introduced and demonstrated an approach for multifaceted domain-specific document embeddings. It is tailored to small document collections of only a few hundred training samples and leverages knowledge graphs to enhance the learned embeddings. Experiments on two benchmark datasets show that our model outperforms state-of-the-art domain-agnostic embeddings and is on par with specialized biomedical document embeddings trained on extensive document collections while only using a tiny fraction of their training data. Our demo provides a faceted view into documents by learning to identify different types of domain knowledge and encoding them into specific dimensions of the embeddings. Thereby, it enables novel ways to compare documents and provides a comparatively high level of interpretability of neural-network-based document similarity measures. A promising path for future work is to remove our neural networks' reliance on ground truth data by designing a semi-supervised approach in which the model learns to update its training goal while discovering new domain terms by itself.

## References


Iz Beltagy, Kyle Lo, and Arman Cohan. 2019. SciBERT: A Pretrained Language Model for Scientific Text. In *Proceedings of the Conference on Empirical Methods in Natural Language Processing and the International Joint Conference on Natural Language Processing (EMNLP-IJCNLP)*, pages 3606–3611.

Piotr Bojanowski, Edouard Grave, Armand Joulin, and Tomas Mikolov. 2017. Enriching Word Vectors with Subword Information. *Transactions of the Association for Computational Linguistics (TACL)*, 5:135–146.

Daniel Cer, Yinfei Yang, Sheng yi Kong, Nan Hua, Nicole Limtiaco, Rhomni St. John, Noah Constant, Mario Guajardo-Céspedes, Steve Yuan, Chris Tar, Yun Hsuan Sung, Brian Strope, and Ray Kurzweil. 2018. Universal Sentence Encoder for English. In *Proceedings of the Conference on Empirical Methods in Natural Language Processing (EMNLP)*, pages 169–174.

Qingyu Chen, Yifan Peng, and Zhiyong Lu. 2019. BioSentVec: Creating Sentence Embeddings for Biomedical Texts. In *Proceedings of the International Conference on Healthcare Informatics (ICHI)*, pages 1–5.

Jacob Devlin, Ming-Wei Chang, Kenton Lee, and Kristina Toutanova. 2019. BERT: Pre-training of Deep Bidirectional Transformers for Language Understanding. In *Proceedings of the Conference of the North American Chapter of the Association for Computational Linguistics (NAACL)*, pages 4171–4186.

Manaal Faruqui, Jesse Dodge, Sujay K. Jauhar, Chris Dyer, Eduard Hovy, and Noah A. Smith. 2015. Retrofitting word vectors to semantic lexicons. In *Proceedings of the Conference of the North American Chapter of the Association for Computational Linguistics (NAACL)*, pages 1606–1615.

Saurav Ghosh, Prithwish Chakraborty, Emily Cohn, John S. Brownstein, and Naren Ramakrishnan. 2016. Characterizing diseases from unstructured text: A vocabulary driven Word2vec approach. In *Proceedings of the International Conference on Information and Knowledge Management (CIKM)*, pages 1129–1138.

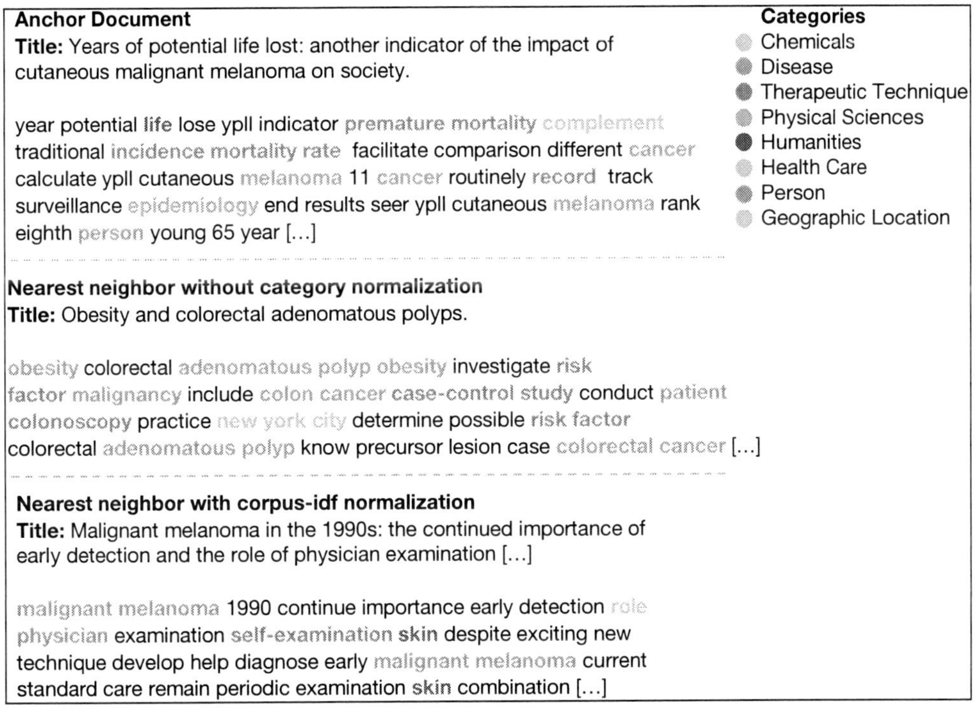


Figure 4: Different weighting of the categories ("facets") changes the distances of the documents in the embedding space and the nearest neighbors of the anchor document. Corpus-idf normalization allows to take into account the frequency of the entities within the corpus. The impact of the most frequent words on the embeddings can thus be reduced. Stop word removal and lemmatization can be turned off for increased readability.


Zhen-Hao Guo, Zhu-Hong You, De-Shuang Huang, Hai-Cheng Yi, Kai Zheng, Zhan-Heng Chen, and Yan-Bin Wang. 2020. MeSHHeading2vec: a new method for representing MeSH headings as vectors based on graph embedding algorithm. *Briefings in Bioinformatics*.

Katikapalli Subramanyam Kalyan and S. Sangeetha. 2020. SECNLP: A survey of embeddings in clinical natural language processing. *Bioinformatics*, 101:1–21.

Ninghao Liu, Qiaoyu Tan, Yuening Li, Hongxia Yang, Jingren Zhou, and Xia Hu. 2019. Is a single vector enough? Exploring node polysemy for network embedding. In *Proceedings of the International Conference on Knowledge Discovery and Data Mining (SIGKDD)*, pages 932–940.

Weijie Liu, Peng Zhou, Zhe Zhao, Zhiruo Wang, Qi Ju, Haotang Deng, and Ping Wang. 2020. K-bert: Enabling language representation with knowledge graph. In *Proceedings of the Conference on Artificial Intelligence (AAAI)*, pages 2901–2908.

Gia Hung Nguyen, Lynda Tamine, Laure Soulier, and Nathalie Souf. 2017. Learning concept-driven document embeddings for medical information search. *Lecture Notes in Computer Science*, 10259(17).

Julian Risch and Ralf Krestel. 2019. Domain-specific word embeddings for patent classification. *Data Technologies and Applications*, 53(1):108–122.

Arpita Roy, Youngja Park, and SHimei Pan. 2017. Learning Domain-Specific Word Embeddings from Sparse Cybersecurity Texts. In *arXiv preprint: 1709.07470*.

Gizem Soğancıoğlu, Hakime Öztürk, and Arzucan Özgür. 2017. BIOSSES: A semantic sentence similarity estimation system for the biomedical domain. *Bioinformatics*, 33(14):49–58.

Yanshan Wang, Naveed Afzal, Sunyang Fu, Liwei Wang, Feichen Shen, Majid Rastegar-Mojarad, and Hongfang Liu. 2020. MedSTS: a resource for clinical semantic textual similarity. *Language Resources and Evaluation*, 54(1):57–72.

Liang Yang, Xiaochun Cao, and Guo Yuanfang. 2018. Multi-facet Network Embedding: Beyond the General Solution of Detection and Representation. In *Proceedings of the Conference on Artificial Intelligence (AAAI)*, pages 499–506.

Yijia Zhang, Qingyu Chen, Zhihao Yang, Hongfei Lin, and Zhiyong Lu. 2019. BioWordVec, improving biomedical word embeddings with subword information and MeSH. *Scientific Data*, 6(1):1–9.

# Improving Evidence Retrieval for Automated Explainable Fact-Checking

Chris Samarinas[1], Wynne Hsu[1,2,3], and Mong Li Lee[1,2,3]

[1]Institute of Data Science, National University of Singapore
[2]NUS Centre for Trusted Internet and Community
[3]School of Computing, National University of Singapore

## Abstract

Automated fact-checking on a large-scale is a challenging task that has not been studied systematically until recently. Large noisy document collections like the web or news articles make the task more difficult. In this paper, we describe the components of a three-stage automated fact-checking system, named Quin+. We demonstrate that using dense passage representations increases the evidence recall in a noisy setting. We experiment with two sentence selection approaches, an embedding-based selection using a dense retrieval model, and a sequence labeling approach for context-aware selection. Quin+ is able to verify open-domain claims using a large-scale corpus or web search results.

## 1 Introduction

With the emergence of social media and many individual news sources online, the spread of misinformation has become a major problem with potentially harmful social consequences. Fake news can manipulate public opinion, create conflicts, elicit unreasonable fear and suspicion. The vast amount of unverified online content led to the establishment of external post-hoc fact-checking organizations, such as PolitiFact, FactCheck.org, Snopes etc, with dedicated resources to verify claims online. However, manual fact-checking is time consuming and intractable on a large scale. The ability to automatically perform fact-checking is critical to minimize negative social impact.

Automated fact checking is a complex task involving evidence extraction followed by evidence reasoning and entailment. For the retrieval of relevant evidence from a corpus of documents, existing systems typically utilize traditional sparse retrieval which may have poor recall, especially when the relevant passages have few overlapping words with the claims to be verified. Dense retrieval models have proven effective in question answering as these models can better capture the latent semantic content of text. The work in (Samarinas et al., 2020) is the first to use dense retrieval for fact checking. The authors constructed a new dataset called Factual-NLI comprising of claim-evidence pairs from the FEVER dataset (Thorne et al., 2018) as well as synthetic examples generated from benchmark Question Answering datasets (Kwiatkowski et al., 2019; Nguyen et al., 2016). They demonstrated that using Factual-NLI to train a dense retriever can improve evidence retrieval significantly.

While the FEVER dataset has enabled the systematic evaluation of automated fact-checking systems, it does not reflect well the noisy nature of real-world data. Motivated by this, we introduce the Factual-NLI+ dataset, an extension of the FEVER dataset with synthetic examples from question answering datasets and noise passages from web search results. We examine how dense representations can improve the first-stage retrieval recall of passages for fact-checking in a noisy setting, and make the retrieval of relevant evidence more tractable on a large scale.

However, the selection of relevant evidence sentences for accurate fact-checking and explainability remains a challenge. Figure 1 shows an example of a claim and the retrieved passage which has three sentences, of which only the last sentence provides the critical evidence to refute the claim. We propose two ways to select the relevant sentences, an embedding-based selection using a dense retrieval model, and a sequence labeling approach for context-aware selection. We show that the former generalizes better with a high recall, while the latter has higher precision, making them suitable for the identification of relevant evidence sentences. Our fact-checking system Quin+ is able



*Proceedings of NAACL-HLT 2021: Demonstrations*, pages 84–91
June 6–11, 2021. 

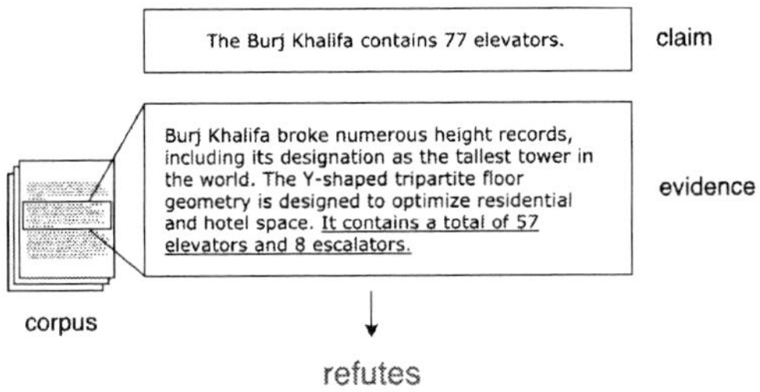


Figure 1: Sample claim and the retrieved evidence passage where only the last sentence is relevant.

to verify open-domain claims using a large corpus or web search results.

## 2 Related Work

Automated claim verification using a large corpus has not been studied systematically until the availability of the Fact Extraction and VERification dataset (FEVER) (Thorne et al., 2018). This dataset contains claims that are supported or refuted by specific evidence from Wikipedia articles. Prior to the work in (Samarinas et al., 2020), fact-checking solutions have relied on sparse passage retrieval, followed by a claim verification (entailment classification) model (Nie et al., 2019). Other approaches used the mentions of entities in a claim and/or basic entity linking to retrieve documents and a machine learning model such as logistic regression or an enhanced sequential inference model to decide whether an article most likely contains the evidence (Yoneda et al.; Chen et al., 2017; Hanselowski et al., 2018).

However, retrieval based on sparse representations and exact keyword matching can be rather restrictive for various queries. This restriction can be mitigated by dense representations using BERT-based language models (Devlin et al., 2019). The works in (Lee et al., 2019; Karpukhin et al., 2020; Xiong et al., 2020; Chang et al., 2020) have successfully used such models and its variants for passage retrieval in open-domain question answering. The results can be further improved using passage re-ranking with cross-attention BERT-based models (Nogueira et al., 2019). The work in (Samarinas et al., 2020) is the first to propose a dense model to retrieve passages for fact-checking.

Apart from passage retrieval, sentence selection is also a critical task in fact-checking. These evidence sentences provide an explanation why a claim has been assessed to be credible or not. Recent works have proposed a BERT-based model for extracting relevant evidence sentences from multi-sentence passages (Atanasova et al., 2020). The authors observe that joint training on veracity prediction and explanation generation performs better than training separate models. The work in (Stammbach and Ash, 2020) investigates how the few-shot learning capabilities of the GPT-3 model (Brown et al., 2020) can be used for generating fact-checking explanations.

## 3 The Quin+ System

The automated claim verification task can be defined as follows: given a textual claim $c$ and a corpus $D = \{d_1, d_2, ..., d_n\}$, where every passage $d$ is comprised of sentences $s_j$, $1 \leq j \leq k$, a system will return a set of evidence sentences $\hat{S} \subset \bigcup d_i$ and a label $\hat{y} \in$ {probably true, probably false, inconclusive}.

We have developed an automated fact-checking system, called Quin+, that verifies a given claim in three stages: passage retrieval from a corpus, sentence selection and entailment classification as shown in Figure 2. The label is determined as follows: we first perform entailment classification on the set of evidence sentences. When the number of retrieved evidence sentences that entail or contradict the claim is low, we label the claim as "inconclusive". If the number of evidence sentences that support the claim exceeds the number of sentences that refute the claim, we assign the label "probably true". Otherwise, we assign the label "probably false".

### 3.1 Passage Retrieval

The passage retrieval model in Quin+ is based on a *dense* retrieval model called QR-BERT (Samarinas et al., 2020). This model is based on BERT and creates dense vectors for passages by calculating their average token embedding. The relevance of a passage $d$ to a claim $c$ is then given by their dot product:

$$r(c, d) = \phi(c)^T \phi(d) \quad (1)$$

Dot product search can run efficiently using an approximate nearest neighbors index implemented using the FAISS library (Johnson et al., 2019). QR-BERT maximizes the sampled softmax loss:

$$L_\theta = \sum_{(c,d) \in D_b^+} r_\theta(c, d) - log(\cdot \sum_{d_i \in D_b} e^{r_\theta(c, d_i)}) \quad (2)$$

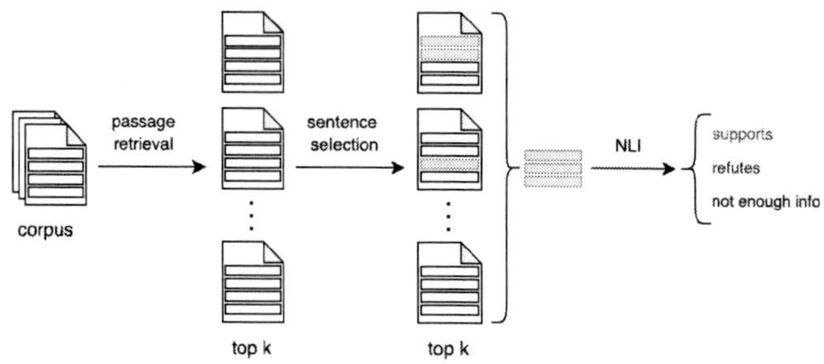


Figure 2: Three stages of claim verification in Quin+.

where $D_b$ is the set of passages in a training batch $b$, $D_b^+$ is the set of positive claim-passage pairs in the batch $b$, and $\theta$ represents the parameters of the BERT model.

The work in (Samarinas et al., 2020) introduced the Factual-NLI dataset that extends the FEVER dataset (Thorne et al., 2018) with more diverse synthetic examples derived from question answering datasets. There are 359,190 new entailed claims with evidence and additional contradicted claims from a rule-based approach. To ensure robustness, we compile a new large-scale *noisy* version of Factual-NLI called Factual-NLI+[1]. This dataset includes all the 5 million Wikipedia passages in the FEVER dataset. We add 'noise' passages as follows. For every claim $c$ in the FEVER dataset, we retrieve the top 30 web results from the Bing search engine and keep passages with the highest BM25 score that are classified as neutral by the entailment model. For claims generated from MSMARCO queries (Nguyen et al., 2016), we include the irrelevant passages that are found in the MSMARCO dataset for those queries. This results in 418,650 additional passages. The new dataset reflects better the nature of a large-scale corpus that would be used by real-world fact-checking system. We trained a dense retrieval model using this extended dataset.

The Quin+ system utilizes a hybrid model that combines the results from the dense retrieval model described above and BM25 sparse retrieval to obtain the final list of retrieved passages. For efficient sparse retrieval, we used the Rust-based Tantivy full text search engine[2].

### 3.2 Sentence Selection

We propose and experiment with two sentence selection methods: an embedding-based selection and context-aware sentence selection method.

The embedding-based selection method relies on the dense representations learned by the dense passage retrieval model QR-BERT. For a given claim $c$, we select the sentences $s_i$ from a given passage $d = \{s_1, s_2, ..., s_k\}$ whose relevance score $r(c, s_i)$ is greater than some threshold $\lambda$ which is set experimentally.

The context-aware sentence selection method uses a BERT-based sequence labeling model. The input of the model is the concatenation of the tokenized claim $C = \{C_1, C_2, ..., C_k\}$, the special [SEP] token and the tokenized evidence passage $E = \{E_1, E_2, ..., E_m\}$ (see Figure 3). For the output of the model, we adopt the BIO tagging format so that all the irrelevant tokens are classified as *O*, the first token of an evidence sentence classified as *B* evidence and the rest tokens of an evidence sentence as *I* evidence. We trained a model based on RoBERTa-large (Liu et al., 2019), minimizing the cross-entropy loss:

$$L_\theta = -\sum_{i=1}^{N}\sum_{j=1}^{l_i} log(p_\theta(y_j^i)) \quad (3)$$

where $N$ is the number of examples in the training batch, $l_i$ the number of non-padding tokens of the $i^{th}$ example, and $p_\theta(y_j^i)$ is the estimated softmax probability of the correct label for the $j^{th}$ token of the $i^{th}$ example. We trained this model on Factual-NLI with batch size 64, Adam optimizer and initial learning rate $5 \times 10^{-5}$ until convergence.

### 3.3 Entailment Classification

Natural Language Inference (NLI), also known as textual entailment classification, is the task of detecting whether a hypothesis statement is entailed by a premise passage. It is essentially a text classification problem, where the input is a

[1]https://archive.org/details/factual-nli

[2]https://github.com/tantivy-search/tantivy

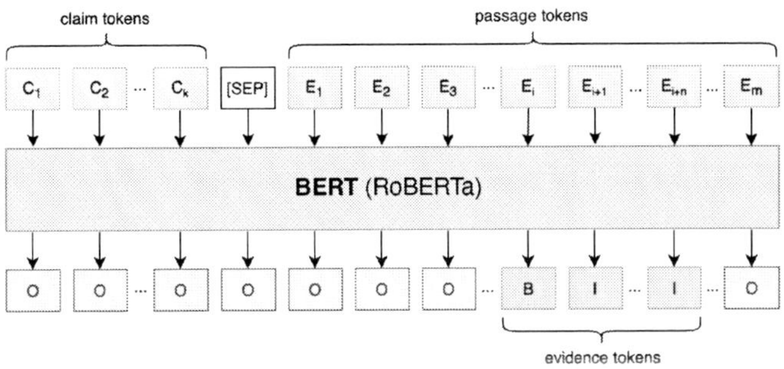


Figure 3: Sequence labeling model for evidence selection from a passage for a given claim.

pair of premise-hypothesis $(P, H)$ and the output a label $y \in$ {entailment, contradiction, neutral}. An NLI model is often a core component of many automated fact-checking systems. Datasets like the Stanford Natural Language Inference corpus (SNLI) (Bowman et al., 2015), Multi-Genre Natural Language Inference corpus (Multi-NLI) (Williams et al., 2018) and Adversarial-NLI (Nie et al., 2020) have facilitated the development of models for this task.

Even though pre-trained NLI models seem to perform well on the two popular NLI datasets (SNLI and Multi-NLI), they are not as effective in a real-world setting. This is possibly due to the bias in these two datasets, which has a negative effect in the generalization ability of the trained models (Poliak et al., 2018). Further, these datasets are comprised of short single-sentence premises. As a result, models trained on these datasets usually do not perform well on noisy real-world data involving multiple sentences. These issues have led to the development of additional more challenging datasets such as Adversarial NLI (Nie et al., 2020).

Our Quin+ system utilizes an NLI model based on RoBERTa-large with a linear transformation of the [CLS] token embedding (Devlin et al., 2019):

$$o = softmax(W \cdot \mathrm{BERT}_{[\mathrm{CLS}]}([P; H]) + a) \quad (4)$$

where $P; H$ is the concatenation of the premise with the hypothesis, $W_{3\times1024}$ is a linear transformation matrix, and $a_{3\times1}$ is the bias. We trained the entailment model by minimizing the cross-entropy loss on the concatenation of the three popular NLI datasets (SNLI, Multi-NLI and Adversarial-NLI) with batch size 64, Adam optimizer and initial learning rate $5 \times 10^{-5}$ until convergence.

## 4 Performance of Quin+

We evaluate the three individual components of Quin+ (retrieval, sentence selection and entailment classification) and finally perform an end-to-end evaluation using various configurations.

Table 1 gives the recall@k and Mean Reciprocal Rank (MRR@100) of the passage retrieval models on FEVER and Factual-NLI+. We also compare the performance on a noisy extension of the FEVER dataset where additional passages from the Bing search engine are included as 'noise' passages. We see that when noise passages are added to the FEVER dataset, the gap between the hybrid passage retrieval model in Quin+ and sparse retrieval widens. This demonstrates the limitations of using sparse retrieval, and why it is crucial to have a dense retrieval model to surface relevant passages from a noisy corpus. Overall, the hybrid passage retrieval model in Quin+ gives the best performance compared to BM25 and the dense retrieval model.

(a) FEVER Dataset

| Model | R@5 | R@10 | R@20 | R@100 | MRR |
|---|---|---|---|---|---|
| BM25 | 50.53 | 58.92 | 67.93 | 82.93 | 0.381 |
| Dense | 65.47 | 69.61 | 72.51 | 75.71 | 0.535 |
| Hybrid | **71.71** | **78.60** | **83.65** | **91.09** | **0.556** |

(b) FEVER with noise passages

| Model | R@5 | R@10 | R@20 | R@100 | MRR |
|---|---|---|---|---|---|
| BM25 | 35.17 | 44.18 | 53.89 | 73.95 | 0.2649 |
| Dense | 54.10 | 62.13 | 68.09 | 75.24 | 0.4053 |
| Hybrid | **54.89** | **64.61** | **73.33** | **86.11** | **0.4074** |

(c) Factual-NLI+ Dataset

| Model | R@5 | R@10 | R@20 | R@100 | MRR |
|---|---|---|---|---|---|
| BM25 | 45.02 | 53.20 | 61.56 | 77.96 | 0.347 |
| Dense | 59.66 | 67.09 | 72.23 | 78.52 | 0.461 |
| Hybrid | **61.29** | **70.03** | **77.51** | **87.90** | **0.465** |

Table 1: Performance of passage retrieval models.

(a) Factual-NLI Dataset

| Model | Precision | Recall | F1 |
|---|---|---|---|
| Baseline | 67.74 | 91.87 | 77.98 |
| Sequence labeling | **94.78** | **92.11** | **93.43** |
| Embedding-based | 66.12 | 90.29 | 76.34 |

(b) SciFact Dataset

| Model | Precision | Recall | F1 |
|---|---|---|---|
| Baseline | 62.21 | 71.54 | 66.55 |
| Sequence labeling | **69.38** | 68.45 | **68.91** |
| Embedding-based | 43.30 | **92.36** | 58.96 |

Table 2: Performance of sentence selection methods.

Table 2 shows the token-level precision, recall and F1 score of the proposed sentence selection methods on the Factual-NLI dataset and a domain-specific (medical) claim verification dataset, SciFact (Wadden et al., 2020). We also compare the performance to a baseline sentence-level NLI approach, where we perform entailment classification (using the model described in Section 3.3) on each sentence of a passage and select the non-neutral sentences as evidence. We observe that the sequence labeling model gives the highest precision, recall and F1 score when tested on the Factual-NLI dataset. Further, the precision is significantly higher than the other methods.

On the other hand, for the SciFact dataset, we see that sequence labeling method remains the top performer in terms of precision and F1 score after fine-tuning, although its recall is lower than the embedding-based method. This shows that sequence labeling model is able to mitigate the high false positive rate observed with the embedding-based selection method by taking into account the surrounding context.

The Factual-NLI+ dataset contains claims with passages that either support or refute the claims with some sentences highlighted as ground truth specific evidence. Table 3 shows the performance of the entailment model to classify the input evidence as supporting or refuting the claims. The input evidence can be in the form of the whole passage, ground truth evidence sentences, or sentences selected by our sequence labeling model. We observe that the entailment classification model performs poorly when whole passages are passed as input evidence. However, when the specific sentences are passed as input, the precision, recall, and F1 measures improve. The reason is that our entailment classification model is trained mostly on short premises. As a result, it does better on sentence-level evidence compared to the longer passages.

(a) Supporting evidence

| Input | Precision | Recall | F1 |
|---|---|---|---|
| Whole passages | 63.40 | 53.93 | 58.28 |
| Highlighted ground truth | 82.15 | 60.05 | 69.38 |
| Selected sentences | 74.40 | 56.68 | 64.34 |

(b) Refuting evidence

| Input | Precision | Recall | F1 |
|---|---|---|---|
| Whole passages | 33.95 | 40.65 | 37.00 |
| Highlighted ground truth | 77.54 | 89.32 | 83.02 |
| Selected sentences | 75.27 | 81.96 | 78.47 |

Table 3: Performance of entailment classification model on different forms of input evidence.

| Passage retrieval | Sentence selection | F1 |
|---|---|---|
| BM25, k=5 | Embedding-based | 52.76 |
| BM25, k=20 | Embedding-based | 47.65 |
| BM25, k=5 | Sequence labeling | 49.65 |
| Dense, k=5 | Embedding-based | 49.03 |
| Dense, k=5 | Sequence labeling | 52.83 |
| **Dense, k=50** | **Sequence labeling** | **58.22** |
| Hybrid, k=6 | Embedding-based | 50.29 |
| **Hybrid, k=6** | **Sequence labeling** | **57.24** |
| Hybrid, k=50 | Sequence labeling | 52.60 |

Table 4: End-to-end claim verification on Factual-NLI+ for different configurations.

Finally, we carry out an end-to-end evaluation of our fact-checking system on Factual-NLI+ using various configurations of top-$k$ passage retrieval (BM25, dense, hybrid, for various values of $k \in [5, 100]$) and evidence selection approaches (embdedding-based and sequence labeling). Table 4 shows the macro-average F1 score for the three classes (supporting, refuting, neutral) for some of the tested configurations. We see that dense or hybrid retrieval with evidence selection using the proposed sequence labeling model gives the best results. Even though hybrid retrieval seems to lead to slightly worse performance, it requires much fewer passages (6 instead of 50) and makes the system more efficient.

## 5 System Demonstration

We have created a demo for verifying open-domain claims using the top 20 results from a web search engine. For a given claim, Quin+ returns relevant text passages with highlighted sentences. The passages are grouped into two sets, supporting and refuting. It computes a veracity rating based on the number of supporting and refuting evidence. It returns "probably true" if there

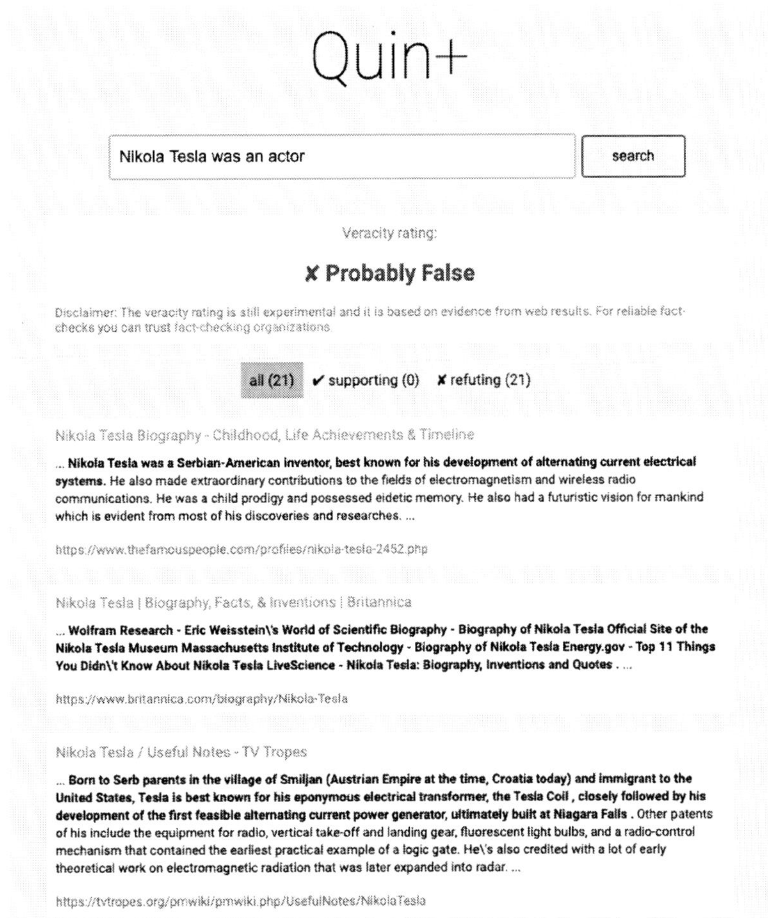


Figure 4: The Quin+ system returning relevant evidence and a veracity rating for a claim.

are more supporting evidence, otherwise it returns "probably false". When the number of retrieved evidence is low, it returns "inconclusive". Figure 4 shows a screen dump of the system with a claim that has been assessed to be probably false based on the overwhelming number of refuting sentence evidence (21 refute versus 0 support). Quin+ can also be used on a large-scale corpus.

## 6 Conclusion & Future Work

In this work, we have presented a three-stage fact-checking system. We have demonstrated how a dense retrieval model can lead to higher recall when retrieving passages for fact-checking. We have also proposed two schemes to select relevant sentences: an embedding-based approach and a sequence labeling model to improve the claim verification accuracy. Quin+ gave promising results in our extended Factual-NLI+ corpus, and is also able to verify open-domain claims using web search results. The source code of our system is publicly available[3].

Even though our system is able to verify multiple open-domain claims successfully, it has some limitations. Quin+ is not able to effectively verify multi-hop claims that require the retrieval of multiple pieces of evidence. For the verification of multi-hop claims, methodologies inspired by multi-hop question answering could be utilized.

For the future development of large-scale fact-checking systems we believe that a new benchmark needs to be introduced. The currently available datasets, including Factual-NLI+, are not suitable for evaluating the verification of claims using multiple sources.

[3]https://github.com/algoprog/Quin

## References


Pepa Atanasova, Jakob Grue Simonsen, Christina Lioma, and Isabelle Augenstein. 2020. Generating fact checking explanations. In *Proceedings of the Annual Meeting of the Association for Computational Linguistics (ACL).*

Samuel R. Bowman, Gabor Angeli, Christopher Potts, and Christopher D. Manning. 2015. A large annotated corpus for learning natural language inference. In *Proceedings of the Conference on Empirical Methods in Natural Language Processing (EMNLP).*

Tom B Brown, Benjamin Mann, Nick Ryder, Melanie Subbiah, Jared Kaplan, Prafulla Dhariwal, Arvind Neelakantan, Pranav Shyam, Girish Sastry, Amanda Askell, et al. 2020. Language models are few-shot learners. *arXiv preprint arXiv:2005.14165.*

Wei-Cheng Chang, Felix X. Yu, Yin-Wen Chang, Yiming Yang, and Sanjiv Kumar. 2020. Pre-training tasks for embedding-based large-scale retrieval. In *International Conference on Learning Representations (ICLR).*

Qian Chen, Xiaodan Zhu, Zhen-Hua Ling, Si Wei, Hui Jiang, and Diana Inkpen. 2017. Enhanced lstm for natural language inference. In *Proceedings of the Annual Meeting of the Association for Computational Linguistics (ACL).*

J. Devlin, Ming-Wei Chang, Kenton Lee, and Kristina Toutanova. 2019. Bert: Pre-training of deep bidirectional transformers for language understanding. In *NAACL-HLT.*

Andreas Hanselowski, Hao Zhang, Zile Li, Daniil Sorokin, Benjamin Schiller, Claudia Schulz, and Iryna Gurevych. 2018. Ukp-athene: Multi-sentence textual entailment for claim verification. In *Proceedings of the First Workshop on Fact Extraction and VERification (FEVER)*, pages 103–108.

Jeff Johnson, Matthijs Douze, and Hervé Jégou. 2019. Billion-scale similarity search with gpus. *IEEE Transactions on Big Data.*

Vladimir Karpukhin, Barlas Oğuz, Sewon Min, Ledell Wu, Sergey Edunov, Danqi Chen, and Wen-tau Yih. 2020. Dense passage retrieval for open-domain question answering. *Proceedings of the Annual Meeting of the Association for Computational Linguistics (ACL).*

Tom Kwiatkowski, Jennimaria Palomaki, Olivia Redfield, Michael Collins, Ankur Parikh, Chris Alberti, Danielle Epstein, Illia Polosukhin, Matthew Kelcey, Jacob Devlin, Kenton Lee, Kristina N. Toutanova, Llion Jones, Ming-Wei Chang, Andrew Dai, Jakob Uszkoreit, Quoc Le, and Slav Petrov. 2019. Natural questions: a benchmark for question answering research. *Transactions of the Association of Computational Linguistics.*

Kenton Lee, Ming-Wei Chang, and Kristina Toutanova. 2019. Latent retrieval for weakly supervised open domain question answering. In *Proceedings of the Annual Meeting of the Association for Computational Linguistics (ACL).*

Yinhan Liu, Myle Ott, Naman Goyal, Jingfei Du, Mandar Joshi, Danqi Chen, Omer Levy, Mike Lewis, Luke Zettlemoyer, and Veselin Stoyanov. 2019. Roberta: A robustly optimized bert pretraining approach. *arXiv preprint arXiv:1907.11692.*

Tri Nguyen, Mir Rosenberg, Xia Song, Jianfeng Gao, Saurabh Tiwary, Rangan Majumder, and Li Deng. 2016. MS MARCO: A human generated machine reading comprehension dataset. *CoRR*, abs/1611.09268.

Yixin Nie, Haonan Chen, and Mohit Bansal. 2019. Combining fact extraction and verification with neural semantic matching networks. In *Proceedings of the AAAI Conference on Artificial Intelligence.*

Yixin Nie, Adina Williams, Emily Dinan, Mohit Bansal, Jason Weston, and Douwe Kiela. 2020. Adversarial NLI: A new benchmark for natural language understanding. In *Proceedings of the Annual Meeting of the Association for Computational Linguistics (ACL).*

Rodrigo Nogueira, W. Yang, Kyunghyun Cho, and Jimmy Lin. 2019. Multi-stage document ranking with bert. *ArXiv*, abs/1910.14424.

Adam Poliak, Jason Naradowsky, Aparajita Haldar, Rachel Rudinger, and Benjamin Van Durme. 2018. Hypothesis only baselines in natural language inference. In *Proceedings of the Joint Conference on Lexical and Computational Semantics.*

Chris Samarinas, Wynne Hsu, and Mong Li Lee. 2020. Latent retrieval for large-scale fact-checking and question answering with nli training. In *IEEE International Conference on Tools with Artificial Intelligence (ICTAI).*

Dominik Stammbach and Elliott Ash. 2020. e-fever: Explanations and summaries for automated fact checking. In *Proceedings of the Conference on Truth and Trust Online (TTO).*

James Thorne, Andreas Vlachos, Christos Christodoulopoulos, and Arpit Mittal. 2018. FEVER: a large-scale dataset for fact extraction and verification. In *NAACL-HLT.*

David Wadden, Kyle Lo, Lucy Lu Wang, Shanchuan Lin, Madeleine van Zuylen, Arman Cohan, and Hannaneh Hajishirzi. 2020. Fact or fiction: Verifying scientific claims. *Proceedings of the Conference on Empirical Methods in Natural Language Processing (EMNLP).*

Adina Williams, Nikita Nangia, and Samuel Bowman. 2018. A broad-coverage challenge corpus for sentence understanding through inference. In *Proceedings of the Conference of the North American Chapter of the Association for Computational Linguistics (NAACL-HLT)*.

Lee Xiong, Chenyan Xiong, Ye Li, Kwok-Fung Tang, Jialin Liu, Paul Bennett, Junaid Ahmed, and Arnold Overwijk. 2020. Approximate nearest neighbor negative contrastive learning for dense text retrieval. *arXiv preprint arXiv:2007.00808*.

Takuma Yoneda, Jeff Mitchell, Johannes Welbl, Pontus Stenetorp, and Sebastian Riedel. Ucl machine reading group: Four factor framework for fact finding (hexaf). In *Proceedings of the First Workshop on Fact Extraction and VERification (FEVER)*.

# Interactive Plot Manipulation using Natural Language

**Yihan Wang, Yutong Shao** and **Ndapa Nakashole**
Computer Science and Engineering
University of California, San Diego
La Jolla, CA 92093
yiw007@ucsd.edu,{yshao, nnakashole}@eng.ucsd.edu

## Abstract

We present an interactive Plotting Agent, a system that enables users to directly manipulate plots using natural language instructions within an interactive programming environment. The Plotting Agent maps language to plot updates. We formulate this problem as a slot-based task-oriented dialog problem, which we tackle with a sequence-to-sequence model. This plotting model while accurate in most cases, still makes errors, therefore, the system allows a feedback mode, wherein the user is presented with a top-k list of plots, among which the user can pick the desired one. From this kind of feedback, we can then, in principle, continuously learn and improve the system. Given that plotting is widely used across data-driven fields, we believe our demonstration will be of interest to both practitioners such as data scientists broadly defined, and researchers interested in natural language interfaces.

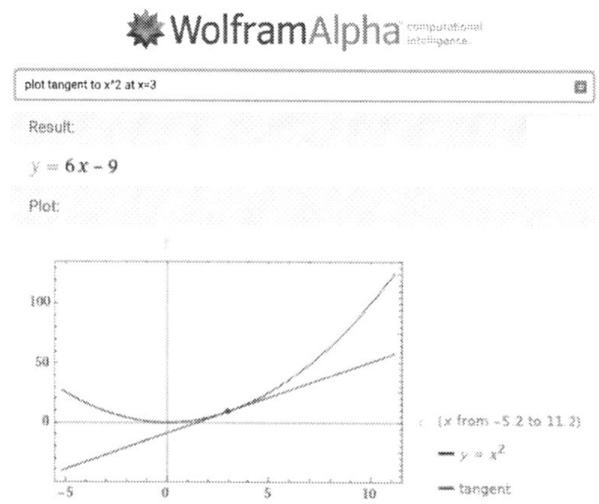


Figure 1: Related to our work is a commercial product, *wolframalpha.com*, which enables users to describe the *function* they would like to visualize, in this example, "plot the tangent to $x^2$ at $x = 3$". However, the user has no control over the plotting details. In contrast, we allow the user to use natural language to manipulate the plot.

## 1 Introduction

**Motivation.** Data can be utilized to improve outcomes in many sectors, for example healthcare, education, and business. However, when presented in its raw form, it is difficult to derive insights from data. Plotting is a simple yet powerful technique for making raw data readable, and exposing trends. Data plotting libraries, such as `matplotlib`, provide operations that enable users to visualize their data. Such libraries support functionalities at different levels, from high-level, "change the X-axis from $linear$ to $log$ scale"; to low-level "color this screen pixel red". However, novice users and expert programmers alike may still find it time-consuming to create plots of interest using these libraries. We therefore propose an interactive natural language interface (NLI) for plotting, that enables users to manipulate plots using natural language. The interactive aspect allows complex plotting needs to be specified and refined in multiple steps.

**Prior Work.** Previous work on NLIs for plotting focused on enabling users to describe the *data* or the *mathematical function* of interest. In contrast, our approach enables users to directly manipulate a *plot.* NLIs that focus on describing the *data* have emerged from Human Computer Interaction (HCI) and related areas (Gao et al., 2015; Setlur et al., 2016; Srinivasan and Stasko, 2017; Yu and Silva, 2019; Sun et al., 2010). Thus the user poses queries such as: "Show me medals for hockey and skating by country." or "Is there a seasonal trend for bike usage?". The system retrieves the relevant data, performs simple data analysis, and produces a visualization. Commercial products such as *wolframalpha.com* enable users to describe the *function*



*Proceedings of NAACL-HLT 2021: Demonstrations*, pages 92–98
June 6–11, 2021. 

they would like to visualize. By leveraging knowledge of functions and mathematical procedures, the system produces meaningful results for queries such as: "plot the tangent to $x^2$ at $x = 3$", as shown in Figure 1.

Our work is also related to conversational image editing (Manuvinakurike et al., 2018b,a), which yields results for queries such as "Can you fix the glare on my dog's eyes". The key difference is that our images are plots, and thus the manipulations are different from those involving photo images.

**Contributions and Demonstration Overview.** We present a Plotting Agent for `matplotlib`, a popular Python plotting library. The Plotting Agent provides users with various ways to manipulate plots in an interactive programming environment, Jupyter Notebooks.

Our demonstration allows the user to explore the Plotting Agent in various ways: **(1)** Upload custom data and interactively manipulating plots on the uploaded data. **(2)** Work in a feedback mode, wherein the user is presented with a top-k list of plots, among which the user can pick the desired one. **(3)** Operate in batch mode where a series of instructions written in a file are loaded and executed sequentially by the system.

**(4)** Have a personalized experience, wherein the system learns user preferences, enabling them to perform certain tasks faster.

In addition to the novel functionality, we also build on ChartDialogs (Shao and Nakashole, 2020) to enable other functionality.

**(5)** Generate synthetic data using on pre-defined random data samplers from ChartDialogs , and interactively manipulate plots on the synthetic data.

**(6)** Load existing dialogs from the ChartDialogs dataset to observe the plot updates for each dialog turn. The user can make further changes to the plot.

In all the above cases, the user can use different lexical items and paraphrases to express the same intent. This demonstrates the advantage of our neural-based model compared to a system that might rely on rules and dictionaries. We have publicly released a live demo system[1] and a screencast showcasing the demo[2].

[1] https://github.com/Bawerlacher/Plotting_Agent

[2] https://youtu.be/a2D77JI7RVs

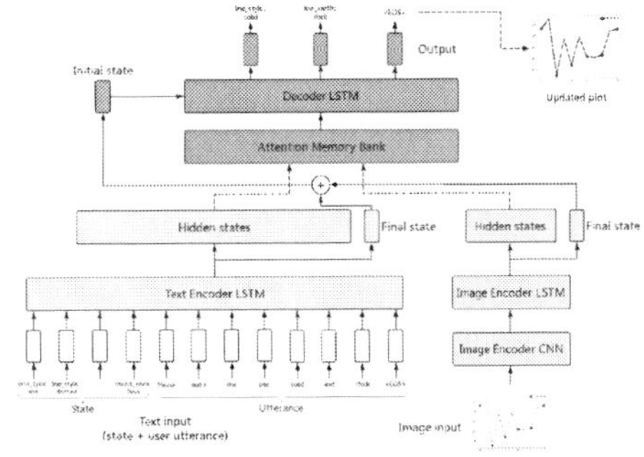


Figure 2: Model for mapping natural language inputs to plot updates.

## 2 The Plotting Agent System

We cast the Plotting Agent problem as a slot-based, task-oriented dialog problem. Each slot represents a plot property, such as *line color, marker size,* etc. Each plot type has different slots. However, some slots are shared and apply to multiple plot types. Consider the slot "X-axis scale", which takes the value "X-axis scale = log", from the request "change the x-axis scale from linear to log". Since the "X-axis scale" slot applies to the x-axis, it is applicable to any plot type with an x-axis, such as line chart, bar plot, or contour plot. Given the slots and their values, we can generate a plot image using `matplotlib`.

**Model for Predicting Updates.** Our model, depicted in Figure 2, for mapping natural language to plot slots and slot values builds on the sequence-to-sequence (seq2seq) framework (Sutskever et al., 2014; Vinyals and Le, 2015). The input to the model is a natural language request, a text-representation of the current plot, the dialog history, formulated as a set of slot-value pairs, and the current plot image[3]. The dialog history consists of prior utterances, which are concatenated and treated as the dialog history.

The model outputs the update needed to go from the current set of slot-value pairs to the new slot-value pairs. For example, if the current slot-value pairs are {*('line_width': 'thin'), ('line_color': 'black')*} and the new slot-value pairs are {*('line_width': 'thin'), ('line_color': 'red')*} after the user utterance that says "change the line color to red", then the corresponding update

[3] Our experiments showed that incorporating the plot image did not improve model performance, thus plot images are omitted in the model we present in this demo.

| Top-k | Exact Match |
|---|---|
| @1 | 0.61 |
| @2 | 0.71 |
| @3 | 0.74 |
| @5 | 0.78 |
| @10 | 0.78 |
| @20 | 0.79 |

Table 1: Top-K exact match (EM) performance

($\Delta$) that the model must predict is $\{$(*'line_color': 'red'*)$\}$. We output decoder predicts $\Delta$ as a sequence.

**Implementation and Training.** The system is implemented in Python and makes use of the Pytorch library for neural network models. We use a 2-layer Bi-LSTM for the text encoder and another 2-layer Bi-LSTM for the decoder. We trained the model on the ChartDialogs (Shao and Nakashole, 2020) dataset which contains dialogs about plots. The dataset was generated by pairs of humans, where one human plays the role of the user, and the other plays the role of the agent. We use the train/dev/test split provided.

## 3 System Evaluation

**Exact Match.** Table 1 shows performance in terms of *Exact Match (EM)*, a measure that reflects how accurate the model is at updating the plots exactly as requested by the natural language utterance. We show performance at top-k ranked predictions, which are obtained from Beam Search. Beam Search keeps track of the $k$ most probable partial predictions (hypotheses). A hypothesis has a score which is its log probability. As can be seen in Table 1, At $k = 1$, EM accuracy is only 61%. However, for $k = 5$, EM accuracy is much higher at 78%. We leveraged this fact, in the feedback mode of our demo, where instead of just showing the highest ranked plot, the top-k plots are shown, and the user selects the one that best corresponds to the intent of their utterance.

**Runtime.** Response times to utterances are on average 0.3s on modest hardware. This is much faster than using a Web search engine which might involve time consuming tasks such as refining the query multiple times and visiting community tutorial websites such as StackOverflow to search for similar questions that might have been answered.

## 4 Plotting Agent Demonstration

Interactive functionality is showcased within Jupyter Notebooks.

**Data points and Instructions.** To generate a plot, the following information must specified: the data points to plot and the slot-value assignments of the plot. The system therefore consists of two parts: data loading and instruction delivery. For data loading, the system supports uploading data files or randomly sampling synthetic data using our pre-defined data samplers. For instruction delivery, the system allows users to instruct the agent interactively or to load instructions from existing dialogs from our ChartDialogs dataset. In both cases, the natural language input and the current plot slot-value assignments (states) are fed into the back-end model to predict a set of slot-value pairs for plot updates.

### 4.1 Data Specification

**Custom Data Upload.** The user can upload a csv file containing the data to visualize. For "clean" csv files in which all the columns are to be plotted, e.g. using the first column for X axis, the second column for Y axis, etc., the data can be automatically loaded without further specifications. For more complex csv files, we also provide a more detailed and customized data specification process. If data loading is successful, the system will output "Data loaded from the csv file!" Figure 3 shows an example of uploading a csv file containing the cumulative COVID-19 daily confirmed cases in the United States until mid June 2020.

**Synthetic Data.** The user can generate data using our pre-defined data samplers for each plot type. After the user specifies the plot type, the system will invoke the corresponding data sampler to generate a group of data suitable for the given plot type. An example of plotting with generated data is shown in the Figure 4.

### 4.2 Plotting Intent Specification

**Interactive Mode.** The user can send instructions directly to the system using the interactive interface. There are two kinds of instructions: special commands and plot descriptions. Special commands are instructions that refer to specific system functionalities, such as "undo", "redo", "load csv", "plot", etc. For example, "plot" will show the plot

```
>: line chart
>: load csv
Please tell me the path of your csv file: time_series_covid19_confirmed_us_sim
plified.csv
Data loaded from the csv file!
```

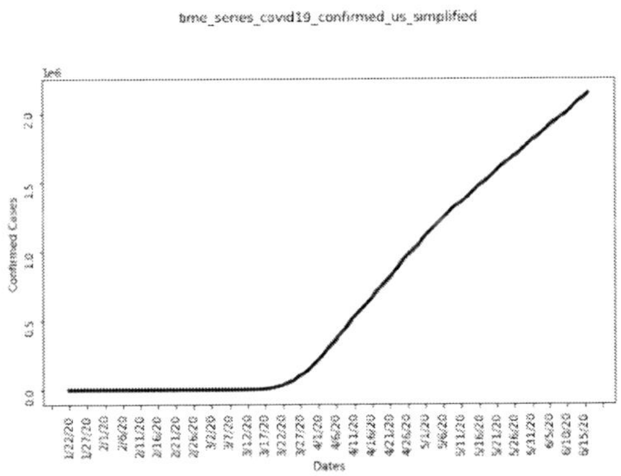


```
>: color the line red, increase the font size and show gridlines
```

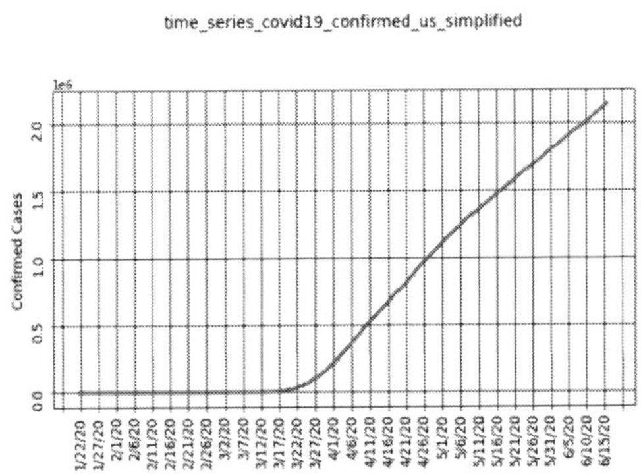


Figure 3: Custom Data with Interactive Instruction Delivery: upload of COVID-19 USA confirmed cases, and one instance of an interactive plot update.

image and "undo" will undo the last change to the plot.

Any other natural language instructions that are not in the special commands set are treated as plot descriptions. A plot description will be fed to the back-end model to predict the plot update, as described above. An example of interactive instruction delivery is shown on the COVID-19 US daily confirmed cases data, in Figure 3.

**Prior Dialog Mode.** In order to get a quick idea of how the system works, the user can choose to load a random dialog from the ChartDialogs dataset. The system treats the utterances in each dialog turn as a natural language instruction and predicts the plot update. The user chooses if they wish to view the updated plot step-by-step or only to obtain the final resulting plot. After the system processes all the dialog turns and shows the result, the user can continue to make further changes to the plot properties through natural language instructions. An example of this use case is shown in Figure 5.

**Batch Mode.** The user can also write their own instructions in a file and send the file path to the system. The system will read the instructions one by one, update the plot correspondingly, and show the final result.

### 4.3 User Feedback

Our plotting model while accurate inmost cases, still makes errors, therefore, the system allows a feedback mode, wherein the user is presented with a top-k list of plots, among which the user can pick the desired one. The top-k results are obtained from Beam search used in our decoder in the architecture shown in 2. At each step of the decoder, Beam

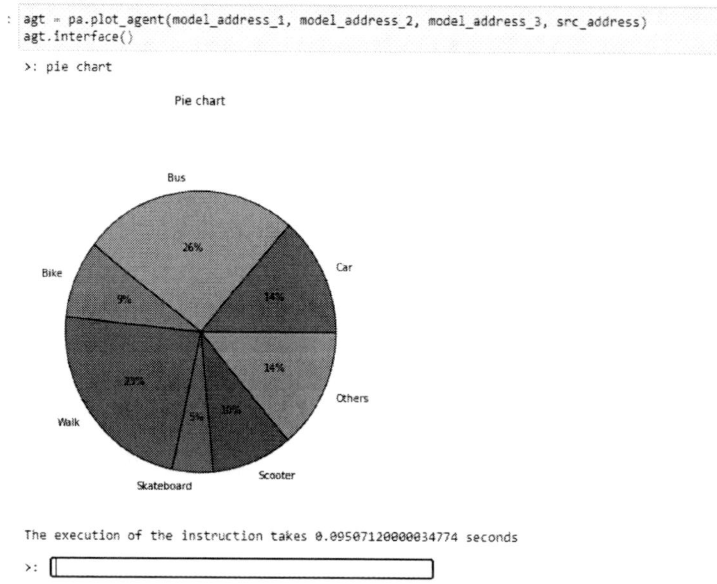


Figure 4: Synthetic Data: example plot of type pie chart generated from our pre-defined data samplers.

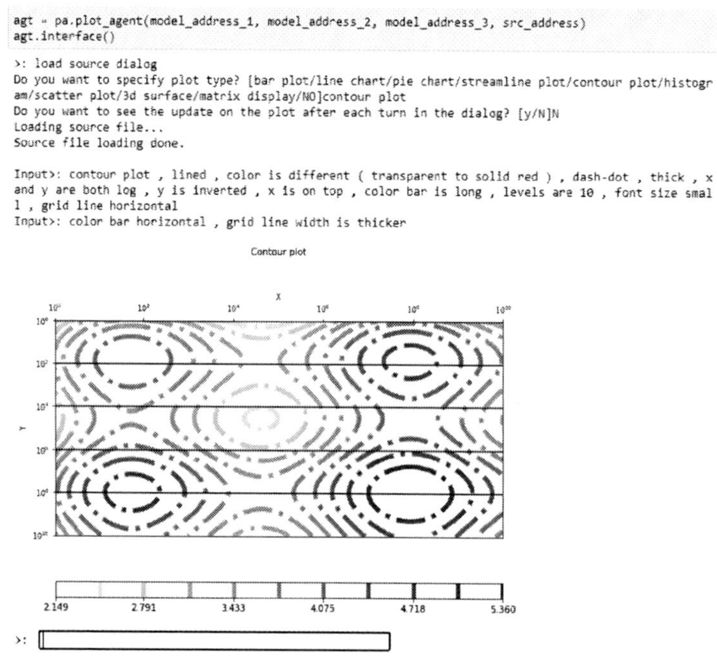


Figure 5: Prior Dialog: an example of executing a dialog taken from the ChartDialogs dataset.

search keeps track of the $k$ most probable partial results, where $k$ is the beam size. As shown in Table 1, the higher the value of $k$, the more likely it is to have the correct plot presented to the user. From this kind of feedback, we can then, in principle, continuously learn and improve the system

### 4.4 Personalization

A useful system should be personalized to an individual user. It should adapt to their unique goals, context, or nuances of the types of visualizations they like to produce. For example, the user can request "change the font size to 16, and the line

```
agt = pa.plot_agent(model_address_1, model_address_2, model_address_3, src_address)
agt.interface()

>: load dialog
What's the path of the dialog file? dialog.txt
Input>: line graph ; solid orange ; round magenta markers ; polarized ; name trajectory
Input>: grid lines both vert and horiz , gray dash/dots ; large markers
Input>: marker interval 3
Input>: larger interval
Input>: grid line width -thin
```

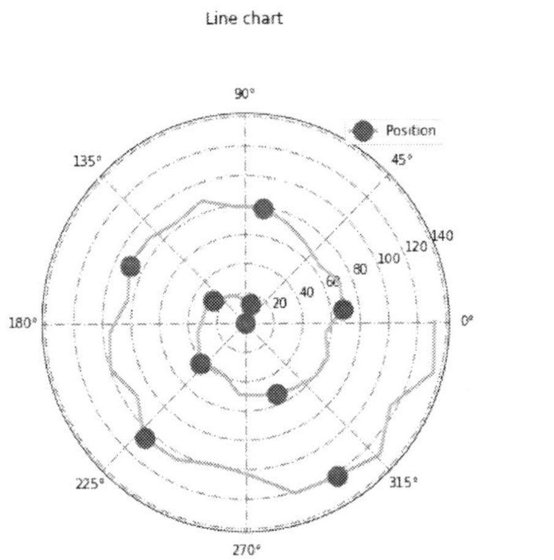


```
The execution of the instruction takes 1.1804163000001608 seconds
>:
```

Figure 6: Batch mode: an example of loading instructions from a file.

color to cyan". But in a personalized form, the user may simply state "fix the fonts and colors", in which case the agent relies on the user prior preferences. Our demo includes a basic notion of personalization.

## 5 Discussion

**Primitive to Complex Plotting Intents.** Interactions with our current plotting agent are limited to manipulating slots preprogrammed by the API developers of the plotting library, such as changing the font size or the color of a particular item. Our goal is to expand commands understood by the plotting agent to include complex slots beyond the API slots (e.g., by teaching the system to "shift the legend so that it does not obscure important parts of the plot" or "make the text labels of a scatter plot to be aesthatically optimized", or "change colors to be colorblind friendly".).

**Limitations of Slot-based Representation.** The current demo system also has limitations due to design choices guided by the goal of task simplification. For example, some plot components that are not easily formulated as slot-value pairs are not supported. This is a research question of representation, while the slot based representation facilitates quick learning, more expressive representations can resolve these limitations.

## 6 Conclusion

In this paper, we introduced an interactive Plotting Agent for mapping natural language instructions to plot updates. The system supports various modes for specifying data and instructing the agent to update plots. Our interactive Plotting Agent is under further research and development to improve its language understanding capabilities, and to expand its functionality to other plot components, and plotting libraries. We hope the demo will be of interest to both practitioners such as data scientists, and researchers interested in natural language interfaces.

## References

Tong Gao, Mira Dontcheva, Eytan Adar, Zhicheng Liu, and Karrie G Karahalios. 2015. Datatone: Managing ambiguity in natural language interfaces for data visualization. In *Proceedings of the 28th Annual*

*ACM Symposium on User Interface Software & Technology*, pages 489–500. ACM.

Ramesh Manuvinakurike, Trung Bui, Walter Chang, and Kallirroi Georgila. 2018a. Conversational image editing: Incremental intent identification in a new dialogue task. In *Proceedings of the 19th Annual SIGdial Meeting on Discourse and Dialogue*, pages 284–295.

Ramesh R. Manuvinakurike, Jacqueline Brixey, Trung Bui, Walter Chang, Doo Soon Kim, Ron Artstein, and Kallirroi Georgila. 2018b. Edit me: A corpus and a framework for understanding natural language image editing. In *Proceedings of the Eleventh International Conference on Language Resources and Evaluation, LREC 2018, Miyazaki, Japan, May 7-12, 2018.*

Vidya Setlur, Sarah E Battersby, Melanie Tory, Rich Gossweiler, and Angel X Chang. 2016. Eviza: A natural language interface for visual analysis. In *Proceedings of the 29th Annual Symposium on User Interface Software and Technology*, pages 365–377. ACM.

Yutong Shao and Ndapa Nakashole. 2020. ChartDialogs: Plotting from Natural Language Instructions. In *ACL*. Association for Computational Linguistics.

Arjun Srinivasan and John Stasko. 2017. Natural language interfaces for data analysis with visualization: Considering what has and could be asked. In *Proceedings of the Eurographics/IEEE VGTC Conference on Visualization: Short Papers*, pages 55–59. Eurographics Association.

Yiwen Sun, Jason Leigh, Andrew E. Johnson, and Sangyoon Lee. 2010. Articulate: A semi-automated model for translating natural language queries into meaningful visualizations. In *Smart Graphics*.

Ilya Sutskever, Oriol Vinyals, and Quoc V Le. 2014. Sequence to sequence learning with neural networks. In *Advances in neural information processing systems*, pages 3104–3112.

Oriol Vinyals and Quoc Le. 2015. A neural conversational model. *arXiv preprint arXiv:1506.05869*.

Bowen Yu and Cláudio T Silva. 2019. Flowsense: A natural language interface for visual data exploration within a dataflow system. *IEEE transactions on visualization and computer graphics*.

# ActiveAnno: General-Purpose Document-Level Annotation Tool with Active Learning Integration

**Max Wiechmann, Seid Muhie Yimam, Chris Biemann**
Language Technology group, Universität Hamburg, Germany
mail@maxwiechmann.de
{yimam,biemann}@informatik.uni-hamburg.de

## Abstract

ACTIVEANNO is a novel annotation tool focused on document-level annotation tasks developed both for industry and research settings. It is designed to be a general-purpose tool with a wide variety of use cases. It features a modern and responsive web UI for creating annotation projects, conducting annotations, adjudicating disagreements, and analyzing annotation results. ACTIVEANNO embeds a highly configurable and interactive user interface. The tool also integrates a RESTful API that enables integration into other software systems, including an API for machine learning integration. ACTIVEANNO is built with extensible design and easy deployment in mind, all to enable users to perform annotation tasks with high efficiency and high-quality annotation results.

## 1 Introduction

Lots of tasks in industry and research require the manual annotation of a potentially large number of documents, for example in content analysis research or supervised machine learning. Existing tools, such as WebAnno (Yimam et al., 2013), allow for span-level annotation tasks like NER and POS tagging. As Neves and Ševa (2019) point out in their review of annotation tools, document-level annotation is a feature missing in most existing tools. ACTIVEANNO is a novel tool created to fill this void. It was created based on five central design goals: 1) Creating annotations of high quality in an efficient manner (**quality**). 2) Support a broad range of use cases without any additional programming effort (**configurability**). 3) provide a good user experience through a modern, responsive web application to be more attractive than specialized prototypes of annotation software (**responsiveness**). 4) Publicly available to extend for future use cases (**open source**). 5) Provide APIs for easy integration into existing software systems and easy deployment to minimize the upfront effort for using ACTIVEANNO (**extensibility**). Through this approach, we would like to put forward ACTIVEANNO as a candidate for the default option for document-level annotation in industry and research.

## 2 Related Work

Neves and Ševa (2019) conducted an extensive review of 78 annotation tools in total, comparing 15 which met their minimum criteria. Five of those tools support document-level annotations: MAT, MyMiner, tagtog, prodigy, and LightTag. MAT[1] (Bayer, 2015) is designed for what they call the "tag-a-little, learn-a-little (TALLAL) loop" to incrementally build up an annotation corpus, but it is only a research prototype and is not ready to be used in production. MyMiner (Salgado et al., 2012) is an online-only tool without a login or user system. Its main purpose is to classify scientific documents in a biomedical context, which is limited in scope and configuration options and not suitable as a general-purpose tool. The tools tagtog[2] (Cejuela et al., 2014), prodigy[3], and LightTag [4] are all feature-rich and support some form of machine learning integration, but are commercial with either no free version or a free version with limited functionality. This makes these tools less accessible for projects with limited monetary resources.

According to Neves and Ševa (2019), WebAnno is the best tool fitting their criteria, however, it does not support document-level annotations. WebAnno is a notable example of an annotation tool which is open-source, widely used and feature-rich. We adapt some of the functionalities into our ACTIVEANNO document-level annotation tool.

[1] http://mat-annotation.sourceforge.net/
[2] https://www.tagtog.net/
[3] https://prodi.gy/
[4] https://www.lighttag.io/



*Proceedings of NAACL-HLT 2021: Demonstrations*, pages 99–105
June 6–11, 2021. ©2021 Association for Computational Linguistics

Another annotation tool with limited support for document-level annotations is Doccano[5] (Nakayama et al., 2018), though it is not mentioned in the evaluation of Neves and Ševa. The open-source tool currently supports three distinct annotation tasks: text classification, sequence labeling, and sequence to sequence tasks.

## 3 Architecture of ACTIVEANNO

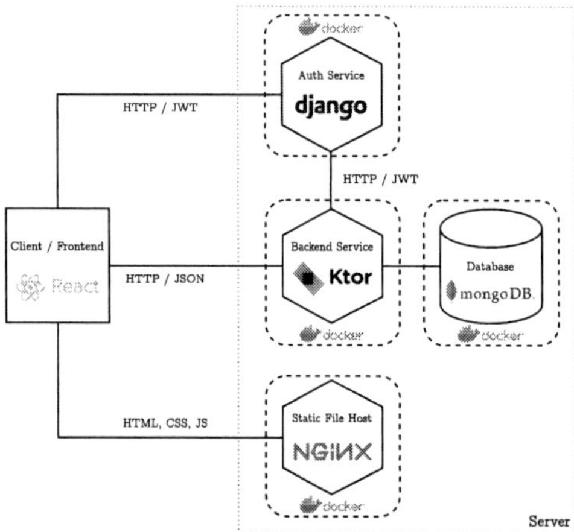


Figure 1: The system architecture of ACTIVEANNO.

ACTIVEANNO is a client-server application as depicted in Figure 1. On the server-side, the main component is a backend service written in Kotlin using the Ktor framework. The backend service is stateless, allowing for horizontal scaling for advanced performance requirements. It is connected to a MongoDB database that is used to store documents and annotation projects. There is also a minimal authentication service written in Python and Django, which provides a simple user management UI and the authentication mechanism of JSON web token (JWT) that is used by the frontend and backend components. The authentication part is extracted into this service such that it can be exchanged for an existing or a more sophisticated user management service, if needed. Finally, the frontend is written in Javascript using React, which is served by an Nginx. All backend components are deployed as Docker containers through existing Docker Compose files. The communication between the client and server is done through HTTP requests via the JSON format.

**ACTIVEANNO documents**: A *document* is represented as a JSON object with a textual field containing the *document text*, for example the text of a tweet or the abstract of a paper. It can optionally have additional fields with *meta data* that can also be displayed to support the annotation process. Metadata examples include the date and username for tweets, the authors and publication for papers, or the number of stars for an app review. Documents are imported through the UI or API in the JSON format and can be annotated for multiple annotation projects afterward.

**Annotation definitions**: Annotation projects define an annotation task for one or more *annotation definitions*. An annotation definition describes the required type and form of the annotation that should be created. The typical example is a tag set annotation, where a document is annotated with one or more predefined tags such as *spam/no spam*, the *sentiment* or the *topic* classification of a text. ACTIVEANNO also supports boolean, number, and text annotations with various configuration options such as minimum/maximum values.

**Annotations and annotation results**: For an annotation project, every document can be annotated for every annotation definition of the annotation project, resulting in one annotation per definition. Together, all annotations for a document from a single annotator form an *annotation result*. Every annotation of the annotation result has a different value structure depending on the type of annotation definition. Additionally, every annotation value can have an associated probability used in the context of automatically generated annotations through the machine learning integration.

**Annotation process**: ACTIVEANNO has a two-step annotation process. In the first step, annotation results are created. They can be created either by annotators, annotation generators (see Section 4), or they can be imported through the import annotation API (see Section 3.2). After every new annotation result, a finalization policy logic is applied to the document and its annotation results. This logic decides if the annotation process is finished for the document and a final annotation result exists. The logic is dependent on the project configuration. The manager of a project can set the number of annotators per document. This is the minimum number of different annotators required for each document until any additional logic is applied. For example, if the number of annotators is set to three, every document will be shown to the annotators until the document is annotated by three users. One annotator can only annotate every

[5] `https://github.com/doccano/doccano`

document once. After three annotation results were created, the finalization policy is applied. Depending on the selected policy, the annotation results will either be exported individually, or the annotations are merged based on a majority calculation. If no majority is observed, the document can either be presented to an additional annotator until a majority is reached, or to a curator to decide on the correct annotation result. It is also possible to always require a curator for use cases with very high-quality requirements.

### 3.1 Web UI

ACTIVEANNO is a modern single-page and responsive web application. It is fully localized, currently supporting English and German. By using a persistent web database, the application state and therefore the created annotations are automatically persisted. A configurable role system allows for the proper authorization of endpoints. The two main roles are *user* and *manager*. A user can be an annotator or curator, a manager has the ability to edit projects as well as analyze the results. There are also the roles *producer* and *consumer* to allow the protection of the API of ACTIVEANNO. Producers are allowed to push data into ACTIVEANNO while consumers are allowed to read the annotation results through the export API. Though slightly modified, the user roles were inspired by WebAnno's user management.

The web interface is composed of the login page, a landing page and pages for annotation, curation, and management. On the landing page, users can see their areas of responsibility and switch the application language. The manage page is for users with the manager role, allowing them to create and edit projects, annotation definitions, annotation generators, and the analysis of annotation results.

Figure 2 (left) shows the UI (Mobile version) for editing the basic properties of an example project, like name and description. Besides, the other parts of the *manage project* component allow configuring the filter condition to query documents from the database, defining which documents are relevant for the project, as well as the field and order of how to sort documents when querying the database. Both the filter and sort inputs translate to MongoDB queries. Additionally, the manager of the project can configure the annotation schema, which is composed of the annotation definitions for the project. From this and the *document mapping* step, where the manager defines which part

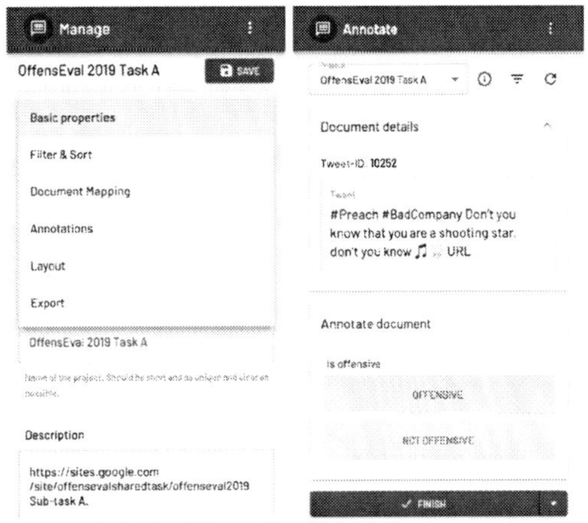


Figure 2: Left: Edit project UI, Right: Annotation UI

(as JSON keys) of the imported documents are relevant for the project, the layout for the annotation task gets generated. The generated layout shows all the metadata, the document text, and the annotation definitions with default input types. Figure 2 (right) shows an example layout for the annotation view (Mobile version). Lastly, the manager can configure how annotation results are able to be exported: either through the REST API, webhooks, or both (see Section 3.2 for the details of the API).

Figure 3 shows the annotation UI for a more complex annotation task, in this case on a desktop layout, with six annotation definitions of different types, including Yes/No annotations, single and multi-select tag set annotations (some displayed as buttons, some as drop-down inputs), a number annotation visualized as a slider, an extensible tag input (where annotators select tags created by other annotators or create their own), and an open text input. After a manager created a project and documents are imported into ACTIVEANNO, the annotators can annotate the documents according to the project set up in the annotate subarea. Depending on how the project is set up, the annotated documents might be checked and possibly overwritten by a curator in the curation subarea. In the curation UI, curators can see all previously created annotation results. Curators have the authority to decide if an annotation created by annotators is correct, to provide a final verdict.

After annotation results are finalized, they can be analyzed by the project managers. In addition to accuracy, the inter-annotator agreement (simple agreement with exact matching), as well as the annotation duration is generated as charts in the UI. There is also a table of individual documents, showing the correctness of every annotator and

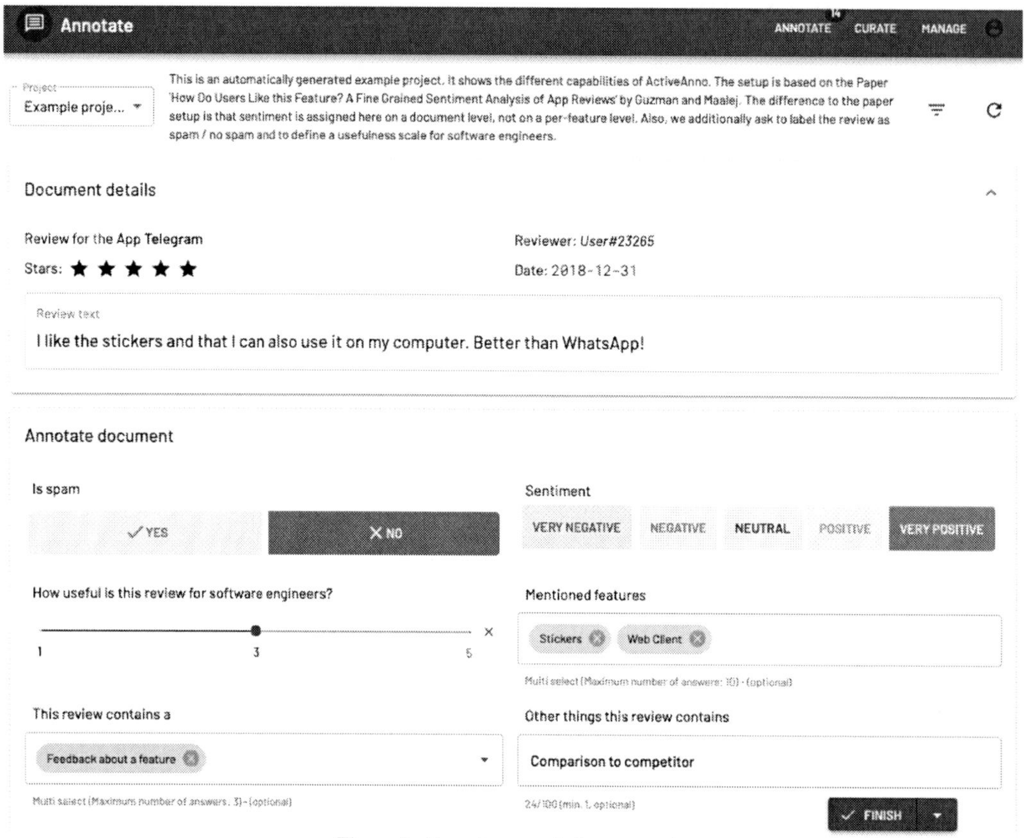


Figure 3: Complex annotation example

their agreements for the document. The UI has filter inputs to restrict analyzed annotation results by *annotator*, *date* range, or more fine-grained filters.

### 3.2 Import and Export API

ACTIVEANNO provides multiple API endpoints to enable automated document processing and integration into larger software systems. The import document endpoint allows uploading any JSON document or an array of JSON documents. Documents will be assigned a unique ID, stored in the MongoDB, and the IDs will be returned to the caller, so they can be used for future reference, e.g. to export from ACTIVEANNO. The ID is also used to import externally created annotations into ACTIVEANNO for a specific project and document. Imported annotations can be treated like any other created annotation in the agreement process, or as pre-annotations for human annotators.

Through a single export endpoint, annotation results can be exported into other applications for further processing. Through the GET parameters, it can be filtered which annotation results will be exported, for example, based on the timestamp or document IDs. As an alternative to the export API, every project can define a list of webhook URLs, which will be called once a document is finalized.

## 4 Annotation Generator

The integration of machine learning and the ability to automate parts of the annotation process are important to increase the efficiency of the annotation process. The basis for automation is the ability to automatically generate annotations without a human annotator. To generalize the concept and to allow for other ways to automatically create annotations, ACTIVEANNO defines the concept of **annotation generators**. An annotation generator is anything capable of creating an annotation for a specific annotation definition given a document and potentially other previously generated annotations for other annotation definitions. An annotation generator is defined through an abstract class with a `generateAnnotation` method that every generator needs to implement. Every annotation generator also has to define what is the input to use for the actual annotation generation. It can be any field from the original document, or it can be any value from another created annotation that is part of the same annotation schema, allowing for chaining or conditional connecting of annotation generators.

Currently, ACTIVEANNO has three inbuilt annotation generator implementations. The first one automatically detects the language of the generator input using the language detection library Lingua[6]. This is an example of a statistical and rule-based annotation generator as compared to a machine learning-based generator. The second annotation generator allows calling an external machine learning service through a URL for tag set annotation definitions, which will take the response and map it into the tag set options from the annotation definition. This can be used when an already trained machine learning model exists. The model would have to be wrapped by an HTTP API to comply with the API definition of ACTIVEANNO for this annotation generator. The API is structured to allow for multiple documents to be predicted at once. The third annotation generator is similar to the second one, but also supports automatically updating the external machine learning model by sending an HTTP request with the training data in the body. To support this functionality, the concept of an **updatable** annotation generator exists. This kind of generator extends the base annotation generator, but also requires its subclasses to implement an `update` method, where the training data will be aggregated and used to train or update the annotation generator. For this, updatable annotation generators also need to define a threshold when to start the training and when to update an existing model. For example, the first model should be trained after 100 training samples are generated, and then it should be updated for every 25 new training samples. An updatable annotation generator is versioned with a version number and an update state, to ensure the version is actually usable to generate new annotations.

Annotation generators can be triggered to generate/re-generate annotations for a project when appropriate, and they can be triggered to update themselves if they are updatable annotation generators and enough new training data is created to allow for a model update.

[6]https://github.com/pemistahl/lingua

### 4.1 Machine Learning Integration

Once the annotation definitions and annotation generators are created and an external machine learning service is provided in compliance with the API of ACTIVEANNO, the last step is to integrate the machine learning module into ACTIVEANNO. For this, a project has multiple configuration possibilities. The first one is the handling policy of generated annotation results. This policy can be set to use the generated annotations as pre-annotations for the annotators. In this case, the annotations will fill out or select the inputs in the annotation panel, giving the annotators the option to just accept the automatically generated annotations, which can reduce the annotation effort. Alternatively, it is possible to set the generator results to be treated equally to an annotator where the results will be included in the finalization logic.

The other important configuration is the sorting policy. With regards to generated annotations, it is possible to overwrite the normal sorting order of the project. This can be set to prefer documents with existing generated annotation results. In this case, if only a subset of documents has received their generated annotations at a point in time, they will be preferred in sending them to the annotators. This means that if pre-annotations are available, they will always be shown before documents without pre-annotations. The second option is to set the sorting to *active learning with uncertainty sampling*. This is used to support active learning, where the documents with the lowest confidence values associated with the generated annotations will be preferred (see Section 4.2). We also have an alternative approach for machine learning integration that relies on the import annotation API. Imported annotations can be used instead of internally generated annotations. For updating a machine learning model, the REST API or webhook support can be used to get the final annotation results. In this case, all the logic regarding how to extract the data and when to update the model need to be implemented externally. This approach might be more useful if the required logic or process is vastly different from the inbuilt annotation generator concept.

### 4.2 Active Learning Process

When there is no existing training data for an annotation definition, ACTIVEANNO can be used to build up a training dataset based on active learning with uncertainty sampling. The training data can either be imported once at the start of the active learning process or continuously, for example, if the data comes from a news crawler or the Twitter API. The active learning process would work as follows: First, when there is no training data, documents get manually labeled by an annotator. If a threshold of the annotation generator is reached, triggering the update of the generator will result in the training data being aggregated and sent to the external service. Triggering the *generate annotations* functionality (from the UI or via an API) will result in the newly trained generator model that will create predictions for all remaining documents in the project. Afterwards, when the *projects sorting* policy is set to active learning, the confidence values from the newly generated annotations will be used to sort the documents for annotation, those with the lowest confidence being presented first.

This process can then be repeated until the machine learning model is performing well enough to be partly or fully automated. This is similar to the "tag-a-little, learn-a-little loop" from MAT (Bayer, 2015). If combined with enabling pre-annotations, it is also very similar to the annotation process of RapTAT (Gobbel et al., 2014). To partly automate the process, the project has to be configured to treat the generator as an annotator and to require one annotator per document. Additionally, the configuration option of the finalize condition has to be set to some confidence threshold, for example, 80%. Then, only the documents with a confidence value below 80% will be required to be annotated further. To fully automate the process, the *finalize* condition should be set to *always* to accept the annotations automatically without additional conditions.

## 5 Use Cases

ACTIVEANNO is designed to be applicable in many settings, including industry and research; for small projects on a local machine and large projects with many users on the internet; for use cases with and without machine learning components. We have used ACTIVEANNO in two industry setups, to test its suitability to collect real-world annotation requirements. It was directly deployed on the service cluster of a company, configured via environment variables, and connected to the existing system via its API with some small additions to the existing software system to get documents into ACTIVEANNO. For the machine learning integration, a small Python service wrapping fastText (Bojanowski et al., 2017) models was employed. The data for the experiments were around 250,000 German textual feedback comments obtained from a retail context.

The first experiment was set up to analyze the effects of pre-annotations on annotation quality and efficiency. Three annotation definitions, namely spam/not spam, sentiment, and topic classification were annotated by two annotators employed at the company. One condition was provided without pre-annotations while the other one was provided with pre-annotations for all three annotation definitions. The annotations were created by pre-trained machine learning models that are integrated into ACTIVEANNO through the annotation generator and the machine learning-related APIs. Through the *analyze* functionality of ACTIVEANNO, the inter-annotator agreement (IAA), annotation duration, and the accuracy of annotators as well as the machine learning models are compared inside the tool. The final result showed a 28% faster annotation without any change of annotation accuracy or annotator agreement for the condition with pre-annotations. ACTIVEANNO enabled the research project itself while the annotators reported a positive user experience using the tool. They reported that the tool is easy, fast, and convenient to use.

The second experiment explored the incremental and active learning capabilities of ACTIVEANNO. A new annotation definition about the utility (or information quality) of a comment with three classes (useful, okay, spam) was created as it was a new business requirement to create such annotations for further aggregation and processing. During the experiment, multiple new machine learning models for different conditions were created by annotating new comments inside ACTIVEANNO and triggering the automatic annotation generator updating and re-annotating functionality. By additionally enabling pre-annotations, annotators had reduced effort for selecting the correct annotation option, once the model had an acceptable level of accuracy. Selecting the best performing model based on the experiment conditions then enables and improves the regular annotation process of the company. Once the model performs well enough while being used for pre-annotation, it could then be used to partly automate the process as described by simply editing the project configuration.

Finally, as both experiments were conducted on non-publicly available data, we created another example project based on the OffensEval 2019 shared task (Zampieri et al., 2019), specifically sub-task A. The task is directly integrated as an example project in ACTIVEANNO, including a machine learning component that can be updated through ACTIVEANNO. Please refer to the demo[7] and video[8] to see this use case in action.

## 6 Conclusion and Future Work

ACTIVEANNO supports several mechanisms to produce high-quality annotations with an efficient annotation process, like the number of annotators per document, a configurable agreement logic, curators, machine learning integration through annotation generators, pre-annotations, treating annotation generators as annotators, partly or fully automating annotations, and updating annotation generators with incremental or active learning. A fully configurable annotation schema with annotation definition types like tag sets, numbers and texts, a modern and responsive web UI, as well as flexible user management allows ACTIVEANNO to be adaptable to many different kinds of annotation process requirements. The RESTful API and webhooks allow for easy integration with other software components.

Future work planned is to add in-app feedback between curators and annotators for improving annotator performance, adding more in-built annotation generators for other types of annotation definitions, UI improvements (layout editor, better display of very long documents) and span-level annotations as well as hybrid-level annotations which can be defined either on a span or document level.

Most importantly, ACTIVEANNO was designed with extensibility and flexibility in mind. It is available as open-source software under the MIT license.

## References

Samuel Bayer. 2015. MITRE Annotation Toolkit (MAT). http://mat-annotation.sourceforge.net/.

Piotr Bojanowski, Edouard Grave, Armand Joulin, and Tomas Mikolov. 2017. Enriching word vectors with subword information. *Transactions of the Association for Computational Linguistics*, 5:135–146.

Juan Miguel Cejuela, Peter McQuilton, Laura Ponting, Steven J. Marygold, Raymund Stefancsik, Gillian H. Millburn, Burkhard Rost, and the FlyBase Consortium. 2014. tagtog: interactive and text-mining-assisted annotation of gene mentions in PLOS full-text articles. *Database*, 2014. Bau033.

Glenn T. Gobbel, Jennifer Garvin, Ruth Reeves, Robert M. Cronin, Julia Heavirland, Jenifer Williams, Allison Weaver, Shrimalini Jayaramaraja, Dario Giuse, Theodore Speroff, Steven H. Brown, Hua Xu, and Michael E. Matheny. 2014. Assisted annotation of medical free text using RapTAT. *Journal of the American Medical Informatics Association*, 21(5):833–841.

Hiroki Nakayama, Takahiro Kubo, Junya Kamura, Yasufumi Taniguchi, and Xu Liang. 2018. doccano: Text annotation tool for human. Software available from https://github.com/doccano/doccano.

Mariana Neves and Jurica Ševa. 2019. An extensive review of tools for manual annotation of documents. *Briefings in Bioinformatics*, 22(1):146–163.

David Salgado, Martin Krallinger, Marc Depaule, Elodie Drula, Ashish V. Tendulkar, Florian Leitner, Alfonso Valencia, and Christophe Marcelle. 2012. MyMiner: a web application for computer-assisted biocuration and text annotation. *Bioinformatics*, 28(17):2285–2287.

Seid Muhie Yimam, Iryna Gurevych, Richard Eckart de Castilho, and Chris Biemann. 2013. WebAnno: A flexible, web-based and visually supported system for distributed annotations. In *Proceedings of the 51st Annual Meeting of the Association for Computational Linguistics: System Demonstrations*, pages 1–6, Sofia, Bulgaria.

Marcos Zampieri, Shervin Malmasi, Preslav Nakov, Sara Rosenthal, Noura Farra, and Ritesh Kumar. 2019. SemEval-2019 Task 6: Identifying and categorizing offensive language in social media (OffensEval). In *Proceedings of the 13th International Workshop on Semantic Evaluation*, pages 75–86, Minneapolis, Minnesota, USA.

[7] Source code, documentation and the link to the demo can be found here: https://github.com/MaxMello/ActiveAnno

[8] Demo Video: https://youtu.be/ryCi4XeReDg

# TextEssence: A Tool for Interactive Analysis of Semantic Shifts Between Corpora

**Denis Newman-Griffis**[1] **Venkatesh Sivaraman**[2] **Adam Perer**[2]
**Eric Fosler-Lussier**[3] **Harry Hochheiser**[1,4]
[1]Department of Biomedical Informatics, University of Pittsburgh
[2]Human-Computer Interaction Institute, Carnegie Mellon University
[3]Department of Computer Science and Engineering, The Ohio State University
[4]Intelligent Systems Program, University of Pittsburgh
dnewmangriffis@pitt.edu vsivaram@andrew.cmu.edu

## Abstract

Embeddings of words and concepts capture syntactic and semantic regularities of language; however, they have seen limited use as tools to study characteristics of different corpora and how they relate to one another. We introduce TextEssence, an interactive system designed to enable comparative analysis of corpora using embeddings. TextEssence includes visual, neighbor-based, and similarity-based modes of embedding analysis in a lightweight, web-based interface. We further propose a new measure of embedding confidence based on nearest neighborhood overlap, to assist in identifying high-quality embeddings for corpus analysis. A case study on COVID-19 scientific literature illustrates the utility of the system. TextEssence can be found at `https://textessence.github.io`.

## 1 Introduction

Distributional representations of language, such as word and concept embeddings, provide powerful input features for NLP models in part because of their correlation with syntactic and semantic regularities in language use (Boleda, 2020). However, the use of embeddings as a lens to investigate those regularities, and what they reveal about different text corpora, has been fairly limited. Prior work using embeddings to study language shifts, such as the use of diachronic embeddings to measure semantic change in specific words over time (Hamilton et al., 2016; Schlechtweg et al., 2020), has focused primarily on quantitative measurement of change, rather than an interactive exploration of its qualitative aspects. On the other hand, prior work on interactive analysis of text collections has focused on analyzing individual corpora, rather than facilitating inter-corpus analysis (Liu et al., 2012; Weiss, 2014; Liu et al., 2019).

We introduce TextEssence, a novel tool that combines the strengths of these prior lines of research by enabling interactive comparative analysis of different text corpora. TextEssence provides a multi-view web interface for users to explore the properties of and differences between multiple text corpora, all leveraging the statistical correlations captured by distributional embeddings. TextEssence can be used both for categorical analysis (i.e., comparing text of different genres or provenance) and diachronic analysis (i.e., investigating the change in a particular type of text over time).

Our paper makes the following contributions:

- We present TextEssence, a lightweight tool implemented in Python and the Svelte JavaScript framework, for interactive qualitative analysis of word and concept embeddings.
- We introduce a novel measure of *embedding confidence* to mitigate embedding instability and quantify the reliability of individual embedding results.
- We report on a case study using TextEssence to investigate diachronic shifts in the scientific literature related to COVID-19, and demonstrate that TextEssence captures meaningful month-to-month shifts in scientific discourse.

The remainder of the paper is organized as follows. §2 lays out the conceptual background behind TextEssence and its utility as a corpus analysis tool. In §3 and §4, we describe the nearest-neighbor analysis and user interface built into TextEssence. §5 describes our case study on scientific literature related to COVID-19, and §6 highlights key directions for future research.

## 2 Background

Computational analysis of text corpora can act as a lens into the social and cultural context in which those corpora were produced (Nguyen et al., 2020). Diachronic word embeddings have been shown to reflect important context behind the corpora they



*Proceedings of NAACL-HLT 2021: Demonstrations*, pages 106–115
June 6–11, 2021. 

are trained on, such as cultural shifts (Kulkarni et al., 2015; Hamilton et al., 2016; Garg et al., 2018), world events (Kutuzov et al., 2018), and changes in scientific and professional practice (Vylomova et al., 2019). However, these analyses have proceeded independently of work on interactive tools for exploring embeddings, which are typically limited to visual projections (Zhordaniya et al.; Warmerdam et al., 2020). TextEssence combines these directions into a single general-purpose tool for interactively studying differences between any set of corpora, whether categorical or diachronic.

### 2.1 From words to domain concepts

When corpora of interest are drawn from specialized domains, such as medicine, it is often necessary to shift analysis from individual words to *domain concepts*, which serve to reify the shared knowledge that underpins discourse within these communities. Reified domain concepts may be referred to by multi-word surface forms (e.g., "Lou Gehrig's disease") and multiple distinct surface forms (e.g., "Lou Gehrig's disease" and "amyotrophic lateral sclerosis"), making them more semantically powerful but also posing distinct challenges from traditional word-level representations.

A variety of embedding algorithms have been developed for learning representations of domain concepts and real-world entities from text, including weakly-supervised methods requiring only a terminology (Newman-Griffis et al., 2018); methods using pre-trained NER models for noisy annotation (De Vine et al., 2014; Chen et al., 2020); and methods leveraging explicit annotations of concept mentions (as in Wikipedia) (Yamada et al., 2020).[1] These algorithms capture valuable patterns about concept types and relationships that can inform corpus analysis (Runge and Hovy, 2020).

TextEssence only requires pre-trained embeddings as input, so it can accommodate any embedding algorithm suiting the needs and characteristics of specific corpora (e.g. availability of annotations or knowledge graph resources). Furthermore, while the remainder of this paper primarily refers to concepts, TextEssence can easily be used for word-level embeddings in addition to concepts.

### 2.2 Why static embeddings?

Contextualized, language model-based embeddings can provide more discriminative features for NLP than static (i.e., non-contextualized) embeddings. However, static embeddings have several advantages for this comparative use case. First, they are less resource-intensive than contextualized models, and can be efficiently trained several times without pre-training to focus entirely on the characteristics of a given corpus. Second, the scope of what static embedding methods are able to capture from a given corpus has been well-established in the literature, but is an area of current investigation for contextualized models (Jawahar et al., 2019; Zhao and Bethard, 2020). Finally, the nature of contextualized representations makes them best suited for context-sensitive tasks, while static embeddings capture aggregate patterns that lend themselves to corpus-level analysis. Nevertheless, as work on qualitative and visual analysis of contextualized models grows (Hoover et al., 2020), new opportunities for comparative analysis of local contexts will provide fascinating future research.

## 3 Identifying Stable Embeddings for Analysis

While embeddings are a well-established means of capturing syntax and semantics from natural language text (Boleda, 2020), the problem of comparing multiple sets of embeddings remains an active area of research. The typical approach is to consider the nearest neighbors of specific points, consistent with the "similar items have similar representations" intuition of embeddings. This method also avoids the conceptual difficulties and low replicability of comparing embedding spaces numerically (e.g. by cosine distances) (Gonen et al., 2020). However, even nearest neighborhoods are often unstable, and vary dramatically across runs of the same embedding algorithm on the same corpus (Wendlandt et al., 2018; Antoniak and Mimno, 2018). In a setting such as our case study, the relatively small sub-corpora we use (typically less than 100 million tokens each) exacerbate this instability. Therefore, to quantify variation across embedding replicates and identify informative concepts, we introduce a measure of *embedding confidence*.[2]

We define embedding confidence as the mean overlap between the top $k$ nearest neighbors of a

[1]The significant literature on learning embeddings from knowledge graph structure is omitted here for brevity.

[2]An *embedding replicate* here refers to the embedding matrix output by running a specific embedding training algorithm on a specific corpus. Ten runs of word2vec on a given Wikipedia dump produce ten replicates; using different Wikipedia dumps would produce one replicate each of ten different sets of embeddings.

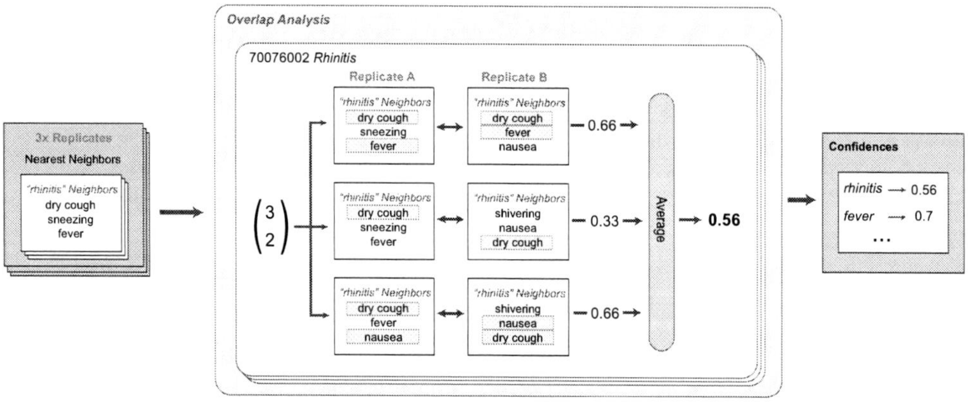


Figure 1: Illustration of embedding confidence calculation, using 3 embedding replicates. Our experiments on CORD-19 used this same process with 10 replicates.

given item between multiple embedding replicates. Formally, let $E^1 \dots E^m$ be $m$ embedding replicates trained on a given corpus, and let $k\text{NN}^i(c)$ be the set of $k$ nearest neighbors by cosine similarity of concept $c$ in replicate $E^i$. Then, the embedding confidence $EC@k$ is defined as:

$$EC@k(c, E^1 \dots E^m) = \frac{1}{m(m-1)} \sum_i^m \sum_{j \neq i} \frac{|kNN^i(c) \cap kNN^j(c)|}{k}$$

An example of this calculation is illustrated in Figure 1.

We can then define the set of *high-confidence* concepts for the given corpus as the set of all concepts with an embedding confidence above a given threshold. A higher threshold will restrict to highly-stable concepts only, but exclude the majority of embeddings. We recommend an initial threshold of 0.5, which can be configured based on observed quality of the filtered embeddings.

### 3.1 Computing aggregate nearest neighbors

After filtering for high-confidence concepts, we summarize nearest neighbors across replicates by computing *aggregate nearest neighbors*. The aggregate neighbor set of a concept $c$ is the set of high-confidence concepts with highest average cosine similarity to $c$ over the embedding replicates. More precisely, let $D^i(c)$ be the vector of pairwise similarities between concept $c$ and all concepts in the embedding vocabulary,[3] as calculated in replicate $E^i$. Then, we calculate the aggregate pairwise distance vector for $c$ as:

$$D_{Agg}(c) = \frac{1}{m} \sum_i^m D^i(c)$$

The $k$ aggregate nearest neighbors of $c$, $kNN_{Agg}(c)$, are then the $k$ concepts with lowest values in $D_{Agg}(c)$. This helps to provide a more reliable picture of the concept's nearest neighbors, while excluding concepts whose neighbor sets are uncertain.

## 4 The TextEssence Interface

The workflow for using TextEssence to compare different corpora is illustrated in Figure 2. Given the set of corpora to compare, the user (1) trains embedding replicates on each corpus; (2) identifies the high-confidence set of embeddings for each corpus; and (3) provides these as input to TextEssence. TextEssence then offers three modalities for interactively exploring their learned representations: (1) Browse, an interactive visualization of the embedding space; (2) Inspect, a detailed comparison of a given concept's neighbor sets across corpora; and (3) Compare, a tool for analyzing the pairwise relationships between two or more concepts.

### 4.1 Browse: visualizing embedding changes

The first interface presented to the user is an overview visualization of one of the embedding spaces, projected into 2-D using t-distributed Stochastic Neighbor Embedding (t-SNE) (van der Maaten and Hinton, 2008). High-confidence concepts are depicted as points in a scatter plot and may be color-coded based on pre-existing groupings; for example, in our case study (§5), we color-coded

[3]All embedding replicates trained on a given corpus will share the same vocabulary.

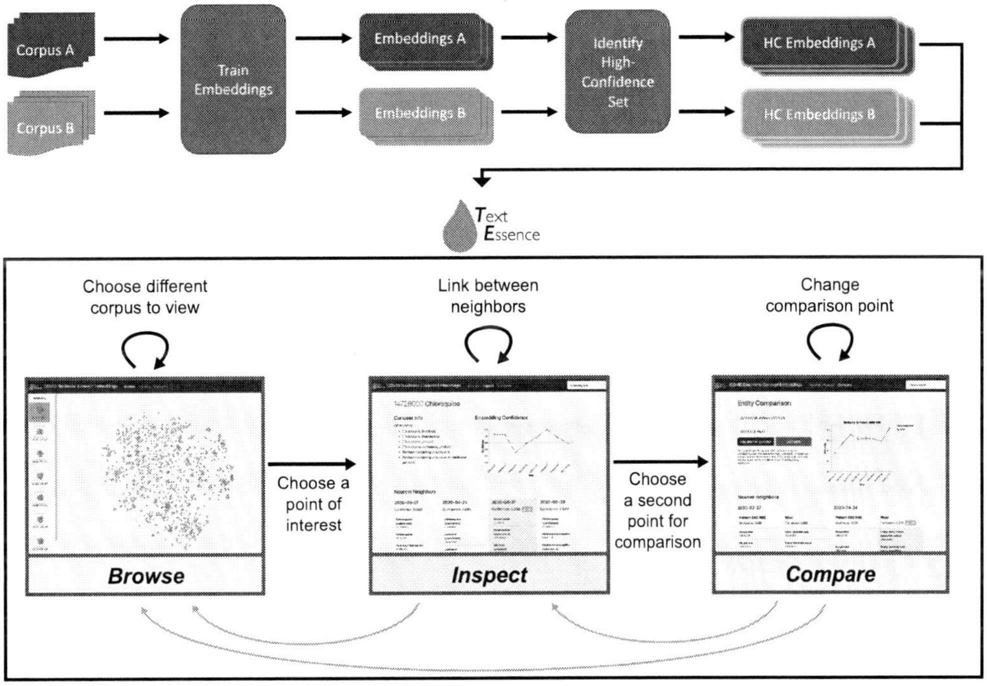


Figure 2: Workflow for comparing corpus embeddings with TextEssence. The system enables three different kinds of interactions: (1) Browse the embedding space for each corpus; (2) Inspect a single concept in each corpus; and (3) Compare two or more concepts across corpora. Each view transitions to the others using the current concept.

medical concepts based on their semantic groups in the UMLS (McCray et al., 2001), such as "Chemicals & Drugs" and "Disorders." The user can select a point to highlight its aggregated nearest neighbors in the high-dimensional space, an interaction similar to TensorFlow's Embedding Projector (Smilkov et al., 2016) that helps distinguish true neighbors from artifacts of the dimensionality reduction process.

The Browse interface also expands upon existing dimensionality reduction tools by enabling visual comparison of multiple corpora (e.g., embeddings from individual months). This is challenging because the embedding spaces are trained separately, and can therefore differ greatly in both high-dimensional and reduced representations. While previous work on comparing projected data has focused on algorithmically aligning projections (Liu et al., 2020; Chen et al., 2018) and adding new comparison-focused visualizations (Cutura et al., 2020), we chose to align the projections using a simple Procrustes transformation and enable the user to compare them using animation.

When the user hovers on a corpus thumbnail, *preview lines* are shown between the positions of each concept in the current and destination corpora. The direction of each line is disambiguated by increasing its width as the line approaches its destination. In addition, the width and opacity of each point's preview line are proportional to the fraction of the point's aggregate nearest neighbors that differ between the source and destination corpora. This serves to draw attention to the concepts that shift the most. Upon clicking the corpus thumbnail, the points smoothly follow their trajectory lines to form the destination plot. In addition, when a concept is selected, the user can opt to *center* the visualization on that point and then transition between corpora, revealing how neighboring concepts move relative to the selected one.

### 4.2 Inspect: tracking individual concept change

Once a particular concept of interest has been identified, the Inspect view presents an interactive table depicting how that concept's aggregated nearest neighbors have changed over time. This view also displays other contextualizing informa-

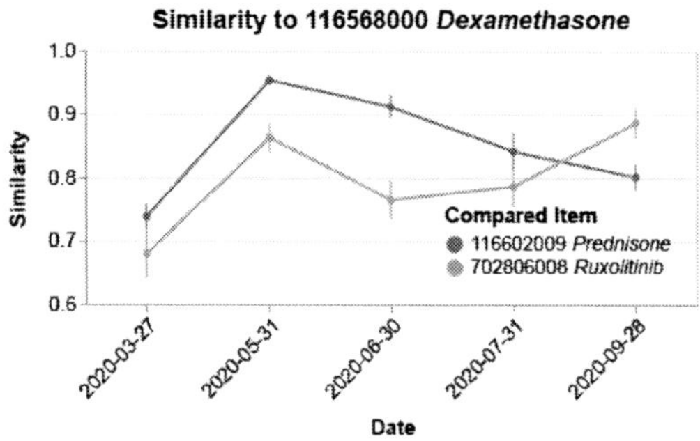


Figure 3: Similarity over time of two drugs to 116568000 *Dexamethasone* in our case study. April, August, and October are omitted as *Dexamethasone* was not high confidence for these months. Similarity values are mean over embedding replicates within each month; error bars indicate standard deviations.

| Month | Docs | Words | Entities | Hi-Conf. |
|---|---|---|---|---|
| March | 41,750 | 158M | 38,451 | 15,100 |
| April | 10,738 | 41M | 25,142 | 1,851 |
| May | 73,444 | 125M | 40,297 | 5,051 |
| June | 24,813 | 34M | 19,749 | 2,729 |
| July | 24,786 | 35M | 19,334 | 2,800 |
| August | 28,642 | 31M | 19,134 | 2,407 |
| September | 33,732 | 38M | 20,947 | 4,381 |
| October | 38,866 | 44M | 21,470 | 1,990 |

Table 1: 2020 monthly snapshots of CORD-19 dataset (documents added each month only; not cumulative). Entities denotes the number of SNOMED CT codes for which embeddings were learned; Hi-Conf. is the subset of these that had confidence above the 0.5 threshold. The high document count in March 2020 included all COVID-19 literature published prior to March 13, 2020 (beginning of CORD-19 dataset); the spike in May 2020 was due to adding arXiv and Medline as data sources for CORD-19.

tion about the concept, including its definitions (derived from the UMLS (Bodenreider, 2004) for our case study[4]), the terms used to refer to the concept (limited to SNOMED CT for our case study), and a visualization of the concept's embedding confidence over the sub-corpora analyzed. For information completeness, we display nearest neighbors from every corpus analyzed, even in corpora where the concept was not designated high-confidence (note that a concept must be high-confidence in at least one corpus to be selectable in the interface). In these cases, a warning is shown that the concept itself is not high-confidence in that corpus; the neighbors themselves are still exclusively drawn from the high-confidence set.

### 4.3 Compare: tracking pair similarity

The Compare view facilitates analysis of the changing relationship between two or more concepts across corpora (e.g. from month to month). This view displays paired nearest neighbor tables, one per corpus, showing the aggregate nearest neighbors of each of the concepts being compared. An adjacent line graph depicts the similarity between the concepts in each corpus, with one concept specified as the reference item and the others serving as comparison items (similar to Figure 3). Similarity between two concepts for a specific corpus is calculated by averaging the cosine similarity between the corresponding embeddings in each replicate.

[4]We included definitions from all English-language sources in the UMLS, as SNOMED CT includes definitions only for a small subset of concepts.

## 5 Case Study: Diachronic Change in CORD-19

The scale of global COVID-19-related research has led to an unprecedented rate of new scientific findings, including developing understanding of the complex relationships between drugs, symptoms, comorbidities, and health outcomes for COVID-19 patients. We used TextEssence to study how the contexts of medical concepts in COVID-19-related scientific literature have changed over time. Table 1 shows the number of new articles indexed in the COVID-19 Open Research Dataset (CORD-19; Wang et al. (2020a)) from its beginning in March 2020 to the end of October 2020; while additions of new sources over time led to occasional jumps in corpus volumes, all are sufficiently large for embedding training. We created disjoint sub-corpora containing the new articles indexed in CORD-19 each month for our case study.

CORD-19 monthly corpora were tokenized using ScispaCy (Neumann et al., 2019), and concept embeddings were trained using JET (Newman-Griffis et al., 2018), a weakly-supervised concept embedding method that does not require explicit corpus annotations. We used SNOMED Clinical Terms (SNOMED CT), a widely-used reference representing concepts used in clinical reporting, as our terminology for concept embedding training, using the March 2020 interim release of SNOMED CT International Edition, which included COVID-19 concepts. We trained JET embeddings using a vector dimensionality $d = 100$ and 10 iterations, to reflect the relatively small size of each corpus. We used 10 replicates per monthly corpus, and a high-confidence threshold of 0.5 for EC@5.

## 5.1 Findings

TextEssence captures a number of shifts in CORD-19 that reflect how COVID-19 science has developed over the course of the pandemic. Table 2 highlights key findings from our preliminary investigation into concepts known *a priori* to be relevant. Please note that while full nearest neighbor tables are omitted due to space limitations, they can be accessed by downloading our code and following the included guide to inspect CORD-19 results.

**44169009** *Anosmia* While associations of anosmia (loss of sense of smell) were observed early in the pandemic (e.g., Hornuss et al. (2020), posted in May 2020), it took time to begin to be utilized as a diagnostic variable (Talavera et al., 2020; Wells et al., 2020). *Anosmia*'s nearest neighbors reflect this, staying stably in the region of other otolaryngological concepts until October (when Talavera et al. (2020); Wells et al. (2020), *inter alia* were included in CORD-19), where we observe a marked shift in utilization to play a similar role to other common symptoms of COVID-19.

**116568000** *Dexamethasone* The corticosteroid dexamethasone was recognized early as valuable for treating severe COVID-19 symptoms (Lester et al. (2020), indexed July 2020), and its role has remained stable since (Ahmed and Hassan (2020), indexed October 2020). This is reflected in the shift of its nearest neighbors from prior contexts of traumatic brain injury (Moll et al., 2020) to a stable neighborhood of other drugs used for COVID-19 symptoms. However, in September 2020, 702806008 *Ruxolitinib* emerges as *Dexamethasone*'s nearest neighbor. This reflects a spike in literature investigating the use of ruxolitinib for severe COVID-19 symptom management (Gozzetti et al., 2020; Spadea et al., 2020; Li and Liu, 2020). As the similarity graph in Figure 3 shows, the contextual similarity between dexamethasone and ruxolitinib steadily increases over time, reflecting the growing recognition of ruxolitinib's new utility (Caocci and La Nasa (2020), indexed May 2020).

**83490000** *Hydroxychloroquine* Hydroxychloroquine, an anti-malarial drug, was misleadingly promoted as a potential treatment for COVID-19 by President Trump in March, May, and July 2020, leading to widespread misuse of the drug (Englund et al., 2020). As a result, a number of studies re-investigated the efficacy of hydroxychloroquine as a treatment for COVID-19 in hospitalized patients (Ip et al. (2020); Albani et al. (2020); Rahmani et al. (2020), all indexed August 2020). This shift is reflected in the neighbors of *Hydroxychloroquine*, adding investigative outcomes such as nosocomial (hospital-acquired) infections and respiratory failure to the expected anti-malarial neighbors.

| Concept | Month(s) | Representative neighbors |
|---|---|---|
| 44169009 **Anosmia** | Mar-Sep | 2553606007 **Gustatory**<br>51388003 **Pharyngeal pain**<br>60707004 **Taste** |
| | Oct | 15387003 **Vomiting**<br>73879007 **Nausea**<br>49727002 **Cough** |
| 116568000 **Dexamethasone** | Mar | 19130008 **Injury**<br>417746004 **Traumatic injury** |
| | May-Jul | 116602009 **Prednisone**<br>108675009 **Infliximab** |
| | Sep | 702806008 **Ruxolitinib** |
| 83490000 **Hydroxychloroquine** | All | 80229008 **Antimalarial agent**<br>96034006 **Azithromycin** |
| | Aug | 198051006 **Nosocomial infection**<br>233765002 **Respiratory failure without hypercapnia** |

Table 2: Representative nearest neighbors (manually selected from top 10) for three concepts in CORD-19, grouped by period of observation. Complete nearest neighbor tables are omitted for brevity, but may be viewed using our released code and data.

# 6 Discussion

Our case study on scientific literature related to COVID-19 demonstrates that TextEssence can be used to study diachronic shifts in usage of domain concepts. We highlight three directions for future work using TextEssence: mining for new shifts and associations in changing literature (§6.1); applications between comparative analysis of corpora (§6.2); and further investigation of embedding confidence as a tool for analysis (§6.3).

## 6.1 Mining shifts in the literature

While our primary focus in developing TextEssence was on its use as a qualitative tool for targeted inquiry, diachronic embeddings have significant potential for knowledge discovery through quantitative measurement of semantic differences. For example, new embeddings could be generated for subsequent months of CORD-19 (or other corpora), and analyzed to determine what concepts shifted the most—indicating current trends—or what concepts are just starting to shift—suggesting potential future developments.

However, quantitative, vector-based comparison of embedding spaces faces significant conceptual challenges, such as a lack of appropriate alignment objectives and empirical instability (Gonen et al., 2020). While nearest neighbor-based change measurement has been proposed (Newman-Griffis and Fosler-Lussier, 2019; Gonen et al., 2020), its efficacy for small corpora with limited vocabularies remains to be determined. Our novel embedding confidence measure offers a step in this direction (see §6.3 for further discussion), but further research is needed.

### 6.2 Other applications of TextEssence

A previous study on medical records (Newman-Griffis and Fosler-Lussier, 2019) showed that the technologies behind TextEssence can be used for categorical comparison as well as analysis of temporal shifts. More broadly, the use of TextEssence is not limited to comparison of text corpora alone. In settings where multiple embedding strategies are available, such as learning representations of domain concepts from text sources (Beam et al., 2020; Chen et al., 2020), knowledge graphs (Grover and Leskovec, 2016), or both (Yamada et al., 2020; Wang et al., 2020b), TextEssence can be used to study the different regularities captured by competing algorithms, providing insight into the utility of different approaches. TextEssence also can function as a tool for studying the properties of different terminologies for domain concepts, something not previously explored in the computational literature.

In addition, the TextEssence interface can provide utility for other types of analyses as well. For example, the Inspect and Compare portions of the interface could be used to interact with topic models learned from different corpora. These components are largely agnostic to the nature of the underlying data, and could be extended for studying a variety of different types of NLP models.

### 6.3 Confidence estimation in embedding analysis

The relatively constrained size of corpora in our analysis motivated our novel embedding confidence measure, to help separate differences due to random effects in embedding training from differences in concept usage patterns. We used a fixed confidence threshold for our analyses; however, increasing or decreasing the threshold for high-confidence embeddings will affect both the set of reported neighbors and the visualization of the embedding space, and can inform the user of TextEssence which observations are more or less stable. We highlight varying this threshold as an important area for future investigation with TextEssence.

More broadly, prior work by Wendlandt et al. (2018), Antoniak and Mimno (2018), and Gonen et al. (2020), among others, has also shown embedding stability to be a concern in models trained on larger corpora than those used in this work. However, the role of random embedding effects on previous qualitative studies using word embeddings (e.g., Kulkarni et al. (2015), Hamilton et al. (2016)) has not been evaluated. A broader investigation of embedding confidence measures in qualitative studies will be invaluable in the continued development of embedding technologies as a tool for linguistics research.

## 7 Conclusion

TextEssence is an interactive tool for comparative analysis of word and concept embeddings. Our implementation and experimental code is available at `https://github.com/drgriffis/text-essence`, and the database derived from our CORD-19 analysis is available at `https://doi.org/10.5281/zenodo.4432958`. A screencast of TextEssence in action is available at `https://youtu.be/1xEEfsMwL0k`. All associated resources for TextEssence may be found at `https://textessence.github.io`.


## Acknowledgments

This work made use of computational resources generously provided by the Ohio Supercomputer Center (Ohio Supercomputer Center, 1987) in support of COVID-19 research. The research reported in this publication was supported in part by the National Library of Medicine of the National Institutes of Health under award number T15 LM007059.

## References


Mukhtar H Ahmed and Arez Hassan. 2020. Dexamethasone for the Treatment of Coronavirus Disease (COVID-19): a Review. *SN Comprehensive Clinical Medicine*, 2(12):2637–2646.

Filippo Albani, Federica Fusina, Alessia Giovannini, Pierluigi Ferretti, Anna Granato, Chiara Prezioso, Danilo Divizia, Alessandra Sabaini, Marco Marri, Elena Malpetti, and Giuseppe Natalini. 2020. Impact of Azithromycin and/or Hydroxychloroquine on Hospital Mortality in COVID-19. *Journal of clinical medicine*, 9(9).

Maria Antoniak and David Mimno. 2018. Evaluating the Stability of Embedding-based Word Similarities. *Transactions of the Association for Computational Linguistics*, 6:107–119.

Andrew L Beam, Benjamin Kompa, Allen Schmaltz, Inbar Fried, Griffin Weber, Nathan Palmer, Xu Shi, Tianxi Cai, and Isaac S Kohane. 2020. Clinical Concept Embeddings Learned from Massive Sources of Multimodal Medical Data. *Pacific Symposium on Biocomputing. Pacific Symposium on Biocomputing*, 25:295–306.

Olivier Bodenreider. 2004. The Unified Medical Language System (UMLS): integrating biomedical terminology. *Nucleic Acids Research*, 32(90001):D267–D270.

Gemma Boleda. 2020. Distributional Semantics and Linguistic Theory. *Annual Review of Linguistics*, 6(1):213–234.

Giovanni Caocci and Giorgio La Nasa. 2020. Could ruxolitinib be effective in patients with COVID-19 infection at risk of acute respiratory distress syndrome (ARDS)?

Juntian Chen, Yubo Tao, and Hai Lin. 2018. Visual exploration and comparison of word embeddings. *Journal of Visual Languages & Computing*, 48:178 – 186.

Qingyu Chen, Kyubum Lee, Shankai Yan, Sun Kim, Chih-Hsuan Wei, and Zhiyong Lu. 2020. BioConceptVec: Creating and evaluating literature-based biomedical concept embeddings on a large scale. *PLOS Computational Biology*, 16(4):e1007617.

Rene Cutura, Michaël Aupetit, Jean-Daniel Fekete, and Michael Sedlmair. 2020. Comparing and exploring high-dimensional data with dimensionality reduction algorithms and matrix visualizations. In *Proceedings of the International Conference on Advanced Visual Interfaces*, AVI '20, New York, NY, USA. Association for Computing Machinery.

Lance De Vine, Guido Zuccon, Bevan Koopman, Laurianne Sitbon, and Peter Bruza. 2014. Medical semantic similarity with a neural language model. In *Proceedings of the 23rd ACM International Conference on Information and Knowledge Management - CIKM '14*, CIKM '14, pages 1819–1822, Shanghai, China. ACM.

Tessa R Englund, Alan C Kinlaw, and Saira Z Sheikh. 2020. Rise and Fall: Hydroxychloroquine and COVID-19 Global Trends: Interest, Political Influence, and Potential Implications. *ACR Open Rheumatology*, 2(12):760–766.

Nikhil Garg, Londa Schiebinger, Dan Jurafsky, and James Zou. 2018. Word embeddings quantify 100 years of gender and ethnic stereotypes. *Proceedings of the National Academy of Sciences*, 115(16):E3635—-E3644.

Hila Gonen, Ganesh Jawahar, Djamé Seddah, and Yoav Goldberg. 2020. Simple, Interpretable and Stable Method for Detecting Words with Usage Change across Corpora. In *Proceedings of the 58th Annual Meeting of the Association for Computational Linguistics*, pages 538–555, Online. Association for Computational Linguistics.

Alessandro Gozzetti, Enrico Capochiani, and Monica Bocchia. 2020. The Janus kinase 1/2 inhibitor ruxolitinib in COVID-19.

Aditya Grover and Jure Leskovec. 2016. Node2Vec: Scalable Feature Learning for Networks. In *Proceedings of the 22Nd ACM SIGKDD International Conference on Knowledge Discovery and Data Mining*, KDD '16, pages 855–864, New York, NY, USA. ACM.

William L. Hamilton, Jure Leskovec, and Dan Jurafsky. 2016. Diachronic Word Embeddings Reveal Statistical Laws of Semantic Change. In *Proceedings of the 54th Annual Meeting of the Association for Computational Linguistics (Volume 1: Long Papers)*, pages 1489–1501, Berlin, Germany. Association for Computational Linguistics.

Benjamin Hoover, Hendrik Strobelt, and Sebastian Gehrmann. 2020. exBERT: A Visual Analysis Tool to Explore Learned Representations in Transformer Models. In *Proceedings of the 58th Annual Meeting of the Association for Computational Linguistics: System Demonstrations*, pages 187–196, Online. Association for Computational Linguistics.

Daniel Hornuss, Berit Lange, Nils Schröter, Siegbert Rieg, Winfried V Kern, and Dirk Wagner. 2020. Anosmia in COVID-19 patients. *medRxiv*, page 2020.04.28.20083311.

Andrew Ip, Donald A Berry, Eric Hansen, Andre H Goy, Andrew L Pecora, Brittany A Sinclaire, Urszula Bednarz, Michael Marafelias, Scott M Berry, Nicholas S Berry, Shivam Mathura, Ihor S Sawczuk, Noa Biran, Ronaldo C Go, Steven Sperber, Julia A Piwoz, Bindu Balani, Cristina Cicogna, Rani Sebti, Jerry Zuckerman, Keith M Rose, Lisa Tank, Laurie G Jacobs, Jason Korcak, Sarah L Timmapuri, Joseph P Underwood, Gregory Sugalski, Carol Barsky, Daniel W Varga, Arif Asif, Joseph C

Landolfi, and Stuart L Goldberg. 2020. Hydroxychloroquine and tocilizumab therapy in COVID-19 patients-An observational study. *PloS one*, 15(8):e0237693.

Ganesh Jawahar, Benoît Sagot, and Djamé Seddah. 2019. What Does BERT Learn about the Structure of Language? In *Proceedings of the 57th Annual Meeting of the Association for Computational Linguistics*, pages 3651–3657, Florence, Italy. Association for Computational Linguistics.

Vivek Kulkarni, Rami Al-Rfou, Bryan Perozzi, and Steven Skiena. 2015. Statistically Significant Detection of Linguistic Change. In *Proceedings of the 24th International Conference on World Wide Web*, WWW '15, pages 625–635, Republic and Canton of Geneva, CHE. International World Wide Web Conferences Steering Committee.

Andrey Kutuzov, Lilja Øvrelid, Terrence Szymanski, and Erik Velldal. 2018. Diachronic word embeddings and semantic shifts: a survey. In *Proceedings of the 27th International Conference on Computational Linguistics*, pages 1384–1397, Santa Fe, New Mexico, USA. Association for Computational Linguistics.

Mohammed Lester, Ali Sahin, and Ali Pasyar. 2020. The use of dexamethasone in the treatment of COVID-19. *Annals of Medicine and Surgery*, 56:218–219.

Hailan Li and Huaping Liu. 2020. Whether the timing of patient randomization interferes with the assessment of the efficacy of ruxolitinib for severe COVID-19. *Journal of Allergy and Clinical Immunology*, 146(6):1453.

S Liu, X Wang, C Collins, W Dou, F Ouyang, M El-Assady, L Jiang, and D A Keim. 2019. Bridging Text Visualization and Mining: A Task-Driven Survey. *IEEE Transactions on Visualization and Computer Graphics*, 25(7):2482–2504.

Shixia Liu, Michelle X Zhou, Shimei Pan, Yangqiu Song, Weihong Qian, Weijia Cai, and Xiaoxiao Lian. 2012. Tiara: Interactive, topic-based visual text summarization and analysis. *ACM Transactions on Intelligent Systems and Technology (TIST)*, 3(2):1–28.

X. Liu, Z. Zhang, R. Leontie, A. Stylianou, and R. Pless. 2020. 2-map: Aligned visualizations for comparison of high-dimensional point sets. In *2020 IEEE Winter Conference on Applications of Computer Vision (WACV)*, pages 2539–2547.

A T McCray, A Burgun, and O Bodenreider. 2001. Aggregating UMLS semantic types for reducing conceptual complexity. *Studies in health technology and informatics*, 84(Pt 1):216–220.

Apolonia Moll, Mónica Lara, Jaume Pomar, Mónica Orozco, Guiem Frontera, Juan A Llompart-Pou, Lesmes Moratinos, Víctor González, Javier Ibáñez, and Jon Pérez-Bárcena. 2020. Effects of dexamethasone in traumatic brain injury patients with pericontusional vasogenic edema: A prospective-observational DTI-MRI study. *Medicine*, 99(43).

Mark Neumann, Daniel King, Iz Beltagy, and Waleed Ammar. 2019. ScispaCy: Fast and Robust Models for Biomedical Natural Language Processing. In *Proceedings of the 18th BioNLP Workshop and Shared Task*, pages 319–327, Florence, Italy. Association for Computational Linguistics.

Denis Newman-Griffis and Eric Fosler-Lussier. 2019. Writing habits and telltale neighbors: analyzing clinical concept usage patterns with sublanguage embeddings. In *Proceedings of the Tenth International Workshop on Health Text Mining and Information Analysis (LOUHI 2019)*, pages 146–156, Hong Kong. Association for Computational Linguistics.

Denis Newman-Griffis, Albert M Lai, and Eric Fosler-Lussier. 2018. Jointly Embedding Entities and Text with Distant Supervision. In *Proceedings of The Third Workshop on Representation Learning for NLP*, pages 195–206. Association for Computational Linguistics.

Dong Nguyen, Maria Liakata, Simon DeDeo, Jacob Eisenstein, David Mimno, Rebekah Tromble, and Jane Winters. 2020. How We Do Things With Words: Analyzing Text as Social and Cultural Data. *Frontiers in Artificial Intelligence*, 3:62.

Ohio Supercomputer Center. 1987. Ohio Supercomputer Center.

Hamid Rahmani, Effat Davoudi-Monfared, Anahid Nourian, Morteza Nabiee, Setayesh Sadeghi, Hossein Khalili, Ladan Abbasian, Fereshteh Ghiasvand, Arash Seifi, Malihe Hasannezhad, Sara Ghaderkhani, Mostafa Mohammadi, and Mir Saeed Yekaninejad. 2020. Comparing outcomes of hospitalized patients with moderate and severe COVID-19 following treatment with hydroxychloroquine plus atazanavir/ritonavir. *Daru : journal of Faculty of Pharmacy, Tehran University of Medical Sciences*, 28(2):625–634.

Andrew Runge and Eduard Hovy. 2020. Exploring Neural Entity Representations for Semantic Information. In *Proceedings of the Third BlackboxNLP Workshop on Analyzing and Interpreting Neural Networks for NLP*, pages 204–216, Online. Association for Computational Linguistics.

Dominik Schlechtweg, Barbara McGillivray, Simon Hengchen, Haim Dubossarsky, and Nina Tahmasebi. 2020. SemEval-2020 Task 1: Unsupervised Lexical Semantic Change Detection. In *Proceedings of the Fourteenth Workshop on Semantic Evaluation*, pages 1–23, Barcelona (online). International Committee for Computational Linguistics.

Daniel Smilkov, Nikhil Thorat, Charles Nicholson, Emily Reif, Fernanda B. Viégas, and Martin Wattenberg. 2016. Embedding projector: Interactive visualization and interpretation of embeddings.

Manuela Spadea, Francesca Carraro, Francesco Saglio, Elena Vassallo, Rosanna Pessolano, Massimo Berger, Carlo Scolfaro, Sergio Grassitelli, and Franca Fagioli. 2020. Successfully treated severe COVID-19 and invasive aspergillosis in early hematopoietic cell transplantation setting.

Blanca Talavera, David García-Azorín, Enrique Martínez-Pías, Javier Trigo, Isabel Hernández-Pérez, Gonzalo Valle-Peñacoba, Paula Simón-Campo, Mercedes de Lera, Alba Chavarría-Miranda, Cristina López-Sanz, María Gutiérrez-Sánchez, Elena Martínez-Velasco, María Pedraza, Álvaro Sierra, Beatriz Gómez-Vicente, Ángel Guerrero, and Juan Francisco Arenillas. 2020. Anosmia is associated with lower in-hospital mortality in COVID-19. *Journal of the Neurological Sciences*, 419.

Laurens van der Maaten and Geoffrey Hinton. 2008. Visualizing data using t-sne. *Journal of Machine Learning Research*, 9(86):2579–2605.

Ekaterina Vylomova, Sean Murphy, and Nicholas Haslam. 2019. Evaluation of Semantic Change of Harm-Related Concepts in Psychology. In *Proceedings of the 1st International Workshop on Computational Approaches to Historical Language Change*, pages 29–34, Florence, Italy. Association for Computational Linguistics.

Lucy Lu Wang, Kyle Lo, Yoganand Chandrasekhar, Russell Reas, Jiangjiang Yang, Darrin Eide, Kathryn Funk, Rodney Kinney, Ziyang Liu, William Merrill, and Others. 2020a. CORD-19: The Covid-19 Open Research Dataset. *arXiv preprint arXiv:2004.10706*.

Qingyun Wang, Manling Li, Xuan Wang, Nikolaus Parulian, Guangxing Han, Jiawei Ma, Jingxuan Tu, Ying Lin, Haoran Zhang, Weili Liu, and Others. 2020b. Covid-19 literature knowledge graph construction and drug repurposing report generation. *arXiv preprint arXiv:2007.00576*.

Vincent Warmerdam, Thomas Kober, and Rachael Tatman. 2020. Going Beyond T-SNE: Exposing whatlies in Text Embeddings. In *Proceedings of Second Workshop for NLP Open Source Software (NLP-OSS)*, pages 52–60, Online. Association for Computational Linguistics.

Rebecca Weiss. 2014. MUCK: A toolkit for extracting and visualizing semantic dimensions of large text collections. In *Proceedings of the Workshop on Interactive Language Learning, Visualization, and Interfaces*, pages 53–58, Baltimore, Maryland, USA. Association for Computational Linguistics.

Philippa M Wells, Katie J Doores, Simon Couvreur, Rocio Martinez Nunez, Jeffrey Seow, Carl Graham, Sam Acors, Neophytos Kouphou, Stuart J D Neil, Richard S Tedder, Pedro M Matos, Kate Poulton, Maria Jose Lista, Ruth E Dickenson, Helin Sertkaya, Thomas J A Maguire, Edward J Scourfield, Ruth C E Bowyer, Deborah Hart, Aoife O'Byrne, Kathryn J A Steel, Oliver Hemmings, Carolina Rosadas, Myra O McClure, Joan Capedevilla-pujol, Jonathan Wolf, Sebastien Ourselin, Matthew A Brown, Michael H Malim, Tim Spector, and Claire J Steves. 2020. Estimates of the rate of infection and asymptomatic COVID-19 disease in a population sample from SE England. *Journal of Infection*, 81(6):931–936.

Laura Wendlandt, Jonathan K Kummerfeld, and Rada Mihalcea. 2018. Factors Influencing the Surprising Instability of Word Embeddings. In *Proceedings of the 2018 Conference of the North American Chapter of the Association for Computational Linguistics: Human Language Technologies, Volume 1 (Long Papers)*, pages 2092–2102. Association for Computational Linguistics.

Ikuya Yamada, Akari Asai, Jin Sakuma, Hiroyuki Shindo, Hideaki Takeda, Yoshiyasu Takefuji, and Yuji Matsumoto. 2020. Wikipedia2Vec: An Efficient Toolkit for Learning and Visualizing the Embeddings of Words and Entities from Wikipedia. In *Proceedings of the 2020 Conference on Empirical Methods in Natural Language Processing: System Demonstrations*, pages 23–30, Online. Association for Computational Linguistics.

Yiyun Zhao and Steven Bethard. 2020. How does BERT's attention change when you fine-tune? An analysis methodology and a case study in negation scope. In *Proceedings of the 58th Annual Meeting of the Association for Computational Linguistics*, pages 4729–4747, Online. Association for Computational Linguistics.

Tamara Zhordaniya, Andrey Kutuzov, and Elizaveta Kuzmenko. Vec2graph: A python library for visualizing word embeddings as graphs. Springer.

# Supporting Spanish Writers using Automated Feedback

Aoife Cahill[1], James V. Bruno[1], James T. Ramey[2], Gilmar Ayala Meneses[2], Ian Blood[1], Florencia Tolentino[1], Tamar Lavee[1] and Slava Andreyev[1]
[1] Educational Testing Service, Princeton, NJ 08541, USA
[2] Universidad Autónoma Metropolitana, Cuajimalpa, Mexico City, Mexico

## Abstract

We present a tool that provides automated feedback to students studying Spanish writing. The feedback is given for four categories: topic development, coherence, writing conventions, and essay organization. The tool is made freely available via a Google Docs add-on. A small user study with post-secondary level students in Mexico shows that students found the tool generally helpful and that most of them plan to continue using it as they work to improve their writing skills. In an analysis of 6 months of user data, we see that a small number of users continue to engage with the app, even outside of planned user studies.

## 1 Motivation and Background

There are a multitude of writing support tools available for students who wish to improve their English writing (e.g. Grammarly,[1] Writing Mentor,[2] Ginger,[3] Microsoft Word, or Revision Assistant[4]). These tools for English vary in complexity from basic feedback on spelling errors to advanced feedback about structure, register, topic development, and use of evidence to support claims. In the context of writing feedback for Spanish, there are automatic grammar checkers available (e.g. LanguageTool[5] or SpanishChecker[6]). However, there are no tools for Spanish that offer the kind of comprehensive writing feedback that tools such as Writing Mentor and Grammarly offer. There is a huge native Spanish-speaking population (almost 500 million globally according to Wikipedia[7]) that we could potentially support by providing advanced NLP tools to help improve writing skills.

## 2 Related Work in Automated Feedback

Studies have shown that automated feedback on student writing can have a positive impact on their learning (Attali, 2004; Shermis et al., 2004; Nagata and Nakatani, 2010; Cotos, 2011; Roscoe et al., 2014). The NLP technologies used to provide feedback on writing have often gone hand-in-hand with the development of automated scoring systems. The intuition is that if the system is "measuring" some aspect of writing in order to be able to grade it, it could also use that same measurement in order to give feedback. However, there are also studies with mixed, or less favourable outcomes when students use tools that provide automated feedback on their writing (Choi, 2010; Bai and Hu, 2017; Ranalli et al., 2017). This is an active area of research, and one that requires significant resources to conduct valid user studies and evaluations.

## 3 Spanish Writing Mentor

Building on previous work that developed comprehensive automated writing feedback for English, we have developed a tool to similarly support Spanish writers by providing automated feedback. `mentormywriting.org/es.html` contains information about the tool, links to the download page, a video describing the main features of the tool, as well as an FAQ section. The tool is implemented as a Google Doc add-on (front-end), freely available to download from the app store, with a server-based

[1] `www.grammarly.com`
[2] `mentormywriting.org`
[3] `www.gingersoftware.com`
[4] `www.revisionassistant.com/`
[5] `https://languagetool.org`
[6] `https://spanishchecker.com/`
[7] `https://en.wikipedia.org/wiki/Spanish_language`



*Proceedings of NAACL-HLT 2021: Demonstrations*, pages 116–124
June 6–11, 2021. 

back-end processing student texts and computing feedback. It is an extension of the original work done for English (Burstein et al., 2018; Madnani et al., 2018a) and the add-on allows users to select either English or Spanish on a per-document basis. Figure 1 shows the language selection screen when the add-on is first started.

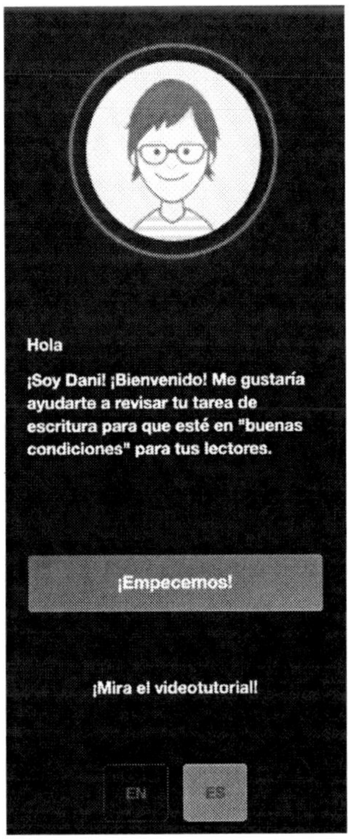


Figure 1: Writing Mentor offers feedback in both English and Spanish. The user makes a selection for each document they write.

The server-based back end of the tool is implemented using a micro-service framework based on Apache Storm[8] – see Madnani et al. (2018b) for more details. The framework allows for robust, scalable, fault-tolerant processing (automatically restarting components if they fail). The back-end engine takes a text as input and returns a JSON representation of feedback. The feedback is computed using a network of micro-services. Each micro-service is defined in terms of inputs (prerequisites) and outputs, and data flows in parallel (automatically managed by Storm) to the final component (Storm *bolt*) that sends JSON-encoded feedback to the front-end of the tool for display to the user.

The design of the back-end feedback engine was based on the corresponding English one. However, in terms of the implementation, much of the functionality naturally differs in order to account for the language differences. Furthermore, we introduce some new functionality – most notably the section on well-organized writing – that could potentially also be made available for the English version of the tool.

We take advantage of a number of publicly available tools to build our feedback components. We use the Spanish Stanford Core NLP[9] for tokenization, tagging and constituency parsing (Manning et al., 2014). We use the Spacy[10] Spanish dependency parser (Honnibal et al., 2020), aligning the dependency relations to the tokenization provided by the Stanford tools. We use the standalone version of Spanish LanguageTool[11] to compute a subset of the feedback relating to writing conventions (spelling and grammatical errors).

### 3.1 Feedback Components

Spanish Writing Mentor gives feedback on four broad areas of writing: topic development, coherence, writing conventions, and essay organization. Figure 2 shows the tool when the user loads the app on an open document.

#### 3.1.1 Topic Development

As in the English version of Writing Mentor, we include feedback on topic development (Beigman Klebanov and Flor, 2013), which relies on a database of pointwise mutual information (PMI) values. In this instance, we are able to re-use the code from the English implementation and simply substitute a Spanish PMI database. We build the database by re-tokenizing the raw version of the Spanish Billion Word Corpus (Cardellino, 2019) with the Stanford tools. This corpus is a union of Spanish resources in a wide range of domains and formats, including legal, financial and medical

[8] `https://storm.apache.org`

[9] `https://stanfordnlp.github.io/CoreNLP/download.html` We use version 3.9.2 which has the linguistically desirable feature of separating clitics from the words they depend on during tokenization. Sadly this feature is not available in the most recent versions of the Stanford Spanish tools, as they have switched to UD tokenization.

[10] `https://spacy.io/models/es`

[11] `https://github.com/languagetool-org/languagetool/`

Figure 2: The Spanish Writing Mentor tool has four categories of feedback: topic development, coherence, writing conventions, and essay organization

documents, books, and movie subtitles. This variety of domains makes it a suitable background database for topic detection in essays on many different subjects. Topic words are identified if they have PMI values higher than a set threshold when paired with all other words in the text, i.e. only the PMI of words in the student's response are considered for this feature. The threshold for identified topic words was tuned by experimenting with a range of values and manually inspecting the output to judge the appropriateness of the topics detected. The tuning was done on a small set of 96 essays written by native-speaker university students as well as a sample of 60 essays representing various levels of proficiency from a publicly available corpus of non-native Spanish essays.[12] A lower threshold yielded many word pairs that were unrelated, while a higher threshold yielded far fewer word pairs. Further threshold tuning and assessment of the background database on a broader dataset remains for future work. The main topic of the essay is identified as the topic word that participates in the most pairs of words over the PMI threshold. As in the English version, users are also able to provide their own topic terms. If these are provided they are highlighted and considered in the automatic identification of the main topic regardless of their PMI values. Users may also manually identify topics of their own choosing, and related topic words are highlighted according to the same rules.

### 3.1.2 Coherence

Spanish Writing Mentor gives feedback on the following aspects of coherence:

**Flow of ideas** The same topic words that are highlighted in the *Topic Development* component are also highlighted in this component, color-coded according to topic. This enables the user to visually understand the extent to which their topics are elaborated in various parts of the document, and they are advised that the most important topics should be represented throughout the entirety of the text.

**Transition terms** We have a fixed list of 100 words and phrases[13] that we highlight. This is intended to prompt users to consider over/under use of transition terms that link ideas and arguments. Examples

[12] https://github.com/ucdaviscl/cowsl2h/blob/master/README.md

[13] Adapted from https://modlang.unl.edu/docs/STC/Palabras_para_ordenar_el_discurso_escrito.pdf

include *porque* (*because*), *primeramente* (*firstly*), *en conclusión* (*in conclusion*), etc.

**Title and section headers** We identify titles and section headers using a set of regular-expression-based rules. These are used both to visually prompt the user about the identified structure of their essay, as well as identify sections of the essay that we do not want to give certain kinds of feedback on. For example, we do not want to highlight spelling or grammatical errors in a list of references.

**Sentence/paragraph length** We highlight complex sentences, which we consider to be sentences containing 2 or more dependent clauses as identified by the constituency parse. This is intended to highlight sentences that could perhaps be broken up to make the text more readable. Using the number of sentences identified by the tokenizer, we also highlight paragraphs that are either too short (choppy, <4 sentences), or too long (>9 sentences), to prompt users to think about elaborating their claims without losing coherence. This extends what is available in the English version which only gives feedback at the sentence level.

**Pronoun use** We highlight a subset of pronouns to help prompt the user to make sure that the references that the pronouns refer to are clear. The POS tags are used to identify the pronouns.

#### 3.1.3 Writing Conventions

We give the following types of feedback on Spanish Writing Conventions:

**Grammar, Usage and Mechanics** We follow a similar categorization of error types to the English Writing Mentor. Some of these errors come directly from the LanguageTool library, though only a subset of errors detected are displayed to the user. We include accent errors, agreement errors, contraction errors, comma errors, spelling errors, and incorrect word usage errors. We also implemented new grammatical error detectors. For example, rules were written to identify fragments and run-ons based on subordinating and coordinating conjunctions and their dependents identified by the dependency parses. Our initial work focused on trying to include only feedback for errors for which we were confident we could achieve reasonable precision, though of course no system is perfect. Future work would extend the coverage of these detectors.

**Unnecessary Words** Related to the concept of pobreza léxica (*lit.* lexical poverty), we highlight occurrences of unnecessary words. These words, when over-used, lead to imprecise and poor writing. This is done by simple regular expression matching from a list that includes words like *absolutamente* (absolutely) and *muy* (very). Future work would build out this functionality to account for more specific guidelines related to this topic.

**Contractions** We highlight sequences of words that should be contracted in Spanish, e.g. *de el* should be written as *del*.

**Accents** We highlight errors related to accent use. This category of errors is new for the Spanish version of the app. These errors are identified using dictionary resources and rules encoded in Language Tool.

#### 3.1.4 Essay organization

A novel aspect of the Spanish tool is that we give feedback on essay organization in the form of a questionnaire. There are 9 main questions, each with a corresponding follow-up question (18 questions total), that prompt the user to think about how they have structured the arguments in their essay. This questionnaire draws on concepts from various rhetoric and composition studies textbooks (e.g. Ramage et al. (2015), Lunsford (2008), Hacker (2006), and Crews (1992)). The questions were chosen to implement insights and recommendations from the writing literature. Figure 3 shows the tool prompting the user to highlight the sentence in the essay containing the main claim. When the user has completed the survey, they are presented with a summary of the aspects that they highlighted, schematized in Figure 4. An obvious extension of this component will be

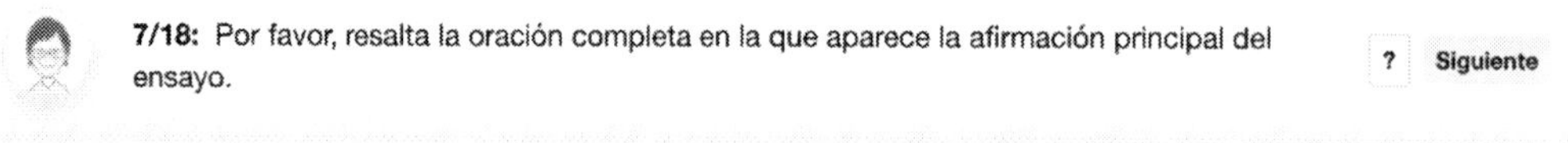


Figure 3: Users are prompted to think about the structure of their essay in the *Well-Organized* questionnaire. Here the users are asked to select the sentence containing the main claim of the essay. This is question 7 of 18 total.

I. Introduction. Thesis Statement: [*Thesis statement as highlighted by the user*]

II. Argumentative Paragraph 1: [*Topic sentence as highlighted by the user*]

III. Argumentative Paragraph 2: [*Topic sentence as highlighted by the user*]

IV. Argumentative Paragraph 3, etc...

V. Conclusion Paragraph: [*Conclusion paragraph as highlighted by the user*]

Figure 4: A schematic of what the user sees after completing the organization questionnaire.

to automate the detection of organizational elements and present an automated *sentence outline* (a formal representation of an essay draft) to the user in the future.

### 3.2 Paragraph-Writing Support

Analogous to the English app, the Spanish app also provides support for paragraph writing. The idea behind the paragraph-writing part of the tool is to support less proficient writers; for example adult learners. The paragraph-writing-support tool includes motivational badges, and provides a subset of the feedback available in the main tool. The focus in the paragraph-writing tool is to help the user understand what aspects of writing lead to a well-written paragraph. Figure 5 shows a screenshot of the paragraph-writing help, which provides scaffolding and guidelines for writing a well-structured paragraph in response to an argumentative question. There are a number of questions available to students to help them practice. The questions come from the New York Times Teaching Resources. (They are translations of

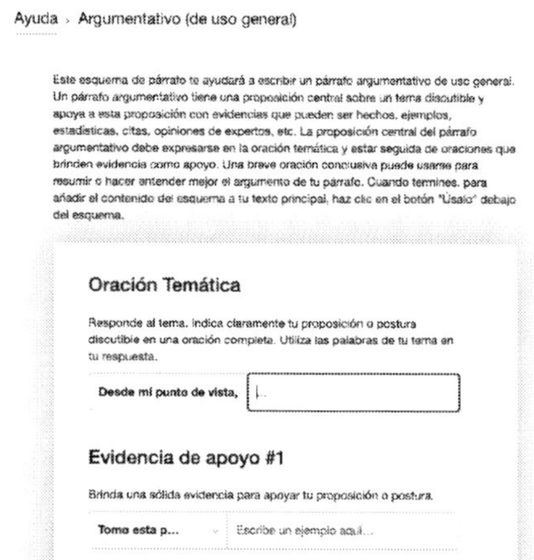


Figure 5: Users are prompted to think about the structure of a paragraph. This interface provides scaffolding to help them write a well-structured paragraph in response to an argumentative prompt.

the original questions supplied by the NYT who approved the translations for use).

## 4 User Study

We conducted a user study to collect initial usage and perception data from the tool. Our participants were students in the Universidad Autónoma Metropolitana, Cuajimalpa, in Mexico City. Participants were recruited from two groups: (1) a group of students taking optional courses in the university Writing Center, which provides support to students who want to improve their writing skills and (2) a group of 3rd and 4th year undergraduate students taking an elective course in Latin American Literature. Participation in the study was optional, and each student who took part received a certificate of participation upon completion. Participants were asked to use Spanish Writing Mentor to support their regular coursework writing assignments. No changes were made to the assignments. Users were given instructions on how to use the tool three weeks before the end of the trimester, and could choose how to use the tool (if at all) during those three weeks. The user study focused only on extended writing. An investigation into the usefulness of the paragraph writing component remains for future work.

Our user study consists of two components: (1) a measure of writing ability before and after using the tool and (2) a user survey completed after the three weeks. In order to measure writing ability before and after using the tool, each participant completed a standardized assessment of writing ability. The assessment is usually administered as a placement test in the Writing Center to assign students to one of four levels: low (0-49), moderate (50-69), acceptable (70-89) or optimum (90-100). Our user survey consisted of 13 questions (see Appendix A) and participants were asked to complete it after they had handed in their final assignments.

## 5 User Data Analysis

Table 1 gives an overview of our participants. We have 13 students in total who completed the entire study; 6 from the Spanish Writing course, and 7 from the Latin American Literature course. All students take the standardized test before their course and after, and receive a score in the range 0-100. We see that the writing ability of all participants, as measured by the standardized test, increases between the pre- and post-tests. Of course, this improvement can be attributed to the content of the courses, and at this point we have no way to measure the direct impact (if any) of using the Writing Mentor tool. A fully randomized controlled experiment would be needed to study this in more depth. For comparison, the average scores of all students (n=94) in the pre-test was 38.7 and this increased to 51.9 in the post-test (n=80 students). The writing proficiency of our participants was, on average, higher than the general population in these classes.

The main findings from the 13 questions in the user survey were as follows:

- The average score for how useful the participants found the tool was 3.7 (on a scale from 1-5, 5 being the most useful; min=2, max=5).

| Student | Course | Initial | Final |
|---|---|---|---|
| 1 | Writing | 39 | 64 |
| 2 | Writing | 44 | 58 |
| 3 | Writing | 58 | 65 |
| 4 | Writing | 37 | 45 |
| 5 | Writing | 72 | 76 |
| 6 | Writing | 38 | 50 |
| 7 | Literature | 36 | 53 |
| 8 | Literature | 28 | 42 |
| 9 | Literature | 58 | 63 |
| 10 | Literature | 72 | 76 |
| 11 | Literature | 50 | 52 |
| 12 | Literature | 58 | 62 |
| 13 | Literature | 51 | 57 |
| Average | | 49.3 | 58.6 |

Table 1: User Study Participants. Initial and Final are the written evaluation results on a standardized test (0-100 scale).

- 12 of 13 participants indicated that by using the tool they had learned something to help them improve their writing.
- The features that were selected as being the most useful were: Coherence (flow of ideas) – 10/13; Well organized – 10/13; Topic development – 9/13.
- The features that were selected as being the least useful were: Coherence (Title and Section headers) – 4/13; Coherence (Use of pronouns) – 3/13; Coherence (Sentence/paragraph length) – 3/13.
- The most useful help article was the one on Coherence (Flow of ideas) – 10/13.
- 12/13 participants plan to use Spanish Writing Mentor again, and 11/13 planned to recommend it to others.
- 11/13 participants indicated that one of the main aspects they liked LEAST about the tool was the interface, but only 2/13 participants commented that the functionality provided by the tool (i.e. what it was presenting as feedback) were what they liked least.

### 5.1 User Behavior

In addition to the user study, we also analyze 6 months of application log data. Figure 6a

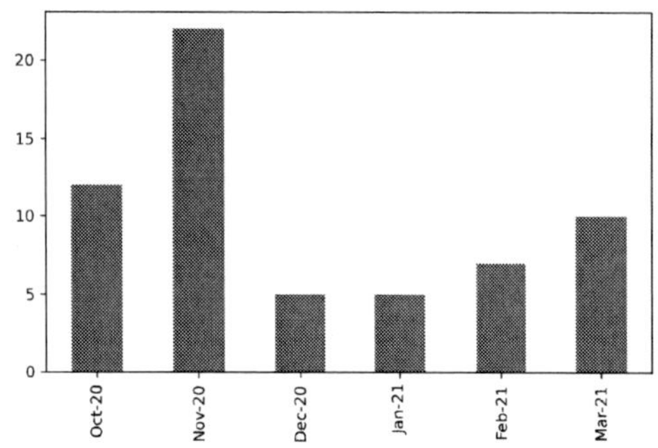


(a) The total number of users by month.

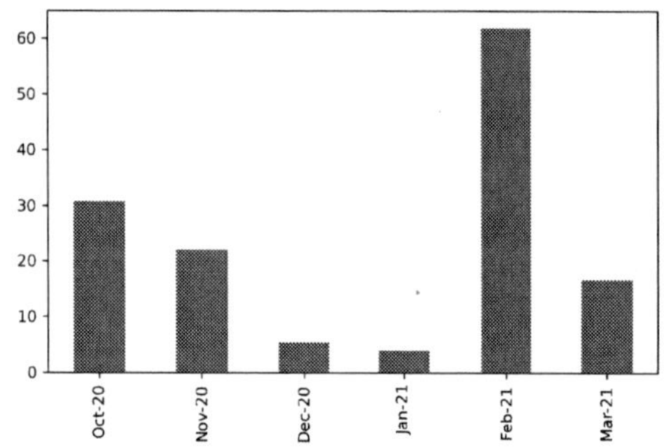


(b) The average length of a Spanish Writing Mentor usage session (in minutes) by month.

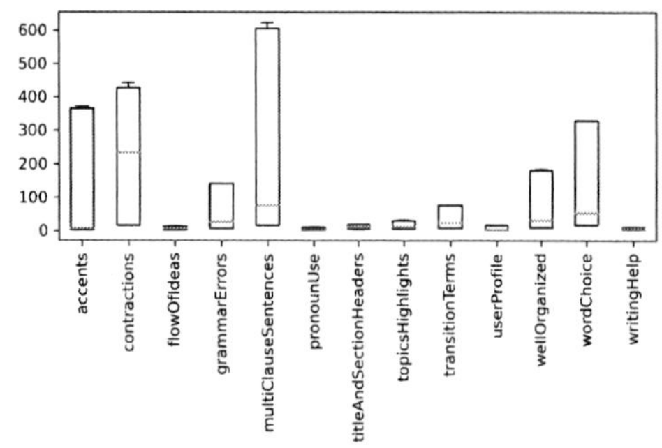


(c) The distribution of the time (in seconds) for each section of the app for the time period October to March.

Figure 6: Analysis of 6 months of user data

shows the number of unique users each month between October 2020 and March 2021. We see that the number of users peaked during our user study, but did not drop off entirely once the study was over. Figure 6b shows the average time (in minutes) for an active session (i.e. we exclude sessions where no text was entered). We see differences in average usage across months, but for the months with the most users, the average time spent using the app was between 15 and 30 minutes. Finally, Figure 6c shows the distribution of the time (in seconds) for each section of the app from the time period October 2020 to March 2021. We restrict the plot to the interquartile range, since there were many extreme outliers (probably due to users switching away from the app and coming back later). Even still, we see quite a range of values for the medial time spent per section. Sections such as contractions, grammar errors, word choice, transition terms, well organized and long sentences engaged the users for longer times, while sections such as flow of ideas, pronoun use, title and section headers engaged the users less.

## 6 Conclusions

We presented a tool to support writers of Spanish by providing them automated feedback within a free Google Docs add-on. The tool was built by adapting an existing tool for English, and implementing Spanish-language-specific components. We conducted a small study with 13 post-secondary level students in Mexico City, and in general found that they considered the tool helpful and were planning to continue using it and also recommend it to others. We see that their writing ability, as measured by a standardized test, improved between the pre- and post-tests, though we cannot yet say whether the Spanish Writing Mentor app contributed to this improvement. We find that a small number of users engage with the app, even outside of planned user studies, which is encouraging.

## References

Yigal Attali. 2004. Exploring the Feedback and Revision Features of *Criterion*. Paper presented at the National Council on Measurement in Education (NCME), Educational Testing Service, Princeton, NJ.

Lifang Bai and Guangwei Hu. 2017. In the face of fallible awe feedback: how do students respond? *Educational Psychology*, 37(1):67–81.

Beata Beigman Klebanov and Michael Flor. 2013. Word association profiles and their use for automated scoring of essays. In *Proceedings of the 51st Annual Meeting of the Association for Computational Linguistics (Volume 1: Long Papers)*, pages 1148–1158.

Jill Burstein, Norbert Elliot, Beata Beigman Klebanov, Nitin Madnani, Diane Napolitano,

Maxwell Schwartz, Patrick Houghton, and Hillary Molloy. 2018. Writing mentor: Writing progress using self-regulated writing support. *Journal of Writing Analytics*, 2:280–284.

Cristian Cardellino. 2019. Spanish Billion Words Corpus and Embeddings.

Jaeho Choi. 2010. *The Impact of Automated Essay Scoring (AES) for Improving English Language Learner's Essay Writing*. Ph.D. thesis, University of Virginia Charlottesville, VA.

Elena Cotos. 2011. Potential of automated writing evaluation feedback. *Calico Journal*, 28(2):420–459.

Frederick Crews. 1992. *The Random House Handbook*, Sixth edition. McGraw Hill.

Diana Hacker. 2006. *The Bedford Handbook*, Seventh edition. Bedford/St. Martin's.

Matthew Honnibal, Ines Montani, Sofie Van Landeghem, and Adriane Boyd. 2020. spaCy: Industrial-strength Natural Language Processing in Python.

Andrea A. Lunsford. 2008. *St. Martin's Handbook*, Sixth edition. Bedford/St. Martin's.

Nitin Madnani, Jill Burstein, Norbert Elliot, Beata Beigman Klebanov, Diane Napolitano, Slava Andreyev, and Maxwell Schwartz. 2018a. Writing mentor: Self-regulated writing feedback for struggling writers. In *Proceedings of the 27th International Conference on Computational Linguistics: System Demonstrations*, pages 113–117, Santa Fe, New Mexico. Association for Computational Linguistics.

Nitin Madnani, Aoife Cahill, Daniel Blanchard, Slava Andreyev, Diane Napolitano, Binod Gyawali, Michael Heilman, Chong Min Lee, Chee Wee Leong, Matthew Mulholland, and Brian Riordan. 2018b. A robust microservice architecture for scaling automated scoring applications. *ETS Research Report Series*, 2018(1).

Christopher D. Manning, Mihai Surdeanu, John Bauer, Jenny Finkel, Steven J. Bethard, and David McClosky. 2014. The Stanford CoreNLP natural language processing toolkit. In *Association for Computational Linguistics (ACL) System Demonstrations*, pages 55–60.

Ryo Nagata and Kazuhide Nakatani. 2010. Evaluating Performance of Grammatical Error Detection to Maximize Learning Effect. In *Proceedings of COLING (Posters)*, pages 894–900, Beijing, China.

John D Ramage, John C Bean, and June Johnson. 2015. *The Allyn & Bacon guide to writing*, Seventh edition. Pearson.

Jim Ranalli, Stephanie Link, and Evgeny Chukharev-Hudilainen. 2017. Automated writing evaluation for formative assessment of second language writing: investigating the accuracy and usefulness of feedback as part of argument-based validation. *Educational Psychology*, 37(1):8–25.

Rod D Roscoe, Laura K Allen, Jennifer L Weston, Scott A Crossley, and Danielle S McNamara. 2014. The writing pal intelligent tutoring system: Usability testing and development. *Computers and Composition*, 34:39–59.

Mark D. Shermis, Jill C. Burstein, and Leonard Bliss. 2004. The Impact of Automated Essay Scoring on High Stakes Writing Assessments. In *Annual Meeting of the National Council on Measurement in Education*.

# Appendix

## A User Survey

The following questions were included (in Spanish) in our final user survey:

| | |
|---|---|
| 1. Overall, how useful was Writing Mentor in helping you with your writing assignment? | 5 point scale (5 being most useful) |
| 2. What (if anything) did you like most about Writing Mentor? | free text |
| 3. What (if anything) did you like the least about Writing Mentor? | free text |
| 4. Do you think you learned anything by using Writing Mentor that will help you improve your writing? | Yes/No |
| a. If so, what? | free text |
| 5. Please mark the features that you found MOST useful (if any): | Multiple-select from list of all possible sections in the tool |
| 6. Please mark the *Writing Help* articles that you found MOST useful (if any) | Multiple-select from list of all help articles |
| 7. Please mark the features that you found LEAST useful (if any): | Multiple-select from list of all possible sections in the tool |
| 8. Please mark the *Writing Help* articles that you found LEAST useful (if any): | Multiple-select from list of all help articles |
| 9. What feature(s) should be added to writing mentor (if any) and why? | free text |
| 10. What other things should be improved in writing mentor (if any), and why? | free text |
| 11. Do you plan to use Writing Mentor again in the future to help you with your writing assignments? | Yes/No |
| 12. Do you plan to recommend Writing Mentor to others? | Yes/No |
| 13. Is there anything else you would like to share about your experience using writing mentor? | free text |

Table 2: Final User Survey Questions

# Alexa Conversations: An Extensible Data-driven Approach for Building Task-oriented Dialogue Systems

Anish Acharya*, Suranjit Adhikari, Sanchit Agarwal, Vincent Auvray, Nehal Belgamwar, Arijit Biswas, Shubhra Chandra, Tagyoung Chung, Maryam Fazel-Zarandi, Raefer Gabriel, Shuyang Gao, Rahul Goel*, Dilek Hakkani-Tur, Jan Jezabek, Abhay Jha, Jiun-Yu Kao, Prakash Krishnan, Peter Ku, Anuj Goyal, Chien-Wei Lin, Qing Liu, Arindam Mandal, Angeliki Metallinou, Vishal Naik, Yi Pan, Shachi Paul*, Vittorio Perera, Abhishek Sethi*, Minmin Shen, Nikko Strom and Eddie Wang

Amazon Alexa AI, Sunnyvale, California, USA[†]

## Abstract

Traditional goal-oriented dialogue systems rely on various components such as natural language understanding, dialogue state tracking, policy learning and response generation. Training each component requires annotations which are hard to obtain for every new domain, limiting scalability of such systems. Similarly, rule-based dialogue systems require extensive writing and maintenance of rules and do not scale either. End-to-End dialogue systems, on the other hand, do not require module-specific annotations but need a large amount of data for training. To overcome these problems, in this demo, we present Alexa Conversations[1], a new approach for building goal-oriented dialogue systems that is scalable, extensible as well as data efficient. The components of this system are trained in a data-driven manner, but instead of collecting annotated conversations for training, we generate them using a novel dialogue simulator based on a few seed dialogues and specifications of APIs and entities provided by the developer. Our approach provides out-of-the-box support for natural conversational phenomena like entity sharing across turns or users changing their mind during conversation without requiring developers to provide any such dialogue flows. We exemplify our approach using a simple pizza ordering task and showcase its value in reducing the developer burden for creating a robust experience. Finally, we evaluate our system using a typical movie ticket booking task and show that the dialogue simulator is an essential component of the system that leads to over 50% improvement in turn-level action signature prediction accuracy.

## 1 Introduction

Goal-oriented dialogue systems enable users to complete specific goals such as making restaurant reservations and buying train tickets. User goals may be complex and may require multiple turns to achieve. Moreover, users can refer to contextual values anaphorically, can correct previously informed preferences and provide additional or fewer entities (over-cooperative or under-cooperative user) than requested by the agent. This presents challenges for building robust dialogue agents that need to understand different kinds of user behavior, gather user requirements split over multiple turns and complete user goals with minimal friction. There is also limited availability of dialogue datasets and they span only a handful of application domains. Designing suitable data collection for dialogue systems is itself a research area.

Traditional dialogue systems follow a pipelined approach that ties together machine learning components for natural language understanding (NLU), dialogue state (belief) tracking, optimal action prediction (policy learning), and natural language generation (Young, 2000). Advances in deep learning techniques have led to the development of more end-to-end neural dialogue systems that combine some or all of the components of the traditional pipeline reducing the need for component-wise annotations and allowing for intermediate representations to be learned and optimized end-to-end (Wen et al., 2017; Liu et al., 2017). On the data side, notable data collection approaches for dialogue systems include the Wizard-of-Oz (WOZ) framework (Asri et al., 2017), rule-based or data-driven user simulators (Pietquin, 2005; Cuayáhuitl et al., 2005; Pietquin and Dutoit, 2006; Schatzmann et al., 2007; Fazel-Zarandi et al., 2017; Gur et al., 2018), and the recently-proposed Machines-Talking-To-Machines (M2M) framework (Shah et al., 2018) where user and system simulators interact with each other to generate dialogue outlines.

In this demo, we present Alexa Conversations, a novel system that enables developers to build ro-

*Work done while at Amazon

[†]Authors are ordered alphabetically

[1]https://tinyurl.com/y3lowd34



*Proceedings of NAACL-HLT 2021: Demonstrations*, pages 125–132
June 6–11, 2021. 

bust goal-oriented dialogue experiences with minimal effort. Our approach is example-driven as it learns from a small number of developer-provided seed dialogues and does not require encoding dialogue flows as rigid rules. Our system contains two core components: a dialogue simulator that generalizes input examples provided by the developer and a neural dialogue system that directly predicts the next optimal action given the conversation history. The dialogue simulator component extends the M2M framework (Shah et al., 2018) in two main directions. First, instead of generating user goals randomly, we use various goal sampling techniques biased towards the goals observed in the seed dialogues in order to support variations of those dialogues robustly. Second, in M2M, the system agent is geared towards database querying applications where the user browses a catalogue, selects an item and completes a transaction. In contrast, our formulation does not require any knowledge of the purpose of the APIs provided by the developer. Moreover, our system can generate a richer set of dialogue patterns including complex goals, proactive recommendations and users correcting earlier provided entities. The proposed neural dialogue model component follows an end-to-end systems approach and bears some similarities with Hybrid Code Networks (HCN) (Williams et al., 2017). However, compared to HCN, our system is more generic in the sense that it directly predicts the full API signature that contains the API name, values of the required API arguments, relevant optional API arguments and their values. The model chooses the API argument values to fill from user mentioned, agent mentioned and API returned entities present in the full dialogue context that includes the current user utterance.

We showcase the significance of our approach in reducing developer burden using the example of a pizza ordering skill. Compared to a rule-based system where a developer would have to code hundreds of dialogue paths to build a robust experience even for such a simple skill, Alexa Conversations requires only a handful of seed dialogues. To evaluate our approach, we build a movie ticket booking experience. On a test set collected via Wizard-of-Oz (WOZ) framework (Asri et al., 2017), we quantify the impact of our novel dialogue simulation approach showing that it leads to over 50% improvement in action signature prediction accuracy.

```
A: nlg:  welcome()
U: "how long is [ la la land | Movie → mt1 ]"
A: call:  GetDuration(movieTitle=$mt1) → d1
A: nlg:  inform_movie_duration(
         duration=$d1, movieTitle=$mt1)
U: "who stars in it"  //anaphoric reference
A: call:  GetCast(movieTitle=$mt1) → gcr1
A: nlg:  inform_movie_cast(
         cast=$gcr1, movieTitle=$mt)
   ...
U: "exit"
A: nlg:  stop()
```

Table 1: A seed dialogue with DML annotations. Note that variables are carried over to resolve anaphoric references.

| Template Name | Template Text |
|---|---|
| *inform_movie_duration* | "$movieTitle is $duration long" |
| *inform_movie_cast* | "$cast.name was in $movieTitle" |
| *offer_recommend_movie* | "Would you like a $genre movie?" |

Table 2: Developer-provided system NLG responses

## 2 System Overview

In Alexa Conversations, we follow a data-driven approach where the developer provides seed dialogues covering the main use cases they want to support, and annotates them in a Dialogue Markup Language (DML). Table 1 shows an example of an annotated conversation. Developers are required to provide their domain-specific APIs and custom Natural Language Generation (NLG) responses for interacting with the user, e.g., for informing an API output response or for requesting an API input argument as shown in Table 2. These APIs and system NLG responses, with their input arguments and output values, define the domain-specific schema of entities and actions that the dialogue system will predict. Developers also provide example user-utterances (as templates with entity-value placeholders) which the users may use to invoke certain APIs or to inform slot values.

To handle the wide variation of conversations a user can have with the dialogue system, Alexa Conversations augments the developer provided seed dialogues through a simulator. This component takes the annotated seed dialogues as input, and simulates different dialogue flows that achieve the same user goals but also include common patterns such as when a user confirms, changes, or repeats an entity or action. Optionally, it uses crowdsourcing through Amazon Mechanical Turk (MTurk) to enrich the natural language variations of user utterances provided by the developer. Overall, the

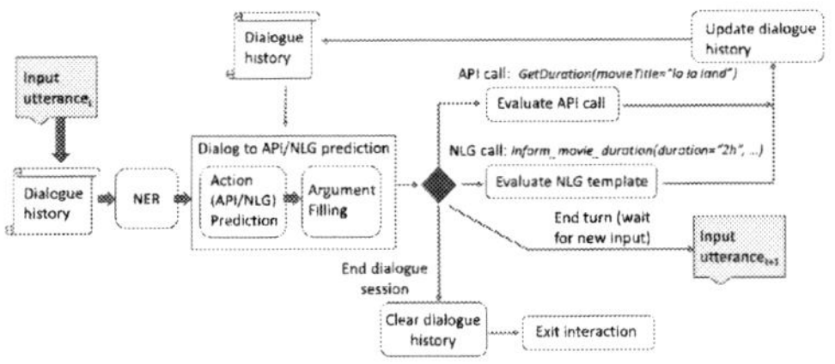


Figure 1: High-level overview of an input utterance's path

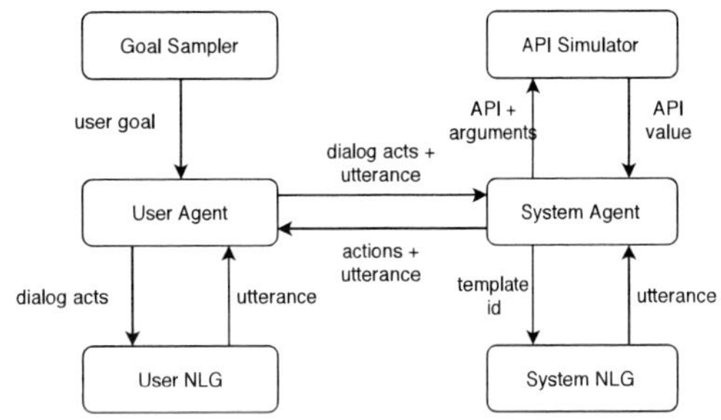


Figure 2: Simulator Architecture

developer provides on the order of 10 seed dialogues and the simulator generates on the order of 10K training dialogues with flow and language variations.

Alexa Conversations consists of three main domain-specific modeling components: 1) a Named-Entity Recognition (NER) model that tags entities in the user utterance (e.g., "La La Land" as a MovieTitle), 2) an Action Prediction (AP) model that predicts which API or NLG response should be executed next (e.g., *GetDuration* or *inform_movie_duration*), and 3) an Argument Filling (AF) model that fills required (and possibly optional) action arguments with entities (e.g., *GetDuration(MovieTitle="La La Land")*). We use the entire dialogue history, i.e., user utterances, system actions and responses, and API return values, as input for all modeling components. In this sense, this dialogue history is used as a generalized state representation from which models can retrieve relevant information. An overview of the runtime flow of a dialogue is illustrated in Figure 1. Each user utterance initiates a turn and is followed by NER, after which one or more actions are predicted. These actions could be either an API or NLG call, or a special action indicating the end of a turn or the end of dialogue. Every new action prediction updates the dialogue history and therefore influences future action predictions. For each API/NLG call the AF model is called to fill in the required arguments. When `<end of turn>` is predicted, the system waits for new user input. When `<end of dialogue>` is predicted, the system ends the interaction.

## 3 Dialogue Simulation

We propose a novel component called simulator to generate diverse but consistent dialogues, which can be used to train robust goal-oriented neural dialogue systems. We presented the simulator details in (Lin et al., 2020) and briefly provide an overview of the overall system here. A high-level simulator architecture is illustrated in Figure 2.

The simulator is structured in two distinct agents that interact turn-by-turn: the user and the system. The user samples a fixed goal at the beginning of the conversation. We propose novel goal-sampling techniques (Lin et al., 2020) to simulate variation in dialogue flows. The agents communicate at the semantic level through dialogue acts. Having the exact information associated with each turn allows us to define a simple heuristic system policy, whose output can be used as supervised training labels to bootstrap models. We note that the user policy is also heuristic-based. In each conversation, the user agent gradually reveals its goal and the system agent fulfills it by calling APIs. The system agent simulates each API call by randomly sampling a return value without actually calling the API and chooses an appropriate response action. Depending on the returned API value, the chosen response is associated with dialogue acts. The system agent gradually constructs an estimate of the user goal and makes proactive offers based on this estimated goal. The dialogue acts generated through self-play are also used to interface between agents and their template-based NLG model. After sampling the dialogue acts from their policy, each agent samples the surface-form from available templates corresponding to the dialogue acts. In addition to enriching the dialogue flows; we use crowd-sourcing through MTurk to enrich the natural language variations of the user utterance templates. Goal sampling and the self-play loop provide dialogue flow variations while crowd-sourcing enriches language variations, both of which are essential for training robust conversational models.

We introduce additional variations to dialogues during simulation for more natural conversation

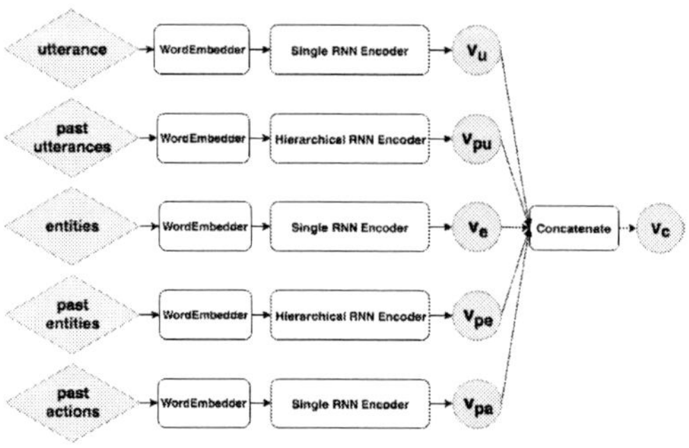


Figure 3: An example of a dialogue context encoder. Different downstream models use slightly different subsets of these features as input.

generation. In goal-oriented conversations, users often change their mind during the course of the conversation. For example, while booking a movie ticket a user may decide to purchase three adult tickets but could eventually change their mind to book only two tickets. We used additional heuristics to introduce such variations to conversations without any additional input requirements from the developer. Another important non-task-specific conversational behavior is the system's ability to suggest an appropriate next action based on the conversation history, without requiring invocation by a specific user utterance. We introduce proactive offers in the system policy of the simulator to facilitate exploration of the available API functionality in a manner consistent with human conversation.

## 4 Models

For each domain, we have three separate models: NER, Action Prediction (AP) and Argument Filling (AF), all of which depend on features extracted from conversation history and encoded using Dialogue Context Encoders.

### 4.1 Dialogue Context Encoders

Given a dialogue, we first apply feature extractors to extract both turn-level, e.g. `current_user_utterance` and `current_entities` (recognized by the NER model), and dialogue-level features, e.g. `past_user_utterances`, `past_actions` and `past_entities`. We pass these extracted features through feature-specific encoders and concatenate the feature representations to obtain the final representation for dialogue context. For encoding turn-level features and dialogue-level features, we use single LSTM and hierarchical LSTM architectures, respectively. For example, for encoding `past_user_utterances`, we use a hierarchical LSTM, where we encode the sequence of words with an inner LSTM and the sequence of turns with an outer LSTM. For `past_actions`, a single LSTM is sufficient. Figure 3 shows an example of our dialogue context encoders. We augment the context encoders with word and sentence embedding vectors from pre-trained language models (Peters et al., 2018; Devlin et al., 2018).

### 4.2 NER

The NER model is used to extract domain-specific entities from user utterances, which are then consumed by downstream models. Our NER model is based on bi-LSTM-CRF (Ma and Hovy, 2016) model. To incorporate dialogue history, we concatenate the encoded dialogue context to the word embedding of each token and use it as the input to our model. To improve NER performance on entities with large and dynamic possible values (e.g. movie titles, restaurant names), we also incorporate catalogue-based features based on domain-specific catalogues of entity values provided by the developer and values returned by APIs. Specifically, catalogue features are computed by scanning the utterance with consecutive windows of size $n$ tokens and detecting any exact matches of the current window with the catalogue entries. For a domain with $K$ domain-specific catalogues, the binary feature will be of dimension $K$, where value 1 indicates an exact match in the catalogue. This approach is inspired by (Williams, 2019), which proposed a generic NER approach but not specific to conversational systems.

### 4.3 Action Prediction (AP)

The goal of the Action Prediction model is to predict the next action the agent should take, given the dialogue history. As illustrated in Figure 1, an action could be an API name (e.g. GetDuration), a system NLG response name (e.g. inform_movie_duration) or a general system action (e.g. `<end of turn>`). The model takes the dialogue context encoding, as described in Section 4.1 and passes it through linear and softmax layers to output a distribution over all actions within the domain. Our system selects $n$-best action hypotheses using a simple binning strategy. We reject actions in the low confidence bins and if there is no actions available in the high-

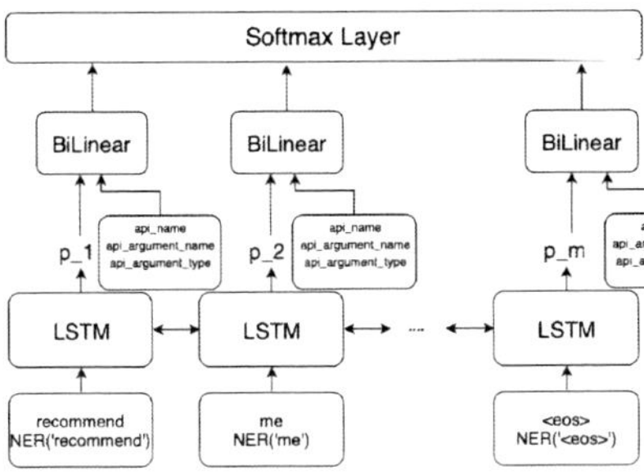


Figure 4: Argument filling model architecture

confidence bin, we randomly sample an action from the medium-confidence bin.

### 4.4 Argument Filling (AF)

The role of the Argument Filling model is to fill the arguments given a particular action and the dialogue history. We formulate the argument filling task as a variation of neural reading comprehension (Chen, 2018) where we treat the dialogue history as a passage to comprehend and ask machine the question "what is the argument value of a particular action?". Specifically, for each argument of an action and each entity mention detected by NER, our model predicts whether to use that entity mention to fill that argument. We do this by encoding all the entities in the dialogue history and use a pointer mechanism to point to the entity position given a particular action and argument combination. The overall architecture for argument filling is shown in Figure 4. Note that a similar method to dialogue state tracking has been proposed by (Gao et al., 2019). We impose constraints to only fill arguments with entities of the correct type according to the action schema provided by the developer. For example, we only consider *Time* entity mentions to fill arguments that accept *Time* type. Finally, we combine the argument filling result with the action prediction result to execute the next system action. API arguments can also be optional. For these type of arguments, we create special `optional` token and insert in the dialogue context and train the model to point to that token when an optional API argument should not be filled.

## 5 Case Study 1: Pizzabot

To showcase how Alexa Conversations improves the skill-building experience of a typical developer, we discuss *Pizzabot*, a pizza ordering skill. *Pizzabot* is provided as one of the template Alexa Conversations skills to help bootstrap a new developer. It allows a user to order a pizza of various sizes, with different kinds of crusts and their choice of any number of toppings. The skill has just one main API *OrderPizza* with four slots types: *toppingsList*, *crust*, *cheese* and *size*. Even with this simple skill, ordering a two topping pizza with a choice of say 10 toppings, 5 crusts and 5 cheese in 4 different sizes results in over hundreds of different possible dialogue paths. With a typical rule-based dialogue manager, a developer would need to code most, if not all, of these flows for building a robust experience. On the other hand, with Alexa Conversations, a *Pizzabot* developer needs to provide just 7 example dialogues to support a total of 3 APIs and 6 entity types. The different variations are automatically generated by the proposed simulator and are consumed by the models, resulting in a robust skill with significantly lower developer effort. Alexa Conversations also provides out-of-the-box support for features like context carryover, entity confirmation, user correction, over/under-cooperative user, and multi-value slots without requiring the developer to write custom rules or logic, making the skill more robust to real user interactions. See Table 3 for an example interaction with *Pizzabot*.

U: I want to order a large pizza
A: You wanted a large pizza, is that correct? *(entity confirmation)*
U: actually make it small *(user correction)*
A: You wanted a small pizza, is that correct?
U: yes
A: What would you like on your pizza?
U: olives tomatoes and green peppers with thin crust and extra cheese *(multi-value slots, over-cooperative user)*
A: So far I have a small olives, tomatoes, green peppers pizza on thin crust with extra cheese. Is that correct? *(context carryover)*
U: yes
A: Great! I placed your order for a total of $5.99.

Table 3: A seed conversation with Pizzabot

## 6 Case Study 2: Ticketbot

To showcase the end-customer impact of Alexa Conversations, we built a movie ticket-booking experience which we call *Ticketbot*. *Ticketbot* allows a user to browse and book movie tickets. Users can browse currently playing movies by various search criteria like date, time, location, theater and movie title. They can specify one or more search criteria either within a single turn or across multiple turns. After finding their choice of movie and theater, users can select a particular showtime, provide booking details like number of tickets and finally confirm booking. The experience was built based on the information provided by the developer. This is a complex experience with 10 APIs, 28 entity types, 10 NLG responses and 35 seed dialogues all provided as an input to the system. This experience was implemented using live APIs that were provided by the developers and thus the users were able to actually achieve their goals and complete ticket-booking transactions.

### 6.1 Evaluation

To evaluate our models, we collected data using a Wizard-of-Oz (WOZ) framework (Asri et al., 2017). These collected dialogues were then annotated by a team of professional annotators using the Dialogue Markup Language. Annotators tagged entities, API and NLG calls and unsupported requests. This is a challenging task and we adopted various methods like inter-annotator agreement and random vetting to ensure high data annotation quality. The test set contained 50 dialogues with an average length of 5.74 turns.

We measure the F1 scores for spans of entities to evaluate NER performance. We also measure the accuracy for action prediction (AP) and full action signature prediction (ASP). The latter metric reflects the performance of both the AP and AF models combined: an action signature is counted as correct when both the action and all the corresponding arguments are predicted correctly. We compute these metrics per turn given fixed dialogue context from previous turns, where a turn can contain one user action and multiple agent actions (multiple api calls, nlg call, wait for user action). Turn-level ASP accuracy most closely reflects the user experience when interacting with the skill. Overall, the system has reasonably high turn-level action signature prediction accuracy, with relatively few failures. We discuss some common failure patterns in 6.2.

We evaluate the proposed dialogue simulation method to establish the impact of this novel component. To do so, we train models with data generated using different simulation approaches and compare their performance on the test set. The baseline approach, Base sampler from (Lin et al., 2020), simply resamples dialogues that are identical in logical structure to the seed dialogues. It generates no new dialogue flows but does add language variations via sampling from developer-provided catalogs and user utterance templates. We observe that models trained on data generated with Sec. 3 significantly outperform the models trained on data generated with baseline as shown in Table 4.

| NER Span Relative F1 | AP Relative Accuracy | ASP Relative Accuracy |
|---|---|---|
| $+18.50\%$ | $+20.92\%$ | $+52.80\%$ |

Table 4: Relative NER span F1-score, AP accuracy and ASP accuracy on Ticket Booking (TB) test set, averaged over 5 runs.

### 6.2 Error Analysis

We conduct an error analysis of our models on the TicketBot test set to investigate performance across different tasks. We showcase a few common error patterns in this section.

#### 6.2.1 NER

We notice that NER model struggles to make correct predictions when the slot value is out of the catalogue vocabulary. As we use fixed slot catalogues during dialogue simulation, it is a difficult task for NER to generalize when real API calls return unseen values. We see that using dynamic catalogue feature significantly improves NER performance, particularly for `Movie` slot. Dynamic catalogues store entities mentioned in system's responses and thus dynamic catalogue feature provides a strong signal to NER when the user later mentions one of those entities. In addition to exact match, the feature also fires for fuzzy matches leading to higher recall without significant drop in precision. Note that, NER model is not run on system utterances; the entities are tagged by the developer in the response NLG templates. Table 5 shows one example in which *"A Star Is Born"* is not recognized as `Movie` without this feature. Overall, by adding dynamic catalogue feature, NER improves by $+11.26\%$ on the `Movie` slot.

#### 6.2.2 ASP

We find that Argument Filling Model makes mistakes when deciding whether or not to carryover a particular argument. In most such failures, either behavior (carryover or not carryover) is logically correct. However, the user might have a specific be-

| U: give me [sunday \| Date] showtimes |
|---|
| A: I found [A Star Is Born \| Movie] playing at ... *(mentioned movie)* |
| U: is [captain marvel \| Movie] playing [sunday \| Date] |
| A: I found showtimes for [Captain Marvel \| Movie] at ... |
| U: is it playing anywhere else |
| A: Sorry, I could not find any matching showtimes |
| U: huh ok what are the showtimes for a star is born again |
| ... |

Table 5: A partial dialogue from Ticketbot test set showing NER mistake

havior in mind, while the model chooses the other path. For example, in Table 6, AF model carryovers theater and date information, while the particular user wanted to know showtimes at all nearby theaters. As evident, this case is ambiguous as both carrying over and not carrying over the theater and date arguments is reasonable. To define the correct carryover behavior, we advise application developers to provide a few examples demonstrating the carryover behavior for each of their use cases. These examples then bias the dialogue simulator to generate data with the desired carryover behavior.

| U: What is playing at Century Cinemas tomorrow? |
|---|
| A: *call: FindMovies(theater="Century Cinemas", date="tomorrow") -> show0* |
| A: Cold Pursuit is playing at Century Cinemas 16 at 8 PM tomorrow |
| U: What are the showtimes for Joker? |
| A: *call: FindMovies(movie="Joker", theater="Century Cinemas", date="tomorrow") -> show1* |
| ... |

Table 6: A partial dialogue from Ticketbot test set showing argument carryover mistake

## 7 Conclusions

We presented Alexa Conversations, a novel data-driven and data-efficient approach for building goal-oriented conversational experiences. Our proposed system significantly reduces developer burden while still allowing them to build robust experiences. We envision that this system will be used by a wide variety of developers who only need to provide seed dialogues and action schema to build conversational experiences[1].

We expect our system to mature in the following directions in future. We aim to reduce developer requirements for providing NLG responses by introducing a statistical NLG system. We will also develop robust mechanisms for incorporating developer feedback through supervised and semi-supervised methods to improve the performance of our simulator and modeling components.

## References


Layla El Asri, Hannes Schulz, Shikhar Sharma, Jeremie Zumer, Justin Harris, Emery Fine, Rahul Mehrotra, and Kaheer Suleman. 2017. Frames: A corpus for adding memory to goal-oriented dialogue systems. *arXiv preprint arXiv:1704.00057*.

Danqi Chen. 2018. *Neural Reading Comprehension and Beyond*. Ph.D. thesis, Stanford University.

Heriberto Cuayáhuitl, Steve Renals, Oliver Lemon, and Hiroshi Shimodaira. 2005. Human-computer dialogue simulation using hidden markov models. In *IEEE Workshop on Automatic Speech Recognition and Understanding, 2005.*, pages 290–295. IEEE.

Jacob Devlin, Ming-Wei Chang, Kenton Lee, and Kristina Toutanova. 2018. Bert: Pre-training of deep bidirectional transformers for language understanding. *arXiv preprint arXiv:1810.04805*.

Maryam Fazel-Zarandi, Shang-Wen Li, Jin Cao, Jared Casale, Peter Henderson, David Whitney, and Alborz Geramifard. 2017. Learning robust dialog policies in noisy environments. *1st Workshop on Conversational AI at NIPS*.

Shuyang Gao, Abhishek Sethi, Sanchit Aggarwal, Tagyoung Chung, and Dilek Hakkani-Tur. 2019. Dialog state tracking: A neural reading comprehension approach. *Proceedings of the 20th Annual SIGdial Meeting on Discourse and Dialogue (SIGDIAL)*.

Izzeddin Gur, Dilek Zeynep Hakkani, Gökhan Tür, and Pararth Shah. 2018. User modeling for task oriented dialogues. *2018 IEEE Spoken Language Technology Workshop (SLT)*, pages 900–906.

Chien-Wei Lin, Vincent Auvray, Daniel Elkind, Arijit Biswas, Maryam Fazel-Zarandi, Nehal Belgamwar, Shubhra Chandra, Matt Zhao, Angeliki Metallinou,


[1] iRobot (`https://tinyurl.com/y5pjp3xn`), BigSky (`https://tinyurl.com/y2ejvd3z`) and Art Museum (`https://tinyurl.com/y3umpqo2`) are some of the external skills that have already been built using Alexa Conversations

Tagyoung Chung, et al. 2020. Dialog simulation with realistic variations for training goal-oriented conversational systems. *1st Workshop on Human in the Loop Dialogue Systems at Neurips.*

Bing Liu, Gokhan Tur, Dilek Hakkani-Tur, Pararth Shah, and Larry Heck. 2017. End-to-end optimization of task-oriented dialogue model with deep reinforcement learning. *arXiv:1711.10712.*

X. Ma and E. Hovy. 2016. End-to-end sequence labeling via bi-directional lstm-cnns-crf. In *Proc. of the 54th Annual Meeting of the ACL (ACL) 2016.*

Matthew E Peters, Mark Neumann, Mohit Iyyer, Matt Gardner, Christopher Clark, Kenton Lee, and Luke Zettlemoyer. 2018. Deep contextualized word representations. *arXiv preprint arXiv:1802.05365.*

Olivier Pietquin. 2005. *A framework for unsupervised learning of dialogue strategies.* Presses univ. de Louvain.

Olivier Pietquin and Thierry Dutoit. 2006. A probabilistic framework for dialog simulation and optimal strategy learning. *IEEE Transactions on Audio, Speech, and Language Processing*, 14(2):589–599.

Jost Schatzmann, Blaise Thomson, Karl Weilhammer, Hui Ye, and Steve Young. 2007. Agenda-based user simulation for bootstrapping a pomdp dialogue system. In *Human Language Technologies 2007: The Conference of the North American Chapter of the Association for Computational Linguistics; Companion Volume, Short Papers*, pages 149–152. Association for Computational Linguistics.

Pararth Shah, Dilek Hakkani-Tür, Gokhan Tür, Abhinav Rastogi, Ankur Bapna, Neha Nayak, and Larry Heck. 2018. Building a Conversational Agent Overnight with Dialogue Self-Play. (i).

Tsung Hsien Wen, David Vandyke, Nikola Mrkšíc, Milica Gašíc, Lina M. Rojas-Barahona, Pei Hao Su, Stefan Ultes, and Steve Young. 2017. A network-based end-to-end trainable task-oriented dialogue system. *15th Conference of the European Chapter of the Association for Computational Linguistics, EACL 2017 - Proceedings of Conference*, 1:438–449.

Jason D Williams, Kavosh Asadi, and Geoffrey Zweig. 2017. Hybrid code networks: practical and efficient end-to-end dialog control with supervised and reinforcement learning. *arXiv preprint arXiv:1702.03274.*

Kyle Williams. 2019. Neural lexicons for slot tagging in spoken language understanding. In *2019 Annual Conference of the North American Chapter of the Association for Computational Linguistics (NAACL '19).*

Steve J Young. 2000. Probabilistic methods in spoken–dialogue systems. *Philosophical Transactions of the Royal Society of London. Series A: Mathematical, Physical and Engineering Sciences*, 358(1769):1389–1402.

# RESIN: A Dockerized Schema-Guided Cross-document Cross-lingual Cross-media Information Extraction and Event Tracking System

**Haoyang Wen[1], Ying Lin[1], Tuan Manh Lai[1], Xiaoman Pan[1], Sha Li[1], Xudong Lin[2], Ben Zhou[3]**
**Manling Li[1], Haoyu Wang[3], Hongming Zhang[3], Xiaodong Yu[3], Alexander Dong[3]**
**Zhenhailong Wang[1], Yi Ren Fung[1], Piyush Mishra[4], Qing Lyu[3], Dídac Surís[2]**
**Brian Chen[2], Susan Windisch Brown[4], Martha Palmer[4], Chris Callison-Burch[3]**
**Carl Vondrick[2], Jiawei Han[1], Dan Roth[3], Shih-Fu Chang[2], Heng Ji[1]**
[1] University of Illinois at Urbana-Champaign [2] Columbia University
[3] University of Pennsylvania [4] University of Colorado, Boulder
hengji@illinois.edu,sc250@columbia.edu,danroth@seas.upenn.edu

## Abstract

We present a new information extraction system that can automatically construct temporal event graphs from a collection of news documents from multiple sources, multiple languages (English and Spanish for our experiment), and multiple data modalities (speech, text, image and video). The system advances state-of-the-art from two aspects: (1) extending from sentence-level event extraction to cross-document cross-lingual cross-media event extraction, coreference resolution and temporal event tracking; (2) using human curated event schema library to match and enhance the extraction output. We have made the dockerlized system publicly available for research purpose at GitHub[1], with a demo video[2].

## 1 Introduction

Event extraction and tracking technologies can help us understand real-world events described in the overwhelming amount of news data, and how they are inter-connected. These techniques have already been proven helpful in various application domains, including news analysis (Glavaš and Štajner, 2013; Glavaš et al., 2014; Choubey et al., 2020), aiding natural disaster relief efforts (Panem et al., 2014; Zhang et al., 2018; Medina Maza et al., 2020), financial analysis (Ding et al., 2014, 2016; Yang et al., 2018; Jacobs et al., 2018; Ein-Dor et al., 2019; Özbayoglu et al., 2020) and healthcare monitoring (Raghavan et al., 2012; Jagannatha and Yu, 2016; Klassen et al., 2016; Jeblee and Hirst, 2018).

However, it's much more difficult to remember event-related information compared to entity-related information. For example, most people in the United States will be able to answer the question "Which city is Columbia University located in?", but very few people can give a complete answer to "Who died from COVID-19?". Progress in natural language understanding and computer vision has helped automate some parts of event understanding but the current, *first-generation*, automated event understanding is overly simplistic since most methods focus on sentence-level sequence labeling for event extraction. Existing methods for complex event understanding also lack of incorporating knowledge in the form of a repository of abstracted event schemas (complex event templates), understanding the progress of time via temporal event tracking, using background knowledge, and performing global inference and enhancement.

To address these limitations, in this paper we will demonstrate a new end-to-end open-source dockerized research system to extract temporally ordered events from a collection of news documents from multiple sources, multiple languages (English and Spanish for our experiment), and multiple data modalities (speech, text, image and video). Our system consists of a pipeline of components that involve schema-guided entity, relation and complex event extraction, entity and event coreference resolution, temporal event tracking and cross-media entity and event grounding. Event schemas encode knowledge of stereotypical structures of events and their connections. Our end-to-end system has been dockerized and made publicly available for research purpose.

## 2 Approach

### 2.1 Overview

The architecture of our system is illustrated in Figure 1. Our system extracts information from multilingual multimedia document clusters. Each docu-

[1]Github: https://github.com/RESIN-KAIROS/RESIN-pipeline-public

[2]Video: http://blender.cs.illinois.edu/software/resin/resin.mp4



*Proceedings of NAACL-HLT 2021: Demonstrations*, pages 133–143
June 6–11, 2021. ©2021 Association for Computational Linguistics

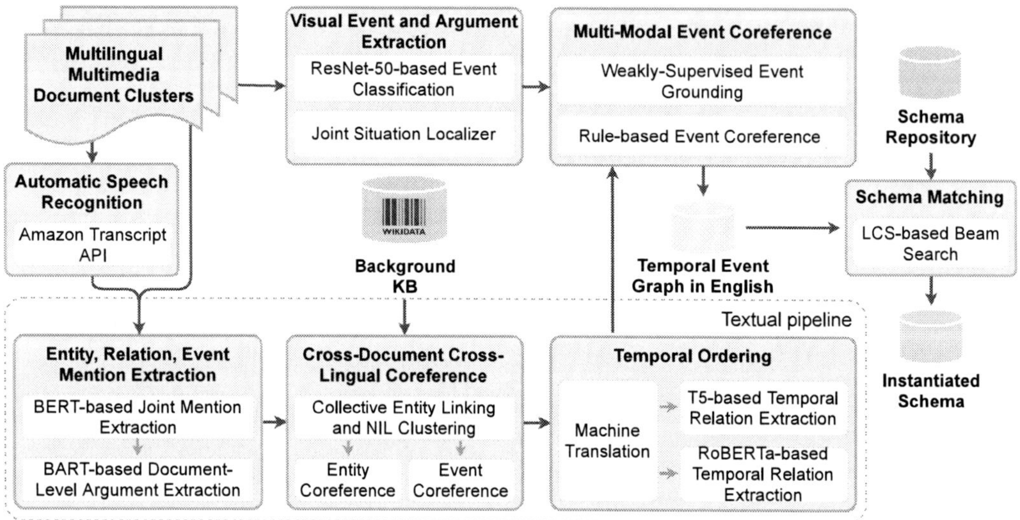


Figure 1: The architecture of RESIN schema-guided information extraction and temporal event tracking system.

ment cluster contains documents about a specific complex event. Our textual pipeline takes input from texts and transcribed speeches. It first extracts entity, relation and event mentions (Section 2.2-2.3) and then perform cross-document cross-lingual entity and event coreference resolution (Section 2.4). The extracted events are then ordered by temporal relation extraction (Section 2.5). Our visual pipeline takes images and videos as input and extracts events and arguments from visual signals and ground the extracted knowledge elements onto our extracted graph via cross-media event coreference resolution (Section 2.6). Finally, our system selects the schema from a schema repository that best matches the extracted IE graph and merges these two graphs (Section 2.7). Our system can extract 24 types of entities, 46 types of relations and 67 types of events as defined in the DARPA KAIROS[3] ontology.

## 2.2 Joint Entity, Relation and Event Mention Extraction and Linking from Speech and Text

For speech input, we apply the Amazon Transcribe API [4] for converting English and Spanish speech to text. When the language is not specified, it is automatically detected from the audio signal. It returns the transcription with starting and ending times for each detected words, as well as potential alternative transcriptions.

Then from the speech recognition results and text input, we extract entity, relation, and event mentions using OneIE (Lin et al., 2020), a state-of-the-art joint neural model for sentence-level information extraction. Given a sentence, the goal of this module is to extract an information graph $G = (V, E)$, where $V$ is the node set containing entity mentions and event triggers and $E$ is the edge set containing entity relations and event-argument links. We use a pre-trained BERT encoder (Devlin et al., 2018) to obtain contextualized word representations for the input sentence. Next, we adopt separate conditional random field-based taggers to identify entity mention and event trigger spans from the sentence. We represent each span, or node in the information graph, by averaging vectors of words in the span. After that, we calculate the label scores for each node or edge using separate task-specific feed forward networks. In order to capture the interactions among knowledge elements, we incorporate schema-guided global features when decoding information graphs. For a candidate graph $G$, we define a global feature vector $\boldsymbol{f} = \{f_1(G), ..., f_M(G)\}$, where $f_i(\cdot)$ is a function that evaluates whether $G$ matches a specific global feature. We compute the global feature score as $\boldsymbol{uf}$, where $\boldsymbol{u}$ is a learnable weight vector. Finally, we use a beam search-based decoder to generate the information graph with the highest global score. After we extract these mentions, we

[3]https://www.darpa.mil/program/knowledge-directed-artificial-intelligence-reasoning-over-schemas

[4]https://aws.amazon.com/transcribe/

apply a syntactic parser (Honnibal et al., 2020) to extend mention head words to their extents. Then we apply a cross-lingual entity linker (Pan et al., 2017) to link entity mentions to WikiData (Vrandečić and Krötzsch, 2014)[5].

### 2.3 Document-level Event Argument Extraction

The previous module can only operate on the sentence level. In particular, event arguments can often be found in neighboring sentences. To make up for this, we further develop a document-level event argument extraction model (Li et al., 2021) and use the union of the extracted arguments from both models as the final output. We formulate the argument extraction problem as *conditional text generation*. Our model can easily handle the case of missing arguments and multiple arguments in the same role without the need of tuning thresholds and can extract all arguments in a single pass. The condition consists of the original document and a blank *event template*. For example, the template for `Transportation` event type is *arg1 transported arg2 in arg3 from arg4 place to arg5 place*. The desired output is a filled template with the arguments.

Our model is based on BART (Lewis et al., 2020), which is an encoder-decoder language model. To utilize the encoder-decoder LM for argument extraction, we construct an input sequence of $\langle \mathrm{s} \rangle$ template $\langle s \rangle \langle /s \rangle$document $\langle /s \rangle$. All argument names (arg1, arg2 etc.) in the template are replaced by a special placeholder token $\langle \mathrm{arg} \rangle$. This model is trained in an end-to-end fashion by directly optimizing the generation probability.

To align the extracted arguments back to the document, we adopt a simple postprocessing procedure and find the matching text span closest to the corresponding event trigger.

### 2.4 Cross-document Cross-lingual Entity and Event Coreference Resolution

After extracting all mentions of entities and events, we apply our cross-document cross-lingual entity coreference resolution model, which is an extension of the e2e-coref model (Lee et al., 2017). We use the multilingual XLM-RoBERTa (XLM-R) Transformer model (Conneau et al., 2020) so that our coreference resolution model can handle non-English data. Second, we port the e2e-coref model to the *cross-lingual cross-document* setting. Given $N$ hybrid English and Spanish input documents, we create $\frac{N(N-1)}{2}$ pairs of documents and treat each pair as a single "mega-document". We apply our model to each mega-document and, at the end, aggregate the predictions across all mega-documents to extract the coreference clusters. Finally, we also apply a simple heuristic rule that prevents two entity mentions from being merged together if they are linked to different entities with high confidence.

Our event coreference resolution method (Lai et al., 2021) is similar to entity coreference resolution, while incorporating additional symbolic features such as the event type information. If the input documents are all about one specific complex event, we apply some schema-guided heuristic rules to further refine the predictions of the neural event coreference resolution model. For example, in a bombing schema, there is typically only one bombing event. Therefore, in a document cluster, if there are two event mentions of type *bombing* and they have several arguments in common, these two mentions will be considered as coreferential.

### 2.5 Cross-document Temporal Event Ordering

Based on the event coreference resolution component described above, we group all mentions into clusters. Next we aim to order events along a timeline. We follow Zhou et al. (2020) to design a component for temporal event ordering. Specifically, we further pre-train a T5 model (Raffel et al., 2020) with distant temporal ordering supervision signals. These signals are acquired through two set of syntactic patterns: 1) before/after keywords in text and 2) explicit date and time mentions. We take such a pre-trained temporal T5 model and finetune it on MATRES (Ning et al., 2018b) and use it as the system for temporal event ordering. We perform pair-wise temporal relation classification for all event mention pairs in a documents.

We further train an alternative model from finetuning RoBERTa (Liu et al., 2019) on MATRES (Ning et al., 2018b). This model has also been successfully applied for event time prediction (Wen et al., 2021; Li et al., 2020a). We only consider event mention pairs which are within neighboring sentences, or can be connected by shared arguments.

Besides model prediction, we also learn high confident patterns from the schema repository. We

[5]`https://www.wikidata.org/`

consider temporal relations that appear very frequently as our prior knowledge. For each given document cluster, we apply these patterns as high-precision patterns before two statistical temporal ordering models separately. The schema matching algorithm will select the best matching from two graphs as the final instantiated schema results.

Because the annotation for non-English data can be expensive and time-consuming, the temporal event tracking component has only been trained on English input. To extend the temporal event tracking capability to cross-lingual setting, we apply Google Cloud neural machine translation [6] to translate Spanish documents into English and apply the FastAlign algorithm (Dyer et al., 2013) to obtain word alignment.

### 2.6 Cross-media Information Grounding and Fusion

**Visual event and argument role extraction:** Our goal is to extract visual events along with their argument roles from visual data, i.e., images and videos. In order to train event extractor from visual data, we have collected a new dataset called **Video M2E2** which contains 1,500 video-article pairs by searching over YouTube news channels using 18 event primitives related to visual concepts as search keywords. We have extensively annotated the the videos and sampled key frames for annotating bounding boxes of argument roles.

Our Visual Event and Argument Role Extraction system consists of an event classification model (ResNet-50 (He et al., 2016)) and an argument role extraction model (JSL (Marasović et al., 2020)). To extract the events and associated argument roles, we leverage a public dataset called Situation with Groundings (SWiG) (Marasović et al., 2020) to pretrain our system. SWiG is designed for event and argument understanding in images with object groundings but has a different ontology. We mapped the event types, argument role types and entity names in SWiG to our ontology (covering 12 event sub-types) so that our model is able to extract event information from both images and videos. For videos, we sample frames at a frame rate of 1 frame per second and process them as individual images. In this way, we have a unified model for both image and video inputs.

[6] `https://cloud.google.com/translate/docs/advanced/translating-text-v3`

**Multimodal event coreference:** We further extended the previous visual event extraction model to find coreference links between visual and text events. For the video frames with detected events, we apply a weakly-supervised grounding model (Akbari et al., 2019) to find sentences and video frames that have high frame-to-sentence similarity, representing the sentence content similar to the video frame content. We apply a rule-based approach to determine if a visual event mention and a textual event mention are coreferential: (1) Their event types match; (2) No contradiction in the entity types for the same argument role across different modalities. (3) The video frame and sentence have a high semantic similarity score. Based on this pipeline, we are able to add visual provenance of events into the event graph. Moreover, we are able to add visual-only arguments to the event graph, which makes the event graph more informative.

### 2.7 Schema Matching

Once we have acquired a large-scale schema repository by schema induction methods (Li et al., 2020c), we can view it as providing a scaffolding that we can instantiate with incoming data to construct temporal event graphs. Based on each document cluster, we need to find the most accurate schema from the schema repository. We further design a schema matching algorithm that can align our extracted event, entities and relations to a schema.

We first perform topological sort for events based on temporal relations for both IE graph and schema graph so that we can get linearized event sequences in chronological order. Then for each pair of IE graph and schema graph, we apply the longest common subsequence (LCS) method to find the best matching. Our schema matching considers coreference and relations, which will break the optimal substructure when only considering event sequences. We extend the algorithm by replacing the best results for subproblems with a beam of candidates with ranking from a scoring metric that considers matched events, arguments and relations. The candidates consist of matched event pairs, and then we greedily match their arguments and relations for scoring. We merge the best matched IE graph and schema graph to form the final instantiated schema.

## 3 Experiments

### 3.1 Data

We have conducted evaluations including schema matching and schema-guided information extraction.

### 3.2 Quantitative Performance

**Schema Induction.** To induce schemas, we collect Wikipedia articles describing complex events related to *improvised explosive device (IED)*, and extract event graphs by applying our IE system. The data statistics are shown in Table 1. We induce schemas by applying the path language model (Li et al., 2020c) over event paths in the training data, and merge top ranked paths into schema graphs for human curation. The statistics of the human curated schema repository are shown in Table 2.

| Split | #Docs | #Events | #Arguments | #Relations |
|---|---|---|---|---|
| **Train** | 5,247 | 41,672 | 136,894 | 122,846 |
| **Dev** | 575 | 4,661 | 15,404 | 13,320 |
| **Test** | 577 | 5,089 | 16,721 | 14,054 |

Table 1: Data statistics of IED Schema Learning Corpus.

| Schema | #Steps | #Arguments | #Temporal Links |
|---|---|---|---|
| **Disease Outbreak** | 20 | 94 | 20 |
| **Disaster Relief** | 15 | 85 | 15 |
| **Medical Treatment** | 8 | 37 | 8 |
| **Search and Rescue** | 11 | 50 | 10 |
| **General Attack** | 21 | 89 | 27 |
| **General IED** | 33 | 144 | 43 |
| **Roadside IED** | 28 | 123 | 36 |
| **Car IED** | 34 | 148 | 45 |
| **Drone Strikes IED** | 32 | 142 | 48 |
| **Backpack IED** | 31 | 138 | 40 |

Table 2: Data statistics of the induced schema library.

**Schema-guided Information Extraction.** The performance of each component is shown in Table 3. We evaluate the end-to-end performance of our system on a complex event corpus (LDC2020E39), which contains multi-lingual multi-media document clusters. The data statistics are shown in Table 4. We train our mention extraction component on ACE 2005 (Walker et al., 2006) and ERE (Song et al., 2015); document-level argument exraction on ACE 2005 (Walker et al., 2006) and RAMS (Ebner et al., 2020); coreference component on ACE 2005 (Walker et al., 2006), EDL 2016[7], EDL 2017[8], OntoNotes (Pradhan et al., 2012), ERE (Song et al., 2015), CoNLL 2002 (Tjong Kim Sang, 2002), DCEP (Dias, 2016) and SemEval 2010 (Recasens et al., 2010); temporal ordering component on MATRES (Ning et al., 2018b); visual event and argument extraction on Video M2E2 and SWiG (Marasović et al., 2020). The statistics of our output are shown in Table 5. The DARPA program's phrase 1 human assessment on about 25% of our system output shows that about 70% of events are correctly extracted.

| Component | | | Benchmark | Metric | Score |
|---|---|---|---|---|---|
| Mention Extraction | En | Trigger | ACE+ERE | $F_1$ | 64.1 |
| | En | Argument | ACE+ERE | $F_1$ | 49.7 |
| | En | Relation | ACE+ERE | $F_1$ | 49.5 |
| | Es | Trigger | ACE+ERE | $F_1$ | 63.4 |
| | Es | Argument | ACE+ERE | $F_1$ | 46.0 |
| | Es | Relation | ACE+ERE | $F_1$ | 46.6 |
| Document-level Argument Extraction | | | ACE | $F_1$ | 66.7 |
| | | | RAMS | $F_1$ | 48.6 |
| Coreference Resolution | En | Entity | OntoNotes | CoNLL | 92.4 |
| | En | Event | ACE | CoNLL | 84.8 |
| | Es | Entity | SemEval 2010 | CoNLL | 67.6 |
| | Es | Event | ERE-ES | CoNLL | 81.0 |
| Temporal Ordering | RoBERTa | | MATRES | F1 | 78.8 |
| | T5 | | MATRES-b | Acc. | 89.6 |
| Visual Event Extraction | | | Video M2E2 | Acc. | 70.0 |

Table 3: Performance (%) of each component. MATRES-b refers to MATRES binary classification that only considers BEFORE and AFTER relations.

| Category | Complex Events | Documents | Images | Videos |
|---|---|---|---|---|
| # | 11 | 139 | 1,213 | 31 |

Table 4: Data statistics for schema matching corpus (LDC2020E39).

| Category | Extracted Events | Schema Steps | Instantiated Steps |
|---|---|---|---|
| # | 3,180 | 1,738 | 958 |

Table 5: Results of schema matching.

### 3.3 Qualitative Analysis

Figure 2 illustrates a subset of examples for the best matched results from our end-to-end system. We

[7]LDC2017E03

[8]LDC2017E52

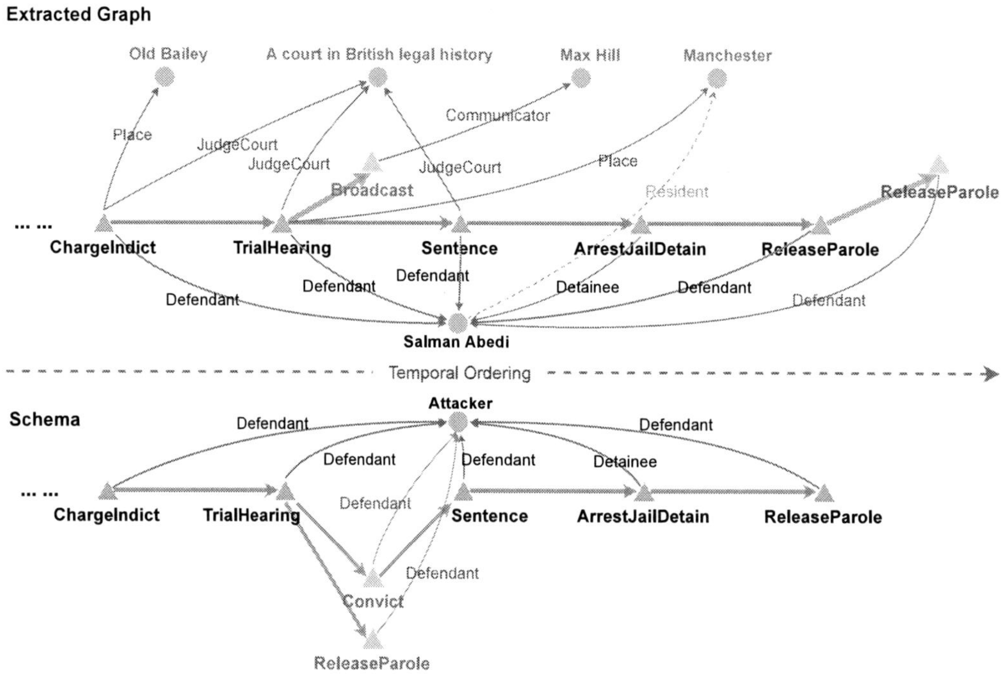


Figure 2: The visualization of schema matching results from extracted graph and schema. The unmatched portions for both extracted graph and schema are blurred.

can see that our system can extract events, entities and relations and align them well with the selected schema. The final instantiated schema is the hybrid of two graphs from merging the matched elements.

## 4 Related Work

**Text Information Extraction.** Existing end-to-end Information Extraction (IE) systems (Wadden et al., 2019; Li et al., 2020b; Lin et al., 2020; Li et al., 2019) mainly focus on extracting entities, events and entity relations from individual sentences. In contrast, we extract and infer arguments over the global document context. Furthermore, our IE system is guided by a schema repository. The extracted graph will be used to instantiate a schema graph, which can be applied to predict future events.

**Multimedia Information Extraction.** Previous multimedia IE systems (Li et al., 2020b; Yazici et al., 2018) only include cross-media entity coreference resolution by grounding the extracted visual entities to text. We are the first to perform cross-media joint event extraction and coreference resolution to obtain the coreferential events from text, images and videos.

**Coreference Resolution.** Previous neural models for event coreference resolution use non-contextual (Nguyen et al., 2016; Choubey et al., 2020; Huang et al., 2019) or contextual word representations (Lu et al., 2020; Yu et al., 2020). We incorporate a wide range of symbolic features (Chen and Ji, 2009; Chen et al., 2009; Sammons et al., 2015; Lu and Ng, 2016, 2017; Duncan et al., 2017), such as event attributes and types, into our event coreference resolution module using a context-dependent gate mechanism.

**Temporal Event Ordering.** Temporal relations between events are extracted for neighbor events in one sentence (Ning et al., 2017, 2018a, 2019; Han et al., 2019), ignoring the temporal dependencies between events across sentences. We perform document-level event ordering and propagate temporal attributes through shared arguments. Furthermore, we take advantage of the schema repository knowledge by using the frequent temporal order between event types to guide the ordering between events.

## 5 Conclusions and Future Work

We demonstrate a state-of-the-art schema-guided cross-document cross-lingual cross-media information extraction and event tracking system. This system is made publicly available to enable users to effectively harness rich information from a variety of sources, languages and modalities. In the future, we plan to develop more advanced graph neural networks based method for schema matching and schema-guided event prediction.

## 6 Broader Impact

Our goal in developing Cross-document Cross-lingual Cross-media information extraction and event tracking systems is to advance the state-of-the-art and enhance the field's ability to fully understand real-world events from multiple sources, languages and modalities. We believe that to make real progress in event-centric Natural Language Understanding, we should not focus only on datasets, but to also ground our work in real-world applications. The application we focus on is navigating news, and the examples shown here and in the paper demonstrate the potential use in news understanding.

For our demo, the distinction between beneficial use and harmful use depends, in part, on the data. Proper use of the technology requires that input documents/images are legally and ethically obtained. We are particularly excited about the potential use of the technologies in applications of broad societal impact, such as disaster monitoring and emergency response. Training and assessment data is often biased in ways that limit system accuracy on less well represented populations and in new domains. The performance of our system components as reported in the experiment section is based on the specific benchmark datasets, which could be affected by such data biases. Thus questions concerning generalizability and fairness should be carefully considered.

A general approach to ensure proper, rather than malicious, application of dual-use technology should: incorporate ethics considerations as the first-order principles in every step of the system design, maintain a high degree of transparency and interpretability of data, algorithms, models, and functionality throughout the system. We intend to make our software available as open source and shared docker containers for public verification and auditing, and explore countermeasures to protect vulnerable groups.

## Acknowledgement

This research is based upon work supported in part by U.S. DARPA KAIROS Program No. FA8750-19-2-1004. The views and conclusions contained herein are those of the authors and should not be interpreted as necessarily representing the official policies, either expressed or implied, of DARPA, or the U.S. Government. The U.S. Government is authorized to reproduce and distribute reprints for governmental purposes notwithstanding any copyright annotation therein. We thank all the annotators who have contributed to the annotations of our training data for the joint IE component (in alphabetical order): Daniel Campos, Anthony Cuff, Yi R. Fung, Xiaodan Hu, Emma Bonnette Hamel, Samual Kriman, Meha Goyal Kumar, Manling Li, Tuan M. Lai, Ying Lin, Sarah Moeller, Ashley Nobi, Xiaoman Pan, Nikolaus Parulian, Adams Pollins, Rachel Rosset, Haoyu Wang, Qingyun Wang, Zhenhailong Wang, Spencer Whitehead, Lucia Yao, Pengfei Yu, Qi Zeng, Haoran Zhang, Hongming Zhang, Zixuan Zhang.

## References

Hassan Akbari, Svebor Karaman, Surabhi Bhargava, Brian Chen, Carl Vondrick, and Shih-Fu Chang. 2019. Multi-level multimodal common semantic space for image-phrase grounding. In *Proceedings of the IEEE Conference on Computer Vision and Pattern Recognition*, pages 12476–12486.

Zheng Chen and Heng Ji. 2009. Graph-based event coreference resolution. In *Proceedings of the 2009 Workshop on Graph-based Methods for Natural Language Processing (TextGraphs-4)*, pages 54–57.

Zheng Chen, Heng Ji, and Robert M Haralick. 2009. A pairwise event coreference model, feature impact and evaluation for event coreference resolution. In *Proceedings of the workshop on events in emerging text types*, pages 17–22.

Prafulla Kumar Choubey, Aaron Lee, Ruihong Huang, and Lu Wang. 2020. Discourse as a function of event: Profiling discourse structure in news articles around the main event. In *Proceedings of the 58th Annual Meeting of the Association for Computational Linguistics*, pages 5374–5386, Online. Association for Computational Linguistics.

Alexis Conneau, Kartikay Khandelwal, Naman Goyal, Vishrav Chaudhary, Guillaume Wenzek, Francisco Guzmán, Edouard Grave, Myle Ott, Luke Zettlemoyer, and Veselin Stoyanov. 2020. Unsupervised cross-lingual representation learning at scale. In

*Proceedings of the 58th Annual Meeting of the Association for Computational Linguistics*, pages 8440–8451, Online. Association for Computational Linguistics.

Jacob Devlin, Ming-Wei Chang, Kenton Lee, and Kristina Toutanova. 2018. Bert: Pre-training of deep bidirectional transformers for language understanding. *arXiv preprint arXiv:1810.04805*.

Francisco Dias. 2016. Multilingual Automated Text Anonymization. Msc dissertation, Instituto Superior Técnico, Lisbon, Portugal, May.

Xiao Ding, Yue Zhang, Ting Liu, and Junwen Duan. 2014. Using structured events to predict stock price movement: An empirical investigation. In *Proceedings of the 2014 Conference on Empirical Methods in Natural Language Processing (EMNLP)*, pages 1415–1425, Doha, Qatar. Association for Computational Linguistics.

Xiao Ding, Yue Zhang, Ting Liu, and Junwen Duan. 2016. Knowledge-driven event embedding for stock prediction. In *Proceedings of COLING 2016, the 26th International Conference on Computational Linguistics: Technical Papers*, pages 2133–2142, Osaka, Japan. The COLING 2016 Organizing Committee.

Chase Duncan, Liang-Wei Chan, Haoruo Peng, Hao Wu, Shyam Upadhyay, Nitish Gupta, Chen-Tse Tsai, Mark Sammons, and Dan Roth. 2017. Ui ccg tac-kbp2017 submissions: Entity discovery and linking, and event nugget detection and co-reference. In *TAC*.

Chris Dyer, Victor Chahuneau, and Noah A Smith. 2013. A simple, fast, and effective reparameterization of ibm model 2. In *Proceedings of the 2013 Conference of the North American Chapter of the Association for Computational Linguistics: Human Language Technologies*, pages 644–648.

Seth Ebner, Patrick Xia, Ryan Culkin, Kyle Rawlins, and Benjamin Van Durme. 2020. Multi-sentence argument linking. In *Proceedings of the 58th Annual Meeting of the Association for Computational Linguistics*.

Liat Ein-Dor, Ariel Gera, Orith Toledo-Ronen, Alon Halfon, Benjamin Sznajder, Lena Dankin, Yonatan Bilu, Yoav Katz, and Noam Slonim. 2019. Financial event extraction using Wikipedia-based weak supervision. In *Proceedings of the Second Workshop on Economics and Natural Language Processing*, pages 10–15, Hong Kong. Association for Computational Linguistics.

Goran Glavaš, Jan Šnajder, Marie-Francine Moens, and Parisa Kordjamshidi. 2014. HiEve: A corpus for extracting event hierarchies from news stories. In *Proceedings of the Ninth International Conference on Language Resources and Evaluation (LREC'14)*, pages 3678–3683, Reykjavik, Iceland. European Language Resources Association (ELRA).

Goran Glavaš and Sanja Štajner. 2013. Event-centered simplification of news stories. In *Proceedings of the Student Research Workshop associated with RANLP 2013*, pages 71–78, Hissar, Bulgaria. INCOMA Ltd. Shoumen, BULGARIA.

Rujun Han, Qiang Ning, and Nanyun Peng. 2019. Joint event and temporal relation extraction with shared representations and structured prediction. In *Proceedings of the 2019 Conference on Empirical Methods in Natural Language Processing and the 9th International Joint Conference on Natural Language Processing, EMNLP-IJCNLP 2019, Hong Kong, China, November 3-7, 2019*, pages 434–444. Association for Computational Linguistics.

Kaiming He, Xiangyu Zhang, Shaoqing Ren, and Jian Sun. 2016. Deep residual learning for image recognition. In *Proceedings of the IEEE conference on computer vision and pattern recognition*, pages 770–778.

Matthew Honnibal, Ines Montani, Sofie Van Landeghem, and Adriane Boyd. 2020. spaCy: Industrial-strength Natural Language Processing in Python. *Zenodo*.

Yin Jou Huang, Jing Lu, Sadao Kurohashi, and Vincent Ng. 2019. Improving event coreference resolution by learning argument compatibility from unlabeled data. In *Proceedings of the 2019 Conference of the North American Chapter of the Association for Computational Linguistics: Human Language Technologies, Volume 1 (Long and Short Papers)*, pages 785–795.

Gilles Jacobs, Els Lefever, and Véronique Hoste. 2018. Economic event detection in company-specific news text. In *Proceedings of the First Workshop on Economics and Natural Language Processing*, pages 1–10, Melbourne, Australia. Association for Computational Linguistics.

Abhyuday N Jagannatha and Hong Yu. 2016. Bidirectional RNN for medical event detection in electronic health records. In *Proceedings of the 2016 Conference of the North American Chapter of the Association for Computational Linguistics: Human Language Technologies*, pages 473–482, San Diego, California. Association for Computational Linguistics.

Serena Jeblee and Graeme Hirst. 2018. Listwise temporal ordering of events in clinical notes. In *Proceedings of the Ninth International Workshop on Health Text Mining and Information Analysis*, pages 177–182, Brussels, Belgium. Association for Computational Linguistics.

Prescott Klassen, Fei Xia, and Meliha Yetisgen. 2016. Annotating and detecting medical events in clinical notes. In *Proceedings of the Tenth International Conference on Language Resources and Evaluation (LREC'16)*, pages 3417–3421, Portorož, Slovenia. European Language Resources Association (ELRA).

Tuan Lai, Heng Ji, Trung Bui, Quan Hung Tran, Franck Dernoncourt, and Walter Chang. 2021. A context-dependent gated module for incorporating symbolic semantics into event coreference resolution. In *Proc. The 2021 Conference of the North American Chapter of the Association for Computational Linguistics - Human Language Technologies (NAACL-HLT2021)*.

Kenton Lee, Luheng He, Mike Lewis, and Luke Zettlemoyer. 2017. End-to-end neural coreference resolution. In *Proceedings of the 2017 Conference on Empirical Methods in Natural Language Processing*, pages 188–197, Copenhagen, Denmark. Association for Computational Linguistics.

Mike Lewis, Yinhan Liu, Naman Goyal, Marjan Ghazvininejad, Abdelrahman Mohamed, Omer Levy, Veselin Stoyanov, and Luke Zettlemoyer. 2020. BART: Denoising sequence-to-sequence pre-training for natural language generation, translation, and comprehension. In *Proceedings of the 58th Annual Meeting of the Association for Computational Linguistics*, pages 7871–7880, Online. Association for Computational Linguistics.

Manling Li, Ying Lin, Joseph Hoover, Spencer Whitehead, Clare Voss, Morteza Dehghani, and Heng Ji. 2019. Multilingual entity, relation, event and human value extraction. In *Proceedings of the 2019 Conference of the North American Chapter of the Association for Computational Linguistics (Demonstrations)*, pages 110–115.

Manling Li, Ying Lin, Tuan Manh Lai, Xiaoman Pan, Haoyang Wen, Sha Li, Zhenhailong Wang, Pengfei Yu, Lifu Huang, Di Lu, Qingyun Wang, Haoran Zhang, Qi Zeng, Chi Han, Zixuan Zhang, Yujia Qin, Xiaodan Hu, Nikolaus Parulian, Daniel Campos, Heng Ji, Brian Chen, Xudong Lin, Alireza Zareian, Amith Ananthram, Emily Allaway, Shih-Fu Chang, Kathleen McKeown, Yixiang Yao, Michael Spector, Mitchell DeHaven, Daniel Napierski, Marjorie Freedman, Pedro Szekely, Haidong Zhu, Ram Nevatia, Yang Bai, Yifan Wang, Ali Sadeghian, Haodi Ma, and Daisy Zhe Wang. 2020a. GAIA at SM-KBP 2020 - a dockerlized multi-media multi-lingual knowledge extraction, clustering, temporal tracking and hypothesis generation system. In *Proceedings of Thirteenth Text Analysis Conference (TAC 2020)*.

Manling Li, Alireza Zareian, Ying Lin, Xiaoman Pan, Spencer Whitehead, Brian Chen, Bo Wu, Heng Ji, Shih-Fu Chang, Clare Voss, Daniel Napierski, and Marjorie Freedman. 2020b. GAIA: A fine-grained multimedia knowledge extraction system. In *Proceedings of the 58th Annual Meeting of the Association for Computational Linguistics: System Demonstrations*, pages 77–86, Online. Association for Computational Linguistics.

Manling Li, Qi Zeng, Ying Lin, Kyunghyun Cho, Heng Ji, Jonathan May, Nathanael Chambers, and Clare Voss. 2020c. Connecting the dots: Event graph schema induction with path language modeling. In *Proc. The 2020 Conference on Empirical Methods in Natural Language Processing (EMNLP2020)*.

Sha Li, Heng Ji, and Jiawei Han. 2021. Document-level event argument extraction by conditional generation. In *Proc. The 2021 Conference of the North American Chapter of the Association for Computational Linguistics - Human Language Technologies (NAACL-HLT2021)*.

Ying Lin, Heng Ji, Fei Huang, and Lingfei Wu. 2020. A joint end-to-end neural model for information extraction with global features. In *Proc. The 58th Annual Meeting of the Association for Computational Linguistics (ACL2020)*.

Yinhan Liu, Myle Ott, Naman Goyal, Jingfei Du, Mandar Joshi, Danqi Chen, Omer Levy, Mike Lewis, Luke Zettlemoyer, and Veselin Stoyanov. 2019. Roberta: A robustly optimized BERT pretraining approach. *CoRR*, abs/1907.11692.

Jing Lu and Vincent Ng. 2016. Event coreference resolution with multi-pass sieves. In *Proceedings of the Tenth International Conference on Language Resources and Evaluation (LREC'16)*, pages 3996–4003.

Jing Lu and Vincent Ng. 2017. Joint learning for event coreference resolution. In *Proceedings of the 55th Annual Meeting of the Association for Computational Linguistics (Volume 1: Long Papers)*, pages 90–101.

Yaojie Lu, Hongyu Lin, Jialong Tang, Xianpei Han, and Le Sun. 2020. End-to-end neural event coreference resolution. *arXiv preprint arXiv:2009.08153*.

Ana Marasović, Chandra Bhagavatula, Jae Sung Park, Ronan Le Bras, Noah A Smith, and Yejin Choi. 2020. Natural language rationales with full-stack visual reasoning: From pixels to semantic frames to commonsense graphs. *arXiv preprint arXiv:2010.07526*.

Salvador Medina Maza, Evangelia Spiliopoulou, Eduard Hovy, and Alexander Hauptmann. 2020. Event-related bias removal for real-time disaster events. In *Findings of the Association for Computational Linguistics: EMNLP 2020*, pages 3858–3868, Online. Association for Computational Linguistics.

Thien Huu Nguyen, Adam Meyers, and Ralph Grishman. 2016. New york university 2016 system for kbp event nugget: A deep learning approach. In *TAC*.

Qiang Ning, Zhili Feng, and Dan Roth. 2017. A structured learning approach to temporal relation extraction. In *Proceedings of the 2017 Conference on Empirical Methods in Natural Language Processing*, pages 1027–1037, Copenhagen, Denmark. Association for Computational Linguistics.

Qiang Ning, Zhili Feng, Hao Wu, and Dan Roth. 2018a. Joint reasoning for temporal and causal relations. In *Proceedings of the 56th Annual Meeting of the Association for Computational Linguistics, ACL 2018, Melbourne, Australia, July 15-20, 2018, Volume 1: Long Papers*, pages 2278–2288. Association for Computational Linguistics.

Qiang Ning, Sanjay Subramanian, and Dan Roth. 2019. An improved neural baseline for temporal relation extraction. In *Proceedings of the 2019 Conference on Empirical Methods in Natural Language Processing and the 9th International Joint Conference on Natural Language Processing, EMNLP-IJCNLP 2019, Hong Kong, China, November 3-7, 2019*, pages 6202–6208. Association for Computational Linguistics.

Qiang Ning, H. Wu, and D. Roth. 2018b. A multi-axis annotation scheme for event temporal relations. *ArXiv*, abs/1804.07828.

Ahmet Murat Özbayoglu, Mehmet Ugur Gudelek, and Omer Berat Sezer. 2020. Deep learning for financial applications : A survey. *Appl. Soft Comput.*, 93:106384.

Xiaoman Pan, Boliang Zhang, Jonathan May, Joel Nothman, Kevin Knight, and Heng Ji. 2017. Cross-lingual name tagging and linking for 282 languages. In *Proc. the 55th Annual Meeting of the Association for Computational Linguistics (ACL2017)*.

Sandeep Panem, Manish Gupta, and Vasudeva Varma. 2014. Structured information extraction from natural disaster events on twitter. In *Proceedings of the 5th International Workshop on Web-scale Knowledge Representation Retrieval & Reasoning, Web-KR@CIKM 2014, Shanghai, China, November 3, 2014*, pages 1–8. ACM.

Sameer Pradhan, Alessandro Moschitti, Nianwen Xue, Olga Uryupina, and Yuchen Zhang. 2012. Conll-2012 shared task: Modeling multilingual unrestricted coreference in ontonotes. In *Joint Conference on Empirical Methods in Natural Language Processing and Computational Natural Language Learning - Proceedings of the Shared Task: Modeling Multilingual Unrestricted Coreference in OntoNotes, EMNLP-CoNLL 2012, July 13, 2012, Jeju Island, Korea*, pages 1–40. ACL.

Colin Raffel, Noam Shazeer, Adam Roberts, Katherine Lee, Sharan Narang, M. Matena, Yanqi Zhou, W. Li, and Peter J. Liu. 2020. Exploring the limits of transfer learning with a unified text-to-text transformer. *J. Mach. Learn. Res.*, 21:140:1–140:67.

Preethi Raghavan, Eric Fosler-Lussier, and Albert Lai. 2012. Temporal classification of medical events. In *BioNLP: Proceedings of the 2012 Workshop on Biomedical Natural Language Processing*, pages 29–37, Montréal, Canada. Association for Computational Linguistics.

Marta Recasens, Lluís Màrquez, Emili Sapena, M. Antònia Martí, Mariona Taulé, Véronique Hoste, Massimo Poesio, and Yannick Versley. 2010. Semeval-2010 task 1: Coreference resolution in multiple languages. In *Proceedings of the 5th International Workshop on Semantic Evaluation, SemEval@ACL 2010, Uppsala University, Uppsala, Sweden, July 15-16, 2010*, pages 1–8. The Association for Computer Linguistics.

Mark Sammons, Haoruo Peng, Yangqiu Song, Shyam Upadhyay, Chen-Tse Tsai, Pavankumar Reddy, Subhro Roy, and Dan Roth. 2015. Illinois ccg tac 2015 event nugget, entity discovery and linking, and slot filler validation systems. In *TAC*.

Zhiyi Song, Ann Bies, Stephanie Strassel, Tom Riese, Justin Mott, Joe Ellis, Jonathan Wright, Seth Kulick, Neville Ryant, and Xiaoyi Ma. 2015. From light to rich ere: annotation of entities, relations, and events. In *Proceedings of the the 3rd Workshop on EVENTS: Definition, Detection, Coreference, and Representation*, pages 89–98.

Erik F. Tjong Kim Sang. 2002. Introduction to the CoNLL-2002 shared task: Language-independent named entity recognition. In *COLING-02: The 6th Conference on Natural Language Learning 2002 (CoNLL-2002)*.

Denny Vrandečić and Markus Krötzsch. 2014. Wikidata: a free collaborative knowledge base. *Communications of the ACM*, 57(10).

David Wadden, Ulme Wennberg, Yi Luan, and Hannaneh Hajishirzi. 2019. Entity, relation, and event extraction with contextualized span representations. In *Proceedings of the 2019 Conference on Empirical Methods in Natural Language Processing and the 9th International Joint Conference on Natural Language Processing (EMNLP-IJCNLP2019)*.

Christopher Walker, Stephanie Strassel, Julie Medero, and Kazuaki Maeda. 2006. Ace 2005 multilingual training corpus. *Linguistic Data Consortium, Philadelphia*, 57.

Haoyang Wen, Yanru Qu, Heng Ji, Qiang Ning, Jiawei Han, Avi Sil, Hanghang Tong, and Dan Roth. 2021. Event time extraction and propagation via graph attention networks. In *Proc. The 2021 Conference of the North American Chapter of the Association for Computational Linguistics - Human Language Technologies (NAACL-HLT2021)*.

Hang Yang, Yubo Chen, Kang Liu, Yang Xiao, and Jun Zhao. 2018. DCFEE: A document-level Chinese financial event extraction system based on automatically labeled training data. In *Proceedings of ACL 2018, System Demonstrations*, pages 50–55, Melbourne, Australia. Association for Computational Linguistics.

Adnan Yazici, Murat Koyuncu, Turgay Yilmaz, Saeid Sattari, Mustafa Sert, and Elvan Gulen. 2018. An intelligent multimedia information system for multi-modal content extraction and querying. *Multimedia Tools and Applications*, 77(2):2225–2260.

Xiaodong Yu, Wenpeng Yin, and Dan Roth. 2020. Paired representation learning for event and entity coreference. *arXiv preprint arXiv:2010.12808*.

Boliang Zhang, Ying Lin, Xiaoman Pan, Di Lu, Jonathan May, Kevin Knight, and Heng Ji. 2018. Elisa-edl: A cross-lingual entity extraction, linking and localization system. In *Proceedings of the 2018 Conference of the North American Chapter of the Association for Computational Linguistics: Demonstrations*, pages 41–45.

Ben Zhou, Kyle Richardson, Qiang Ning, Tushar Khot, A. Sabharwal, and D. Roth. 2020. Temporal reasoning on implicit events from distant supervision. *ArXiv*, abs/2010.12753.

# MUDES: Multilingual Detection of Offensive Spans

**Tharindu Ranasinghe**
University of Wolverhampton
Wolverhampton, UK
tharindu.ranasinghe@wlv.ac.uk

**Marcos Zampieri**
Rochester Institute of Technology
Rochester, NY, USA
mazgla@rit.edu

## Abstract

The interest in offensive content identification in social media has grown substantially in recent years. Previous work has dealt mostly with post level annotations. However, identifying offensive spans is useful in many ways. To help coping with this important challenge, we present MUDES, a multilingual system to detect offensive spans in texts. MUDES features pre-trained models, a Python API for developers, and a user-friendly web-based interface. A detailed description of MUDES' components is presented in this paper.

## 1 Introduction

Offensive and impolite language are widespread in social media posts motivating a number of studies on automatically detecting the various types of offensive content (e.g. aggression (Kumar et al., 2018, 2020), cyber-bullying (Rosa et al., 2019), hate speech (Malmasi and Zampieri, 2018), etc.). Most previous work has focused on classifying full instances (e.g. posts, comments, documents) (e.g. offensive vs. not offensive) while the identification of the particular spans that make a text offensive has been mostly neglected.

Identifying offensive spans in texts is the goal of the SemEval-2021 Task 5: Toxic Spans Detection (Pavlopoulos et al., 2021). The organisers of this task argue that highlighting toxic spans in texts helps assisting human moderators (e.g. news portals moderators) and that this can be a first step in semi-automated content moderation. Finally, as we demonstrate in this paper, addressing offensive spans in texts will make the output of offensive language detection systems more interpretable thus allowing a more detailed linguistics analysis of predictions and improving the quality of such systems.

With these important points in mind, we developed MUDES: **Mu**ltilingual **De**tection of Offensive **S**pans. MUDES is a multilingual framework for offensive language detection focusing on text spans. The main contributions of this paper are the following:

1. We introduce MUDES, a new Python-based framework to identify offensive spans with state-of-the-art performance.

2. We release four pre-trained offensive language identification models: en-base, en-large models which are capable of identifying offensive spans in English text. We also release Multilingual-base and Multilingual-large models which are able to recognise offensive spans in languages other than English.

3. We release a Python Application Programming Interface (API) for developers who are interested in training more models and performing inference in the code level.

4. For general users and non-programmers, we release a user-friendly web-based User Interface (UI), which provides the functionality to input a text in multiple languages and to identify the offensive span in that text.

## 2 Related Work

Early approaches to offensive language identification relied on traditional machine learning classifiers (Dadvar et al., 2013) and later on neural networks combined with word embeddings (Majumder et al., 2018; Hettiarachchi and Ranasinghe, 2019). Transformer-based models like BERT (Devlin et al., 2019) and ELMO (Peters et al., 2018) have been recently applied to offensive language detection achieving competitive scores (Wang et al., 2020; Ranasinghe and Hettiarachchi, 2020) in recent SemEval competitions such as HatEval (Basile et al., 2019) OffensEval (Zampieri et al., 2020).

In terms of languages, the majority of studies on this topic deal with English (Malmasi and Zampieri,

WARNING: This paper contains text excerpts and words that are offensive in nature.



*Proceedings of NAACL-HLT 2021: Demonstrations*, pages 144–152
June 6–11, 2021. ©2021 Association for Computational Linguistics

| Post | Offensive Spans |
|---|---|
| Stupid hatcheries have completely fucked everything | [0, 1, 2, 3, 4, 5, 34, 35, 36, 37, 38, 39] |
| Victimitis: You are such an asshole. | [28, 29, 30, 31, 32, 33, 34] |
| So is his mother. They are silver spoon parasites. | [] |
| You're just silly. | [12, 13, 14, 15, 16] |

Table 1: Four comments from the dataset, with their annotations. The offensive words are displayed in red and the spans are indicated by the character position in the instance.

2017; Yao et al., 2019; Ridenhour et al., 2020; Rosenthal et al., 2020) due to the the wide availability of language resources such as corpora and pre-trained models. In recent years, several studies have been published on identifying offensive content in other languages such as Arabic (Mubarak et al., 2020), Dutch (Tulkens et al., 2016), French (Chiril et al., 2019), Greek (Pitenis et al., 2020), Italian (Poletto et al., 2017), Portuguese (Fortuna et al., 2019), and Turkish (Çöltekin, 2020). Most of these studies have created new datasets and resources for these languages opening avenues for multilingual models as those presented in Ranasinghe and Zampieri (2020). However, all studies presented in this section focused on classifying full texts, as discussed in the Introduction. MUDES' objective is to fill this gap and perform span level offensive language identification.

## 3 Data

The main dataset used to train the machine learning models presented in this paper is the dataset released within the scope of the aforementioned SemEval-2021 Task 5: Toxic Spans Detection for English. The dataset contains posts (comments) from the publicly available Civil Comments dataset (Borkan et al., 2019). The organisers have randomly selected 10,000 posts, out of a total of 1,2 million posts in the original dataset. The offensive spans have been annotated using a crowd-annotation platform, employing three crowd-raters per post. By the time of writing this paper, only the trial set and the training set have been released and the gold labels for the test set have not yet been released. Therefore, training of the machine learning models presented in MUDES was done on the training set which we refer to as *TSDTrain* and the evaluation was conducted on the trial set which we refer to as *TSDTrial* set. In Table 1 we show four randomly selected examples from the *TSDTrain* dataset with their annotations.

The general idea is to learn a robust model from this dataset and generalize to other English datasets which do not contain span annotation. Another goal is to investigate the feasibility of annotation projection to other languages.

**Other Datasets** In order to evaluate our framework in different domains and languages we used three publicly available offensive language identification datasets. As an off-domain English dataset, we choose the Offensive Language Identification Dataset (OLID) (Zampieri et al., 2019a), used in OffensEval 2019 (SemEval-2019 Task 6) (Zampieri et al., 2019b), containing over 14,000 posts from Twitter. To evaluate our framework in different languages, we selected a Danish (Sigurbergsson and Derczynski, 2020) and a Greek (Pitenis et al., 2020) dataset. These two datasets have been provided by the organisers of OffensEval 2020 (SemEval-2020 Task 12) (Zampieri et al., 2020) and were annotated using OLID's annotation guidelines. The Danish dataset contains over 3,000 posts from Facebook and Reddit while the Greek dataset contains over 10,000 Twitter posts, allowing us to evaluate our dataset in an off-domain, multilingual setting. As these three datasets have been annotated at the instance level, we followed an evaluation process explained in Section 5.

## 4 Methodology

The main motivation behind this methodology is the recent success that transformer models had in various NLP tasks (Devlin et al., 2019) including offensive language identification (Ranasinghe and Zampieri, 2020; Ranasinghe et al., 2019; Wiedemann et al., 2020). Most of these transformer-based approaches take the final hidden state of the first token ([CLS]) from the transformer as the representation of the whole sequence and a simple softmax classifier is added to the top of the transformer model to predict the probability of a class label (Sun et al., 2019). However, as previously men-

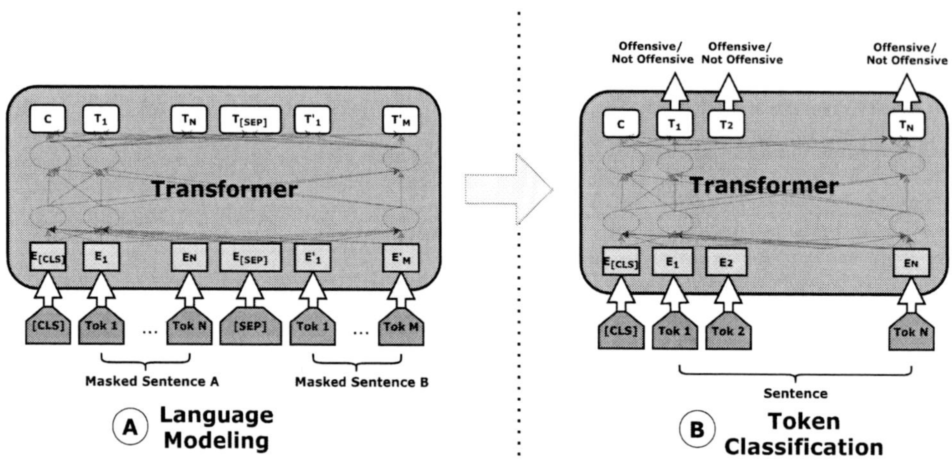


Figure 1: Model Architecture. Architecture consists of two parts. Part A is the language modelling and Part B is the token classification.

tioned, these models classify whole comments or documents and do not identify the spans that make a text offensive. Since the objective of this task is to identify offensive spans rather than classifying the whole comment, we followed a different architecture.

As shown in Figure 1, the complete architecture contains two main parts; Language Modeling (LM) and Token Classification (TC). In the LM part, we used a pre-trained transformer model and retrained it on the *TSDTrain* dataset using Masked Language Modeling (MLM). In the second part of the architecture, we used the saved model from the LM part and we perform a token classification. We added a token level classifier on top of the transformer model as shown in Figure 1. The token-level classifier is a linear layer that takes the last hidden state of the sequence as the input and produce a label for each token as the output. In this case each token can have two labels; offensive and not offensive. We have listed the training configurations in the Appendix.

We experimented with several popular transformer models like BERT (Devlin et al., 2019), XLNET (Yang et al., 2019), ALBERT (Lan et al., 2020), RoBERTa (Liu et al., 2019) etc. From the pre-trained transformer models we selected, we grouped the large models and base models separately in order to release two English models. A large model; en-large which is more accurate, but has a low efficiency regarding space and time. The base model; en-base is efficient, but has a comparatively low accuracy than the en-large model. All the experiments have been executed for five times with different random seeds and we took the mode of the classes predicted by each random seed as the final result (Hettiarachchi and Ranasinghe, 2020).

**Multilingual models** - The motivation behind the use of multilingual models comes from recent works (Ranasinghe and Zampieri, 2020, 2021; Ranasinghe et al., 2020) which used transfer learning and cross-lingual embeddings. These studies show that cross-lingual transformers like XLM-R (Conneau et al., 2019) can be trained on an English dataset and have the model weights saved to detect offensive language in other languages outperforming monolingual models trained on the target language dataset. We used a similar methodology but for the token classification architecture instead. We used XLM-R cross-lingual transformer model (Conneau et al., 2019) as the Transformer in Figure 1 on *TSDTrain* and carried out evaluations on the Danish and Greek datasets. We release two multilingual models; multilingual-base based on XLM-R base model and multilingual-large based on XLM-R large model.

## 5 Evaluation and Results

We followed two different evaluation methods. In Section 5.1 we present the methods used to evaluate offensive spans on the TSDTrial set. In Section 5.2 we presented the methods used to evaluate the other three datasets which only contained post level annotations.

### 5.1 Offensive Spans Evaluation

For the Toxic Spans Detection dataset, we followed the same evaluation procedure of the SemEval Toxic Spans Detection competition. The organisers have used F1 score mentioned in Da San Martino et al. (2019) to evaluate the systems. Let system $A_i$ return a set $S^t_{A_i}$ of character offsets, for parts of the post found to be toxic. Let $G_t$ be the character offsets of the ground truth annotations of t. We compute the F1 score of system $A_i$ with respect to the ground truth G for post t as mentioned in Equation 1, where $|\cdot|$ denotes set cardinality.

$$F^t_1(A_i, G) = \frac{2 \cdot P^t(A_i, G) \cdot R^t(A_i, G)}{P^t(A_i, G) + R^t(A_i, G)} \quad (1)$$

$$P^t(A_i, G) = \frac{\left|S^t_{A_i} \cap S^t_G\right|}{\left|S^t_{A_i}\right|} \quad R^t(A_i, G) = \frac{\left|S^t_{A_i} \cap S^t_G\right|}{\left|S^t_G\right|}$$

We present the results along with the baseline provided by the organisers in Table 2. The baseline is implemented using a spaCy NER pipeline. The spaCy NER system contains a word embedding strategy using sub word features and Bloom embedding (Serrà and Karatzoglou, 2017), and a deep convolution neural network with residual connections. Additionally, we compare our results to a lexicon-based word match approach mentioned in Ranasinghe et al. (2021) where the lexicon is based on profanity words from online resources[1,2].

| Model Name | Base Model | F1 score |
|---|---|---|
| en-large | roberta-large | 0.6886 |
| en-base | xlnet-base-cased | 0.6734 |
| multilingual-large | XLM-R-large | 0.6338 |
| multilingual-base | XLM-R-base | 0.6160 |
| spaCy baseline | NA | 0.5976 |
| Lexicon word match (Ranasinghe et al., 2021) | NA | 0.3378 |

Table 2: Results ordered by F1 score for TSD Trial.

The results show that all MUDES' models outperform the spaCy baseline and the lexicon-based word match. From all of the large transformer models we experimented roberta-large performed better than others. Therefore, we released it as en-large model in MUDES. From the base models we experimented, XLNet-base-cased model outperformed all the other base models so we released it as en-base model. We also released two multilingual models; multilingual-base and multilingual-large based on XLM-R-base and XLM-R-large respectively. All the pre-trained MUDES' models are available to download from HuggingFace model hub [3] (Wolf et al., 2020).

### 5.2 Off-Domain and Multilingual Evaluation

For the English off-domain and multilingual datasets we followed a different evaluation process. We used a pre-trained MUDES' model trained on *TSDTrain* to predict the offensive spans for all texts in the test sets of two non-English datasets (Danish, and Greek) and English off-domain dataset, OLID, which is annotated at the document level. If a certain text contains at least one offensive span we marked the whole text as offensive following the OLID annotation guidelines described in Zampieri et al. (2019a). We compared our results to the best systems submitted to OffensEval 2020 in terms of macro F1 reported by the task organisers (Zampieri et al., 2020). We present the results along with the majority class baseline for each dataset in Table 3. For English off domain dataset (OLID) we only used the MUDES en models while for Danish and Greek datasets we used the MUDES multilingual models.

| Language | Model | M F1 |
|---|---|---|
| Danish | Pàmies et al. (2020) | 0.8119 |
| | multilingual-large | 0.7623 |
| | multilingual-base | 0.7143 |
| | Majority Baseline | 0.4668 |
| English | Wiedemann et al. (2020) | 0.9204 |
| | en-large | 0.9023 |
| | en-base | 0.8892 |
| | Majority Baseline | 0.4193 |
| Greek | Ahn et al. (2020) | 0.8522 |
| | multilingual-large | 0.8143 |
| | multilingual-base | 0.7820 |
| | Majority Baseline | 0.4202 |

Table 3: Results ordered by macro (M) F1 for Danish, English and Greek datasets

Results show that despite the change of domain and the language, MUDES perform well in all the datasets and compares favourably to the best systems submitted. It should be noted that the best

[1] https://www.cs.cmu.edu/~biglou/resources/bad-words.txt

[2] https://github.com/RobertJGabriel/Google-profanity-words

[3] MUDES' models are available on https://huggingface.co/mudes

systems have been predominantly trained on offensive languages identification task on post level while MUDES' objective is different. Yet MUDES come closer to the best systems in all the datasets.

From the results, it is clear that MUDES english models can perform in a different domain like Twitter. Also the results show that MUDES multilingual models are capable of identifying offensive spans in other languages too. Since XLM-R supports 104 languages, this approach will benefit all those languages without any training data at all.

## 6 System Demonstration

### 6.1 Application Programming Interface

MUDES is available as a Python package in the Python Package Index (PyPI)[4]. The package is related to MUDES GitHub repository[5]. Users can install it easily with the following command after installing PyTorch (Paszke et al., 2019).

```
$ pip install mudes
```

The Python package contains the following functionalities.

**Get offensive spans with a pretrained model** The library provides the functionality to load a pretrained model and use it to identify offensive spans. The following code segment downloads and loads MUDES' en-base model in a CPU only environment and identifies offensive spans in the the text; *"This is fucking crazy!!"*. If the users prefer a GPU, the argument *use_cuda* should be set to True.

**Listing 1** English Inference Example

```
from mudes.app.mudes_app
                  import MUDESApp

sentence = "This is fucking crazy!!"

app = MUDESApp("en-base",
                  use_cuda=False)
app.predict_toxic_spans(sentence)
```

**Train a MUDES model** The library provides the functionality to train a MUDES model from scratch using the code segment present next. It takes a Pandas dataframe in the format of *TSDTrain*, formats it for the token classification task and train a MUDES model from scratch. MUDES support popular transformer types as bert, xlnet, roberta etc. as the MODEL_TYPE and name of the model as appear in Hugging Face (Wolf et al., 2020) model repository. [6]

**Listing 2** Training Example

```
from mudes.algo.mudes_model
                import MUDESModel
from mudes.algo.preprocess
                import read_datafile,
                       format_data

train_df = format_data(train)
tags = train_df['labels']
            .unique().tolist()

model = MUDESModel(MODEL_TYPE,
            MODEL_NAME, labels=tags)
model.train(train_df)
```

### 6.2 User Interface

We developed a prototype of the User Interface (UI) to demonstrate the capabilities of the system. The UI is based on Streamlit[7] which provides functionalities to easily develop dashboards for machine learning projects. The code base for the UI is available in GitHub [8]. This UI is hosted in a Linux server. [9] We also release a Docker container image of the UI in Docker Hub[10] for those who are interested in self hosting the UI. Docker enables developers to easily deploy and run any application as a lightweight, portable, self-sufficient container, which can run virtually anywhere. The released Docker container image follows Continuous Integration/Continuous Deployment (CI/CD) from the GitHub repository which allows sharing and deploying the code quickly and efficiently.

Once Docker is installed, one can easily run our UI with this command.

```
$ docker run tharindudr/mudes
```

This command will automatically install all the required packages, download and load the pre-trained models and open the system in the default browser. We provide the following functionalities from the user interface.

**Switch through pretrained models** - The users can switch through the pre-trained models using the radio buttons available in the left side of the UI under Available Models section. They can select

[4] https://pypi.org/project/mudes/

[5] https://github.com/tharindudr/MUDES

[6] https://huggingface.co/models

[7] www.streamlit.io

[8] https://github.com/tharindudr/MUDES-UI.

[9] http://rgcl.wlv.ac.uk/mudes/

[10] Docker Hub is a hosted repository service provided by Docker for finding and sharing container images.

(a) Example from Civil Comments Dataset (b) Example from Tamil. (Pussy like this !!!!)

Figure 2: Examples in English and in a low-resource languages. The experiments were conducted with en-large and the multilingual-large models respectively.

an option from en-base, en-large, multilingual-base and multilingual-large. These models have been already downloaded from the HuggingFace model hub and they are loaded in to the random-access memory of the hosting computer.

**Switch through available datasets** - We have made the four datsets used in this paper available from the UI for the users to experiment with (Borkan et al., 2019; Zampieri et al., 2019a; Pitenis et al., 2020; Sigurbergsson and Derczynski, 2020). Once the user selects a particular option, the system will automatically load the test set of the selected dataset. Once it is loaded the user can iterate through the dataset using the scrollbar. For each text the UI will display the offensive spans in red.

**Get offensive spans for a custom text** - The users can also enter a custom text in the text box, hit ctrl+enter and see the offensive spans available in the input text. Once processed through the system, any offensive spans available in the text will be displayed in red. Figure 2 shows several screenshots from the UI. It illustrates an example on English for the texts taken from civil comments dataset (Borkan et al., 2019) conducted with en-large model. To show that MUDES framework works on low resource language too, Figure 2 also displays an example from Tamil.

### 6.3 System Efficiency

The time taken to predict the offensive spans for a text will be critical in an online system developed for real time use. Therefore, we evaluated the time MUDES takes to predict the offensive spans in 100 texts for all the released models in a CPU and GPU environment. The results show that large models take around 3 seconds for a sentence in a CPU and take around 1 second for a sentence in a GPU on average while the base models take approximately one third of that time in both environments. From these results it is clear that MUDES is capable of predicting toxic spans efficiently in any environment. The full set of results are reported in the Appendix. We used a batch size of one, in order to mimic the real world scenario. The full specifications of the CPU and GPU environments are listed in the Appendix.

## 7 Conclusion

This paper introduced *MUDES:* **Mu**ltilingual **D**etection of Offensive **S**pans. We evaluated MUDES on the recently released SemEval-2021 Toxic Spans Detection dataset. Our results show that MUDES outperforms the strong baselines of the competition. Furthermore, we show that once MUDES is trained on English data using state of the art cross-lingual transformer models, it is capable of detecting offensive spans in other languages. With MUDES, we release a Python library, four pre-trained models and an user interface. We show that MUDES is efficient to use in real time scenarios even in a non GPU environment. In future work, we would like to further evaluate MUDES on other datasets. Finally, we would like to implement a flexible multitask architecture capable of detecting offense at both span and post level.

## Acknowledgments

We would like to thank the SemEval-2021 Toxic Spans Detection shared task organisers for making this interesting dataset available. We further thank the anonymous reviewers for their insightful feedback.

## References


Hwijeen Ahn, Jimin Sun, Chan Young Park, and Jungyun Seo. 2020. NLPDove at SemEval-2020 task 12: Improving offensive language detection with cross-lingual transfer. In *Proceedings of SemEval*.

Valerio Basile, Cristina Bosco, Elisabetta Fersini, Debora Nozza, Viviana Patti, Francisco Manuel Rangel Pardo, Paolo Rosso, and Manuela Sanguinetti. 2019. Semeval-2019 task 5: Multilingual detection of hate speech against immigrants and women in twitter. In *Proceedings of SemEval*.

Daniel Borkan, Lucas Dixon, Jeffrey Sorensen, Nithum Thain, and Lucy Vasserman. 2019. Nuanced metrics for measuring unintended bias with real data for text classification. In *Proceedings of WWW*.

Çağrı Çöltekin. 2020. A Corpus of Turkish Offensive Language on Social Media. In *Proceedings of LREC*.

Patricia Chiril, Farah Benamara Zitoune, Véronique Moriceau, Marlène Coulomb-Gully, and Abhishek Kumar. 2019. Multilingual and multitarget hate speech detection in tweets. In *Proceedings of TALN*.

Alexis Conneau, Kartikay Khandelwal, Naman Goyal, Vishrav Chaudhary, Guillaume Wenzek, Francisco Guzmán, Edouard Grave, Myle Ott, Luke Zettlemoyer, and Veselin Stoyanov. 2019. Unsupervised cross-lingual representation learning at scale. In *Proceedings of ACL*.

Giovanni Da San Martino, Seunghak Yu, Alberto Barrón-Cedeño, Rostislav Petrov, and Preslav Nakov. 2019. Fine-grained analysis of propaganda in news article. In *Proceedings of EMNLP-IJCNLP*.

Maral Dadvar, Dolf Trieschnigg, Roeland Ordelman, and Franciska de Jong. 2013. Improving Dyberbullying Detection with User Context. In *Proceedings of ECIR*.

Jacob Devlin, Ming-Wei Chang, Kenton Lee, and Kristina Toutanova. 2019. BERT: Pre-training of Deep Bidirectional Transformers for Language Understanding. In *Proceedings of NAACL*.

Paula Fortuna, Joao Rocha da Silva, Leo Wanner, Sérgio Nunes, et al. 2019. A Hierarchically-labeled Portuguese Hate Speech Dataset. In *Proceedings of ALW*.

Hansi Hettiarachchi and Tharindu Ranasinghe. 2019. Emoji powered capsule network to detect type and target of offensive posts in social media. In *Proceedings of RANLP*.

Hansi Hettiarachchi and Tharindu Ranasinghe. 2020. InfoMiner at WNUT-2020 task 2: Transformer-based covid-19 informative tweet extraction. In *Proceedings of W-NUT*.

Ritesh Kumar, Atul Kr Ojha, Shervin Malmasi, and Marcos Zampieri. 2018. Benchmarking aggression identification in social media. In *Proceedings of TRAC*.

Ritesh Kumar, Atul Kr. Ojha, Shervin Malmasi, and Marcos Zampieri. 2020. Evaluating Aggression Identification in Social Media. In *Proceedings of TRAC*.

Zhenzhong Lan, Mingda Chen, Sebastian Goodman, Kevin Gimpel, Piyush Sharma, and Radu Soricut. 2020. ALBERT: A Lite BERT for Self-supervised Learning of Language Representations. In *Proceedings of ICLR*.

Yinhan Liu, Myle Ott, Naman Goyal, Jingfei Du, Mandar Joshi, Danqi Chen, Omer Levy, Mike Lewis, Luke Zettlemoyer, and Veselin Stoyanov. 2019. Roberta: A robustly optimized bert pretraining approach. *arXiv preprint arXiv:1907.11692*.

Prasenjit Majumder, Thomas Mandl, et al. 2018. Filtering Aggression from the Multilingual Social Media Feed. In *Proceedings TRAC*.

Shervin Malmasi and Marcos Zampieri. 2017. Detecting Hate Speech in Social Media. In *Proceedings of RANLP*.

Shervin Malmasi and Marcos Zampieri. 2018. Challenges in Discriminating Profanity from Hate Speech. *Journal of Experimental & Theoretical Artificial Intelligence*, 30:1 – 16.

Hamdy Mubarak, Ammar Rashed, Kareem Darwish, Younes Samih, and Ahmed Abdelali. 2020. Arabic offensive language on twitter: Analysis and experiments. *arXiv preprint arXiv:2004.02192*.

Marc Pàmies, Emily Öhman, Kaisla Kajava, and Jörg Tiedemann. 2020. LT@Helsinki at SemEval-2020 task 12: Multilingual or language-specific BERT? In *Proceedings of SemEval*.

Adam Paszke, Sam Gross, Francisco Massa, Adam Lerer, James Bradbury, Gregory Chanan, Trevor Killeen, Zeming Lin, Natalia Gimelshein, Luca Antiga, Alban Desmaison, Andreas Kopf, Edward Yang, Zachary DeVito, Martin Raison, Alykhan Tejani, Sasank Chilamkurthy, Benoit Steiner, Lu Fang, Junjie Bai, and Soumith Chintala. 2019. Pytorch: An imperative style, high-performance deep learning library. In *Proceedings of NeurIPS*.

John Pavlopoulos, Léo Laugier, Jeffrey Sorensen, and Ion Androutsopoulos. 2021. Semeval-2021 task 5: Toxic spans detection. In *Proceedings of SemEval*.

Matthew Peters, Mark Neumann, Mohit Iyyer, Matt Gardner, Christopher Clark, Kenton Lee, and Luke Zettlemoyer. 2018. Deep Contextualized Word Representations. In *Proceedings of NAACL*.

Zeses Pitenis, Marcos Zampieri, and Tharindu Ranasinghe. 2020. Offensive Language Identification in Greek. In *Proceedings of LREC*.

Fabio Poletto, Marco Stranisci, Manuela Sanguinetti, Viviana Patti, and Cristina Bosco. 2017. Hate Speech Annotation: Analysis of an Italian Twitter Corpus. In *Proceedings of CLiC-it*.

Tharindu Ranasinghe, Sarthak Gupte, Marcos Zampieri, and Ifeoma Nwogu. 2020. WLV-RIT at HASOC-Dravidian-CodeMix-FIRE2020: Offensive Language Identification in Code-switched YouTube Comments. In *Proceedings of FIRE*.

Tharindu Ranasinghe and Hansi Hettiarachchi. 2020. BRUMS at SemEval-2020 task 12: Transformer based multilingual offensive language identification in social media. In *Proceedings of SemEval*.

Tharindu Ranasinghe, Diptanu Sarkar, Marcos Zampieri, and Alex Ororbia. 2021. WLV-RIT at SemEval-2021 Task 5: A Neural Transformer Framework for Detecting Toxic Spans. In *Proceedings of SemEval*.

Tharindu Ranasinghe and Marcos Zampieri. 2020. Multilingual Offensive Language Identification with Cross-lingual Embeddings. In *Proceedings of EMNLP*.

Tharindu Ranasinghe and Marcos Zampieri. 2021. Multilingual Offensive Language Identification for Low-resource Languages. *ACM Transactions on Asian and Low-Resource Language Information Processing (TALLIP)*.

Tharindu Ranasinghe, Marcos Zampieri, and Hansi Hettiarachchi. 2019. BRUMS at HASOC 2019: Deep Learning Models for Multilingual Hate Speech and Offensive Language Identification. In *Proceedings of FIRE*.

Michael Ridenhour, Arunkumar Bagavathi, Elaheh Raisi, and Siddharth Krishnan. 2020. Detecting Online Hate Speech: Approaches Using Weak Supervision and Network Embedding Models. *arXiv preprint arXiv:2007.12724*.

Hugo Rosa, N Pereira, Ricardo Ribeiro, Paula Costa Ferreira, Joao Paulo Carvalho, S Oliveira, Luísa Coheur, Paula Paulino, AM Veiga Simão, and Isabel Trancoso. 2019. Automatic cyberbullying detection: A systematic review. *Computers in Human Behavior*, 93:333–345.

Sara Rosenthal, Pepa Atanasova, Georgi Karadzhov, Marcos Zampieri, and Preslav Nakov. 2020. A Large-Scale Weakly Supervised Dataset for Offensive Language Identification. In *arXiv preprint arXiv:2004.14454*.

Joan Serrà and Alexandros Karatzoglou. 2017. Getting deep recommenders fit: Bloom embeddings for sparse binary input/output networks. In *Proceedings of RecSys*.

Gudbjartur Ingi Sigurbergsson and Leon Derczynski. 2020. Offensive Language and Hate Speech Detection for Danish. In *Proceedings of LREC*.

Chi Sun, Xipeng Qiu, Yige Xu, and Xuanjing Huang. 2019. How to fine-tune bert for text classification? In *Proceedings of CCL*.

Stéphan Tulkens, Lisa Hilte, Elise Lodewyckx, Ben Verhoeven, and Walter Daelemans. 2016. A Dictionary-based Approach to Racism Detection in Dutch Social Media. In *Proceedings of TA-COS*.

Shuohuan Wang, Jiaxiang Liu, Xuan Ouyang, and Yu Sun. 2020. Galileo at SemEval-2020 task 12: Multi-lingual learning for offensive language identification using pre-trained language models. In *Proceedings of SemEval*.

Gregor Wiedemann, Seid Muhie Yimam, and Chris Biemann. 2020. UHH-LT at SemEval-2020 task 12: Fine-tuning of pre-trained transformer networks for offensive language detection. In *Proceedings of SemEval*.

Thomas Wolf, Lysandre Debut, Victor Sanh, Julien Chaumond, Clement Delangue, Anthony Moi, Pierric Cistac, Tim Rault, Remi Louf, Morgan Funtowicz, Joe Davison, Sam Shleifer, Patrick von Platen, Clara Ma, Yacine Jernite, Julien Plu, Canwen Xu, Teven Le Scao, Sylvain Gugger, Mariama Drame, Quentin Lhoest, and Alexander Rush. 2020. Transformers: State-of-the-art natural language processing. In *Proceedings of EMNLP*.

Zhilin Yang, Zihang Dai, Yiming Yang, Jaime Carbonell, Russ R Salakhutdinov, and Quoc V Le. 2019. XLNet: Generalized Autoregressive Pretraining for Language Understanding. In *Proceedings of NeurIPS*.

Mengfan Yao, Charalampos Chelmis, and Daphney-Stavroula Zois. 2019. Cyberbullying Ends Here: Towards Robust Detection of Cyberbullying in Social Media. In *Proceedings of WWW*.

Marcos Zampieri, Shervin Malmasi, Preslav Nakov, Sara Rosenthal, Noura Farra, and Ritesh Kumar. 2019a. Predicting the type and target of offensive posts in social media. In *Proceedings of NAACL*.

Marcos Zampieri, Shervin Malmasi, Preslav Nakov, Sara Rosenthal, Noura Farra, and Ritesh Kumar. 2019b. SemEval-2019 Task 6: Identifying and Categorizing Offensive Language in Social Media (OffensEval). In *Proceedings of SemEval*.

Marcos Zampieri, Preslav Nakov, Sara Rosenthal, Pepa Atanasova, Georgi Karadzhov, Hamdy Mubarak, Leon Derczynski, Zeses Pitenis, and Çağrı Çöltekin. 2020. SemEval-2020 Task 12: Multilingual Offensive Language Identification in Social Media (OffensEval 2020). In *Proceedings of SemEval*.

## Appendix

i **Training Configurations** We used an Nvidia Tesla K80 GPU to train the models. We divided the dataset into a training set and a validation set using 0.8:0.2 split. We fine tuned the learning rate and number of epochs of the model manually to obtain the best results for the validation set. We obtained $1e^{-}5$ as the best value for learning rate and 3 as the best value for number of epochs for all the languages. We performed *early stopping* if the validation loss did not improve over 10 evaluation steps. Training large models took around 30 minutes while training base models took around 10 minutes. In addition to the learning rate and number of epochs we used the parameter values mentioned in Table 4. We kept these values as constants.

| Parameter | Value |
|---|---|
| adam epsilon | 1e-8 |
| warmup ratio | 0.1 |
| warmup steps | 0 |
| max grad norm | 1.0 |
| max seq. length | 140 |
| gradient accumulation steps | 1 |

Table 4: Parameter Specifications.

ii **Hardware Specifications**

In Table 5 and in Table 6 we mention the specifications of the GPU and CPU we used for the experiments of the paper. For the training of the MUDES models, we mainly used the GPU. For the efficiency experiments mentioned in Section 6.3 we used both GPU and CPU environments.

| Parameter | Value |
|---|---|
| GPU | Nvidia K80 |
| GPU Memory | 12GB |
| GPU Memory Clock | 0.82GHz |
| Performance | 4.1 TFLOPS |
| No. CPU Cores | 2 |
| RAM | 12GB |

Table 5: GPU Specifications.

iii **Run time**

As expected base models perform efficiently than the large models in both environments. Large models take around 3 seconds for a sentence in a CPU and take around 1 second for a sentence in a GPU while the base models take approximately one third of that time in both environments. From these results it is clear that MUDES is capable of predicting toxic spans efficiently in any environment.

| Parameter | Value |
|---|---|
| CPU Model Name | Intel(R) Xeon(R) |
| CPU Freq. | 2.30GHz |
| No. CPU Cores | 2 |
| CPU Family | Haswell |
| RAM | 12GB |

Table 6: CPU Specifications.

| Model | GPU Time | CPU Time |
|---|---|---|
| en-base | 35.51 | 100.81 |
| en-large | 100.36 | 315.72 |
| multilingual-base | 36.23 | 115.98 |
| multilingual-large | 120.54 | 335.65 |

Table 7: Time taken to do predictions on 100 sentences in seconds.

## Ethics Statement

MUDES is essentially a web-based visualization tool with predictive models trained on multiple publicly available datasets. The authors of this paper used datasets referenced in this paper which were previously collected and annotated. No new data collection has been carried out as part of this work. We have not collected or processed writers'/users' information nor have we carried out any form of user profiling protecting users' privacy and identity.

We understand that every dataset is subject to intrinsic bias and that computational models will inevitably learn biased information from any dataset. We believe that MUDES will help coping with biases in datasets and models as it features: (1) a freely available Python library that other researchers can use to train new models on other datasets; (2) a web-based visualizing tool that can help efforts in reducing biases in offensive language identification as they can be used to process and visualize potentially offensive spans new data. Finally, unlike models trained at the post level, the projected annotation of spans allows users to understand which part of the instance is considered offensive by the models.

**Association for Computational Linguistics**
209 N. Eighth Street
Stroudsburg, Pennsylvania 18360

ISBN 978-1-7138-3011-5

CURRAN ASSOCIATES INC.
proceedings.com